Strategic Intervention Teacher Guide

Grade 4

Harcourt School Publishers

www.harcourtschool.com

Copyright © by Harcourt, Inc.

All rights reserved. No part of this publication may be reproduced or transmitted in any form or by any means, electronic or mechanical, including photocopy, recording, or any information storage and retrieval system, without permission in writing from the publisher.

Requests for permission to make copies of any part of the work should be addressed to School Permissions and Copyrights, Harcourt, Inc., 6277 Sea Harbor Drive, Orlando, Florida 32887-6777. Fax: 407-345-2418.

STORYTOWN is a trademark of Harcourt, Inc. HARCOURT and the Harcourt Logo are trademarks of Harcourt, Inc., registered in the United States of America and/or other jurisdictions.

Printed in the United States of America

ISBN 10: 0-15-365500-3
ISBN 13: 978-0-15-365500-5

6 7 8 9 10 0877 16 15 14 13 12 11 10 09

If you have received these materials as examination copies free of charge, Harcourt School Publishers retains title to the materials and they may not be resold. Resale of examination copies is strictly prohibited and is illegal.

Possession of this publication in print format does not entitle users to convert this publication, or any portion of it, into electronic format.

CONTENTS

What Are Intervention Strategies?..........................vi

Components..vi

Using the *Strategic Intervention Teacher Guide*...........vii

Suggested Lesson Planners...............................viii

Fluency..x

Fluency Practice and Assessment...........................xi

Phonemic Awareness Activities...........................xii

Vocabulary Activities....................................xvi

LESSON 1
The Cake Game 2
by Linda Barr

LESSON 2
Drive Fast!... 14
by Linda Barr

LESSON 3
Clusters of Hope 26
by Luis Berrios

LESSON 4
The Best Time.. 38
by Eva Ramos

LESSON 5
The Flan Plan 50
by Kathryn Powers

LESSON 6
Close Call 62
by Pam Barrett

LESSON 7

You Have Mail! 74
by Amber Anderson

LESSON 8

The Pigs, the Wolf, and a Laptop 86
by Pamela K. Jennett

LESSON 9

Raising a Barn 98
by Linda Barr

LESSON 10

Joan's Eagle 110
by Kathryn Powers

LESSON 11

Born for Snow 122
by Linda Barr

LESSON 12

When the Earth Moves 134
by Linda Barr

LESSON 13

Mom in Control 146
by Sam Nori

LESSON 14

Just Down the Road 158
by Linda Barr

LESSON 15

The Camping Club 170
by Linda Barr

Table of Contents   iii

CONTENTS

LESSON 16
Inventors at Work 182
by Shannon Gilliam

LESSON 17
The Artist's Life 194
by Jimmy Aguilar

LESSON 18
Troy Bright Saves the Day 206
by Bill McMahon

LESSON 19
An Awful Mess 218
Retold by Jimmy Aguilar

LESSON 20
The Case of the Seashore Crook 230
by Shannon Gilliam

LESSON 21
My New Dog 242
by Guadalupe V. Lopez

LESSON 22
Dear Diary 254
by Guadalupe V. Lopez

LESSON 23
Phil in the City 266
by Guadalupe V. Lopez

LESSON 24
Where Land and Sea Meet 278
by Guadalupe V. Lopez

LESSON 25
Monterey County Fair **290**
by Guadalupe V. Lopez

LESSON 26
Rough and Tough Enough........................ **302**
by Keith Maynard

LESSON 27
Along the Mighty Mississippi **314**
by Shannon Gilliam

LESSON 28
The Untold Story of Texas Kate **326**
by Amy Vu

LESSON 29
Caught in the Ice!............................... **338**
by Shannon Gilliam

LESSON 30
Beneath the Sands **350**
by Shannon Gilliam

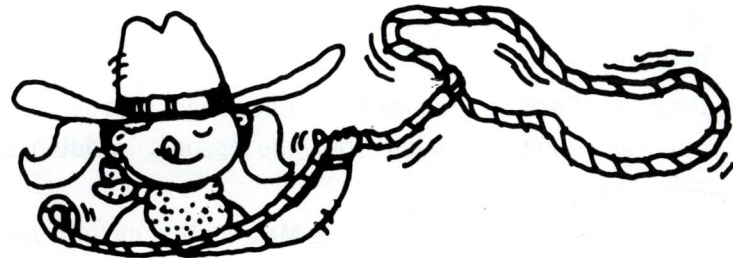

Table of Contents   v

INTRODUCTION

What Are Intervention Strategies?

Intervention strategies are designed to facilitate learning for those students who might experience some difficulty no matter how well we have planned our curriculum. These strategies offer support and guidance to the student who is struggling. The strategies themselves are no mystery. They are based on the same time-honored techniques that effective teachers have used for years—teaching students on their instructional reading level; modeling previewing and predicting; and directed instruction in strategic reading, vocabulary, phonics, fluency, and writing.

Intervention works best in conjunction with a strong core program. For an intervention program to be effective, instruction should focus on specific needs of students, as determined by systematic monitoring of progress.

Components of the Strategic Intervention Resource Kit

The goal of this *Strategic Intervention Resource Kit* is to provide the scaffolding, extra support, and extra reading practice that struggling readers need to succeed. Each kit in grades 2–6 includes the following components:

- *Teacher Guide* with lessons directly aligned with and correlated to the lessons in the *StoryTown* Teacher Edition.
- *Interactive Reader* that provides accessible reading material with built-in support for the student.
- *Skill Cards* to teach each lesson's Focus Skill.
- *Practice Book* with the following practice pages that accompany each lesson:
  - *Fluency Practice Page* with word lists and phrase-cued sentences that reinforce vocabulary and decoding skills and parallel the reading level of the *Interactive Student Edition* selection.
  - *Grammar Practice Page* that reinforces the lesson's grammar skill and can be used as a teacher-directed or independent activity.
  - *Writing Trait Practice Page* that reinforces the writing trait taught in the lesson.
  - *Decoding/Spelling Practice Page* that provides an additional opportunity to practice and apply the lesson's decoding/spelling skill.
- *Teacher Resource Book* with Copying Masters that include Vocabulary Word Cards and activities providing additional reinforcement of decoding/spelling, word attack, comprehension, grammar, and writing skills.
- *Assessment Book* to monitor progress and ensure success.

Using the Strategic Intervention Teacher Guide

The *Strategic Intervention Teacher Guide* gives support for struggling readers in key instructional strands, plus prerequisite phonics skills and oral-reading fluency. Each five-day lesson plan includes the following resources:

- *Vocabulary* lessons and Student-Friendly Explanations to preteach and reteach key vocabulary that appears in the *Interactive Reader* selection.
- *Robust Vocabulary* lessons to enrich students' listening and speaking vocabularies and help them master the language of school.
- *Decoding/Spelling* lessons to systematically preteach and reteach basic phonics skills and connect spelling and phonics.
- *Decoding/Word Attack* lessons to preteach and reteach phonics and word analysis skills.
- *Fluency* activities that reinforce key vocabulary, decoding/spelling, and word attack skills, while providing reading practice and promoting oral reading fluency.
- *Comprehension Focus Skill* lessons to ensure that struggling readers get the in-depth instruction they need to reach grade-level standards.
- *Directed Reading Lesson* for the *Interactive Reader* selection to reinforce basic comprehension skills, using questions and teacher modeling.
- *Interactive Writing Support* that reinforces key writing traits and forms.
- *Review Lessons* that provide cumulative reviews of skills.

Depending on your individual classroom and school schedules, you can tailor the instruction to suit your needs. The following pages show two options for pacing the instruction in this guide.

Introduction vii

SUGGESTED LESSON PLANNERS

Grade 4: For Use with *StoryTown*

DAY 1

RETEACH

VOCABULARY
- Reteach the Vocabulary Words that were introduced on Day 1 in *StoryTown*.

COMPREHENSION
 Preteach the skill that will be introduced on Day 2 in *StoryTown*.

DECODING/SPELLING
- Reteach the skill that was introduced on Day 1 in *StoryTown*.

GRAMMAR/WRITING
- Preteach the aspect of the grammar skill that will be introduced on Day 2 in *StoryTown*.

FLUENCY
- Begin fluency practice for the current week.

DAY 2

RETEACH

VOCABULARY
- Provide guided practice of the week's Vocabulary Words.

COMPREHENSION
 Read the *Turn It Up!* selection.
- Build Background
- Monitor Comprehension
- Have students answer the *Think Critically* questions

DECODING/SPELLING
- Reteach the decoding/spelling skill.

GRAMMAR/WRITING
- Preteach the aspect of the grammar skill that will be introduced on Day 3 in *StoryTown*.

FLUENCY
- Continue fluency practice for the current week.

Grade 4 OPTION: As a stand-alone program

DAY 1

VOCABULARY
- Reteach the Vocabulary Words.

COMPREHENSION
 Reteach the comprehension focus skill.

DECODING/SPELLING
- Reteach the decoding/spelling skill.

GRAMMAR/WRITING
- Teach another aspect of the grammar/writing skill.

FLUENCY
- Begin fluency practice for the current week.

DAY 2

VOCABULARY
- Provide guided practice of the Vocabulary Words.

COMPREHENSION
 Read the *Turn It Up!* selection.
- Build Background
- Monitor Comprehension
- Have students answer the *Think Critically* questions

DECODING/SPELLING
- Reteach the decoding/spelling skill.

GRAMMAR/WRITING
- Teach another aspect of the grammar/writing skill.

FLUENCY
- Continue fluency practice for the current week.

Strategic Intervention Teacher Guide

DAY 3

RETEACH

COMPREHENSION
- Preteach the skill that will be introduced on Day 4 in *StoryTown*.
- Reread and Summarize the *Turn It Up!* selection.

DECODING/SPELLING
- Reteach the skill that is reviewed on Day 3 in *StoryTown*.

BUILD ROBUST VOCABULARY
- Teach additional vocabulary from the *Turn It Up!* selection.

GRAMMAR/WRITING
- Reteach the writing trait that is taught this week in *StoryTown*.

FLUENCY
- Continue fluency practice for the current week.

DAY 4

RETEACH

COMPREHENSION
- Reteach the skill that was introduced on Day 4 in *StoryTown*.

DECODING/SPELLING
- Provide guided practice of the skill that is reviewed on Day 4 in *StoryTown*.

BUILD ROBUST VOCABULARY
- Review additional vocabulary from the *Turn It Up!* selection.

GRAMMAR/WRITING
- Reteach the writing form that is taught this week in *StoryTown*.

FLUENCY
- Continue fluency practice for the current week.

DAY 5

PRETEACH for next week's *StoryTown* lesson

VOCABULARY
- Preteach the Vocabulary Words that will be introduced next week in *StoryTown*.

COMPREHENSION
- Preteach the skill that will be introduced on Day 2 next week in *StoryTown*.

DECODING/WORD ATTACK
- Preteach the skill that will be introduced on Day 1 next week in *StoryTown*.

DECODING/SPELLING
- Preteach the skill that will be introduced on Day 1 next week in *StoryTown*.

GRAMMAR/WRITING
- Preteach the aspect of the grammar skill that will be introduced on Day 1 next week in *StoryTown*.

FLUENCY
- Evaluate students' fluency performance for the current week.

DAY 3

COMPREHENSION
- Teach the comprehension skill.
- Reread and Summarize the *Turn It Up!* selection.

DECODING/SPELLING
- Reteach the decoding/spelling skill.

BUILD ROBUST VOCABULARY
- Teach additional vocabulary from the *Turn It Up!* selection.

GRAMMAR/WRITING
- Teach the writing trait. (This is labeled Reteach in our actual lessons.)

FLUENCY
- Continue fluency practice for the current week.

DAY 4

COMPREHENSION
- Reteach the comprehension skill.

DECODING/SPELLING
- Provide guided practice of the decoding/spelling skill.

BUILD ROBUST VOCABULARY
- Review additional vocabulary from the *Turn It Up!* selection.

GRAMMAR/WRITING
- Teach the writing form. (This is labeled Reteach in our lessons.)

FLUENCY
- Continue fluency practice for the current week.

DAY 5

VOCABULARY
- Teach the Vocabulary Words.

COMPREHENSION
- Teach the comprehension focus skill.

DECODING/WORD ATTACK
- Teach the decoding/word attack skill.

GRAMMAR/WRITING
- Teach one aspect of the grammar/writing skill.

FLUENCY
- Evaluate students' fluency performance for the current week.

Suggested Lesson Planners ix

FLUENCY

Fluency

"So that students will understand why rereading is done, we have involved them in a discussion of how athletes develop skill at their sports. This discussion brings out the fact that athletes spend considerable time practicing basic skills until they develop speed and smoothness at their activity. Repeated readings uses this same type of practice."

S. Jay Samuels
The Reading Teacher, February 1997
(originally published January 1979)

In the years since S. Jay Samuels pioneered the technique of repeated reading to improve fluency, continuing research has confirmed and expanded upon his observations. Ideally, oral reading mirrors the pacing, smoothness, and rhythms of normal speech. Fluency in reading can be defined as a combination of these key elements.

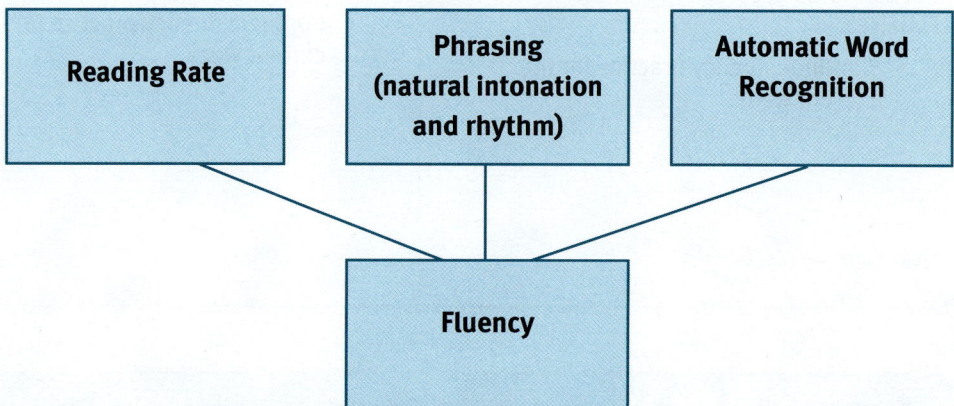

How Do Students Become More Fluent Readers?

Research and the experiences of classroom teachers make it clear that certain practices can and do lead to significant improvements in reading fluency. Techniques that have been shown to be successful include

- **Teacher modeling**
- **Repeated reading of short passages**
- **Daily monitoring of progress**

A program that incorporates these three elements will help struggling readers gain fluency and improve their comprehension.

x   Strategic Intervention Teacher Guide

Fluency Practice and Assessment

The plan for each lesson in the *Strategic Intervention Teacher Guide* includes daily fluency practice that incorporates the elements of teacher modeling, repeated reading, and self-monitoring.

The fluency portion of the lesson is designed to be completed in five minutes, though you may adjust the time according to students' needs and as your schedule allows.

About the *Strategic Intervention Practice Book* Fluency Page

The *Strategic Intervention Practice Book* Fluency page is designed to correlate with the phonics elements taught in the *Strategic Intervention Teacher Guide*, as well as with key vocabulary from the *Interactive Reader* selections. A total of twenty words that fall into these three categories are listed at the top of the Fluency page for each lesson.

On the bottom half of the page, you will find a set of numbered sentences that incorporate the words from the lists. Slashes are used to divide each sentence into phrases. To help students improve natural phrasing, model reading each phrase smoothly, as a unit, and encourage students to follow the same procedure in their repeated-reading practice.

This chart gives an overview of the fluency portion of the Intervention Program.

Day	Material	Explanation
1	*Practice Book* Fluency page	Teacher models reading aloud word lists. Students then practice reading aloud the word lists with partners.
2	*Practice Book* Fluency page	Teacher models reading aloud the phrased fluency sentences. Students then practice repeated rereadings of the sentences with partners.
3	*Practice Book* Fluency page	Students read the fluency sentences to improve pacing and tone.
4	*Interactive Reader* selection	Students read aloud a selected short passage from the *Interactive Reader* selection three times, monitoring their progress after each reading.
5	*Interactive Reader* selection	Students read the same passage aloud to the teacher. Both teacher and student assess the student's progress.

PHONEMIC AWARENESS ACTIVITIES

Rhyming Activities

Rhyme-a-Day
Start each day by teaching students a short rhyme. Periodically throughout the day, repeat the rhyme with them. Say the rhyme together, have them say it alone, pause and leave out words for them to insert, or ask volunteers to say each line. Students will develop a repertoire of favorite rhymes that can serve as a storehouse for creating their own rhymes.

Rhyme Sort
Place on a tabletop pictures of items that rhyme. Have students sort the pictures into groups, according to names that rhyme. You also might want to try an "open sort" by having students create categories of their own to sort the picture cards.

Rhyme Pairs
To assess students' ability to recognize pairs of words that rhyme, say a list of twenty or more pairs of words. Half of the word pairs should rhyme. Students tell which word pairs rhyme and which do not. Have students indicate *yes* with a card marked *Y* or another symbol.

What Word Rhymes?
Use theme-related words from across the curriculum to focus on words that rhyme. For example, if you are studying animals, ask: **What rhymes with *snake? bear? fox? deer? ant? frog? goat? hen? fish? whale?*** If a special holiday is approaching, ask: **What rhymes with *flag, year,* or *heart?*** Use these word groups for sound-matching, sound-blending, or sound-segmenting activities.

Sound-Matching Activities

Odd Word Out
Form a group of four students. Say a different word for each group member to repeat. The student with the word that does not begin (or end) like the other words must step out of the group. For example, say *basket, bundle, cost,* and *bargain*. The student whose word is *cost* steps out of the group. The odd-word-out player then chooses three students to form a new group and the procedure continues.

Head or Toes, Finger or Nose?
Teach students the following rhyme. Be sure to say the sound, not the letter, at the beginning of each line. Recite the rhyme together several times while touching the body parts.

/h/ is for *head*.
/t/ is for *toes*.
/f/ is for *finger*.
/n/ is for *nose*.

Explain that you will say a list of words. Students are to touch the head when you say a word that begins with /h/, the toes for the words that begin with /t/, a finger for words that begin with /f/, and the nose for words that begin with /n/. Say words such as *fan, ten, horn, hat, feet, nut, ham, nest, toy, fish, note, tub, nail, time, fox,* and *house*.

xii Strategic Intervention Teacher Guide

Souvenir Sound-Off

Have students imagine that a friend has traveled to a special place and has brought them a gift. Recite the following verse, and ask a volunteer to complete it. The names of the traveler, the place, and the gift must begin with the same letter and sound.

- My friend [person]
- who went to [place]
- brought me back a [gift].

Example: *My friend Hannah
who went to Hawaii
brought me back a hula skirt.*

After repeating this activity a few times, ask partners to recite the missing words. As an alternative, you can focus on words with initial blends and digraphs. Students can focus on social studies and phonics skills by using a world map or globe to find names of places.

Match My Word

Have students match beginning or ending sounds in words. Seat students in pairs, sitting back to back. One student in each pair will say a word. His or her partner will repeat the word and say another word that begins with the same sound. Repeat the activity, reversing the roles of partners and focusing on ending sounds.

Sound Isolation Activities

What's Your Name N-N-N-Name?

Invite students to say their names by repeating the initial phoneme in the name, such as *M-M-M-M-Michael,* or by drawing out and exaggerating the initial sound, such as *Sssss-erena*. Have students say the names of others, such as friends or family members.

Singling Out the Sounds

Form groups of three students. Students can decide who will name the beginning, the middle, and the ending sounds in one-syllable picture names. Given a set of pictures, the group identifies a picture name, and then each group member isolates and says the sound he or she is responsible for. Group members can check one another's responses.

Chain Reaction

Have students form a circle. The student who begins will say a word, such as *bus*. The next student must isolate the ending sound in the word, /s/, and say a word that begins with that sound, such as *sun*. If the word is correct, the two students link arms, and the procedure continues with the next student isolating the final sound in *sun* and giving a word that begins with /n/. You will want all students to be able to link arms and complete the chain, so provide help when needed.

Phonemic Awareness Activities   xiii

PHONEMIC AWARENESS ACTIVITIES

Sound-Addition, -Deletion, or -Substitution Activities

Add-a-Sound

Explain that the beginning sound is missing in each of the words you will say. Students must add the missing sound and say the new word. Some examples follow. Add:

/b/ to *at* (*bat*)	/f/ to *ox* (*fox*)
/k/ to *art* (*cart*)	/f/ to *ace* (*face*)
/p/ to *age* (*page*)	/h/ to *air* (*hair*)
/w/ to *all* (*wall*)	/j/ to *am* (*jam*)
/r/ to *an* (*ran*)	/b/ to *and* (*band*)
/d/ to *ark* (*dark*)	/f/ to *arm* (*farm*)
/d/ to *ash* (*dash*)	/s/ to *it* (*sit*)
/s/ to *oak* (*soak*)	/h/ to *eel* (*heel*)
/b/ to *end* (*bend*)	/m/ to *ice* (*mice*)
/n/ to *ear* (*near*)	/f/ to *east* (*feast*)
/b/ to *each* (*beach*)	/f/-/l/ to *at* (*flat*)
/sk/ to *ate* (*skate*)	/t/-/r/ to *eat* (*treat*)
/g/-/r/ to *ill* (*grill*)	/sh/ to *out* (*shout*)
/p/-/l/ to *ant* (*plant*)	

Remove-a-Sound

Reinforce rhyme while focusing on the deletion of initial sounds in words to form new words. Ask students to say:

hat without the /h/ (*at*)
fin without the /f/ (*in*)
tall without the /t/ (*all*)
box without the /b/ (*ox*)
will without the /w/ (*ill*)
peach without the /p/ (*each*)
nice without the /n/ (*ice*)
meat without the /m/ (*eat*)
band without the /b/ (*and*)

Continue with other words in the same manner.

Mixed-Up Tongue Twisters

Think of a simple tongue twister, such as *ten tired toads*. Say the tongue twister for students, but replace the initial letter in each word with another letter, such as *p*, to create nonsense words: *pen pired poads*. Explain to students that you need their help to make sense of the tongue twister by having them replace /p/ with /t/ and say the new tongue twister. Use the same procedure for other tongue twisters.

- *copper coffee cups*
- *nine new nails*
- *two ton tomatoes*
- *long lean legs*

Then ask partners to continue this activity together.

The Name Game

Occasionally when a new sound is introduced, students might enjoy substituting the first sound of their names for the name of a classmate. Students will have to stop and think when they call one another by name, including the teacher. For example, Paul would call Ms. Vega *Ms. Pega*; *Carmen* becomes *Parmen*; *Jason* becomes *Pason*; and *Kiyo* becomes *Piyo*. Just make certain beforehand that all names will be agreeable.

Take Away

New words can be formed by deleting an initial phoneme from a word. Have students say the new word that is formed.

- *flake* without the /f/ (*lake*)
- *bring* without the /b/ (*ring*)
- *swing* without the /s/ (*wing*)
- *swell* without the /s/ (*well*)
- *shrink* without the /sh/ (*rink*)
- *shred* without the /sh/ (*red*)
- *spread* without the /s/-/p/ (*read*)
- *gloom* without the /g/ (*loom*)
- *fright* without the /f/ (*right*)
- *snout* without the /s/-/n/ (*out*)
- *score* without the /s/ (*core*)
- *slip* without the /s/ (*lip*)
- *bride* without the /b/ (*ride*)
- *block* without the /b/ (*lock*)
- *spoke* without the /s/ (*poke*)
- *snail* without the /s/ (*nail*)

Sound Blending Activities

I'm Thinking of a Word

Play a guessing game with students. Tell students that you will give them clues to a word. Have them listen closely to blend the sounds to say the word.

- I'm thinking of something that has words—/b/-/oo/-/k/. (*book*)
- I'm thinking of something that comes in bunches—/g/-/r/-/ā/-/p/-/s/. (*grapes*)
- I'm thinking of something that shines in the night sky—/s/-/t/-/är/-/z/. (*stars*)
- I'm thinking of something that moves very slowly—/s/-/n/-/ā/-/l/. (*snail*)

What's in the Box?

Place various objects in a box or bag. Play a game with students by saying: **In this box is a /k/-/r/-/ā/-/o/-/n/. What do you think is in the box?** (*crayon*) Continue with the other objects in the box, segmenting the phonemes for students to blend and say the word.

Sound-Segmenting Activities

Sound Game

Have partners play a word-guessing game using a variety of pictures that represent different beginning sounds. One student says the name on the card, separating the beginning sound, as in *p-late*. The partner blends the sounds and guesses the word. After students are proficient with beginning sounds, you could have them segment all the sounds in a word when they give their clues, as in *d-o-g*.

Count the Sounds

Tell students that you are going to say a word. Have them listen and count the number of sounds they hear in that word. For example, say the word *task*. Have students repeat the word and tell how many sounds they hear. Students should reply *four*.

tone (3)	*four* (3)
great (4)	*peak* (3)
pinch (4)	*sunny* (4)
stick (4)	*clouds* (5)
flake (4)	*feel* (3)
rain (3)	*paint* (4)

Phonemic Awareness Activities   xv

VOCABULARY ACTIVITIES

The six activities on the following pages provide additional opportunities for vocabulary practice and application. Two activities are offered for individual students, two for pairs of students working together, and two for small groups of three or four students. All require a minimum of preparation and call for materials that are readily available in the classroom.

Word Book

MATERIALS
- paper
- markers
- stapler
- simple binding materials

INDIVIDUAL ACTIVITY As students progress through a theme, encourage them to identify new vocabulary that they find interesting or that they think will be useful to them. Have students create a page for each of the special words they choose. Encourage them to check the spelling of the word and to include the definition and other information they might find helpful, such as how the word is divided into syllables, whether it has a prefix or a suffix, how it is pronounced, synonyms and antonyms, and how the word is related to other words they know. Students can also draw pictures and include captions and labels.

Upon completion of the theme, have students make a cover for the book. Staple the pages together, or help students use simple materials to bind them. Encourage them to share their word books with classmates and to use them as a resource for their writing.

xvi Strategic Intervention Teacher Guide

Draw a Smile

MATERIALS
- list of Vocabulary Words from a complete theme
- two sheets of paper and markers or chalk and chalkboard
- dictionary

PARTNER ACTIVITY Pairs of students can play this game on paper or on the board. Players should be designated Player 1 and Player 2. Player 1 begins by choosing a Vocabulary Word from the list for Player 2 to define. If Player 2 defines the word correctly, he or she gets to draw one part of a smiling face. If Player 2 cannot define the word correctly, he or she cannot draw on that turn. Players take turns choosing words for each other to define and adding parts to their drawings each time they define a word correctly. Encourage students to use a dictionary to check definitions as necessary.

A completed drawing has five parts, to be drawn in this order: (1) head, (2) one eye, (3) the other eye, (4) nose, (5) smile. The first player to draw a complete smiling face wins the game.

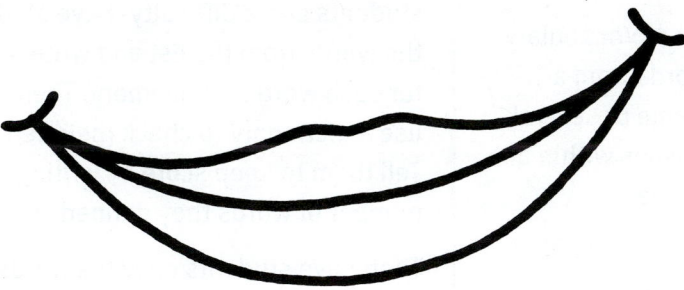

Vocabulary Activities xvii

VOCABULARY ACTIVITIES

Make a Word Garden

MATERIALS
- bulletin board
- colored construction paper
- markers
- scissors
- masking tape
- pencil
- paper

SMALL GROUP ACTIVITY Students can create a word garden by drawing and cutting out large flowers from construction paper. Encourage them to use their imaginations to create flowers in a variety of shapes and colors. Have students use markers to write a Vocabulary Word on each flower and then arrange the flowers to make a garden on the bulletin board.

Then have students create a key on a separate sheet of paper by making a small drawing of each of the large flowers and writing the definition of the word that appears on the matching large flower. Students should display the key on the bulletin board with their garden.

What's the Score?

MATERIALS
- list of Vocabulary Words from a theme or several lessons within a theme
- pencil and paper
- dictionary

INDIVIDUAL ACTIVITY Make a list of six to eight Vocabulary Words that may have given students some difficulty. Have students copy the words from the list and write a definition for each word from memory. Then have them use a dictionary to check their definitions. Tell them to keep score by writing down the number of words they defined correctly.

Then have students copy the words from the list in reverse order, beginning at the bottom. Have them again write a definition for each word from memory, check the definitions in a dictionary, and count the words they defined correctly. Tell students to compare this score to their first score to see how much they improved.

xviii Strategic Intervention Teacher Guide

Finger Puppets

MATERIALS
- finger puppet pattern
- construction paper
- markers
- scissors
- tape
- list of Vocabulary Words from a theme

SMALL GROUP ACTIVITY Give students a simple pattern that they can trace to make finger puppets. Have students use construction paper and markers to create puppets that represent favorite characters from a particular theme.

Have students work together to make up simple dramatizations using the finger puppets. Challenge students to use as many words as possible from the vocabulary list. They can keep track of the words they use by checking them off the list.

Guess My Word

MATERIALS
- list of Vocabulary Words from a theme
- scrap paper
- pencils

PARTNER ACTIVITY Display the list of Vocabulary Words where both players can see it. Students take turns choosing a word from the list for each other to guess. The student who is guessing may ask questions about the meaning of the word, how it is spelled, the number of syllables, or any other information they think may help them, as long as the questions can be answered with *yes* or *no.* Encourage students to jot down information that they find out about the word that can help narrow down the list. You may want to give examples of questions that players might ask and explain how they can use the information they obtain.

QUESTION: Does the word begin with a consonant?

INFORMATION: If the answer is *yes,* you can look at the words that begin with consonants and ask more questions to figure out which of those is the correct word. If the answer is *no,* you can rule out the words that begin with consonants and focus on those that begin with vowels.

QUESTION: Does the word have an *-ed* ending?

INFORMATION: If the answer is *no,* you can rule out all words with *-ed* endings. If the answer is *yes,* focus on the words with *-ed* endings. Ask more questions to figure out which of those words is the correct one.

Vocabulary Activities **xix**

DAY AT A GLANCE
Day 1

VOCABULARY
Reteach *pact, queasy, foisted, venture, annoyed, depriving*

COMPREHENSION
Reteach Character's Traits and Motivations

DECODING/SPELLING
Reteach Words with Short Vowels and Vowel Digraphs

GRAMMAR/WRITING
Preteach Declarative Sentences

FLUENCY
Fluency Practice

Materials Needed: *Turn It Up!*

| Student Edition pp. 10–11 | Practice Book p. 3 | Skill Card 1 | Copying Master 2 |

LESSON 1

RETEACH
Vocabulary

Lesson 1 Vocabulary Read aloud the Vocabulary Words and the Student-Friendly Explanations. Then have students turn to page 10 of their books and read the story. Guide them to fill in the blanks on page 11 by selecting the correct word in dark type. Have volunteers read the sentences, adding the word they chose. If some students are unable to complete the questions, refer to the Student-Friendly Explanations. (Answers for page 11: 2. *depriving*, 3. *venture*, 4. *pact*, 5. *foisted*, 6. *queasy*, Possible responses: 7. They were eating all the cake. 8. You make someone take it even if they don't want any.)

RETEACH
Comprehension

Character's Traits and Motivations Have students look at side A of *Skill Card 1: Character's Traits and Motivations*. Read the explanation of a character's traits and motivations. Then read the passage aloud as students follow along. Ask:

- **Who are the characters in the story?** (Amy and Li)
- **What are they doing?** (getting ready for a hike)
- **How would you describe Amy based on what she does and says?** (likes to eat healthful foods, is a careful planner, tries to think of everything)
- **How would you describe Li based on what she does and says?** (likes sweet things, is also a good planner)

Guide students through the graphic organizer, pointing out where the information they have just provided is placed. Have students find each listed answer in the paragraph. If necessary, go over the difference between traits and motivations.

GUIDED PRACTICE Now have students look at side B of *Skill Card 1: Character's Traits and Motivations*. Read the Skill Reminder. Then have a volunteer read the passage aloud as students follow along. Guide students as they copy the graphic organizer and complete it with details from the story. (Possible responses: Jason's Trait: is neat and tidy; Jason's Motivation: doesn't want his pals to be mad, Tina's Trait: is messy, Tina's Motivation: likes her big brother and wants to be with him)

2 Lesson 1 • *Turn It Up!*

Day 1

RETEACH

Decoding/Spelling

Copying Master 2

Words with Short Vowels and Vowel Digraphs Distribute *Copying Master 2*. Write these words on the board: *dread* and *check*. Point out that the short *e* sound, as in *check*, can also be spelled *ea* as in *dread*. Explain that when two vowels together make up one sound, it is called a vowel digraph. Have students identify the short vowel sound in each Spelling Word.

PRETEACH

Grammar/Writing

Declarative Sentences Remind students that a complete sentence has two parts: a subject that tells who or what the sentence is about and a predicate that tells about the subject or what happened. If a sentence does not contain both of these, it is a sentence fragment.

Now explain that a declarative sentence expresses a complete thought. It is a statement that begins with a capital letter and ends with a period. Write the following sentences and fragments on the board:

> studies every night
> Dan asks a question.
> Sasha and Liz

Guide students to identify each example as a fragment or a declarative sentence. (fragment; declarative sentence; fragment)

VOCABULARY
Student-Friendly Explanations

pact A pact is an agreement between people or countries in which they promise to do certain things.

queasy If you feel queasy, you have a sick feeling in your stomach.

foisted If something is foisted on you, it is given to you whether you want it or not.

venture A new venture is a project that is exciting and even risky.

annoyed To be annoyed means to be somewhat angry about something.

depriving If someone is depriving you of something, they are keeping you from having it.

Fluency

Practice Book 3

Fluency Practice Have students turn to *Practice Book* page 3. Read the words in the first column aloud. Invite students to track each word and repeat the words after you. Then have students work in pairs to read the words in the first column aloud to each other. Follow the same procedure with each of the remaining columns. After partners have practiced reading aloud the words in each of the columns, have them practice reading all of the words.

"The Cake Game" 3

LESSON 1

DAY AT A GLANCE — Day 2

VOCABULARY
Reteach pact, queasy, foisted, venture, annoyed, depriving

COMPREHENSION
"The Cake Game"
Build Background
Monitor Comprehension
Answers to *Think Critically* Questions

DECODING/SPELLING
Reteach Words with Short Vowels and Vowel Digraphs

GRAMMAR/WRITING
Preteach Interrogative Sentences

FLUENCY
Fluency Practice

Materials Needed: *Turn It Up!*

Student Edition pp. 12–19   Practice Book pp. 3, 4   Copying Masters 1, 2

 30+ Minutes

RETEACH

Vocabulary

Copying Master 1

Lesson 1 Vocabulary Distribute a set of Vocabulary Word Cards to each pair of students. Hold up the card for the first word, and ask a volunteer to read it aloud. Have students repeat the word and hold up the matching card. Give the explanation for the word. Then ask students the first question below and discuss their responses. Continue for each of the Vocabulary Words.

- Have you ever made a **pact** with a friend? What was it about?
- What is something that makes you feel **queasy**?
- Has someone ever **foisted** something on you? What happened?
- What is a new **venture** you'd like to try?
- When was the last time you were **annoyed**? What was the reason?
- Have you ever felt that someone was **depriving** you of something? How did you react?

Comprehension

Build Background: "The Cake Game"

Ask students to describe a time when they had some sort of contest with a friend or family member. What was the contest? How did it turn out? Do they think the competition was a good idea? Why or why not?

pp. 12–13

Monitor Comprehension: "The Cake Game"

Read the title of the story aloud. Then have students read pages 12–13 to find out who the main characters are and what kind of contest they are about to have.

After reading the pages, ask: **Who are the main characters of this story? What does Dave tell Jake?** (Dave, Jake, and Ann; Dave tells Jake that he can eat all of the cake.) **NOTE DETAILS**

Model setting a purpose for reading the story.

THINK ALOUD The title of this story is "The Cake Game." What do I know from that? I know that there's a cake, as well as some kind of game with the cake. As I read, I want to find out what game they're playing with a cake. **MAKE INFERENCES**

Discuss the Stop and Think question on page 12: **What do you know about Jake and Dave so far?** (I know that Jake and Dave are friends. I know Dave is annoyed that Ann is there. I know Jake is glad to see Ann.) Guide students in writing the answer to this question. **NOTE DETAILS**

4 Lesson 1 • Turn It Up!

Day 2

Ask: **Why do you think Ann does not take any cake?** (Possible responses: She's not hungry. She doesn't like cake.) **MAKE INFERENCES**

Discuss the Stop and Think question on page 13: **Why do you think Dave and Jake both want all the cake?** (Possible response: I think they want all the cake because they are showing off for Ann.) Guide students in writing the answer to this question. **CHARACTER'S TRAITS AND MOTIVATIONS**

 Discuss the Stop and Think question on page 14: **What happens when Jake eats too fast?** (When Jake eats too fast, he gags on the cake. Ann has to hit him on the back.) Guide students in writing the answer to this question. **CAUSE AND EFFECT**

Ask: **What reason might Jake have for offering some cake to Ann?** (Possible response: He might be getting full and could want to end the contest.) **CHARACTER'S TRAITS AND MOTIVATIONS**

Discuss the Stop and Think question on page 15: **Do you think Ann will have some cake? Explain your answer.** (Possible response: I think Ann will not have any cake. She said earlier that she did not want any.) Guide students in writing the answer to this question. **MAKE PREDICTIONS**

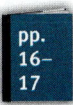 Ask: **What do you think Jake is thinking as he gazes at the cake?** (Possible response: He might be thinking that he couldn't eat another crumb and is glad the contest is over.) **DRAW CONCLUSIONS**

Discuss the Stop and Think question on page 16: **The cake game is over. Who wins? Explain your answer.** (When the cake game is over, nobody wins. Jake and Dave tie. Each boy ate four pieces of cake.) Guide students in writing the answer to this question. **DRAW CONCLUSIONS**

Discuss the Stop and Think question on page 17: **How do you think Ann feels about the boys' cake game? What makes you think that?** (Possible response: I think Ann feels the cake game is silly. She says she's glad the game is over.) Guide students in writing the answer to this question. **MAKE INFERENCES**

 Discuss the Stop and Think question on page 18: **Why does Ann say "Blame it on the cake"?** (Ann says "Blame it on the cake" because the boys don't want to go skating now. They don't think they can go fast.) Guide students in writing the answer to this question. **MAKE INFERENCES**

VOCABULARY
Student-Friendly Explanations

pact A pact is an agreement between people or countries in which they promise to do certain things.

queasy If you feel queasy, you have a sick feeling in your stomach.

foisted If something is foisted on you, it is given to you whether you want it or not.

venture A new venture is a project that is exciting and even risky.

annoyed To be annoyed means to be somewhat angry about something.

depriving If someone is depriving you of something, they are keeping you from having it.

"The Cake Game" 5

Day 2

Spelling Words: Lesson 1

1. pact	11. dread
2. brand	12. spend
3. brick	13. past
4. crop	14. plot
5. broad	15. check
6. tread	16. split
7. film	17. sting
8. else	18. strap
9. gram	19. task
10. gum	20. twin

 Answers to *Think Critically* Questions Help students read and answer the *Think Critically* questions on page 19. Have students copy the graphic organizer in question 1 onto a separate sheet of paper. Then guide students in writing the answer to each question. Possible responses are provided.

1. [2.] The boys race to eat the most cake; [3.] No one wins the cake game; [4.] Dave decides that Ann is okay. **PLOT**

2. In the beginning of the story, Dave thinks he does not like Ann. By the end of the story, Dave decides that Ann might be a good friend.  **CHARACTER**

3. I think the author did this because she feels that kids shouldn't eat that much cake. **AUTHOR'S PURPOSE**

RETEACH

Decoding/Spelling

Words with Short Vowels and Vowel Digraphs Distribute *Copying Master 2*. Model reading the Spelling Words and have students repeat them. Then write the words on the board. Ask students to identify the sounds they hear in the middle of each word and the letter or combination of letters that stands for each sound. Then have students complete the following activity based on the traditional Memory Game. Pairs of students make game cards using the lesson's Spelling Words with vowels missing; a dash appears in place of each vowel. After a student matches two cards, he or she must supply the correct missing letters to keep the game cards. If the wrong letter is supplied, the opponent gets the game cards and the next turn.

6 Lesson 1 • Turn It Up!

| Day
| 2

PRETEACH

Grammar/Writing

Interrogative Sentences Review declarative sentences with students. Explain that an interrogative sentence is another type of sentence. An interrogative sentence asks a question. It begins with a capital letter and ends with a question mark. Write the following sentences on the board:

> will Dave eat the cake
>
> Dave will eat the cake

Invite students to read each sentence aloud. Guide them to identify the first example as an interrogative sentence and the second one as a declarative sentence. Invite volunteers to capitalize and punctuate each sentence correctly. (Will Dave eat the cake? Dave will eat the cake.)

GUIDED PRACTICE Direct students' attention to page 4 in their *Practice Books*. Have students complete the page. Allow time to discuss their answers.

Practice Book 4

Fluency

Fluency Practice Invite students to look at the bottom half of *Practice Book* page 3. These sentences have been broken into natural phrases. Tell students to repeat each phrase after you, mirroring your expression, phrasing, and pace. After students have repeated each sentence, invite them to practice reading the sentences to a partner.

Practice Book 3

"The Cake Game" 7

LESSON 1

DAY AT A GLANCE
Day 3

COMPREHENSION
Preteach Synonyms and Antonyms
Reread and Summarize "The Cake Game"

DECODING/SPELLING
Reteach Listen to the Sounds

BUILD ROBUST VOCABULARY
Teach Words from "The Cake Game"

GRAMMAR/WRITING
Reteach Writing Trait: Voice

FLUENCY
Fluency Practice

Materials Needed: *Turn It Up!*

  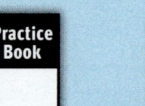

Student Edition pp. 12–18 | Practice Book pp. 3, 5 | Copying Master 3

30+ Minutes

PRETEACH

Comprehension

Synonyms and Antonyms Tell students that a synonym is a word whose meaning is the same or nearly the same as another word. Point out that the word *huge* is a synonym for *big*. Then explain that an antonym is a word whose meaning is the opposite of another word. *Small* is an antonym for *big*. Distribute *Copying Master 3,* and have a volunteer read aloud the instructions. Have students offer other examples of synonyms and antonyms.

GUIDED PRACTICE Guide students in completing the sentences using the chart. Allow time for students to share their responses with others. Have them explain why they made each choice.

Reread and Summarize Have students reread and summarize "The Cake Game" in sections, as described below.

pp. 12–13
Let's reread pages 12–13 to recall who is in this story, where they are, and what they are doing.
Summary: Dave, Jake, and Ann are in the back yard. Dave is annoyed that Jake seems to be friendly with Ann. Dave and Jake start to brag about how much cake they can eat.

pp. 14–15
Now let's reread pages 14–15 to remember how the contest goes.
Summary: Jake and Dave eat cake while Ann watches. Jake gags on some cake, and Ann has to hit him on the back. Then the boys start to feel a little sick from too much cake.

pp. 16–18
Last, let's reread pages 16–18 to find out how the contest ends.
Summary: The cake game ends in a tie, and the boys take the rest of the cake away. By now, Dave thinks Ann is OK, and they talk about going skating. But the boys are too full—blame it on the cake!

RETEACH

Decoding/Spelling

Listen to the Sounds Tell students that they need to listen carefully for how many sounds they hear before and after the vowel in each Spelling Word. Say *brick* and identify the /b/ /r/ blend before the vowel and the /k/ sound after the vowel. Point out that the *c* and *k* make one sound, /k/.

Then say *split*. Identify the /s/, /p/, and /l/ sounds before the vowel and the /t/ sound after it. Point out how each sound at the beginning of the word is made by a different letter.

---

8 Lesson 1 • Turn It Up!

Day 3

TEACH
Build Robust Vocabulary

pp. 13–15 **Words from "The Cake Game"** Have students locate the word *blabs* on page 13 of "The Cake Game." Ask a volunteer to read aloud the sentence in which this word appears. (First sentence: *"My dad baked a cake," Jake blabs to Ann.*) Explain that this means that Jake told something that was supposed to be a secret. Continue by asking students to locate and read aloud the sentence on page 14 in which *crams* appears. (Line 2: *Dave crams his cake down.*) Explain that this sentence means that Dave stuffed his cake into his mouth. He put more into his mouth than was polite. Then ask students to locate and read aloud the sentence on page 15 in which *jabs* appears. (Line 3: *Dave jabs at the cake on his plate.*) Explain that this sentence means that Dave poked his cake with something pointed, probably his fork.

Have students work in groups of three. Ask them to decide how to act out each word. Allow one person in each group to act out one of the words while the rest of the students guess the word.

RETEACH
Grammar/Writing

Practice Book 5 **Writing Trait: Voice** Have students turn to page 5 in their *Practice Book*. Tell students that an author's personal voice reveals his or her personality or attitude. Invite volunteers to take turns reading the instructions aloud. Point out how the author of "The Cake Game" uses lighthearted dialogue to show humor.

GUIDED PRACTICE Guide students in completing the activities. Invite volunteers to read aloud each passage. Allow time for students to share their rewrites with the group.

Fluency

Practice Book 3 **Fluency Practice** Tell students that today they will reread the sentences on the bottom of *Practice Book* page 3. Have students locate and point to the first sentence. Tell students that everyone is going to read the sentence together. This choral reading will give students an opportunity to hear others and listen to the natural phrasing of the sentences. Choral-read each of the sentences several times.

"The Cake Game" 9

LESSON 1

DAY AT A GLANCE
Day 4

COMPREHENSION
Reteach Synonyms and Antonyms

DECODING/SPELLING
Reteach Words with Short Vowels and Vowel Digraphs

BUILD ROBUST VOCABULARY
Reteach Words from "The Cake Game"

GRAMMAR/WRITING
Reteach Writing Form: Character Description

FLUENCY
Fluency Practice

Materials Needed: *Turn It Up!*

 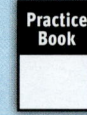 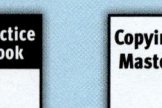

Student Edition pp. 12–18 | Practice Book p. 6 | Copying Master 4

Spelling Words: Lesson 1

1. pact	11. dread
2. brand	12. spend
3. brick	13. past
4. crop	14. plot
5. broad	15. check
6. tread	16. split
7. film	17. sting
8. else	18. strap
9. gram	19. task
10. gum	20. twin

30+ Minutes

RETEACH
Comprehension

pp. 12–18 **Synonyms and Antonyms**   Review with students what they have learned about synonyms and antonyms. Write the following words from "The Cake Game," and the page on which they occur, on the board.

annoyed (p. 12)	*glad* (p. 12)
queasy (p. 15)	*pale* (p. 17)

Have volunteers find each word in the story and read the sentence in which it appears. Then have other students suggest a synonym and an antonym for each word. (Possible responses: *annoyed*: synonym—*irritated*, antonym—*pleased*; *glad*: synonym—*happy*, antonym—*sad*; *queasy*: synonym—*sick*, antonym—*healthy*; *pale*: synonym—*white*, antonym—*rosy*)

GUIDED PRACTICE   Have students work in pairs to find synonyms or antonyms for these words from the story: *pact, grabs, whacks,* and *depriving*. Have one student find the word, read the sentence in which it appears, and say "synonym" or "antonym." The other student supplies an appropriate word. Have students switch roles. Conclude by asking volunteers to share their synonyms and antonyms.

RETEACH
Decoding/Spelling

Practice Book 6 **Words with Short Vowels and Vowel Digraphs**   Have students number a sheet of paper 1–18. Write *crop* on the board and circle the *o*. Explain that *o* makes the short *o* sound. Point out that the next 16 words you say have a short vowel sound spelled with one vowel. Repeat for *tread*, circling the digraph. Remind students that short vowel sounds can also be spelled with vowel digraphs, such as in the last two words. After students write each word, display it so they can proofread their work.

1. plot	2. brick	3. twin	4. film
5. sting	6. split	7. strap	8. brand
9. past	10. gram	11. task	12. pact
13. gum	14. check	15. spend	16. else
17. dread	18. broad		

Have students turn to page 6 in their *Practice Book*. Ask them to complete the items. Go over the correct answers with the group. If necessary, have volunteers describe the pictures.

10   Lesson 1 • Turn It Up!

Day 4

RETEACH

Build Robust Vocabulary

Words from "The Cake Game" Review the meanings of *blabs*, *crams*, and *jabs*. Then say these sentences and ask which word each sentence describes. Have students explain why.

- Jenny stuffs so many things in her desk that they spill out. (crams)
- My little sister always tells people what their birthday presents are before they open them. (blabs)
- The bee expert pokes at the hive with a stick to see if any bees are still in it. (jabs)

RETEACH

Grammar/Writing

Copying Master 4

Writing Form: Character Description Tell students that a character description, or sketch, describes a person. A character description includes the character's words and actions. Distribute *Copying Master 4* and have a volunteer read the instruction aloud. Then read the Student Model together. Write the following sentence from the passage on the board:

> It usually means there's something baking in Aunt Nicole's oven.

Model for students how the sentence can be improved by adding colorful details and expressing the author's personal voice.

> It usually means there's a mouth-watering, cake, pie, or batch of cookies in Aunt Nicole's oven.

GUIDED PRACTICE Complete the activity by having students answer the questions at the bottom of *Copying Master 4*. Allow time for students to share and explain their answers with the group.

Fluency

pp. 12–18

Fluency Practice Have each student work with a partner to read passages from "The Cake Game" aloud to each other. Students may select a passage that they enjoyed or choose one of the following options:

- Read page 14. (Total: 43 words)
- Read page 18. (Total: 63 words)

Encourage students to read the selected passage aloud to their partner three times. Have the student rate his or her reading on the 1–4 scale.

1	Need more practice
2	Pretty good
3	Good
4	Great!

"The Cake Game" 11

Preteach for LESSON 2

DAY AT A GLANCE
Day 5

VOCABULARY
Preteach legendary, muttered, gaped, flinched, snickering, glared, stunned, fluke

COMPREHENSION
Preteach Character's Traits and Motivations

DECODING/WORD ATTACK
Preteach Decode Longer Words

DECODING/SPELLING
Preteach Long Vowels and Vowel Digraphs

GRAMMAR/WRITING
Preteach Imperative Sentences

FLUENCY
Fluency Performance

Materials Needed: *Turn It Up!*

Student Edition pp. 12–18

Copying Master 5

30+ Minutes

PRETEACH

Vocabulary

 Copying Master 5

Lesson 2 Vocabulary Distribute a set of Vocabulary Word Cards to each student. Hold up the first word, and ask a volunteer to read it aloud. Have students repeat the word and hold up the matching card. Give the explanation for the word. Ask students the first question below and discuss their responses. Continue for each Vocabulary Word.

- Who are some examples of **legendary** people?
- How can a spoken sentence be **muttered**?
- What would your face look like if you just **gaped** at something?
- Have you ever **flinched** when something scared you?
- Why is **snickering** an unkind thing to do?
- If someone **glared** at you, how might that person be feeling?
- Why might a **stunned** person be silent in response to shocking news?
- What kinds of events might be called a **fluke**?

PRETEACH

Comprehension

 pp. 12–18

Character's Traits and Motivations Review with students that a character is a person in a story. A character's traits show what a character is like through his or her words, thoughts, and actions. A character's motive is the reason he or she acts in a certain way. Ask students to recall "The Cake Game." Then ask

- **How would you describe Jake and Dave?** (like to play games, competitive, selfish)
- **How is Ann different from Jake and Dave?** (She is cooperative, understanding, and giving.)
- **Why did Jake and Dave act a certain way toward Ann?** (Jake and Dave made a pact not to like Ann, but then they grew to like her.)

Remind students that the setting is where a story takes place. Explain that a setting can have an effect on how a character feels, acts, or develops as a person. Then ask:

- **Why do you think Ann said "We can go skate now"?** (She wants the boys to know that there are things she wants to do with them.)

GUIDED PRACTICE Tell students that the setting has been changed to a bake sale at the children's school to raise money for the homeless. Discuss how Ann, Jake, and Dave might act differently in this setting and why. (Possible response: They may not play the cake game. They would be selling the cake, not eating it.)

12 Preteach for Lesson 2 • *Turn It Up!*

Day 5

PRETEACH

Decoding/Word Attack

Decode Longer Words Write these word pairs on the board: *fat/fate, kit/kite, cub/cube, cop/cope.* Have students echo-read each pair. Point out that words with the CVCe pattern usually have a long vowel sound.

Point out that a vowel pair usually stands for a long vowel sound. Write *braid, coat, beak,* and *steep* on the board. Identify the letters that stand for the long vowel sound as you read each word aloud. Finally, tell students that a syllable that ends with a vowel is called an open syllable. An open syllable usually has a long vowel sound, such as the first syllable in *major* or *music.*

PRETEACH

Decoding/Spelling

Long Vowels and Vowel Digraphs Tell students that long vowel sounds are spelled in different ways. Write the chart on the board:

Long *a*	Long *e*	Long *o*	Long *u*	Long *i*
gape (a-e)	cheese (e-e)	woke (o-e)	fluke (u-e)	ripen (i-e)
aim (ai)	season (ea)	boast (oa)		
crayon (ay)	heel (ee)			

Point to the letter or letters that stand for the long *a* sound in the first column. Have students echo-read the words. Repeat for other columns.

PRETEACH

Grammar/Writing

Imperative Sentences Write the following sentence on the board:

> Park the car on Spring Street.

Read the sentence aloud. Explain that an imperative sentence gives a command. Point out that it begins with a verb. In the example above, the verb is *park.*

VOCABULARY

Student-Friendly Explanations

legendary Someone who is legendary has a special fame for something he or she has done.

muttered If you muttered, you said something very quietly because you did not want it to be heard.

gaped If you gaped at something, you stared open-mouthed in surprise.

flinched If a person flinched, he or she quickly moved away from something dangerous or painful.

snickering Snickering is laughing quietly in an unkind way at what someone says or does.

glared If you glared at someone, you stared at the person in an angry way.

stunned When someone is stunned by something amazing, she is shocked and sometimes even speechless.

fluke A fluke is something unusual that happens by accident.

Fluency

Fluency Performance

pp. 12–18

Invite students to read aloud the passages from "The Cake Game" that they selected and practiced earlier. Note the number of words each student reads correctly and incorrectly. Have students rate their own oral reading on the 1–4 scale. Give students the opportunity to continue practicing and then to read the passage to you again.

"The Cake Game" 13

DAY AT A GLANCE
Day 1

LESSON 2

VOCABULARY
Reteach legendary, muttered, gaped, flinched, snickering, glared, stunned, fluke

COMPREHENSION
Reteach Character's Traits and Motivations

DECODING/SPELLING
Reteach Long Vowels and Vowel Digraphs: Long *a* and Long *o*

GRAMMAR/WRITING
Preteach Exclamatory Sentences

FLUENCY
Fluency Practice

Materials Needed: *Turn It Up!*

Student Edition pp. 20–21 | Practice Book p. 7 | Skill Card 2 | Copying Master 6

RETEACH
Vocabulary

pp. 20–21

Lesson 2 Vocabulary Read aloud the Vocabulary Words and the Student-Friendly Explanations. Then have students read the story on page 20 of their books. Guide students as they complete the sentences on page 21. Explain that they should select the word in dark type that best completes the sentence. Have a volunteer read each completed sentence aloud. Then have students read the completed sentences along with you. (Answers for page 21: 2. *glared*, 3. *flinched*, 4. *muttered*, 5. *stunned*, 6. *fluke*, 7. *legendary*, 8. *snickering*)

RETEACH
Comprehension

Skill Card 2

Character's Traits and Motivations Have students look at side A of *Skill Card 2: Character's Traits and Motivations*. Read the definitions of a character's traits and motivations. Then read the passage aloud as students follow along. Ask:

- **Who are the characters in this story?** (Alex, the coach)
- **How are Alex's traits different from those of the coach?** (Alex is more willful, willing to take a chance. The coach is more cautious, careful.)
- **Why did Alex say "I'll do what it takes to get better"?** (He will take care of his leg and do what he is told so he can be in the competition.)

Remind students that the setting can have an effect on how a character feels and acts in a story. Discuss how the characters might act differently if the story took place in the doctor's office after the accident rather than at the ice rink.

GUIDED PRACTICE Now have students look at side B of *Skill Card 2: Character's Traits and Motivations*. Have a volunteer read the information at the top of the Skill Card aloud. Then have a student read the story aloud as others follow along. Guide students as they copy the chart and complete it with the information from the story. (His Actions: John meets Emma at the park to ride bikes. John gives his sunglasses to Emma. His Words: "Here, you can have them. I've got another pair I like, too." His Traits: friendly, generous)

14 Lesson 2 • *Turn It Up!*

Day 1

RETEACH
Decoding/Spelling

Long Vowels and Vowel Digraphs: Long *a*, Long *o* Distribute *Copying Master 6*. Read aloud the Spelling Words that contain the long *a* sound and have students repeat them after you. List the different spellings for long *a* on the board (*a-e, ai, ay*) and next to each write the Spelling Words that contain the same letter combination. Repeat this process with the Spelling Words that contain the long *o* sound spelled *o-e, ow,* and *oa.* Point out that *rainbow* contains both the long *a* and long *o* sounds. Ask a volunteer to identify the letters that make up each sound.

PRETEACH
Grammar/Writing

Exclamatory Sentences Tell students that an exclamatory sentence is a statement that expresses a strong feeling. It begins with a capital letter and ends with an exclamation mark. Write the following sentence on the board:

> What an exciting basketball player!

Ask a volunteer to read the sentence aloud. Explain that this sentence is exclamatory. The exclamation mark helps show the strong feeling.

GUIDED PRACTICE Write the following sentences on the board and read each aloud. Have students tell which sentences are exclamatory and how they know.

> That's an amazing art project!
> Come to art class at ten o'clock.
> This is the biggest mess ever!
> Will you help me clean up?

VOCABULARY
Student-Friendly Explanations

legendary Someone who is legendary has a special fame for something he or she has done.

muttered If you muttered, you said something very quietly because you did not want it to be heard.

gaped If you gaped at something, you stared open-mouthed in surprise.

flinched If a person flinched, he or she quickly moved away from something dangerous or painful.

snickering Snickering is laughing quietly in an unkind way at what someone says or does.

glared If you glared at someone, you stared at the person in an angry way.

stunned When someone is stunned by something amazing, she is shocked and sometimes even speechless.

fluke A fluke is something unusual that happens by accident.

Fluency

Fluency Practice Have students turn to *Practice Book* page 7. Read the words in the first column aloud. Invite students to track each word and repeat the words after you. Then have students work in pairs to read the words in the first column aloud to each other. Follow the same procedure with each of the remaining columns. After partners have practiced reading aloud the words in each of the columns, have them practice reading all of the words.

"Drive Fast!" 15

LESSON 2

DAY AT A GLANCE
Day 2

VOCABULARY
Reteach legendary, muttered, gaped, flinched, snickering, glared, stunned, fluke

COMPREHENSION
"Drive Fast!"
Build Background
Monitor Comprehension
Answers to *Think Critically* **Questions**

DECODING/SPELLING
Reteach Long Vowels and Vowel Digraphs: Long *e*

GRAMMAR/WRITING
Preteach Interjections

FLUENCY
Fluency Practice

Materials Needed: *Turn It Up!*

Student Edition pp. 22–29

Practice Book pp. 7, 8

Copying Masters 5, 6

RETEACH

Vocabulary

Copying Master 5

Lesson 2 Vocabulary Distribute a set of Word Cards to each pair of students. Ask each pair to set all the cards face-up on a desk. Have one student silently choose a word and say a sentence using the word. Have the other student point to the correct Word Card. Continue until the students have used all the words.

Comprehension

Build Background: "Drive Fast!"
Ask students to share experiences about taking on a new challenge such as learning a new sport. Discuss the problems they faced and the things that helped them succeed in meeting the challenges.

pp. 22–23

Monitor Comprehension: "Drive Fast!"
Read the title of the story aloud. Then have students read pages 22–23 to find out about the problem Danica faced.

After reading the pages, ask: **What problem did Danica face?** (Some people thought she could not race cars because she is a woman.) **PROBLEM/SOLUTION**

Discuss the Stop and Think question on page 22: **Why did some people think Danica could not win?** (Some people thought Danica could not win because she is a woman and is too small.) Guide students in writing the answer to this question. **DRAW CONCLUSIONS**

Discuss the Stop and Think question on page 23: **Some drivers snickered or glared at Danica. How would that make you feel?** (Possible response: It would make me feel sad or angry if someone snickered or glared at me.) Guide students in writing the answer to the question. **IDENTIFY WITH CHARACTERS**

Ask: **Why do you think that the other drivers don't snicker at Danica anymore?** (They know that Danica wins sometimes, and that she drives fast.) **MAKE INFERENCES**

pp. 24–25

Ask students to make a prediction based on the Stop and Think question on page 24. **Do you think Danica will win this race? Explain your answer.** (Possible response: I think Danika will not win because she was in a pile-up.) Guide students in writing the answer to this question. **MAKE PREDICTIONS**

16 Lesson 2 • *Turn It Up!*

Ask: **How did Danica react when she slid into the big pile-up on the track?** (She didn't give up.) CHARACTER'S TRAITS AND MOTIVATIONS

Discuss the Stop and Think question on page 25: **What would happen if Danica stopped for gas?** (If Danica stopped for gas, then the other cars would get ahead of her.) Guide students in writing the answer to this question. CAUSE AND EFFECT

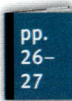
pp. 26–27

Ask students to read pages 26–27 to find out what happens to Danica. After reading the pages, ask: **Does Danica win the Indy 500? Does this surprise you? Explain your answer.** (Danica does not win. Possible response: This surprises me because the story made it seem as if she would win.) MAIN IDEA AND DETAILS

Discuss the Stop and Think question on page 26: **The author says that what Danica did was *legendary*. Why does the author say this?** (Possible response: The author says this because it was the first time a woman almost won the Indy 500.) Guide students in writing the answer to this question. AUTHOR'S PURPOSE

Discuss the Stop and Think question on page 27: **Why do you think Danica knows she will win the big one some day?** (Possible response: I think Danica knows she will win the big one some day because she really wants to win. She keeps trying to get faster.) Guide students in writing the answer to this question. MAKE INFERENCES

Read aloud the first two sentences on page 27. Model identifying a character's traits and motivations for doing something.

THINK ALOUD **When I read the first two sentences, I learn that Danica is very caring. I think she likes to bring joy to others who are not as lucky as she is. That tells me something about the kind of person she is.** CHARACTER'S TRAITS AND MOTIVATIONS

page 28

Discuss the Stop and Think Question on page 28: **Traits are words that describe people. What are some words that tell about Danica?** (Possible responses: determined, brave, caring) Guide students in writing the answer to this question. CHARACTER'S TRAITS AND MOTIVATIONS

Ask: **What does it mean to be fit and trim?** (Possible response: It means that Danica is healthy. Point out that the sentence that follows is the context clue: She skates for miles at a time.) CONTEXT CLUES

VOCABULARY

Student-Friendly Explanations

legendary Someone who is legendary has a special fame for something he or she has done.

muttered If you muttered, you said something very quietly because you did not want it to be heard.

gaped If you gaped at something, you stared open-mouthed in surprise.

flinched If a person flinched, he or she quickly moved away from something dangerous or painful.

snickering Snickering is laughing quietly in an unkind way at what someone says or does.

glared If you glared at someone, you stared at the person in an angry way.

stunned When someone is stunned by something amazing, she is shocked and sometimes even speechless.

fluke A fluke is something unusual that happens by accident.

"Drive Fast!" 17

Day 2

Spelling Words: Lesson 2

1. cheese	11. eagle
2. heel	12. throw
3. season	13. rose
4. boast	14. student
5. chief	15. goal
6. gape	16. woke
7. aim	17. ripen
8. brain	18. cube
9. fluke	19. rainbow
10. crayon	20. scrape

page 29 — Answers to *Think Critically* Questions Help students read and answer the *Think Critically* questions on page 29. Have students copy the graphic organizer in question 1 on a separate sheet of paper. Then guide students in writing the answer to each question. Possible responses are provided.

1. [Her Traits] works hard, tries her best, kind to others **CHARACTER**
2. The main thing that this selection tells me about Danica Patrick is that she wants to be a great race car driver. **MAIN IDEA AND DETAILS**
3. Danica might win a big race one day because she will not give up until she does. **CAUSE AND EFFECT**

RETEACH
Decoding/Spelling

Copying Master 6 — Long Vowels and Vowel Digraphs: Long *e* Explain that /ē/ can be spelled *ee*, *ea*, and sometimes *ie*. Distribute *Copying Master 6*. Read the Spelling Words that contain the long *e* sound and have students repeat them after you. List the different spellings for the long *e* sound on the board (*ee, ea, ie*). Then write *cheese* next to *ee*, *season* next to *ea*, and so on for all five of the long *e* words in the list. Read the words aloud and have students repeat them after you.

18 Lesson 2 • Turn It Up!

Day 2

PRETEACH
Grammar/Writing

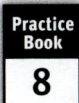 **Interjections** Tell students that an interjection is a word or phrase that expresses strong feeling. It is set apart by a comma or an exclamation mark. Write these sentences on the board:

> Oh, I forgot to get my math book.
> Wow! She hit a home run!

Guide students to notice the punctuation after the interjections. Point out that if an exclamation point follows an interjection, the next word begins with a capital letter. Have students say, then write, sentences that begin with *yes, hooray,* and *yikes*.

GUIDED PRACTICE Direct students to page 8 in their *Practice Book*. Have students recall what they have learned about imperative and exclamatory sentences. Review how they can identify an interjection. Read the activity directions together. Then ask students to complete the page.

Fluency

Fluency Practice Invite students to look at the bottom half of *Practice Book* page 7. These sentences have been broken into natural phrases. Tell students to repeat each phrase after you, mirroring your expression, phrasing, and pace. After students have repeated each sentence, invite them to practice reading the sentences to a partner.

"Drive Fast!" 19

LESSON 2

Day 3

COMPREHENSION
Preteach Synonyms and Antonyms
Reread and Summarize "Drive Fast!"

DECODING/SPELLING
Reteach Long Vowels and Vowel Digraphs: Long *i*, Long *u*

BUILD ROBUST VOCABULARY
Teach Words from "Drive Fast!"

GRAMMAR/WRITING
Reteach Writing Trait: Voice

FLUENCY
Fluency Practice

Materials Needed: *Turn It Up!*

Student Edition pp. 22–28 | Practice Book pp. 7, 9 | Copying Masters 6, 7

PRETEACH
Comprehension

Synonyms and Antonyms Distribute *Copying Master 7* and have students listen as you read the information at the top of the page. Ask a volunteer to read the first sentence pair. Tell students that knowing what *shouted* means can help them figure out the meaning of *muttered*. Point out how the context of the sentences helps you figure out that the underlined words are opposites.

GUIDED PRACTICE Have pairs of students work together to complete the rest of the page. Allow time for students to share their answers.

Reread and Summarize Have students reread and summarize "Drive Fast!" in sections, as described below.

 Let's reread pages 22–23 to recall what problem Danica faced at the beginning of the story.
Summary: Some people thought that Danica could not race cars because she is a woman and she is small.

 Now let's reread pages 24–25 to find out what happens as Danica drives in the Indy 500.
Summary: Danica drives very fast, and she slides into a big pile-up on the track. She doesn't give up, though, and she gets back on the track. She doesn't have time to get gas, and so she slips back.

 Last, let's reread pages 26–28 to find out if Danica wins the Indy 500.
Summary: Danica does not win the Indy 500. However, her fans are proud of her hard work.

RETEACH
Decoding/Spelling

Long Vowels and Vowel Digraphs: Long *i*, Long *u* Refer students to *Copying Master 6*. Model reading aloud the Spelling Words that contain the long *u* and long *i* sounds, and have students repeat them after you. List spellings for long *u* and long *i* on the board, and write the Spelling Word examples next to each.

Refer students to the activity at the bottom of *Copying Master 6*. This activity is based on the traditional Memory Game. Pairs of students make game cards using the lesson's Spelling Words with the vowels missing; a dash appears in place of each vowel. After a student matches two cards, he or she must supply the correct missing letters to keep the game cards. If the wrong letters are supplied, the opponent gets the game cards and the next turn.

20 Lesson 2 • Turn It Up!

Day 3

TEACH

Build Robust Vocabulary

Words from "Drive Fast!" Have students locate the word *pile-up* on page 24 of "Drive Fast!" Ask a volunteer to read aloud the sentence in which this word appears. (Line 6: *Then Danica slid into a big pile-up.*) Explain that this means that Danica's car slid into several cars that had crashed into each other. Continue by asking students to locate and read aloud the sentence in which *staff* appears on page 25. (First sentence: *Her pit staff fixed her car.*) Explain that this sentence means that a team of workers helped Danica fix her car. Then ask students to locate and read aloud the sentence in which *laps* first appears on page 25. (Line 4: *Nine laps to go!*) Explain that this sentence means that Danica had to drive her car around the racetrack nine more times.

pp. 24–25

Ask each student to write the words on cards or slips of paper. Give an explanation of each word and have students hold up the correct word.

RETEACH

Grammar/Writing

Writing Trait: Voice Have students turn to page 9 in their *Practice Book*. Explain that good writers let their own personal voice come through when they write. Ask a volunteer to read the information at the top of the page. Then read aloud the story beginning in Part A as students read along. Invite students to point out the vivid details and the expressive words that the author uses.

Practice Book 9

GUIDED PRACTICE Complete Part B on page 9 of the *Practice Book* together. Guide students to find details to complete the section. Then have pairs of students work together to complete Part C. Remind them to use details from the chart as they think about their responses.

Fluency

Fluency Practice Tell students that today they will reread the sentences on the bottom of *Practice Book* page 7. Have students locate and point to the first sentence. Tell students that everyone is going to read the sentence together. This choral reading will give students an opportunity to hear others and listen to the natural phrasing of the sentences. Choral-read each of the sentences several times.

Practice Book 7

"Drive Fast!" 21

LESSON 2

Day 4

COMPREHENSION
Reteach Synonyms and Antonyms

DECODING/SPELLING
Reteach Long Vowel and Vowel Digraphs

BUILD ROBUST VOCABULARY
Reteach Words from "Drive Fast!"

GRAMMAR/WRITING
Reteach Writing Form: Descriptive Paragraph

FLUENCY
Fluency Practice

Materials Needed: *Turn It Up!*

Student Edition pp. 22–28 | Practice Book p. 10 | Copying Master 8

Spelling Words: Lesson 2

1. cheese	11. eagle
2. heel	12. throw
3. season	13. rose
4. boast	14. student
5. chief	15. goal
6. gape	16. woke
7. aim	17. ripen
8. brain	18. cube
9. fluke	19. rainbow
10. crayon	20. scrape

30+ Minutes

RETEACH
Comprehension

Synonyms and Antonyms Remind students that they can sometimes use synonyms and antonyms as clues to the meaning of a new word. Ask students to define a synonym (a word that means the same or nearly the same) and an antonym (a word that means the opposite).

Write the following sentences on the board. Have students find a synonym for the underlined word. Remind them that this word will help them figure out the meaning of the underlined word. (ducked)

> Pat flinched as the ball sailed past. She ducked because she thought it was going to hit her.

GUIDED PRACTICE Write these sentences on the board:

> Mr. Thompson thought the uniforms were extravagant. He wanted to buy the simple uniforms instead.

Have students find the antonym that helps them understand the meaning of the underlined word. (simple)

RETEACH
Decoding/Spelling

Long Vowels and Vowel Digraphs Have students number a sheet of paper 1–17. Write the Spelling Words *gape, brain,* and *crayon* on the board. Point out how the long *a* sound is spelled in different ways. Dictate the rest of the long *a* words, followed by Spelling Words with long *e,* long, *o,* long *u,* and long *i* as shown below:

1. aim	2. rainbow	3. scrape	4. cheese
5. heel	6. season	7. chief	8. eagle
9. boast	10. throw	11. rose	12. goal
13. woke	14. fluke	15. student	16. cube
17. ripen			

After the students have written each word, display it so they can proofread their work. Then have students turn to page 10 in their *Practice Books*. Ask a volunteer to read the instructions at the top of the page. Have students work together to complete the activities.

22 Lesson 2 • Turn It Up!

Day 4

RETEACH
Build Robust Vocabulary

Words from "Drive Fast!" Review the meanings of the words *pile-up*, *staff*, and *laps*. Then say these sentences and ask which word each sentence describes. Have students explain why.

- **Cars were stopped on the road because of a crash involving several other cars.** (pile-up)
- **The school's team of cleaning helpers made the classrooms look great.** (staff)
- **The girl ran around the track five times.** (laps)

RETEACH
Grammar/Writing

Copying Master 8 — **Writing Form: Descriptive Paragraph (Setting)** Tell students that a descriptive paragraph of a setting describes a particular place. The description should include details about sights, sounds, smells, and actions. A writer may include statements, thoughts, and feelings that let the reader know what the place means to him or her personally. Distribute *Copying Master 8*. Have students read the information at the top of the page. Then read the Student Model together.

Write the following sentence on the board:

> The park was full of colorful flowers.

Point out that this sentence offers some description but does not have a sense of the writer's voice. Model for students how the sentence can be revised to reflect a more personal voice:

> I am surrounded by a rainbow of blossoms as I skip through the park.

GUIDED PRACTICE Complete the activity by having students identify examples of details that reveal the writer's personality, voice, and viewpoint.

Fluency

pp. 22–28 **Fluency Practice** Have each student work with a partner to read aloud passages from "Drive Fast!" Students may select a passage that they enjoyed or choose one of the following options:

- Read page 23. (Total: 70 words)
- Read page 28. (Total: 63 words)

Encourage students to read the selected passage aloud to their partner three times. Have the student rate his or her reading on the 1–4 scale.

1	Need more practice
2	Pretty good
3	Good
4	Great!

"Drive Fast!" 23

Preteach for **LESSON 3**

DAY AT A GLANCE
Day 5

VOCABULARY
Preteach surrender, clusters, sparkling, particular, sizzles, stroll

COMPREHENSION
 Preteach Compare and Contrast

DECODING/WORD ATTACK
Preteach Decode Longer Words

DECODING/SPELLING
Preteach Variant Vowels and Vowel Diphthongs

GRAMMAR/WRITING
Preteach Sentences: Subjects

FLUENCY
Fluency Performance

Materials Needed: *Turn It Up!*

Student Edition pp. 22–28

Copying Master 9

PRETEACH
Vocabulary

Copying Master 9 — **Lesson 3 Vocabulary** Tell students that they are going to learn six new words that they will see again when they read a story called "Clusters of Hope." Distribute a set of Vocabulary Word Cards to each pair of students. Hold up the first word and ask a volunteer to read it aloud. Have students repeat the word and hold up the matching card. Give the explanation for the word. Ask students the first question below and discuss their responses. Continue this way until students have answered a question about each of the Vocabulary Words.

- What has happened to make you **surrender**?
- What is something that comes in **clusters**?
- What kind of **sparkling** object can make you smile? Why?
- What is a **particular** activity or hobby you enjoy?
- If something **sizzles**, what might be happening?
- When is the last time you took a **stroll**? Where did you go?

PRETEACH
Comprehension

pp. 22–28  **Compare and Contrast** Tell students that to compare means to look for the ways things are alike. To contrast means to look for the ways things are different. Have students name two foods, animals, sports, or comparable household or classroom items. Ask:

- **Compare the two items. How are they alike?**
- **Contrast the two items. How are they different?**

Ask students to recall what they read in "Drive Fast!" Then ask:

- **Compare Danica Patrick and her pit staff. What are some ways they are alike?** (Possible responses: Both want to win; both love car racing.)
- **Now contrast Danica and her pit staff. What are some ways they are different?** (Possible responses: She drives, but they work on her car; she takes the risks, but they stay safer; they may all be men, but she is a woman.)

GUIDED PRACTICE Have students work in pairs to find other elements in "Drive Fast!" to compare and contrast. (Danica's childhood and their own childhoods, Danica's experience of a race and that of her fans, or Danica's work at the racetrack and her time away from the track) Have volunteers share their responses with the class.

24 Preteach for Lesson 3 • *Turn It Up!*

Day 5

PRETEACH

Decoding/Word Attack

Decode Longer Words Write the following word sets on the board and have volunteers read them aloud: *choice/toy, awful/auto, down/house, /new/blue/tool, took/look.* Then review these generalizations:

- The /ô/ sound can be spelled *au* and *aw.*
- The /oi/ sound can be spelled *oy* and *oi.*
- The /o͞o/ sound can be spelled *ew, ue,* and *oo.*
- The /ow/ sound can be spelled *ow* and *ou.*

GUIDED PRACTICE Write the following words on the board. Guide students to identify the vowel sound in each word.

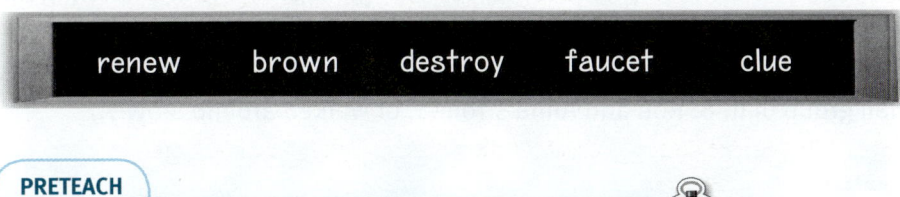

renew   brown   destroy   faucet   clue

PRETEACH

Decoding/Spelling

Variant Vowels and Vowel Diphthongs Write these incomplete words on the board. Have students copy and complete each word by writing the correct vowel variant—*au, aw, ew,* or *oo*—in each blank.

shamp__   bl__   __ful   d__ghter

Help students understand that the same vowel sound can be formed by different, or varied, letter combinations.

PRETEACH

Grammar/Writing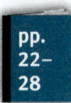

Sentences: Subjects Write the following sentence on the board:

Mark ate the hot dog.

Read the sentence aloud. Tell students that the subject of the sentence is who or what the sentence is about. Ask the class to identify the subject **(Mark)** and have a volunteer underline the word. Now ask students to suggest different subjects to insert into the sentence. **(Possible responses: I, you, they, Shawn, Ms. Roberts)** Write each suggestion and read the new sentence.

VOCABULARY

Student-Friendly Explanations

surrender When you surrender, you stop fighting something or someone.

particular Something that is particular is one specific thing of its kind.

sparkling Something that is sparkling is shining, clear, and bright.

clusters Clusters are small groups of people or things that are close together.

sizzles If something sizzles, it is very hot and makes a hissing sound.

stroll To stroll is to walk in a slow, relaxed way.

Fluency

pp. 22–28 **Fluency Performance** Invite students each to read aloud from "Drive Fast!" a passage that they selected and practiced earlier. Note the number of words each student reads correctly and incorrectly. Have students rate their own oral reading on the 1–4 scale. Give each student the opportunity to continue practicing and then to read the passage to you again.

"Drive Fast!" 25

LESSON 3

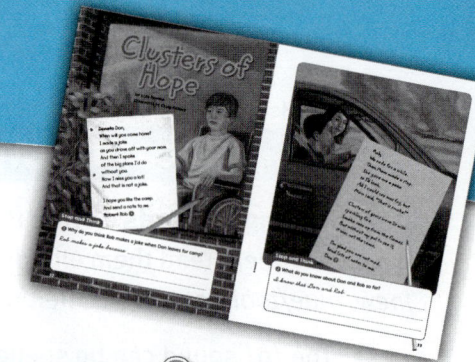

DAY 1

VOCABULARY
Reteach *surrender, clusters, sparkling, particular, sizzles, stroll*

COMPREHENSION
 Reteach Compare and Contrast

DECODING/SPELLING
Reteach Vowel Diphthongs /oi/

GRAMMAR/WRITING
Preteach Sentences: Predicates

FLUENCY
Fluency Practice

Materials Needed: *Turn It Up!*

Student Edition pp. 30–31 | Practice Book p. 11 | Skill Card 3 | Copying Master 10

RETEACH
Vocabulary

Lesson 3 Vocabulary Read aloud the Vocabulary Words and Student-Friendly Explanations. Write the words on the board. Then ask a volunteer to read aloud the story on pages 30 and 31 as students follow along. At each blank, ask a student to choose the correct term. Have a volunteer read each completed sentence. Then guide students in answering the questions on page 31. (Answers for pages 30–31: 2. *sparkling,* 3. *surrender,* 4. *stroll,* 5. *particular,* 6. *sizzles,* Possible responses: 7. A cluster of grass is a small group of it. 8. Rob and Anna strolled, or walked around slowly.)

RETEACH
Comprehension

Compare and Contrast Have students look at side A of *Skill Card 3: Compare and Contrast*. Read the explanation of compare and contrast. Then read the passage aloud as students follow along. Refer students to the chart and ask these questions:

- What two things are being compared and contrasted?
- What are some ways the two cats are alike?
- What are some ways the cats are different?

Remind students that they can compare and contrast almost anything using these skills. Ask them to think how they might compare and contrast their own pets, two friends, two books or movies, or other comparable pairs.

GUIDED PRACTICE Now have students look at side B of *Skill Card 3: Compare and Contrast*. Read the Skill Reminder aloud. Then read the passage aloud as students follow along. Guide students as they copy the chart and complete it with the details from the story. (Tennis: hit a ball with a racquet, ball is small and yellow, divided into sets, individual sport; Both: Sasha's favorite sports, both use balls, players hit balls over a net; Volleyball: hit the ball with hands, ball is large and white, divided into games, team sport)

26 Lesson 3 • Turn It Up!

Day 1

RETEACH
Decoding/Spelling

Vowel Diphthongs /oi/ Read aloud the Spelling Words. Help students identify those words with the /oi/ sound. Model reading these Spelling Words and have students repeat them: *toil, foist, choice, royal, destroy, boyhood,* and *annoyed*. Then write the words on the board and have students copy them onto a sheet of paper. Read each word one more time and have students circle the letter combination in each word that stands for the /oi/ sound.

Copying Master 10

PRETEACH
Grammar/Writing

Sentences: Predicates Write the following sentence on the board:

> Darren played the game.

Ask a volunteer to read the sentence aloud. Tell students that the predicate tells what the subject, Darren, did. Ask the class to identify the predicate (played the game) and have a volunteer circle the words.

Now ask students to suggest different predicates to insert into the sentence to replace the word *played*. (Possible responses: saw, bought, won, lost, loved) Write each suggestion in a new sentence and have a volunteer read it.

GUIDED PRACTICE Ask students to suggest new predicates to replace the last three words in the sentence. (Possible responses: drank the milk, watched a movie, rode his bike) Invite students to explain how they know the words they chose form the predicate.

VOCABULARY
Student-Friendly Explanations

surrender When you surrender, you stop fighting something or someone.

particular Something that is particular is one specific thing of its kind.

sparkling Something that is sparkling is shining, clear, and bright.

clusters Clusters are small groups of people or things that are close together.

sizzles If something sizzles, it is very hot and makes a hissing sound.

stroll To stroll is to walk in a slow, relaxed way.

Fluency

Fluency Practice Have students turn to *Practice Book* page 11. Read the words in the first column aloud. Invite students to track each word and repeat the words after you. Then have students work in pairs to read the words in the first column aloud to each other. Follow the same procedure with each of the remaining columns. After partners have practiced reading aloud the words in each of the columns, have them practice reading all of the words.

Practice Book 11

"Clusters of Hope" 27

LESSON 3

DAY AT A GLANCE — Day 2

VOCABULARY
Reteach surrender, clusters, sparkling, particular, sizzles, stroll

COMPREHENSION
"Clusters of Hope"
Build Background
Monitor Comprehension
Answers to Think Critically **Questions**

DECODING/SPELLING
Reteach Variant Vowels /aw/

GRAMMAR/WRITING
Preteach Sentences: Subjects and Predicates

FLUENCY
Fluency Practice

Materials Needed: Turn It Up!

Student Edition pp. 32–39 | Practice Book pp. 11, 12 | Copying Masters 9, 10

RETEACH

Vocabulary

Lesson 3 Vocabulary Distribute a set of Word Cards to each student. Then have students work in small groups. Have two students sit next to each other, while a third reads aloud the definition of one word. Have the two students try to identify the word being defined and hold up the card for that word. The first student to hold up the correct word gives the definition for the next round. Have the groups continue until all the students in the group have had a turn.

Comprehension

Build Background: "Clusters of Hope"
Ask students to share experiences they may have had spending time away from friends. Who went away? How did they stay in touch, if at all? How did they renew their friendship at the end of the separation?

Monitor Comprehension: "Clusters of Hope"
Read the title of the story aloud. Then have students read pages 32–33 to find out who the characters are and what they are doing.

After reading the pages, ask: **Who are the two main characters?** (Don and Rob) **What do you know about where they are?** (Rob is at home, while Don is on a trip to summer camp.) Note Details/Summarize

Discuss the Stop and Think question on page 32: **Why do you think Rob makes a joke when Don leaves for camp?** (Possible response: Rob makes a joke because he doesn't want anyone to know that he feels sad.) Guide students in writing the answer to this question. Character's Motivations

Ask: **Why do you think Rob says that it is not a joke that he misses Don?** (Possible response: He made jokes when Don was leaving, but now he is serious.) Character's Motivations

Discuss the Stop and Think question on page 33: **What do you know about Don and Rob so far?** (Possible response: I know that Don and Rob are good friends and they write letters to each other.) Guide students in writing the answer to the question. Summarize

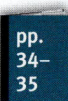

Discuss the Stop and Think question on page 34: **Do you think Cole will become Rob's new best friend? Explain your answer.** (Possible response: I think Cole will not become Rob's best friend because Rob does not like Cole's jokes.) Guide students in writing the answer to this question. Make Predicitons

28 Lesson 3 • Turn It Up!

Read aloud the first paragraph on page 34. Model the strategy of using context and previous knowledge to confirm the meaning of a word.

(THINK ALOUD) **When I read this page I was not sure what *bank* meant: "as we sit on the bank picking up tadpoles and frogs." I know they're not sitting on a building where you keep your money. What other meanings does this word have? I know—it's like the bank of a river, which means the land next to the river. They're sitting on the edge of the pond.** CONTEXT CLUES

Ask: **Why do you think Don starts his next letter by talking about frogs?** (Rob mentioned catching tadpoles and frogs in his letter.) AUTHOR'S CRAFT

Discuss the Stop and Think question on page 35: **What do Rob and Don do that is the same?** (Possible response: Rob and Don both do something with frogs.) Guide students in writing the answer to this question.  COMPARE AND CONTRAST

pp. 36–37

Ask: **What kinds of things might Rob write about in his next letter?** (Possible responses: different friends, other activities he does, how he hopes Don will come home soon) MAKE PREDICITONS

Discuss the Stop and Think question on page 36: **Why do you think the author repeats the word *hope* in italics at the end of Rob's notes?** (Possible response: I think the author repeats the word because he wants us to see how strongly Rob feels.) Guide students in writing the answer to this question. AUTHOR'S CRAFT

Discuss the Stop and Think question on page 37: **Don says "Now it's time to go home." What does he mean?** (Possible responses: When Don says "Now it's time to go home," he means he's ready to be back home; camp is over.) Guide students in writing the answer to this question. MAKE INFERENCES

page 38

Ask: **What do you think will happen after this story ends?** (Possible response: I think Rob's new friends will meet Don and they will all become friends.) MAKE PREDICTIONS

Discuss the Stop and Think question on page 38: **What does Rob mean when he says his "hopes" got Don home?** (Possible response: When Rob says his "hopes" got Don home, he means that each time he used the word *hope*, he was wishing for Don to come home. His wish came true.) Guide students in writing the answer to this question. MAKE INFERENCES

Day 2

VOCABULARY

Student-Friendly Explanations

surrender When you surrender, you stop fighting something or someone.

particular Something that is particular is one specific thing of its kind.

sparkling Something that is sparkling is shining, clear, and bright.

clusters Clusters are small groups of people or things that are close together.

sizzles If something sizzles, it is very hot and makes a hissing sound.

stroll To stroll is to walk in a slow, relaxed way.

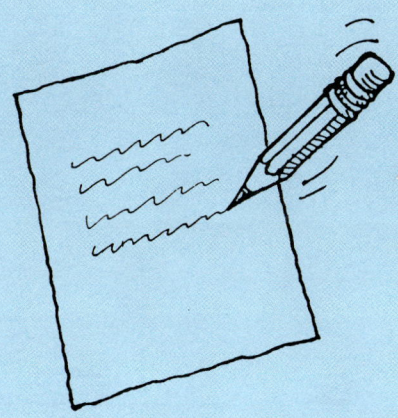

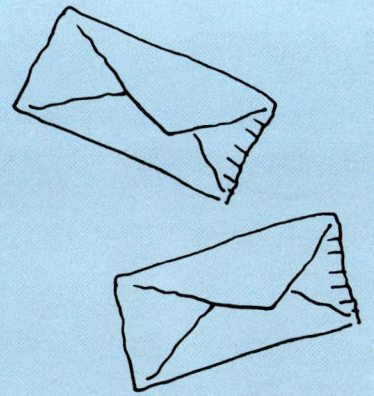

"Clusters of Hope" 29

Day 2

Spelling Words: Lesson 3

1. toil	11. royal
2. faucet	12. allow
3. boyhood	13. destroy
4. choice	14. blew
5. dawn	15. spoon
6. awful	16. shampoo
7. foist	17. brown
8. daughter	18. renew
9. flaw	19. wooden
10. annoyed	20. auction

page 39 **Answers to *Think Critically* Questions** Help students read and answer the *Think Critically* questions on page 39. Have students copy the graphic organizer in question 1 on a separate sheet of paper. Then guide students in writing the answer to each question. Possible responses are provided.

1. 1. Don and Rob missed each other a lot. 2. Don and Rob did things with other friends. 3. When Don comes back from camp, they are friends again. **PLOT**

2. I think Rob would be the kind of friend who likes to do fun things and cares about people. **CHARACTER**

3. I think the author wants me to see that friends can be apart and still be best friends. **THEME**

RETEACH
Decoding/Spelling

Copying Master 10 **Variant Vowels /aw/** Draw students' attention to the /aw/ words on *Copying Master 10*. Model reading these Spelling Words and have students repeat them: *faucet, dawn, awful, daughter, flaw,* and *auction*. Then write the words on the board and have students copy them on a separate sheet of paper. Read each word one more time and have students circle the letter combination in each word that creates the /aw/ sound.

30 Lesson 3 • Turn It Up!

Day 2

PRETEACH
Grammar/Writing

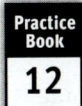 **Sentences: Subjects and Predicates**   Remind students that if a sentence is missing a subject or a predicate, it is a sentence fragment. Write these fragments on the board:

> Hopes to go on her uncle's boat.
> Anna and her uncle, Jake.

Help students understand that the first sentence is missing a subject and the second is missing a predicate. Ask volunteers to provide possible subjects and predicates for the sentences so they are complete. Rewrite the complete sentences and have students identify the subjects and predicates.

GUIDED PRACTICE   Direct students' attention to page 12 in their *Practice Book*. Ask a volunteer to read and answer item 1. Ask for several other possible predicates from other students. Make sure all understand that the phrase is a fragment because it is missing a predicate. Continue in the same way with each of the remaining items.

Fluency

Fluency Practice   Invite students to look at the bottom half of *Practice Book* page 11. These sentences have been broken into natural phrases. Tell students to repeat each phrase after you, mirroring your expression, phrasing, and pace. After students have repeated each sentence, invite them to practice reading the sentences to partners.

"Clusters of Hope"   31

LESSON 3

DAY AT A GLANCE — Day 3

COMPREHENSION
Preteach Make Judgments
Reread and Summarize "Clusters of Hope"

DECODING/SPELLING
Reteach Variant Vowels and Vowel Diphthongs /o͞o/, /o͝o/, /ow/

BUILD ROBUST VOCABULARY
Teach Words from "Clusters of Hope"

GRAMMAR/WRITING
Reteach Writing Trait: Word Choice

FLUENCY
Fluency Practice

Materials Needed: *Turn It Up!*

Student Edition pp. 32–38 | Practice Book pp. 11, 13 | Copying Master 11

30+ Minutes

PRETEACH

Comprehension

Copying Master 11

Make Judgments Distribute *Copying Master 11* and have students listen as you read the information at the top of the page. Have students give examples of judgments they can make about movies, TV shows, and books they are familiar with.

GUIDED PRACTICE Ask students to read the story and fill out the chart. Allow time for students to share their judgments with others.

Reread and Summarize Have students reread and summarize "Clusters of Hope" in sections, as described below.

pp. 32–33

Let's reread pages 32–33 to find out what we know at the beginning of the story.
Summary: Rob and Don are friends. Don has gone off to summer camp, while Rob stays at home. On the way to camp, Don and his mother see a brush fire.

pp. 34–35

Now let's reread pages 34–35 to see what Don and Rob write about to each other.
Summary: Rob goes to the park with his friend Cole. They skip stones and catch tadpoles and frogs. Don rides on a raft and eats five hot dogs at camp. The boys miss each other.

pp. 36–38

Now let's reread pages 36–38. What happens on these pages and how does the story end?
Summary: Rob goes for a stroll with Anna. Don goes fishing at camp. Don says he's ready to come home. Rob admits that, while Anna and Cole are fun, Don is still his best friend.

RETEACH

Decoding/Spelling

Variant Vowels and Vowel Diphthongs /o͞o/, /o͝o/, /ow/ Focus students' attention on the /o͞o/, /o͝o/, and /ow/ words from this lesson's Spelling Words. Model reading these Spelling Words and have students repeat them: *boyhood, allow, blew, spoon, shampoo, brown, renew,* and *wooden.* Then ask volunteers to write each word on the board. Read each word one more time and have students circle the letter combinations in each word that stand for the /o͞o/, /o͝o/, and /ow/ sounds.

32 Lesson 3 • Turn It Up!

Day 3

TEACH

Build Robust Vocabulary

Words from "Clusters of Hope" Have students locate the word *poke* on page 33 of "Clusters of Hope." Ask a volunteer to read aloud the sentence in which this word appears. (Line 4: *She gave me a poke so I'd look.*) Explain that this sentence means that Mom gave Don a push with her finger. Continue by asking students to locate and read aloud the sentence in which the word *bank* appears on page 34. (Line 6: *I tell him what we like to do as we sit on the bank picking up tadpoles and frogs.*) Explain that this means that the boys sat on the land at the edge of the pond. Then ask students to locate and read aloud the sentence in which *cracks* appears on page 34. (Line 8: *Cole cracks jokes a lot.*) Explain that this sentence means that Cole tells many jokes.

Ask volunteers to use the words in sentences they make up.

RETEACH

Grammar/Writing

Practice Book 13 **Writing Trait: Word Choice** Have students turn to page 13 in their *Practice Book*. Explain that when they write a poem or story, it is important to use specific and interesting words so readers can picture what they are saying and describing. Ask a volunteer to read the information in the graphic organizer. Point out how the author of "Clusters of Hope" uses vivid words to describe the characters' actions and experiences.

GUIDED PRACTICE Complete the page together. Have volunteers share their answers to Parts B and C. Discuss other possible vivid words and phrases.

Fluency

Practice Book 11 **Fluency Practice** Tell students that today they will reread the sentences on the bottom of *Practice Book* page 11. Have students locate and point to the first sentence. Tell students that everyone is going to read the sentence together. This choral reading will give students an opportunity to hear others and listen to the natural phrasing of the sentences. Choral-read each of the sentences several times.

"Clusters of Hope" **33**

LESSON 3

DAY AT A GLANCE — Day 4

COMPREHENSION
Reteach Make Judgments

DECODING/SPELLING
Reteach Variant Vowels and Vowel Diphthongs

BUILD ROBUST VOCABULARY
Reteach Words from "Clusters of Hope"

GRAMMAR/WRITING
Reteach Writing Form: Narrative Poem

FLUENCY
Fluency Practice

Materials Needed: *Turn It Up!*

 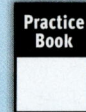 

Student Edition pp. 32–38 | Practice Book p. 14 | Copying Master 12

Spelling Words: Lesson 3

1. toil	11. royal
2. faucet	12. allow
3. boyhood	13. destroy
4. choice	14. blew
5. dawn	15. spoon
6. awful	16. shampoo
7. foist	17. brown
8. daughter	18. renew
9. flaw	19. wooden
10. annoyed	20. auction

30+ Minutes

RETEACH
Comprehension

Make Judgments Remind students that when we form our own ideas or opinions about something, we are making judgments. When we read, we use details from the text, along with what we know from our own experiences, to make judgments about the characters, events, and setting of a story.

Ask students to listen carefully as you read aloud the following story. Then ask for volunteers each to make a judgment about the fox's actions. Discuss reasons for the judgments, based on both the text and students' experiences.

> **The fox was walking through the woods.** *I sure am hungry,* he thought. **Suddenly, he spied some juicy grapes hanging from a high branch. The grapes made his mouth water. He tried to jump for them, but couldn't come close. Then he tried to climb the tree. After many tries, the fox was all worn out. He sighed and said, "Those stupid grapes are probably sour anyway. I really didn't want them."**

(Possible response: The fox was foolish to say he didn't really want the grapes; he just said that because he couldn't get them.)

GUIDED PRACTICE Have students form pairs. Assign each pair one letter from "Clusters of Hope." Have them make a judgment about the poem, the characters, or the events the letter describes. Have students share their judgments about the poems and discuss their supporting reasons.

RETEACH
Decoding/Spelling

 Variant Vowels and Vowel Diphthongs Have students number a sheet of paper 1–16. Write the Spelling Word *auction* on the board and point to the *au* letter combination. Then have students write the first five words below. After students have written each word, display it so that they can proofread their work. Repeat for each of the other letter sounds using these examples: *royal, spoon,* and *brown*. Give *wooden* as the last word.

1. flaw	2. dawn	3. awful	4. daughter
5. faucet	6. toil	7. choice	8. foist
9. boyhood	10. destroy	11. annoyed	12. blew
13. shampoo	14. renew	15. allow	16. wooden

Have students turn to page 14 in their *Practice Books* and read the story, circling each word as directed. Then ask volunteers to read aloud the story and tell which words they circled. When students have correctly identified each word, have them complete the second part of the activity.

34 Lesson 3 • Turn It Up!

Day 4

RETEACH
Build Robust Vocabulary

Words from "Clusters of Hope" Review the meanings of *poke, bank,* and *cracks*. Then say these sentences and ask which word each sentence describes. Have students explain why.

- **The boy pushed his friend with his finger and said, "You go next!"** (poke)
- **The ducks lined up on the edge of the river.** (bank)
- **Dad always tells jokes at dinner.** (cracks)

RETEACH
Grammar/Writing

Copying Master 12 **Writing Form: Narrative Poem** Tell students that poets use colorful, precise language to help readers form a vivid picture in their minds. By carefully choosing words, poets help readers imagine what people, places, events, and experiences are like. Distribute *Copying Master 12.* Have a volunteer read the description of a narrative poem. Then read the student model together. Tell students that the passage is one student's effort to write a narrative poem. Write on the board the following sentence from the passage.

> My friends and I get out of our sleeping bags.

Model for students how the sentence can be improved by the addition of vivid language.

> My friends and I tumble out of our sleeping bags.

GUIDED PRACTICE Complete the activity by having students revise three more sentences from the student model. Allow time for students to share their revised sentences with the group.

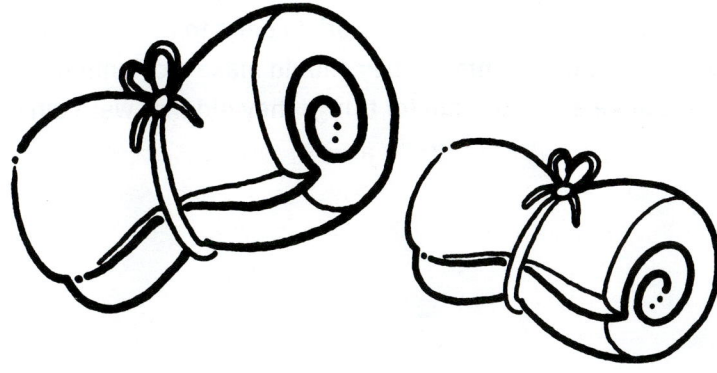

Fluency

pp. 32–38 **Fluency Practice** Have each student work with a partner to read passages from "Clusters of Hope" aloud to each other. Students may select a passage that they enjoyed or choose one of the following options:

- Read page 33. (Total: 70 words)
- Read page 34. (Total: 63 words)

Encourage students to read the selected passage aloud to their partner three times. Have the student rate his or her reading on the 1–4 scale.

1	Need more practice
2	Pretty good
3	Good
4	Great!

"Clusters of Hope" 35

Preteach for LESSON 4

DAY AT A GLANCE — Day 5

VOCABULARY
Preteach averted, fury, interrogation, stern, accusing, solemnly, cringed, craned

COMPREHENSION
 Preteach Compare and Contrast

DECODING/WORD ATTACK
Preteach Decode Using Structural Patterns

DECODING/SPELLING
Preteach Inflections -ed, -ing

GRAMMAR/WRITING
Preteach Complete and Simple Subjects

FLUENCY
Fluency Performance

Materials Needed: Turn It Up!

Student Edition pp. 32–38

Copying Master 13

30+ Minutes

PRETEACH — Vocabulary

Copying Master 13

Lesson 4 Vocabulary Distribute a set of Vocabulary Word Cards to each pair of students. Hold up the card for the first word, and ask a volunteer to read it. Have students repeat the word and hold up the matching card. Give the explanation for the word. Then ask students the first question below and discuss their responses. Continue for each of the Vocabulary Words.

- Have you ever **averted** your eyes from something? What was it?
- What might make you react with **fury**?
- What happens when police on TV perform an **interrogation**?
- When was the last time someone gave you a **stern** look?
- How would you look if you were **accusing** someone of something?
- What is something that people do **solemnly**?
- When was the last time you **cringed**? Why?
- What have you **craned** your neck to see?

PRETEACH — Comprehension

pp. 32–38 Focus Skill

Compare and Contrast Authors compare people, places, and things by telling and showing how they are alike. Authors contrast people, places, and things by telling and showing how they are different. Remind students that comparing and contrasting setting, characters, and events can help them better understand the stories they read. Ask students to think about how Rob and Don spent their summers in "Clusters of Hope." Ask:

- **What are some ways the boys' summers were alike?** (Possible responses: They both wrote notes, they both missed a friend, they both saw frogs.)
- **What are some ways the boys' summers were different?** (Possible responses: Don went to camp, while Rob stayed home; Rob skipped stones and went for a stroll, while Don rode on a raft and went fishing.)

GUIDED PRACTICE Have students work in pairs to makes similar lists of how they spent the last summer. They should make a column for things they did that were alike and a column for things they did that were different.

Day 5

PRETEACH

Decoding/Word Attack

Decode Using Structural Patterns Write the word *counting* on the board. Cover the *-ing* and pronounce the root word. Do the same with the word *pushed*. Point out that the inflection *-ing* forms its own syllable, and the ending *-ed* forms its own syllable when it is added to some words.

GUIDED PRACTICE Write the following words on the board: *burned, cracked, shopping, visited, flapping*. Have students read each word, tell whether *-ed* or *-ing* forms its own syllable, and tell how many syllables the whole word has.

PRETEACH

Decoding/Spelling

Inflections -ed, -ing Tell students that inflections are endings added to words. Write the words below on the board and read them aloud. Then make the changes necessary to form the words in parentheses.

beg	count	return	shop	move
(begging)	(counting)	(returned)	(shopping)	(moving)

Help students understand that adding *-ed* and *-ing* sometimes requires spelling changes, such as doubling the final consonant or dropping the final *e*.

PRETEACH

Grammar/Writing

Complete and Simple Subjects Remind students that the subject of a sentence tells who or what is doing the action. The predicate tells what the subject is doing. Then write the following sentence on the board:

> The large boat passed near the docks.

Tell students that *The large boat* is the complete subject because all these words name what the sentence is about. *Boat* is the simple subject. It names the specific thing the sentence is about. Ask students to help you do the same for this sentence:

> **The boat's whistle made a loud sound.** (The boat's whistle; whistle)

VOCABULARY

Student-Friendly Explanations

averted If you averted your eyes, you looked away from something instead of directly at it.

fury Fury is extremely strong anger.

interrogation An interrogation is a long period of intense questioning to get information from someone.

stern Someone who is stern is very serious and strict.

accusing When you look at someone in an accusing way, you are showing that you think he or she has done something wrong.

solemnly When you say something solemnly, you say it in a very serious way.

cringed If you cringed, you moved or flinched slightly because of discomfort or fear.

craned If you craned your neck, you stretched it to let you see or hear something better.

Fluency

pp. 32–38 Fluency Performance Invite students each to read aloud from "Clusters of Hope" a passage that they selected and practiced earlier. Note the number of words each student reads correctly and incorrectly. Have students rate their own oral reading on the 1–4 scale. Give each student the opportunity to continue practicing and then to read the passage to you again.

LESSON 4

Day 1 — Day at a Glance

30+ Minutes

VOCABULARY
Reteach *averted, fury, interrogation, stern, accusing, solemnly, cringed, craned*

COMPREHENSION
 Reteach Compare and Contrast

DECODING/SPELLING
Reteach Inflections *-ed, -ing*

GRAMMAR/WRITING
Preteach Complete and Simple Predicates

FLUENCY
Fluency Practice

Materials Needed: *Turn It Up!*

| Student Edition pp. 40–41 | Practice Book p. 15 | Skill Card 4 | Copying Master 14 |

RETEACH
Vocabulary

pp. 40–41 **Lesson 4 Vocabulary** Read aloud the Vocabulary Words, writing each word on the board, and the Student-Friendly Explanations. Have students write down each word and make notes about the definition. Then ask a volunteer to read the first sentence on page 40 of their books. Have another student give a definition of the word in boldface type. Do the same for each remaining sentence on page 40. Then guide students in completing the sentences on page 41 by selecting the correct word. Have a volunteer read each completed sentence along with you. *(Answers for page 41: 2. cringed, 3. interrogation, 4. fury, 5. averted, 6. solemnly, 7. stern, 8. accusing)*

RETEACH
Comprehension

  **Compare and Contrast** Have students look at side A of *Skill Card 4: Compare and Contrast*. Read the explanation of compare and contrast. Then have a volunteer read the passage aloud as students follow along. Ask:

- **What two things are being compared and contrasted?** *(travel by boat and travel by airplane)*

- **How are the ways of traveling different?** *(Boats were more popular in the past and are slow. Airplanes are fast and are more popular today.)* **In which part of the Venn diagram can you find descriptions of traveling by boat and airplane?** *(under the headings "Boats" and "Airplanes")*

- **How are the ways of traveling alike?** *(Both can carry many people and will continue to serve travelers' needs.)* **In which part of the Venn diagram can you find out?** *(under the heading "Both")*

Ask students how they might compare and contrast two other ways of traveling, two relatives, or two music groups.

GUIDED PRACTICE Now have students look at side B of *Skill Card 4: Compare and Contrast*. Read the Skill Reminder aloud. Then have a student read the passage aloud as others follow along. Guide students in copying the Venn diagram and completing it. *(Rachel: rakes leaves into piles, wears gloves; Both: rake leaves to earn money, think they work well together, happy when they split the money; Mei: puts leaves in bags, doesn't wear gloves)*

38 Lesson 4 • *Turn It Up!*

Day 1

RETEACH
Decoding/Spelling

 **Inflections -ed, -ing** Distribute *Copying Master 14*. Focus on the *-ed* words in the list. Model reading these Spelling Words, and have students repeat them: *craned, seemed, burned, chopped, cracked, begged, slipped, trimmed, returned, pushed, visited, cringed,* and *screamed*. Then write the words on the board. Ask students to identify each root word and which root words have changed when they added *-ed* (*craned, chopped, begged, slipped, trimmed, cringed*). Have volunteers explain the change to each root. (Some doubled the final consonant; others dropped the final *e*.) Read each word one more time and have volunteers circle the root in each word.

PRETEACH
Grammar/Writing

Complete and Simple Predicates Remind students that the predicate of a sentence tells what the subject is doing. The subject tells who or what is doing the action. Then write the following sentence on the board:

> The large boat passed near the docks.

Underline *passed near the docks* and circle *passed*. Tell students that *passed near the docks* is the complete predicate because all these words name what the subject is doing. *Passed* is the simple predicate because it is the specific thing the subject, the boat, is doing.

GUIDED PRACTICE Write these sentences on the board:

> The boat's whistle made a loud sound.
> The people on the dock waited for their friends.
> The ship's captain waved to the passengers.

Have students take turns identifying the complete predicate and simple predicate in each sentence. (made a loud sound; waited for their friends; waved to the passengers)

VOCABULARY
Student-Friendly Explanations

averted If you averted your eyes, you looked away from something instead of directly at it.

fury Fury is extremely strong anger.

interrogation An interrogation is a long period of intense questioning to get information from someone.

stern Someone who is stern is very serious and strict.

accusing When you look at someone in an accusing way, you are showing that you think he or she has done something wrong.

solemnly When you say something solemnly, you say it in a very serious way.

cringed If you cringed, you moved or flinched slightly because of discomfort or fear.

craned If you craned your neck, you stretched it to let you see or hear something better.

Fluency

 **Fluency Practice** Have students turn to *Practice Book* page 15. Read the words in the first column aloud. Invite students to track each word and repeat the words after you. Then have students work in pairs to read the words in the first column aloud to each other. Follow the same procedure with each of the remaining columns. After partners have practiced reading aloud the words in each of the columns, have them practice reading all of the words.

"The Best Time" 39

LESSON 4

DAY AT A GLANCE — Day 2

VOCABULARY
Reteach *averted, fury, interrogation, stern, accusing, solemnly, cringed, craned*

COMPREHENSION
"The Best Time"
Build Background
Monitor Comprehension
Answers to *Think Critically* Questions

DECODING/SPELLING
Reteach Inflections *-ed* and *-ing*

GRAMMAR/WRITING
Preteach Complete and Simple Subjects and Predicates

FLUENCY
Fluency Practice

Materials Needed: *Turn It Up!*

Student Edition pp. 42–49 | Practice Book pp. 15, 16 | Copying Masters 13, 14

30+ Minutes

RETEACH

Vocabulary

Copying Master 13

Lesson 4 Vocabulary Have students make on a sheet of paper a tic-tac-toe form with a total of nine boxes. Ask them to write an *X* in the center box. Then have them write the eight vocabulary words in the outer boxes in any order. Read aloud the definitions of the words and have students place an *X* on the word that is being defined. Have students raise their hands when they have completed a horizontal, vertical, or diagonal row.

Comprehension

Build Background: "The Best Time"
Ask students to share experiences they may have had about moving. What feelings did they have? How does their new home or neighborhood compare and contrast with the old home or neighborhood?

pp. 42–43

Monitor Comprehension: "The Best Time"
Read the title of the story aloud. Then have students read pages 42–43 to find out where Meg and her mother are and what they are doing.

After reading the pages, ask: **Where are Meg and her mother as the story begins? What are they doing?** (They are on a ship entering a harbor; they are moving to the United States.) NOTE DETAILS

Discuss the Stop and Think question on page 42: **Where do you think Meg and her mom lived before?** (Possible response: I think Meg and her mom lived in Europe somewhere. I think this because she had to travel across the sea to get to the United States.) Guide students in writing the answer to this question. MAKE INFERENCES

Discuss the Stop and Think question on page 43: **How do you think Meg feels as she looks for her dad? Why?** (Possible response: I think Meg feels a little sad because her dad is not there yet.) Guide students in writing the answer to this question. IDENTIFY WITH CHARACTERS

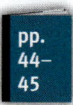
pp. 44–45

Tell students: Think about the vocabulary term *interrogation*. Then ask: **What do you predict might happen after the interrogation?** (Possible response: I predict that Meg and her mom will either pass or not pass the interrogation.) MAKE PREDICTIONS

---

40 Lesson 4 • *Turn It Up!*

Day 2

Discuss the Stop and Think question on page 44: **Why are Meg and her mom tired and weak?** (Possible response: Meg and her mom are tired and weak because they just finished a long journey, on a ship.) Guide students in writing the answer to this question. **DRAW CONCLUSIONS**

Discuss the Stop and Think question on page 45: **How is Meg's test like the ones you take at school?** (Possible response: Meg's test is like the ones I take at school because it's important to pass, they need to be passed before moving on to the next part.) Guide students in writing the answer to this question. **COMPARE AND CONTRAST**

pp. 46–47

Ask: **Why is it important for Meg to say she is not sick?** (Sick people are not allowed to come into the United States and are sent back home.) **NOTE DETAILS**

Discuss the Stop and Think question on page 46: **Why does the author tell you about the husband and wife?** (Possible response: The author tells me about the husband and wife so I know how hard it was for some to come to the United States.) Guide students in writing the answer to this question. **AUTHOR'S PURPOSE**

Ask: **How do you think Meg felt when the man said they were free to go into the United States?** (Possible response: She was probably very happy, a little scared, and excited to see her dad.) **CHARACTER'S EMOTIONS**

Discuss the Stop and Think question on page 47: **Once Meg and her mom pass their tests, what do they do next?** (Once Meg and her mom pass their tests, they leave the testing site and go toward the docks.) Guide students in writing the answer to this question. **SEQUENCE**

Read aloud the last paragraph on page 47. Point out that Meg and her mother have still not seen Meg's dad. Then tell students that one way authors can hold readers' interest is by creating suspense, or making readers wonder what will happen next. Model the strategy of analyzing suspense in a story.

(**THINK ALOUD**) The story is almost over, and they still don't know if Meg's dad will be there. Maybe something happened to him. After all, they haven't seen him in a year. He could be hurt, or maybe he couldn't come to meet them. I hope the author clears it all up on the last page. **USE STORY STRUCTURE**

VOCABULARY

Student-Friendly Explanations

averted If you averted your eyes, you looked away from something instead of directly at it.

fury Fury is extremely strong anger.

interrogation An interrogation is a long period of intense questioning to get information from someone.

stern Someone who is stern is very serious and strict.

accusing When you look at someone in an accusing way, you are showing that you think he or she has done something wrong.

solemnly When you say something solemnly, you say it in a very serious way.

cringed If you cringed, you moved or flinched slightly because of discomfort or fear.

craned If you craned your neck, you stretched it to let you see or hear something better.

"The Best Time" 41

Day 2

Spelling Words: Lesson 4

1. counting	11. trimmed
2. craned	12. shopping
3. seemed	13. returned
4. burned	14. watching
5. chopped	15. pushed
6. cracked	16. visited
7. begged	17. cringed
8. moving	18. screamed
9. slipped	19. scratching
10. sailing	20. flapping

 page 48 Discuss the Stop and Think question on page 48: **Do you think Meg will want to leave the United States and go back home? Explain your answer.** (Possible response: I think Meg will not want to leave. Both of her parents are in the United States; they worked hard to get there.) Guide students in writing the answer to this question. **MAKE PREDICTIONS**

Tell students: **The author says that Meg has tears on her cheeks, yet she seems to be happy.** Then ask: **Have you ever cried because you were happy? Describe the situation.** (Responses will vary.) **IDENTIFY WITH CHARACTERS**

page 49 **Answers to Think Critically Questions** Help students read and answer the Think Critically questions on page 49. Have students copy the graphic organizer in question 1 onto a separate sheet of paper. Then guide students in writing the answer to each question. Possible responses are provided.

1. [Event 1] Meg and her Mom come on a ship to the United States. [Event 2] They must pass tests to get in. [Event 3] They pass the tests. [Event 4] Meg's dad is waiting for them. **PLOT**

2. The main idea of this story is that many people wanted to come to the United States, but not all of them were allowed to. **MAIN IDEA AND DETAILS**

3. I think people tried to pass the tests so they could have a better life in the United States. **MAKE INFERENCES**

RETEACH

Decoding/Spelling

Copying Master 14 **Inflections -ed, -ing** Distribute Copying Master 14. Direct students' attention to the -ing words in this lesson's list. Model reading these Spelling Words and have students repeat them: *counting, moving, sailing, shopping, watching, scratching,* and *flapping.* Then write the words on the board. Ask students to identify each root word and which root words changed when -ing was added. (moving, shopping, flapping) Have volunteers explain the change to each root. (Two doubled the final consonant, while one dropped the final e.) Read each word one more time and have students circle the root in each word.

42 Lesson 4 • Turn It Up!

Day 2

PRETEACH

Grammar/Writing

Practice Book 16 **Complete and Simple Subjects and Predicates** Direct students' attention to page 16 in their *Practice Books*. Share with students this information about complete and simple subjects and predicates, and examine the examples together. Ask students to suggest other possible complete subjects and predicates for the example sentence.

- The complete subject of a sentence is all the words that name the person or thing the sentence is about.
- The simple subject is the main word or words within the complete subject.

Meg's long (trip) ended in the United States.

- The complete predicate includes all the words that tell what the subject is or does.
- The simple predicate is the main word or words within the complete predicate.

Meg's long trip (ended) in the United States.

GUIDED PRACTICE Ask a volunteer to read and answer item 1. Continue in the same manner with each of the remaining items. Invite volunteers to rewrite sentences with different subjects or predicates on the board and have other students identify the complete and simple subjects and predicates.

Fluency

Practice Book 15 **Fluency Practice** Invite students to look at the bottom half of *Practice Book* page 15. These sentences have been broken into natural phrases. Tell students to repeat each phrase after you, mirroring your expression, phrasing, and pace. After students have repeated each sentence, invite them to practice reading the sentences to a partner.

"The Best Time" 43

LESSON 4

DAY AT A GLANCE
Day 3

COMPREHENSION
Preteach Make Judgments
Reread and Summarize: "The Best Time"

DECODING/SPELLING
Reteach Inflections -ed, -ing

BUILD ROBUST VOCABULARY
Teach Words from "The Best Time"

GRAMMAR/WRITING
Reteach Writing Trait: Word Choice

FLUENCY
Fluency Practice

Materials Needed: *Turn It Up!*

Student Edition pp. 42–48

Practice Book pp. 15, 17

Copying Master 15

PRETEACH
Comprehension

Make Judgments Distribute *Copying Master 15*. Have students read aloud the information about making judgments at the top of the page.

GUIDED PRACTICE Have students look at the cartoon and complete the activity. Allow time for students to share what they have added to the chart.

Reread and Summarize Have students reread and summarize "The Best Time" in sections, as described below.

pp. 42–43 **Let's reread pages 42–43 to find out what we know at the beginning of the story.**
Summary: Meg and her mother have arrived in the United States after a long trip. They are meeting Meg's dad, who moved to the United States a year ago. But before they can enter, they have to pass some tests.

pp. 44–45 **Let's reread pages 44–45 to find out about the tests they must pass.**
Summary: At the testing site, a weak and tired Meg and her mother have to answer questions about their health. They learn that sick people are sent back home.

pp. 46–48 **Let's reread pages 46–48 to find out how Meg's story turns out.**
Summary: Although some around them do not pass their tests, Meg and her mother are cleared to enter the United States. Finally, they find Meg's dad, and the family is together again.

RETEACH
Decoding/Spelling

Inflections -ed, -ing Review with students the *-ed* and *-ing* words from the Spelling Words. Write each of the words below on the board.

| count (+ing) | crane (+ed) | chop (+ing) | return (+ed) |
| move (+ing) | beg (+ed) | sail (+ing) | cringe (+ed) |

Have students add the indicated inflection to the roots. Then have volunteers explain whether or how the root word changed when they added *-ed* or *-ing*. (counting, craned, chopping, returned, moving, begged, sailing, cringed) Conclude by having students read each word along with you.

44 Lesson 4 • Turn It Up!

Day 3

TEACH
Build Robust Vocabulary

pp. 46–47 **Words from "The Best Time"** Have students locate the words *revealed* and *disease* on page 46 of "The Best Time." Ask a volunteer to read aloud the sentence in which these words appear. (Line 2: *A test revealed that she had a disease.*) Explain that this sentence means that a test showed that the man's wife had a sickness. *Reveal* means to show something that was secret or unknown. *Disease* is another word for *sickness*. Continue by asking students to locate and read aloud the sentence in which the word *grim* appears on page 47. (Line 3: *Life was grim there.*) Explain that this means that life at the testing spot was serious and sad.

Guide students to act out the meaning of each word.

RETEACH
Grammar/Writing

Practice Book 17 **Writing Trait: Word Choice** Have students turn to page 17 in their *Practice Book*. Explain that when writers write a story, it is important to use vivid, specific, and interesting words so readers can more easily imagine what the characters experience. Ask a volunteer to read the information at the top of the page.

GUIDED PRACTICE Complete the page together. Have volunteers share their answers to Parts B and C. Discuss other possible vivid words and phrases.

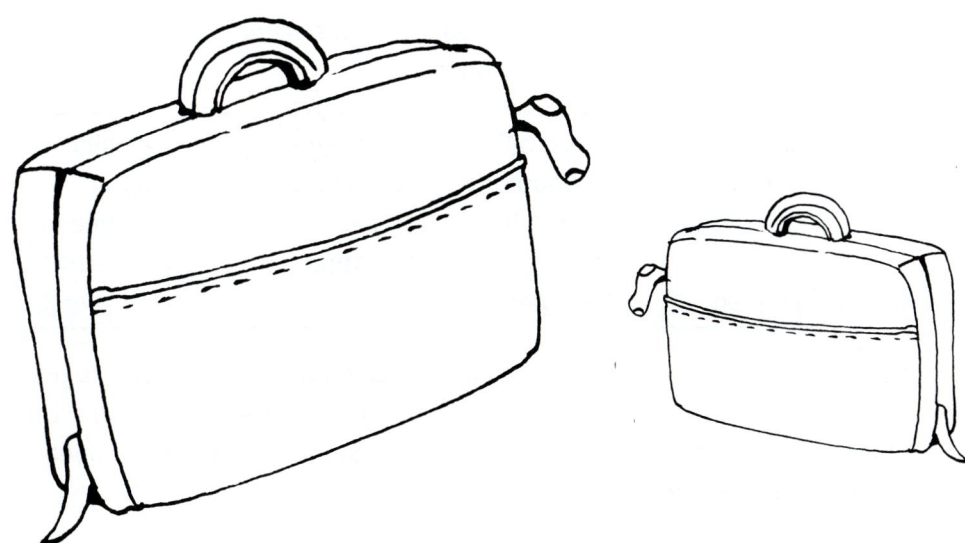

Fluency

Practice Book 15 **Fluency Practice** Tell students that today they will reread the sentences on the bottom of *Practice Book* page 15. Have students locate and point to the first sentence. Tell students that everyone is going to read the sentence together. This choral reading will give students an opportunity to hear others and listen to the natural phrasing of the sentences. Choral-read each of the sentences several times.

"The Best Time" 45

LESSON 4

DAY AT A GLANCE — Day 4

COMPREHENSION
Reteach Make Judgments

DECODING/SPELLING
Reteach Inflections -ed, -ing

BUILD ROBUST VOCABULARY
Reteach Words from "The Best Time"

GRAMMAR/WRITING
Reteach Writing Form: Journal Entry

FLUENCY
Fluency Practice

Materials Needed: Turn It Up!

Student Edition pp. 42–48 | Practice Book p. 18 | Copying Master 16

Spelling Words: Lesson 4

1. counting
2. craned
3. seemed
4. burned
5. chopped
6. cracked
7. begged
8. moving
9. slipped
10. sailing
11. trimmed
12. shopping
13. returned
14. watching
15. pushed
16. visited
17. cringed
18. screamed
19. scratching
20. flapping

30+ Minutes

RETEACH
Comprehension

Make Judgments pp. 42–48   Give students the following information about making judgments:

- When you form your own opinion, you are making a judgment.
- Use details from the story, along with what you already know, to make judgments when reading.
- Different readers can make different judgments.

Ask students to reread the first paragraph on page 47 in "The Best Time." Have them think about why some people were kept at the testing spot for weeks. Remind them to consider details from the story as well as their own knowledge. Then have them each discuss with a partner a judgment they could make about the difficult situation. Have volunteers share their judgments and what they based their judgments on. (Possible response: The people at the testing spot were not trying to be cruel. They were just doing their jobs, trying to keep sick people from entering the United States and making sure that the ones who did come in were healthy and without diseases that could harm other Americans.)

GUIDED PRACTICE Have students reread page 43 in "The Best Time." Then ask them to make a judgment about what kind of person Meg's dad is. Have volunteers share their judgments and explain what information they used to make them.

RETEACH
Decoding/Spelling

Inflections -ed, -ing Practice Book 18   Have students number a sheet of paper 1–18. Write *craned* on the board and circle the *-ed* inflection. Then do the same for *counting*, pointing to the *-ing* inflection. Remind students that when they spell a word with an *-ed* or *-ing* inflection, they sometimes have to change the spelling of the root word.

1. chopped	2. moving	3. returned	4. trimmed
5. cringed	6. shopping	7. seemed	8. sailing
9. begged	10. scratching	11. visited	12. screamed
13. watching	14. burned	15. flapping	16. cracked
17. pushed	18. slipped		

Have students turn to page 18 in their *Practice Book*. Read the story together. Then have students answer the questions that follow the story. Review the answers. Have students identify this lesson's Spelling Words that appear in the story and questions.

46   Lesson 4 • Turn It Up!

Day 4

RETEACH
Build Robust Vocabulary

Words from "The Best Time" Review the meanings of *revealed, disease,* and *grim*. Then say these sentences and ask which word each sentence describes. Have students explain why.

- **Opening the box showed that the present was a new baseball glove.** (revealed)
- **Doctors help cure sickness.** (disease)
- **The television show about the lost dog was sad and serious.** (grim)

RETEACH
Grammar/Writing

Copying Master 16

Writing Form: Journal Entry Remind students that writers use colorful, precise language to help readers form a vivid picture in their minds. By carefully choosing words, writers can help readers imagine what people, places, events, and experiences are like. Distribute *Copying Master 16*. Have a volunteer read the description of a journal entry. Tell students that this passage is a journal entry written by a student who took a sailing trip. Then read the Student Model together. Guide students to identify examples of specific words and effective word choices. Ask students how the choice of words helps them to picture what the writer is describing. Write the following sentence on the board:

> Our sailboat was moving along much faster than I could move on land.

Model for students how the sentence can be improved by the addition of vivid language.

> Our sailboat was zipping along much faster than I could run on land.

GUIDED PRACTICE Complete the activity by having students answer the three questions about the Student Model. Allow time for students to share and discuss their answers with the group.

Fluency

pp. 42-48 **Fluency Practice** Have each student work with a partner to read passages from "The Best Time" aloud to each other. Students may select a passage that they enjoyed or choose one of the following options:

- Read page 42. (Total: 61 words)
- Read page 45. (Total: 76 words)

Encourage students to read the selected passage aloud to their partner three times. Have the student rate his or her reading on the 1–4 scale.

1	Need more practice
2	Pretty good
3	Good
4	Great!

"The Best Time" 47

Preteach for LESSON 5

DAY AT A GLANCE — Day 5

VOCABULARY
Preteach culinary, downcast, consternation, vivid, extensive, serenely, reminiscent, pensive, recruit, commencing

COMPREHENSION
 Reteach Character's Traits and Motivations

DECODING/WORD ATTACK
Reteach Decode Longer Words

DECODING/SPELLING
Reteach Words with Short Vowels and Vowel Digraphs

GRAMMAR/WRITING
Reteach Sentences

FLUENCY
Fluency Performance

Materials Needed: *Turn It Up!*

Student Edition pp. 42–48 | Practice Book p. 20 | Skill Card 5 | Copying Master 17

 30+ Minutes

PRETEACH
Vocabulary

Copying Master 17 **Lesson 5 Vocabulary** Distribute a set of Vocabulary Word Cards to each pair of students. Hold up the card for the first word, and ask a volunteer to read it aloud. Have students repeat the word and hold up the matching card. Give the explanation for the word. Then ask students the first question below and discuss their responses. Continue for each Vocabulary Word.

- What **culinary** skills do you have?
- What could you do to cheer up a **downcast** friend?
- What might cause **consternation** at a surprise party?
- What **vivid** color of clothing do you like to wear?
- If you had an **extensive** collection of something, what would it be?
- If you sit **serenely** in your seat, will you do well on a test?
- What book or story is **reminiscent** of when you were younger?
- Are you ever **pensive** during your school day?
- What activity do your friends **recruit** you to do with them?
- After school, will you be **commencing** to do your homework?

RETEACH
Comprehension

  **Character's Traits and Motivations** Have students look at side A of *Skill Card 5: Review: Character's Traits and Motivations*. Ask a volunteer to read aloud the information. Invite other students to read aloud the passage. Then ask:

- **Why does Kevin practice so hard?** (He wants to win his Ping Pong contest.)
- **Why does Kevin show the first-place trophy to his mom?** (He thinks it is big and shiny, and he wants to win it.)
- **How would you describe Kevin?** (He works hard and he is a good athlete.)

GUIDED PRACTICE Guide students in copying the chart onto a separate sheet of paper. Have them use the story information to determine the character's traits and motivations and complete the chart. (His Motivation: Kevin wants to win the first-place trophy; His Actions: He practices every day. He practices hitting and quick moving; His Thoughts and Words: He says "I want to win that trophy!" and asks his friends for help. He thinks "I better start practicing," and he remembers everything he practiced; His Traits: Kevin is athletic and determined. He is a hard worker.)

48 Preteach for Lesson 5 • Turn It Up!

Day 5

RETEACH
Decoding/Word Attack

Decode Longer Words Write *dreadful* and *fretted* on the board. Say the words aloud and have students repeat them. With students, divide *dreadful* into syllables. Point out that both syllables end with consonant sounds, so they are called closed syllables. Help students identify the short vowel sounds in the syllables and tell them that closed syllables usually have short vowel sounds. Repeat with *fretted*. Note that the short vowel sound is sometimes made by a vowel digraph—two vowels that stand for one sound. Have students identify which word has a vowel digraph in one of its closed syllables. (the *ea* in *dreadful*)

RETEACH
Decoding/Spelling

Words with Short Vowels and Vowel Digraphs Write *tread* on the board. Underline the vowel digraph. (*ea*) Remind students that a vowel digraph can stand for a short vowel sound. Point out that a vowel in a VCV pattern can also stand for a short vowel sound. Then guide students to repeat the activity with the following words: *broad, split*.

RETEACH
Grammar/Writing

Sentences Have students review subjects, predicates, and types of sentences by examining these sentences:

1. The pool is ready.
2. Hooray!
3. Do you like to swim?
4. The pool is open!
5. Put your suit on.

Have students identify the sentence type or the interjection. Ask volunteers to write *declarative, interrogative, imperative, exclamatory,* or *interjection* next to each. (1. declarative, 2. interjection, 3. interrogative, 4. exclamatory, 5. imperative)

VOCABULARY
Student-Friendly Explanations

culinary Culinary describes anything that is related to cooking.

downcast Someone who is downcast is feeling sad or depressed.

consternation Someone who shows consternation is feeling anxious or worried about something.

vivid Something that is vivid has intensely bright colors.

extensive Something extensive includes many items, details, or ideas.

serenely Serenely means "calmly" or "quietly."

reminiscent If an object or experience is reminiscent of something, it brings back memories of a place or a time.

pensive Someone who is pensive is deep in thought.

recruit When you recruit people, you get them to join a group for a purpose.

commencing Something that is commencing is beginning.

Fluency

pp. 42–49 **Fluency Performance** Invite students each to read aloud from "The Best Time" a passage that they selected and practiced earlier. Note the number of words each student reads correctly and incorrectly. Have students rate their own oral reading on the 1–4 scale. Have each student practice and then read the passage to you again.

"The Best Time" 49

LESSON 5

Day 1

VOCABULARY
Reteach culinary, downcast, consternation, vivid, extensive, serenely, reminiscent, pensive, recruit, commencing

COMPREHENSION
 Reteach Compare and Contrast

DECODING/WORD ATTACK
Reteach Decode Longer Words

DECODING/SPELLING
Reteach Words with Long Vowels and Vowel Digraphs

GRAMMAR/WRITING
Reteach Sentences

FLUENCY
Fluency Practice

Materials Needed: *Turn It Up!*

Student Edition pp. 50–51 | Practice Book pp. 19, 20 | Skill Card 5 | Copying Master 18

RETEACH

Vocabulary

Lesson 5 Vocabulary Read aloud the Vocabulary Words and the Student-Friendly Explanations. Then have students turn to pages 50–51 in their books. Ask a volunteer to read the directions aloud. Remind students that they should read each sentence to themselves with the word they chose to be sure it makes sense. If students have difficulty choosing the correct word, refer to the Student-Friendly Explanations. After students have completed the pages, have volunteers take turns reading aloud each sentence. (Answers for pages 50–51: 2. *commencing*, 3. *pensive*, 4. *reminiscent*, 5. *consternation*, 6. *extensive*, 7. *vivid*, 8. *recruit*, 9. *serenely*, 10. *culinary*, 11.–12. Responses will vary.)

RETEACH

Comprehension

Review: Compare and Contrast Have students look at side B of *Skill Card 5: Review: Compare and Contrast.* Ask a volunteer to read the instructions. Then read the passage aloud with students.

GUIDED PRACTICE Guide students in copying the Venn diagram on a separate sheet of paper to compare and contrast the way the girls made their posters. (Barb's Poster: big black letters; drew a brownie picture; picture on sides; "where" and "when" at bottom; Both Posters: "Bake Sale Today" at the top; picture of a cookie; Elana's Poster: bright red letters; "In the Lunchroom"; smiling faces in yellow and pink; pictures of lemon bars)

50 Lesson 5 • Turn It Up!

Day 1

RETEACH

Decoding/Word Attack

Decode Longer Words Write *destroy* and *reason* on the board, and say the words. Ask students to say them, divide them into syllables, and say them again. Help students hear that the first syllables end with vowel sounds. Note that these syllables are open syllables. Point out that the vowel sound is sometimes made by one vowel and sometimes by a vowel digraph—two vowels that stand for a single sound. Next, write the words *nature, peanut,* and *vibration.* Have students say the words, divide them into syllables, identify the open syllables, and circle the vowels in the open syllables.

RETEACH

Decoding/Spelling

Copying Master 18

Words with Long Vowels and Vowel Digraphs Distribute *Copying Master 18.* Echo-read the Spelling Words with students. Then ask students to identify the words with long vowel sounds and identify the letters that stand for those sounds in each word. (*ie, ea, ai, ow, oa, a–e*) Write *chief, season, brain, throw, goal,* and *scrape* on the board. Invite volunteers to underline the letters that stand for the long vowel sounds.

RETEACH

Grammar/Writing

Practice Book 20

Sentences Review the types of sentences and the correct punctuation mark for each type. Also review that each sentence begins with a capital letter, and some sentences may also include an interjection. Write the following sentence on the board:

> What time does the bus arrive!

Identify the sentence as an interrogative sentence. Point out the punctuation mark at the end and the capital letter at the beginning. Ask: **Is this the correct punctuation to use here?** (no) Erase the exclamation point and invite a volunteer to name and write the correct punctuation. (?)

GUIDED PRACTICE Have students turn to page 20 in their *Practice Books.* Invite a volunteer to read aloud the activity directions. Have students work in pairs to proofread each sentence and make corrections. Ask volunteers to share their responses.

VOCABULARY
Student-Friendly Explanations

culinary Culinary describes anything that is related to cooking.

downcast Someone who is downcast is feeling sad or depressed.

consternation Someone who shows consternation is feeling anxious or worried about something.

vivid Something that is vivid has intensely bright colors.

extensive Something extensive includes many items, details, or ideas.

serenely Serenely means "calmly" or "quietly."

reminiscent If an object or experience is reminiscent of something, it brings back memories of a place or a time.

pensive Someone who is pensive is deep in thought.

recruit When you recruit people, you get them to join a group for a purpose.

commencing Something that is commencing is beginning.

Fluency

Practice Book 19

Fluency Practice Have students turn to *Practice Book* page 19. Read the words in the first column aloud. Invite students to track each word and repeat after you. Then have students work in pairs to read the words in the first column aloud to each other. Follow the same procedure with the remaining columns. After partners have practiced reading aloud the words in each column, have them practice reading all of the words.

"The Flan Plan" 51

LESSON 5

 30+ Minutes

DAY AT A GLANCE — Day 2

VOCABULARY
Reteach culinary, downcast, consternation, vivid, extensive, serenely, reminiscent, pensive, recruit, commencing

COMPREHENSION
"The Flan Plan"
Build Background
Monitor Comprehension
Answers to *Think Critically* Questions

DECODING/WORD ATTACK
Reteach Decode Longer Words

DECODING/SPELLING
Reteach Words with Variant Vowels and Diphthongs

GRAMMAR/WRITING
Reteach Subjects and Predicates

FLUENCY
Fluency Practice

Materials Needed: *Turn It Up!*

Student Edition pp. 52–59

Practice Book p. 19

Copying Masters 17, 18

RETEACH

Vocabulary

 Copying Master 17

Lesson 5 Vocabulary Distribute a set of Vocabulary Word Cards to each student or pair of students. Have a volunteer choose one card and use the word on it in a sentence. Then ask the next volunteer to choose another card and create a sentence using that word. Challenge students to link each sentence to the content of the preceding sentence in some way.

Comprehension

Build Background: "The Flan Plan"
Invite students to share their experiences with food from other cultures. Are there any special foods from their families' cultures that they enjoy? Do they help to make these foods?

Monitor Comprehension: "The Flan Plan"
pp. 52–53

Read the title of the story aloud. Then have students read pages 52–53 to find out what Snack Week is and how Ruben feels about it.

After reading the pages, ask: **What is Snack Week? How does Ruben feel about it?** (Snack Week is a time when students bring snacks from their homeland to class. Ruben feels downcast and pensive about Snack Week.) **CHARACTER'S EMOTIONS**

Discuss the Stop and Think question on page 52: **What is another word for *downcast*? What is the opposite of *downcast*?** (Possible responses: Another word for *downcast* is *sad*, *unhappy*, or *upset*. The opposite of *downcast* is *happy* or *glad*.) Guide students in writing the answer to this question. **VOCABULARY**

Ask: **What is Ruben's homeland?** (Ruben's homeland is Cuba.) **Could a person have more than one homeland?** (Yes, a person could have more than one homeland if his or her ancestors come from different countries.) **VOCABULARY**

Discuss the Stop and Think question on page 53: **Why does Ruben think about taking black beans?** (Possible response: Ruben thinks about taking black beans because that is a popular dish in Cuba.) Guide students in writing the answer to this question. **MAKE INFERENCES**

---

52 Lesson 5 • Turn It Up!

Day 2

pp. 54–55

Discuss the Stop and Think question on page 54: **How are Ruben and Amanda the same?** (Possible responses: Ruben and Amanda are the same because they are about the same age; they live in the same neighborhood; they probably go to the same school.) Guide students in writing the answer to this question. **COMPARE AND CONTRAST**

Discuss the Stop and Think question on page 55: **How would you describe Amanda?** (Possible responses: Amanda is kind; friendly; helpful.) Guide students in writing the answer to this question.
 CHARACTER'S TRAITS AND MOTIVATIONS

pp. 56–57

Discuss the Stop and Think question on page 56: **Is Ruben really thinking about taking frog's legs? Explain your answer.** (Possible response: Ruben is not really thinking about taking frog's legs to school. He is just teasing Tucker.) Guide students in writing the answer to this question. **MAKE JUDGMENTS**

Have a volunteer reread the first five lines on page 56. Model for students how to discover a character's traits from what the character says and does.

> **THINK ALOUD** When I read Ruben's teasing words to Tucker, I wonder why he says this. First, I think he is a mean person. Then I read that he is grinning when he says this, so I think that Ruben likes to make jokes. I think Ruben has a good sense of humor.
> **CHARACTER'S TRAITS**

Discuss the Stop and Think question on page 57: **How can you tell Ruben knows what flan is?** (I can tell Ruben knows what flan is because he quickly agrees to take flan for Snack Week.) Guide students in writing the answer to this question. **MAKE INFERENCES**

page 58

Discuss the Stop and Think question on page 58: **How are flan and cake the same?** (Possible responses: Here is how they are the same: both are desserts; both contain milk and eggs; both are round.) Guide students in writing the answer to this question. **COMPARE AND CONTRAST**

Ask: Why do you think Tucker asks Ruben's mom to make two? (Possible response: I think Tucker asks because he likes food and likes to eat. Earlier, Tucker said that he has an extensive list of food he likes to eat. I think he wants to add flan to his list.) **CHARACTER'S TRAITS AND MOTIVATIONS**

VOCABULARY
Student-Friendly Explanations

culinary Culinary describes anything that is related to cooking.

downcast Someone who is downcast is feeling sad or depressed.

consternation Someone who shows consternation is feeling anxious or worried about something.

vivid Something that is vivid has intensely bright colors.

extensive Something extensive includes many items, details, or ideas.

serenely Serenely means "calmly" or "quietly."

reminiscent If an object or experience is reminiscent of something, it brings back memories of a place or a time.

pensive Someone who is pensive is deep in thought.

recruit When you recruit people, you get them to join a group for a purpose.

commencing Something that is commencing is beginning.

"The Flan Plan" 53

Day 2

Spelling Words: Lesson 5

1. tread
2. broad
3. split
4. chief
5. season
6. brain
7. throw
8. goal
9. scrape
10. choice
11. allow
12. auction
13. flaw
14. daughter
15. destroy
16. renew
17. boyhood
18. returned
19. chopped
20. counting

 page 59 **Answers to *Think Critically* Questions**
Help students read and answer the *Think Critically* questions on page 59. Then guide students in writing the answer to each question. Possible responses are provided.

1. Ruben's mom likes that rule because she is proud of her homeland. **CHARACTER**
2. I think the class will like his snack because it sounds like a sweet treat. **MAKE PREDICTIONS**
3. Two purposes the author might have had to write this play are to entertain readers and to tell about foods from different countries. **AUTHOR'S PURPOSE**

RETEACH
Decoding/Word Attack

Decode Longer Words Remind students that two vowels sometimes stand for a single sound. List the following words across the board:

> roaming   fifteen   eastern

Read each word aloud and point out the vowel combinations that stand for the long *e* and long *o* sounds (*oa, ee, ea*). Then write *approach* on the board. Ask a student to read the word aloud and rewrite it below the word with the same vowel sound. (*roaming*) Invite students to work in pairs and repeat this activity with each word in the following list: *weakened, sleepiness, dreaming, reproachful, creeping.*

54 Lesson 5 • Turn It Up!

Day 2

RETEACH

Decoding/Spelling

Copying Master 18

Words with Variant Vowels and Diphthongs Review with students that *au* and *aw* stand for the /aw/ sound, *oi* and *oy* stand for the /oi/ sound, and *oo* stands for the /o͞o/ in *hoot* and the /o͝o/ in *hood*. Direct students to look at *Copying Master 18* and to read aloud the Spelling Words that include these letter pairs. Write these letter combinations on the board: *au, aw, oi, oy, oo*. Tell students that when you say a Spelling Word, volunteers should point to the corresponding letter pair. Then say *flaw, destroy, daughter, choice, auction,* and *boyhood*.

RETEACH

Grammar/Writing

Subjects and Predicates Have students recall that a complete sentence has a subject and a predicate, and a fragment is missing a subject or a predicate. Write the following two items on the board:

> Most children eat snacks.
> This girl.

Underline the subject (children) and the predicate (eat) in the first sentence. Point out that the second item is a fragment. Then write this sentence:

> Some tasty snacks are made from fish.

Help students locate the complete subject and circle it. (Some tasty snacks) Repeat for the complete predicate. (are made from fish) Explain that the simple subject is *snacks* and draw a box around the word. Finally, draw a box around the simple predicate. (made)

GUIDED PRACTICE Write these sentences:

> My mother brought a special treat to school.
> The students enjoyed the sweet snack.

Guide students to circle the complete subject and underline the complete predicate in each sentence. Then have students draw a box around the simple subject and around the simple predicate.

Fluency

Practice Book 19

Fluency Practice Invite students to look at the bottom half of *Practice Book* page 19. These sentences have been broken into natural phrases. Tell students to repeat each phrase after you, mirroring your expression, phrasing, and pace. After students have repeated each sentence, invite them to practice reading the sentences to partners.

"The Flan Plan" 55

LESSON 5

DAY AT A GLANCE — Day 3

COMPREHENSION
Reteach Synonyms and Antonyms
Reread and Summarize "The Flan Plan"

DECODING/WORD ATTACK
Reteach Decode Longer Words

DECODING/SPELLING
Reteach Words with Inflection: -ed, -ing

BUILD ROBUST VOCABULARY
Teach Words from "The Flan Plan"

GRAMMAR/WRITING
Reteach Subjects and Predicates

FLUENCY
Fluency Practice

Materials Needed: *Turn It Up!*

Student Edition
pp. 52–58

Practice Book
pp. 19, 21

Copying Master
18

30+ Minutes

RETEACH
Comprehension

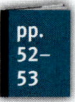 pp. 52–58

Synonyms and Antonyms Help students recall that a synonym is a word that means the same or nearly the same as another word, and an antonym is a word that means the opposite of another word. Have students read what Ruben says to his mom in the middle of page 53 in "The Flan Plan." Then ask:

- **What is a synonym for the word *stumped*?** (Possible responses: *baffled, confused, dazed, flustered, lost, muddled, speechless, stuck*)
- **What is an antonym for the word *stumped*?** (Possible responses: *clear, understanding, certain, talkative, clearheaded, aware*)

GUIDED PRACTICE Guide pairs of students to use a thesaurus to find synonyms and antonyms for these words from "The Flan Plan:" *snack, pensive, grin, puzzled*. Invite students to share their lists.

Reread and Summarize
Have students reread and summarize "The Flan Plan" in sections, as described below.

 pp. 52–53

Let's reread pages 52–53 to recall who the characters are and what problem the main character has.
Summary: Ruben needs to take a snack from his homeland to class for Snack Week. Mom tries to help him, and the Narrator and Chorus add thoughts and comments.

 pp. 54–55

Now let's reread pages 54–55 to remember who tries to help Ruben and what they offer.
Summary: Amanda suggests her dad's snack from Japan. Tucker offers his extensive food list, especially hot dogs and buns.

 pp. 56–58

Last, let's reread pages 56–58 to find out if anyone else tries to help and how the problem is solved.
Summary: June offers to take her grandma's sweet pumpkin cakes. Then Mom suggests flan. Ruben likes that idea and is happy there is a plan to make flan.

RETEACH
Decoding/Word Attack

Decode Longer Words Review with students that inflections *-ed* and *-ing* are added to some verbs. Note that while *-ing* always forms its own syllable, *-ed* only sometimes forms its own syllable. Write *shopped* and *bounding* on the board. Help students discover that *shopped* is a one-syllable word and *bounding* is a two-syllable word. Then guide students to sort the following

---

56 Lesson 5 • Turn It Up!

words by number of syllables and to note when the inflected ending forms a syllable and when it doesn't: *shopping* (2), *bounded* (2), *reprimanding* (4), *stumped* (1), *puzzled* (2), *commencing* (3), *kidding* (2).

TEACH

Build Robust Vocabulary

page 53 **Words from "The Flan Plan"** Have students locate the word *stumped* on page 53 of "The Flan Plan." Ask a volunteer to read aloud the sentence in which this word appears. (Line 5: *I'm stumped!*) Explain that this sentence means that Ruben can't figure out what to do.

Ask volunteers to use the word in sentences about themselves, such as sharing something that has them stumped.

RETEACH

Decoding/Spelling

Copying Master 18 **Words with Inflection: *-ed*, *-ing*** Remind students that for inflected *-ed* and *-ing* endings, we sometimes double the final consonant, drop the final *e*, or add the ending to the root word. Have students review *Copying Master 18* and identify words on the list that include the inflected endings *-ed* and *-ing*. Then have pairs of students write the Spelling Words on index cards. Have one student draw a card and read its word aloud. The other student writes the word. Then partners switch roles. When a student spells a word correctly, he or she initials the card and returns it to the pile. Have students write down words they do not spell correctly to study later.

RETEACH

Grammar/Writing

Practice Book 21 **Complete Subjects and Predicates** Review the key points about simple and complete subjects and predicates. Write the following sentence fragment on the board:

> Played in the snow.

Guide students to proofread to determine if the subject or predicate is missing, and then add one to make a sentence. (missing subject; Possible response: That little boy played in the snow.)

GUIDED PRACTICE Have students turn to page 21 in their *Practice Book*. Have students work in pairs to proofread each sentence. Encourage students to share their responses.

Fluency

Practice Book 19 **Fluency Practice** Tell students that today they will reread the sentences on the bottom of *Practice Book* page 19. Have students locate and point to the first sentence. Tell students that everyone is going to read the sentence together. This choral reading will give students an opportunity to hear others and listen to the natural phrasing of the sentences. Choral-read each of the sentences several times.

"The Flan Plan" 57

LESSON 5

DAY AT A GLANCE — Day 4

COMPREHENSION
Reteach Make Judgments

DECODING/SPELLING
Cumulative Review

BUILD ROBUST VOCABULARY
Reteach Words from "The Flan Plan"

GRAMMAR/WRITING
Cumulative Review

FLUENCY
Fluency Practice

Materials Needed: *Turn It Up!*

 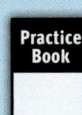 

Student Edition pp. 52–58 | Practice Book p. 22 | Copying Master 20

Spelling Words: Lesson 5

1. tread	11. allow
2. broad	12. auction
3. split	13. flaw
4. chief	14. daughter
5. season	15. destroy
6. brain	16. renew
7. throw	17. boyhood
8. goal	18. returned
9. scrape	19. chopped
10. choice	20. counting

30+ Minutes

RETEACH
Comprehension

Make Judgments Review with students that making judgments means forming their own opinions about something. Remind students that they use details from the text and knowledge they already have. Read aloud page 52 in "The Flan Plan" with students. Ask: **Mom tells Ruben "That's not so bad." Was this a good thing to say to Ruben?** Guide students to make a judgment about Mom's words to Ruben. (Possible responses: Yes, I think this was good because a mom should be trying to make her son worry less like my mom does.)

GUIDED PRACTICE Have students reread the text on page 58 of "The Flan Plan." Then ask: **Do you think that it was polite for Tucker to ask Ruben's mom to make a flan for them? Why or why not?** Guide students in small groups to discuss and make judgments by telling whether they think this was polite behavior.

RETEACH
Decoding/Spelling

Cumulative Review Have students number a sheet of paper 1–16. Write *tread* on the board, and point out that *ea* stands for a short vowel sound. Tell students that the first two words you will dictate include a short vowel or vowel digraph. After students write each word, display it so they can proofread their work. Repeat this activity using the word *chief* for long vowel and vowel digraphs; *choice* for variant vowels and diphthongs; and *returned* for *-ed* and *-ing* inflections.

1. broad	2. split	3. season	4. brain
5. throw	6. goal	7. scrape	8. allow
9. auction	10. flaw	11. daughter	12. destroy
13. renew	14. boyhood	15. chopped	16. counting

Have students turn to page 22 in their *Practice Books*. Ask a volunteer to read the directions aloud. Point out that students need to choose the answer that best describes the story events.

58 Lesson 5 • Turn It Up!

Day 4

RETEACH
Build Robust Vocabulary

Words from "The Flan Plan" Review the meaning of *stumped*. Then say these sentences and ask which one relates to the meaning of *stumped*. Have students explain why.

- **I have worked on this math problem for fifteen minutes, but I can't figure out the answer.** (stumped)
- **I love building things, and Mom says I have a real gift for it.**

RETEACH
Grammar/Writing

Copying Master 20

Cumulative Review Have students recall the grammar skills they reviewed in this lesson:

- kinds of sentences
- correct end marks or punctuation
- simple subjects and simple predicates
- complete subjects and complete predicates

Have students give examples of declarative, interrogative, imperative, and exclamatory sentences, and interjections. Use their examples, and ask volunteers to identify the complete and simple subjects and predicates in each.

GUIDED PRACTICE Distribute *Copying Master 20* to each student. Ask volunteers to read the directions. Have students complete the page independently. Allow time to review students' responses as a group.

Fluency

pp. 52–58

Fluency Practice Have each student work with a partner to read passages from "The Flan Plan" aloud to each other. Remind students to:

- read each word accurately when reading aloud.
- adjust their reading rate to reflect what is happening in the story.

Encourage partners to read the selected passage aloud three times. Have the students rate their own reading on the 1–4 scale.

1	Need more practice
2	Pretty good
3	Good
4	Great!

"The Flan Plan"

Preteach for **LESSON 6**

VOCABULARY
Preteach responsible, darted, jostling, swerved, attentive, pounced, contradicting

COMPREHENSION
 Preteach Plot: Conflict/Resolution

DECODING/WORD ATTACK
Preteach Decode Longer Words

DECODING/SPELLING
Preteach Words with Consonant *-le*

GRAMMAR/WRITING
Preteach Compound Subjects and Predicates

FLUENCY
Fluency Performance

Materials Needed: *Turn It Up!*

Student Edition pp. 52–58

Copying Master 21

PRETEACH

Vocabulary

Copying Master 21 — **Lesson 6 Vocabulary** Distribute a set of Vocabulary Word Cards to each pair of students. Hold up the card for the first word, and ask a volunteer to read it aloud. Have students repeat the word and hold up the matching card. Give the explanation for the word. Then ask students the first question below and discuss their responses. Continue for each of the Vocabulary Words.

- What kinds of things does a **responsible** person do?
- Imagine you saw an animal as it **darted** past you. What kind of animal might it have been?
- When was the last time you were in a crowd of **jostling** people?
- Show how you **swerved** to get out of the way.
- How does an **attentive** person listen to someone talk?
- If your cat **pounced** on something, what would it do?
- How do you react when people are **contradicting** you?

PRETEACH

Comprehension

pp. 52–58

Plot: Conflict/Resolution Tell students that the series of events in a story or play make up the plot. The plot includes a conflict and a resolution. The conflict is usually identified at the beginning of the story or play. It is a problem or challenge faced by the main character or characters. The events of the story or play center around this conflict. The conflict may be resolved suddenly or over time. Often, the conflict gets worse before it gets better. Have students recall what they read in "The Flan Plan." Ask:

- **What problem does Ruben face at the beginning of the play?** (He has to bring a treat from his homeland to school next week.)
- **Why is this the conflict of the play?** (because he doesn't know what to bring and has to think of something)

GUIDED PRACTICE Have volunteers explain how the events of "The Flan Plan" revolve around this conflict. (Ruben's mom and his friends all try to help him figure out what to take.) Then ask students how the conflict in the play is resolved. (His mom suggests flan, and Ruben thinks it's a great idea.)

Day 5

PRETEACH

Decoding/Word Attack

Decode Longer Words Write *cradle* on the board, define it, and divide it into syllables between the *a* and the *d*. Ask students what sound they hear in the second syllable. (/del/) Explain that when the /el/ sound follows a consonant, the /el/ sound is often spelled with the letters *le*. Repeat with *circle* and *juggle*.

PRETEACH

Decoding/Spelling

Words with Consonant *-le* Write the following word pairs on the board: *castel/castle, ruffle/ruffal, ankel/ankle, battul/battle, riddle/riddil, jungle/jungel*. Guide students to determine the correct spellings. Conclude by asking what the correct spellings have in common. (They are all spelled with the consonant *-le* combination.)

PRETEACH

Grammar/Writing

Compound Subjects and Predicates Write these sentences on the board:

> My brother likes cookies. My sister likes cookies.

Read the sentences aloud. Point out that simple sentences with the same predicate can be combined to make one sentence with a **compound subject**, two or more subjects joined by a coordinating conjunction, such as *and* or *or*.

> My brother and sister like cookies.

Read the new sentence aloud. Ask a volunteer to explain what changes were made in the first sentences to form the new sentence. (The word *and* joins *brother* and *sister*, the second *my* drops out, the verb changes from the singular to the plural.)

Now write these sentences:

> My sister baked. My sister ate the cookies.

Help students understand that the sentences have the same subject and can be combined to make one sentence with a **compound predicate**. Like compound subjects, compound predicates are joined by *and* or *or*. Combine the sentences and have students identify the compound predicate. (My sister baked and ate the cookies.)

VOCABULARY

Student-Friendly Explanations

responsible If someone is responsible, that person can be trusted to do a job on their own.

darted An animal that darted moved suddenly and quickly in a particular direction.

jostling If the people in a crowd push or knock against you, they are jostling you.

swerved If a car swerved, it turned suddenly to avoid hitting something.

attentive If someone is attentive, that person is carefully listening to or watching something.

pounced A person or animal that pounced on something jumped on it eagerly in order to take it.

contradicting Contradicting someone is saying that what the person has said is wrong.

Fluency

pp. 52–58 **Fluency Performance** Invite partners to read aloud the passages from "The Flan Plan" that they selected and practiced earlier. Have students rate their own oral reading on the 1–4 scale. Give partners the opportunity to continue practicing and then to read the passage to you again.

"The Flan Plan" 61

DAY AT A GLANCE

Day 1

LESSON 6

VOCABULARY
Reteach responsible, darted, jostling, swerved, attentive, pounced, contradicting

COMPREHENSION
Reteach Plot: Conflict and Resolution

DECODING/SPELLING
Reteach Words with Consonant -le

GRAMMAR/WRITING
Preteach Combining Sentences: Compound Subjects

FLUENCY
Fluency Practice

Materials Needed: *Turn It Up!*

Student Edition pp. 60–61 | Practice Book p. 23 | Skill Card 6 | Copying Master 22

RETEACH
Vocabulary

Lesson 6 Vocabulary Read aloud the Vocabulary Words, writing each word on the board, and say the Student-Friendly Explanations. Then have students read the story. Guide them to fill in the blanks on pages 60–61 of their books by selecting the correct word in dark type. Have volunteers read the sentences, adding the word they chose. If students are unable to complete the questions, refer to the Student-Friendly Explanations. (Answers for pages 60–61: 2. *jostling*, 3. *responsible*, 4. *darted*, 5. *attentive*, 6. *contradicting*, 7. *pounced*, 8.–9. Responses will vary.)

RETEACH
Comprehension

Plot: Conflict and Resolution Have students look at side A of *Skill Card 6: Plot: Conflict and Resolution*. Read the explanation of plot conflict and how it is resolved. Then read the passage aloud as students follow along. Ask:

- **Who are the characters in the story?** (Matt and his dog Rufus)
- **What is the problem, or conflict, in the story? Who has the problem? Why is it a problem?** (Rufus's feet get muddy; Matt has the problem because his parents don't like mud all over the house.)
- **What two unsuccessful steps does Matt take to resolve the conflict?** (He puts socks on Rufus, he keeps Rufus inside all the time.)
- **How is the conflict finally resolved?** (Matt washes and dries Rufus's feet when he gets muddy.)

Now guide students through the graphic organizer, pointing out where the information they have just provided is placed.

GUIDED PRACTICE Now have students look at side B of *Skill Card 6: Plot: Conflict and Resolution*. Read the Skill Reminder. Then read the passage aloud as students follow along. Guide students in copying the graphic organizer and completing it with details from the story. (Problem: Martin needs to choose socks that match; Problem-Solving Steps: 1. He tried to set socks out before bed, but always forgot; 2. He put socks under his pillow, but they made lumps; Resolution: He put a flashlight in his sock drawer.)

62 Lesson 6 • Turn It Up!

Day 1

RETEACH

Decoding/Spelling

Copying Master 22 **Words with Consonant–*le*** Distribute *Copying Master 22*. Model reading the Spelling Words and have students repeat them. Then write the words on the board and have students copy them. Ask students to identify the sound they hear at the end of each word (/el/) and the letter combination that represents the sound. (-le) Then have students complete the activity. Have pairs of students write the Spelling Words on index cards. Have one student draw a card and read its word aloud and the other student write the word; then have partners switch roles. When a student spells a word correctly, he or she initials the card and returns it to the pile. Students should work through the pile twice. Have students write down each word they do not spell correctly to study later.

PRETEACH

Grammar/Writing

Combining Sentences: Compound Subjects Review compound subjects:

- A compound subject is made up of two or more subjects joined by a coordinating conjunction, such as *and* or *or*.
- Simple sentences that have the same predicate can be combined to make one sentence with a compound subject.

Write the following sentences on the board:

> Cake tastes very good.
> Ice cream tastes very good.

Have a volunteer read the sentences and circle the parts that are the same. (tastes very good) Ask another student to rewrite the sentences on the board as a single sentence with a compound subject. (Cake and ice cream taste very good.)

GUIDED PRACTICE Write these sentences on the board:

> The book is new. The magazine is new.
> Ducks nest at the lake. Geese nest at the lake.

Have students work in pairs to rewrite the two sentences as a single sentence with a compound subject. (The book and magazine are new. Ducks and geese nest at the lake.)

VOCABULARY

Student-Friendly Explanations

responsible If someone is responsible, that person can be trusted to do a job on their own.

darted An animal that darted moved suddenly and quickly in a particular direction.

jostling If the people in a crowd push or knock against you, they are jostling you.

swerved If a car swerved, it turned suddenly to avoid hitting something.

attentive If someone is attentive, that person is carefully listening to or watching something.

pounced A person or animal that pounced on something jumped on it eagerly in order to take it.

contradicting Contradicting someone is saying that what the person has said is wrong.

Fluency

Practice Book 23 **Fluency Practice** Have students turn to *Practice Book* page 23. Read the words in the first column aloud. Invite students to track each word and repeat the words after you. Then have students work in pairs to read the words in the first column aloud to each other. Follow the same procedure with each of the remaining columns. After partners have practiced reading aloud the words in each of the columns, have them practice reading all of the words.

"Close Call" 63

LESSON 6

DAY AT A GLANCE
Day 2

VOCABULARY
Reteach responsible, darted, jostling, swerved, attentive, pounced, contradicting

COMPREHENSION
"Close Call"
Build Background
Monitor Comprehension
Answers to *Think Critically* **Questions**

DECODING/SPELLING
Reteach Words with Consonant -le

GRAMMAR/WRITING
Preteach Combining Sentences: Compound Predicates

FLUENCY
Fluency Practice

Materials Needed: *Turn It Up!*

Student Edition pp. 62–69

Practice Book pp. 23, 24

Copying Masters 21, 22

30+ Minutes

RETEACH

Vocabulary

Copying Master 21

Lesson 6 Vocabulary List the Vocabulary Words on the board. Then write *adjective* and *verb* at the top of two columns and have students sort the words into the correct categories. (adjectives: *responsible, attentive;* verbs: *darted, jostling, swerved, pounced, contradicting*) After the lists are made, have students use each Vocabulary Word in a sentence.

Comprehension

Build Background: "Close Call"
Ask students what they think the phrase "close call" means. Then ask them to describe a time when they had a close call. What were the circumstances? How much danger were they in? What did they learn from the incident?

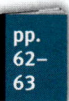

pp. 62–63

Monitor Comprehension: "Close Call"
Read the title of the story aloud. Then have students read pages 62–63 to find out who the main character is and what he is doing.

Ask: **Who is the main character? What is he doing?** (a boy named Walt; he is plowing a field with two oxen) **NOTE DETAILS**

After reading the pages, ask: **The story says that Walt is a responsible lad. What evidence can you find in the text that this is true?** (Possible response: Walt is allowed to plow with two large oxen all by himself; this shows his parents trust him with a challenging task.) **DRAW CONCLUSIONS**

Discuss the Stop and Think question on page 62: **What do you think is upsetting the oxen?** (Possible response: I think the oxen are upset by something in the tall grass, maybe a snake.) Guide students in writing the answer to this question. **MAKE INFERENCES**

Ask: **The phrase "snake in the grass" means an unseen or surprise enemy. How does this story illustrate the meaning of this phrase?** (Possible response: The snake is unseen until Walt is almost on top of it; it surprised him and the oxen.) **FIGURATIVE LANGUAGE**

Discuss the Stop and Think question on page 63: **Where do you think the story takes place? Explain.** (Possible response: I think the story takes place on a farm, long ago. People used to use oxen to work their fields.) Guide students in writing the answer to this question. **SETTING**

64 Lesson 6 • Turn It Up!

Read aloud the next to the last paragraph on page 63. Model the strategy of identifying with characters.

THINK ALOUD People have said this to me before, that scary animals are just as scared of me as I am of them. But sometimes I have a hard time believing it. I bet Walt feels the same as I do. It's a little hard to believe a rattlesnake would be scared of me. IDENTIFY WITH CHARACTERS

Ask: **Have you ever seen a snake or other dangerous animal in the wild? How did you feel?** (Responses will vary.) PERSONAL RESPONSE

Discuss the Stop and Think question on page 64: **What do you think Walt's dad wants him to see?** (Possible response: I think Walt's dad wants him to see something that has to do with the rattlesnake Jude killed.) Guide students in writing the answer to this question. MAKE PREDICTIONS

Discuss the Stop and Think question on page 65: **Walt's dad says he kept the rattle for luck so snakes would leave him alone. Is this statement a fact or an opinion? Explain.** (Possible response: This statement is an opinion because it cannot be proven.) Guide students in writing the answer to this question. FACT AND OPINION

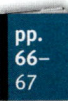

Discuss the Stop and Think question on page 66: **Why do you think Walt has trouble falling asleep? Explain your answer.** (Possible responses: I think Walt has trouble falling asleep because he is too excited about seeing the snake in the field; he is too excited about getting a rattle from his dad.) Guide students in writing the answer to this question. CAUSE AND EFFECT

Ask: **Think about what you know about snakes. Do you think Walt really hears a snake near his bed? Why or why not?** (Possible response: It's unlikely there's a snake in Walt's room because snakes stay outside most of the time.) USE PRIOR KNOWLEDGE

Discuss the Stop and Think question on page 67: **What problem does Walt have now? How could he solve it?** (Possible response: Now Walt's problem is he thinks he hears a snake, but his dad doesn't think it's there. Walt could solve this problem by looking to see where the rattle is coming from.) Guide students in writing the answer to this question. CONFLICT/RESOLUTION

Discuss the Stop and Think question on page 68: **Does Walt really have a close call? Explain your answer.** (Possible response: Walt does not have a close call because there is no snake under his bed.) Guide students in writing the answer to this question. DRAW CONCLUSIONS

VOCABULARY

Student-Friendly Explanations

responsible If someone is responsible, that person can be trusted to do a job on their own.

darted An animal that darted moved suddenly and quickly in a particular direction.

jostling If the people in a crowd push or knock against you, they are jostling you.

swerved If a car swerved, it turned suddenly to avoid hitting something.

attentive If someone is attentive, that person is carefully listening to or watching something.

pounced A person or animal that pounced on something jumped on it eagerly in order to take it.

contradicting Contradicting someone is saying that what the person has said is wrong.

Day 2

Spelling Words: Lesson 6

1. circle		11. fable	
2. angle		12. riddle	
3. cradle		13. icicle	
4. ladle		14. sparkle	
5. castle		15. jungle	
6. ruffle		16. tangle	
7. juggle		17. marble	
8. ankle		18. sizzle	
9. battle		19. paddle	
10. candle		20. handle	

page 69 **Answers to *Think Critically* Questions**
Help students read and answer the *Think Critically* questions on page 69. Have students copy the graphic organizer in question 1 on a separate sheet of paper. Then guide students in writing the answer to each question. Possible responses are provided.

1. [2.] Walt's dad tells him a story and gives him a rattle. [3.] Walt hears a rattle in his room. [4.] His dad shows him how the wind moves the rattle.  **PLOT**

2. Walt dreams about a snake because he saw one in the field that day; he hears a rattle under his bed. **CAUSE AND EFFECT**

3. The author included this information so readers would also know how to stay safe if they hear a rattle from a rattlesnake. **AUTHOR'S PURPOSE**

RETEACH

Decoding/Spelling

Copying Master 22 **Words with Consonant -*le*** Have students copy the following chart in their notebooks and write each Spelling Word in the correct category.

-cle	-gle	-dle	-tle
circle icicle	angle juggle jungle tangle	cradle ladle candle riddle paddle handle	castle battle

-fle	-kle	-ble	-zle
ruffle	ankle sparkle	fable marble	sizzle

66 Lesson 6 • Turn It Up!

PRETEACH

Grammar/Writing

Combining Sentences: Compound Predicates (Practice Book 24)

Tell students that two simple sentences that have the same subject can be combined. The result will be a sentence with a compound predicate. The words *and, but,* or *or* join compound predicates.

> The snake raised its head. The snake rattled its tail.
>
> The snake raised its head and rattled its tail.

GUIDED PRACTICE Direct students' attention to page 24 in their *Practice Books*. Invite volunteers to rewrite each pair of sentences and explain their answers.

Fluency

Fluency Practice (Practice Book 23) Invite students to look at the bottom half of *Practice Book* page 23. These sentences have been broken into natural phrases. Tell students to repeat each phrase after you, mirroring your expression, phrasing, and pace. After students have repeated each sentence, invite them to practice reading the sentences to partners.

"Close Call" 67

LESSON 6

DAY AT A GLANCE

Day 3

COMPREHENSION
Preteach Prefixes, Suffixes, and Roots
Reread and Summarize "Close Call"

DECODING/SPELLING
Reteach Words with Consonant -le

BUILD ROBUST VOCABULARY
Teach Words from "Close Call"

GRAMMAR/WRITING
Reteach Writing Trait: Ideas

FLUENCY
Fluency Practice

Materials Needed: *Turn It Up!*

Student Edition pp. 62–68

Practice Book pp. 23, 25

Copying Master 23

30+ Minutes

PRETEACH

Comprehension

Prefixes, Suffixes, and Roots Distribute *Copying Master 23*. Have students listen as you read the information at the top of the page about prefixes, suffixes, and roots. Have them tell what each listed prefix and suffix means and give examples of words that use them.

GUIDED PRACTICE Have students read the story and complete the activity. Allow time for students to share their answers to the questions.

Reread and Summarize Have students reread and summarize "Close Call" in sections, as described below.

pp. 62–63

Let's reread pages 62–63 to recall who is in this story, where they are, and what their lives are like.
Summary: Walt is a farm boy. He helps his parents on their farm. He is plowing a field when his oxen see a rattlesnake and become restless. Walt's dad comes running and warns the boy to be attentive.

pp. 64–65

Now let's reread pages 64–65 to see what Walt's father says and what he shows Walt.
Summary: Walt's father describes a big rattlesnake that his cat once killed. He shows Walt the snake's rattle, explaining that he keeps it for protection. He gives the rattle to Walt.

pp. 66–68

Finally, let's reread pages 66–68 to recall what happens to Walt that night.
Summary: That night, Walt hears a rattle. Scared that a snake is near, he calls his father. His father shows Walt that the sound he heard was the rattle in the box as the wind blew in the window.

RETEACH

Decoding/Spelling

Words with Consonant -le Divide the group into two teams. Explain that you are going to play a game with this lesson's Spelling Words. Write on the board "_____le." Tell Team A to choose a word from the list. One member of the team will give a clue about the word. A member of Team B will write in the letters that precede the -le and correctly spell the word. If Team B correctly spells the word based on Team A's clue, both sides score a point. If Team B guesses the right word but misspells it, Team A gets a point if a team member correctly fills in the missing letters. Have teams alternate until all the words have been correctly spelled.

68 Lesson 6 • *Turn It Up!*

Day 3

TEACH
Build Robust Vocabulary

Words from "Close Call" Have students locate the word *plodded* on page 62 of "Close Call." Ask a volunteer to read aloud the sentence in which this word appears. (Line 1: *Walt plodded along*.) Explain that this sentence means that Walt walked along in a slow, tired, heavy way. Continue by asking students to locate and read aloud the sentence in which the word *halted* appears on page 62. (Line 4: *All of a sudden, one ox halted, peered at its feet, and grunted*.) Explain that this sentence means that the ox stopped, looked at its feet, and grunted. Then ask students to locate and read aloud the sentence in which the word *gasped* appears on page 62. (Last line: *When he looked down, he gasped*.) Explain that this sentence means that he was so surprised that he took in breath suddenly and made a sound.

Ask students to demonstrate each action as you call out the word.

RETEACH
Grammar/Writing

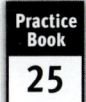 **Writing Trait: Ideas** Have students turn to page 25 in their *Practice Book*. Have a volunteer read aloud the information at the top of the page. Point out that in focused writing, every sentence stays on topic.

GUIDED PRACTICE Complete Parts A, B, and C together. Have volunteers share their paragraphs for Part C.

Fluency

Fluency Practice Tell students that today they will reread the sentences on the bottom of *Practice Book* page 23. Have students locate and point to the first sentence. Tell students that everyone is going to read the sentence together. This choral reading will give students an opportunity to hear others and listen to the natural phrasing of the sentences. Choral-read each of the sentences several times.

"Close Call" **69**

LESSON 6

DAY AT A GLANCE
Day 4

COMPREHENSION
Reteach Prefixes, Suffixes, and Roots

DECODING/SPELLING
Reteach Words with Consonant -le

BUILD ROBUST VOCABULARY
Reteach Words from "Close Call"

GRAMMAR/WRITING
Reteach Writing Form: Summary

FLUENCY
Fluency Practice

Materials Needed: Turn It Up!

 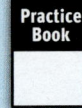 

Student Edition pp. 62–68 | Practice Book p. 26 | Copying Master 24

Spelling Words: Lesson 6

1. circle	11. fable
2. angle	12. riddle
3. cradle	13. icicle
4. ladle	14. sparkle
5. castle	15. jungle
6. ruffle	16. tangle
7. juggle	17. marble
8. ankle	18. sizzle
9. battle	19. paddle
10. candle	20. handle

30+ Minutes

RETEACH
Comprehension

Prefixes, Suffixes, and Roots Draw this chart of common prefixes and suffixes on the board:

Common Prefixes	Common Suffixes
dis, un, re, im, in, non, pre, over	able, ible, less, ful, ist, ian, ness, er, ous

Then say these root words: *farm, hope, art, happy, stress, comfort, help, act, possible, music, eat, visible, short, view, danger, fiction, flex.* As you say each word, have students match its root with a prefix or suffix from the list. Write the new words on the board. There may be more than one new word formed from each root.

GUIDED PRACTICE Have students work in pairs. Have them use the meaning of the prefixes and suffixes to determine the meanings of the words they formed. Have volunteers write sentences on the board for some of the newly formed words.

RETEACH
Decoding/Spelling

Practice Book 26

Words with Consonant -le Have students number a sheet of paper 1–18. Write the Spelling Word *circle* on the board and circle the *le* that makes the ending /el/ sound. Then do the same for the Spelling Word *angle*. Remind students that the /el/ sound is often spelled *-le*. Read aloud the remaining Spelling Words, and have students write each word. After students write each word, display it so they can proofread their work.

1. juggle	2. castle	3. sparkle	4. candle
5. fable	6. tangle	7. cradle	8. handle
9. jungle	10. icicle	11. marble	12. sizzle
13. ladle	14. battle	15. ruffle	16. riddle
17. ankle	18. paddle		

Have students turn to page 26 in their *Practice Books*. Ask them to draw in the items described at the bottom of the page. Have the class identify the target Spelling Words in the sentences.

70 Lesson 6 • Turn It Up!

Day 4

RETEACH
Build Robust Vocabulary

Words from "Close Call" Review the meanings of *plodded*, *halted*, and *gasped*. Then say these sentences and ask which word describes each sentence. Have students explain why.

- **Stan walked slowly and heavily as he tried to finish the long hike.** (plodded)
- **The police officer told the children to stop at the corner and look both ways for traffic.** (halted)
- **Maria breathed in a gulp of air suddenly when everyone yelled, "Surprise!"** (gasped)

RETEACH
Grammar/Writing

Copying Master 24

Writing Form: Summary Tell students that a summary includes only the main ideas and the most important details in the information. For example, a summary of a story or movie briefly mentions its characters, setting, conflict, main events, and resolution. Distribute *Copying Master 24* and have a volunteer read the description of a summary. Then read the Student Model together. Write on the board the following sentences from the summary:

> Walt went to bed that night. Walt couldn't sleep.

Model for students how the sentence can be improved by rewriting it as one sentence with a compound predicate.

> Walt went to bed that night but couldn't sleep.

GUIDED PRACTICE Complete the activity by having students complete the questions at the bottom of *Copying Master 24*. Allow time for students to share and explain their answers to the group.

Fluency

Fluency Practice Have each student work with a partner to read passages from "Close Call" aloud to each other. Students may select a passage that they enjoyed or choose one of the following options:

pp. 62–68

- Read page 63. (Total: 86 words)
- Read page 68. (Total: 83 words)

Encourage students to read the selected passage aloud to their partner three times. Have the student rate his or her reading on the 1–4 scale.

1	Need more practice
2	Pretty good
3	Good
4	Great!

"Close Call" 71

Preteach for LESSON 7

DAY AT A GLANCE
Day 5

VOCABULARY
Preteach reluctant, rumpled, surge, inspecting, taut, untangled, resounded, lurked

COMPREHENSION
 Preteach Plot: Conflict and Resolution

DECODING/WORD ATTACK
Preteach Decode Longer Words

DECODING/SPELLING
Preteach Words with VCCV: Same Medial Consonant

GRAMMAR/WRITING
Preteach Compound Sentences

FLUENCY
Fluency Performance

Materials Needed: *Turn It Up!*

Student Edition
pp. 62–68

Copying Master 25

30+ Minutes

PRETEACH
Vocabulary

Copying Master 25

Lesson 7 Vocabulary Distribute a set of Vocabulary Word Cards to each student. Hold up the first Vocabulary Word Card, and ask a volunteer to read the word aloud. Have students repeat the word and hold up the matching card. Give the explanation for the word. Ask students the first question below and discuss their responses. Continue for each Vocabulary Word.

- What sport are you **reluctant** to try?
- What would you do if your favorite shirt were **rumpled**?
- What caused you to feel a **surge** of happiness?
- Was there a time when you were **inspecting** a new toy or game?
- Do you play any games with a **taut** string or rope?
- Is it easy or hard to **untangle** a ball of string?
- Can you describe a place that has **resounded** with music?
- What happened to make you think something **lurked** in your closet?

PRETEACH
Comprehension

pp. 62–68

Plot: Conflict and Resolution Tell students that being able to identify the conflict, plot events, and resolution in a story will help them better understand it. Ask students to recall "Close Call." Then ask:

- **What is the conflict, or what problem does Walt have?** (Walt is frightened by a rattlesnake.)
- **What plot events tell you this is the conflict?** (Walt calls his dad for help when he sees a rattlesnake; Walt gets scared when he dreams about the snake and hears the rattle sound.)
- **What events lead to a resolution, or solution, to the conflict?** (Dad tells Walt a story; Dad gives Walt the snake's rattle.)
- **How is the problem solved at the end of the story?** (Walt's Dad discovers that the wind is causing the rattle to make noise.)

Have students discuss how the plot would be different if Walt's problem were solved in a different way. For example, ask students to consider the differences if Walt had expected his dad to get a cat. (Walt might have taken the cat everywhere as protection. The cat might have caught all the rattlesnakes.)

GUIDED PRACTICE Have the group discuss how the plot might have been different if Walt's dad didn't want him to plow the fields anymore. (Walt might have felt bad because his dad had to do the plowing; he might be responsible for other chores instead.)

72 Preteach for Lesson 7 • *Turn It Up!*

PRETEACH

Decoding/Word Attack

Decode Longer Words   Write the word *flutter* on the board. Explain that the two consonants stand for one sound, but the syllables are divided between the two consonants. (flut/ter) Write *fluttering* on the board. Point out that knowing how to divide the syllables in VCCV words with the double consonant will help them read longer words. (flut/ter/ing) Repeat with *splatter* and *splattering*. (splat/ter, splat/ter/ing)

PRETEACH

Decoding/Spelling

Words with VCCV: Same Medial Consonant   Explain to students that many words have a VCCV pattern. The first vowel usually has a short sound. Write each of the words below on the board and read them aloud. Have students identify what short vowel sounds they hear in the first syllable.

| rabbit | winter | hunger | college |
| better | hollow | lesson | accent |

Tell students that words with the VCCV pattern are divided into syllables between two like consonants.

PRETEACH

Grammar/Writing

Compound Sentences   Write the following sentences on the board:

> The puppy barked. The bird chirped.

Read the sentences aloud. Point out that each is a simple sentence. Each has a subject and predicate. Then ask a volunteer to read this sentence:

> The puppy barked, and the bird chirped.

Note that two simple sentences can be joined with a comma and a conjunction. Explain that *and* is used to join sentences with similar ideas, *but* is used for contrasting ideas, *or* is used for alternatives, and *for* is used to show cause and effect.

Day 5

VOCABULARY

Student-Friendly Explanations

reluctant   If someone is reluctant to do something, he or she does not want to do it.

rumpled   Something is rumpled if it is wrinkled or messy.

surge   If you feel a surge of a particular feeling, you feel it suddenly and very strongly.

inspecting   Someone who is inspecting something is looking at it very carefully.

taut   Something that is taut has been stretched or pulled very tightly.

untangled   If you untangled something, you untied knots in it or straightened it if it was twisted.

resounded   If a place resounded with a sound, it became filled with that sound.

lurked   If something lurked somewhere, it waited there quietly hidden, usually before doing something bad.

Fluency

pp. 62–68

Fluency Performance   Invite students each to read aloud from "Close Call" a passage that they selected and practiced earlier. Note the number of words each student reads correctly and incorrectly. Have students rate their own oral reading on the 1–4 scale. Give each student the opportunity to continue practicing and then to read the passage to you again.

"Close Call!"   73

DAY AT A GLANCE

Day 1

VOCABULARY
Reteach reluctant, rumpled, surge, inspecting, taut, untangled, resounded, lurked

COMPREHENSION
Reteach Plot: Conflict and Resolution

DECODING/SPELLING
Reteach Words with VCCV: Same Medial Consonant

GRAMMAR/WRITING
Preteach Simple and Compound Sentences

FLUENCY
Fluency Practice

Materials Needed: *Turn It Up!*

Student Edition pp. 70–71 | Practice Book p. 27 | Skill Card 7 | Copying Master 26

LESSON 7

RETEACH
Vocabulary

Lesson 7 Vocabulary Read aloud the Vocabulary Words and the Student-Friendly Explanations. Have a volunteer read the story on page 70 aloud as students follow along. Guide students to complete the sentences on page 71 by choosing the correct Vocabulary Word. Invite volunteers to read each completed sentence aloud. If students need additional guidance, refer to the Student-Friendly Explanations. (Answers for page 71: 2. *reluctant*, 3. *rumpled*, 4. *inspecting*, 5. *untangled*, 6. *taut*, 7. *surge*, 8. *resounded*)

pp. 70–71

RETEACH
Comprehension

Skill Card 7

Plot: Conflict and Resolution Have students look at side A of *Skill Card 7: Plot: Conflict and Resolution*. Read the definitions of plot, conflict, and resolution. Then read the passage aloud as students follow along. Direct students to look at the chart to answer the following questions:

- What is the conflict in this story?
- What are the plot events?
- What is the resolution of the problem?

Remind students that the resolution might be different than what the main character wants or expects. Discuss how the plot events would be different if the kite had pulled free when Beth tugged on it the first time. (Her brother wouldn't have helped her.)

GUIDED PRACTICE Have students look at side B of *Skill Card 7: Plot: Conflict and Resolution*. Have volunteers read aloud the information at the top of the card and the story. Assist students in copying the chart and completing it with the conflict, plot events, and resolution. Then ask students to discuss whether or not the problem was solved in the way that Josh expected. (Conflict: Josh's little brother Tommy really wants a turn driving his remote control car. Plot Events: 1. Josh teaches Tommy how to use the controls. 2. Josh lets Tommy drive the car on his own. Resolution: Tommy drives the car even better than his brother does.)

74 Lesson 7 • *Turn It Up!*

Day 1

RETEACH

Decoding/Spelling

Copying Master 26

Words with VCCV: Same Medial Consonant Distribute *Copying Master 26*. Read aloud the Spelling Words as students read along. Review the instruction for recognizing the VCCV pattern. Have students complete the following activity. Have pairs of students write the Spelling Words on index cards. Have one student draw a card and read its word aloud and the other student write the word; then have partners switch roles. When a student spells a word correctly, he or she initials the card and returns it to the pile. Students should work through the pile twice or until each student has had the opportunity to spell each of the words. Have students write down each word they do not spell correctly to study later.

PRETEACH

Grammar/Writing

Simple and Compound Sentences Tell students that a simple sentence can have a compound subject, a compound predicate, or both. Write this sentence on the board:

> Ducks and geese swim in the pond.

Ask a student to read the sentence. Point out that this is a simple sentence with a compound subject. Then write the following sentence on the board:

> Ducks and geese swim in the pond, and frogs jump and leap on the shore.

Ask a volunteer to read aloud the sentence. Remind students that a compound sentence can have a compound subject and a compound predicate in each simple sentence part. Have students draw one line under the compound subject and two lines under the compound predicate. (single line: *Ducks and geese*; double line: *jump and leap on the shore.*) Point out the two simple sentences that are joined to make this compound sentence. (Ducks and geese swim in the pond; frogs jump and leap on the shore.)

VOCABULARY

Student-Friendly Explanations

reluctant If someone is reluctant to do something, he or she does not want to do it.

rumpled Something is rumpled if it is wrinkled or messy.

surge If you feel a surge of a particular feeling, you feel it suddenly and very strongly.

inspecting Someone who is inspecting something is looking at it very carefully.

taut Something that is taut has been stretched or pulled very tightly.

untangled If you untangled something, you untied knots in it or straightened it if it was twisted.

resounded If a place resounded with a sound, it became filled with that sound.

lurked If something lurked somewhere, it waited there quietly hidden, usually before doing something bad.

Fluency

Practice Book 27

Fluency Practice Have students turn to *Practice Book* page 27. Read the words in the first column aloud. Invite students to track each word and repeat the words after you. Then have students work in pairs to read the words in the first column aloud to each other. Follow the same procedure with each of the remaining columns. After partners have practiced reading aloud the words in each of the columns, have them practice reading all of the words.

"You Have Mail!" 75

LESSON 7

30+ Minutes

RETEACH
Vocabulary

Lesson 7 Vocabulary Provide a set of Vocabulary Word Cards for each student. Read aloud the meaning of one Vocabulary Word. Write a space on the board for each letter of the word. Ask students to match the correct Word Card to the definition. Ask a volunteer to write the word in the spaces. Continue for all of the words.

(Copying Master 25)

Comprehension

Build Background: "You Have Mail!"
Invite students to share their experiences with e-mail. Have they ever helped someone else learn to use an electronic device? How did the other person feel about learning something new?

Monitor Comprehension: "You Have Mail!"
(pp. 72–73) Read the title of the story aloud. Then have students read pages 72–73 to find out who the characters are and what they want to do.

After reading the pages, ask: **Who are the main characters in the story and what do they want to do?** (Jay and Grandma; Jay wants to go to the mall. Grandma wants to write a letter.) NOTE DETAILS

Discuss the Stop and Think question on page 72: **How do you think Jay felt when his Grandma sat down to write her letter? Why?** (Possible response: I think Jay felt unhappy because he would have to wait a long time.) Guide students in writing the answer to this question. CHARACTER'S EMOTIONS

Ask: **Why do you think Grandma's letter would be called "snail mail"?** (Possible response: Grandma's letter would go slow if it is mailed, just like a snail moves slowly.) FIGURATIVE LANGUAGE

Discuss the Stop and Think question on page 73: **Why do you think Grandma says that e-mail is just for kids?** (Possible response: I think Grandma says e-mail is just for kids because sometimes kids know more about computers than grown-ups do.) Guide students in writing the answer to this question. MAKE INFERENCES

(pp. 74–75) Read aloud page 74. Model the strategy of reading ahead.

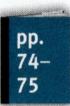 **THINK ALOUD** When I read the first paragraph, I was not sure what the laptop was. Then, as I read ahead, I learned that Jay "untangled and plugged in the cord." This told me that it might be a machine. I read ahead again and found out that Jay "flipped it on" and Grandma "peered at the screen." Now I think it is a computer because it has a screen to look at like computers do. READ AHEAD

VOCABULARY
Reteach reluctant, rumpled, surge, inspecting, taut, untangled, resounded, lurked

COMPREHENSION
"You Have Mail!"
Build Background
Monitor Comprehension
Answers to *Think Critically Questions*

DECODING/SPELLING
Reteach Words with VCCV: Same Medial Consonant

GRAMMAR/WRITING
Preteach Run-On Sentences and Comma Splices

FLUENCY
Fluency Practice

Materials Needed: *Turn It Up!*

Student Edition pp. 72–79 | Practice Book pp. 27, 28 | Copying Masters 25, 26

76 Lesson 7 • Turn It Up!

Day 2

Discuss the Stop and Think question on page 74: **Why does Grandma say, "Wait"?** (Possible response: Grandma says "Wait" because she isn't sure that Jay is allowed to use his father's laptop.) Guide students in writing the answer to this question. CAUSE AND EFFECT

Discuss the Stop and Think question on page 75: **What problem does Jay have?** (Possible response: Jay's problem is he needs a ride to the mall.) Guide students in writing the answer to this question.
🌀 PLOT: CONFLICT/RESOLUTION

 pp. 76–77 After reading the pages, ask: **Did Grandma learn how to send an e-mail?** (Yes, Grandma does learn to send e-mail because she types on the keys and then presses the "send" key.) NOTE DETAILS

Ask: **What was Grandma doing when "her clicking keys resounded in the small den"?** (Possible response: She was typing fast. As she typed her note, the clicking sound was made when she pressed down on each letter key.) CONTEXT CLUES

Discuss the Stop and Think question on page 76: **Why doesn't Grandma have Gail's e-mail address?** (Possible response: Grandma doesn't have Gail's e-mail address because she has never sent her an e-mail before.) Guide students in writing the answer to this question. DRAW CONCLUSIONS

Ask: **Grandma says "I did it!" And she feels a surge of pride. What have you done that made you say these words or feel a surge of pride?** (Responses will vary.) PERSONAL RESPONSE

Discuss the Stop and Think question on page 77: **Do you think Grandma will use only e-mail from now on? Explain your answer.** (Possible response: I think Grandma will use e-mail sometimes, but she will also still write notes.) Guide students in writing the answer to this question. MAKE PREDICTIONS

page 78 Ask: **Why do you think Grandma is smiling when they go to the mall?** (Possible response: She is happy because she learned something new.) MAKE INFERENCES/CHARACTERS' EMOTIONS

Discuss the Stop and Think question on page 78: **What did this story teach you?** (Possible response: This story teaches me that it is important to try new things; it is important to help others try new things.) Guide students in writing the answer to this question. AUTHOR'S PURPOSE

VOCABULARY
Student-Friendly Explanations

reluctant If someone is reluctant to do something, he or she does not want to do it.

rumpled Something is rumpled if it is wrinkled or messy.

surge If you feel a surge of a particular feeling, you feel it suddenly and very strongly.

inspecting Someone who is inspecting something is looking at it very carefully.

taut Something that is taut has been stretched or pulled very tightly.

untangled If you untangled something, you untied knots in it or straightened it if it was twisted.

resounded If a place resounded with a sound, it became filled with that sound.

lurked If something lurked somewhere, it waited there quietly hidden, usually before doing something bad.

"You Have Mail!" 77

Day 2

Spelling Words: Lesson 7

1. letter	11. officer
2. ladder	12. lettuce
3. appear	13. better
4. lesson	14. slipper
5. soccer	15. bottom
6. classic	16. ribbon
7. hollow	17. summer
8. supper	18. college
9. accent	19. occur
10. pizza	20. rabbit

page 79 **Answers to *Think Critically* Questions** Help students read and answer the *Think Critically* questions on page 79. Have students copy the graphic organizer in question 1 onto a separate sheet of paper. Then guide students in writing the answer to each question. Possible responses are provided.

1. [solution to Jay's Problem] teaches Grandma how to write an e-mail so she can now take him to the mall; [Grandma's problem] learns how to send an e-mail to her friend Gail. **CONFLICT/RESOLUTION**

2. In the beginning, Grandma is afraid to use e-mail because she doesn't know how. At the end, Grandma is proud that she has learned how to send e-mail. **MAKE COMPARISONS**

3. Jay smiles because Grandma is taking him to the mall; he is proud of Grandma. **CAUSE AND EFFECT**

RETEACH

Decoding/Spelling

Copying Master 26 **Words with VCCV: Same Medial Consonant** Remind students that when a word has the VCCV pattern, the first syllable often has a short vowel sound. Then point out that there are a few words that do not follow this pattern. Write the following headings across the board: *short a, short e, short i, short o, short u, other*. Invite teams of students to choose a word from the Spelling Words on *Copying Master 26*. Have a student read aloud the word and write it on the board under the correct heading. Alternate teams until all words are placed in the columns. (short *a*: ladder, classic, accent, rabbit; short *e*: letter, lesson, lettuce, better; short *i*: slipper, ribbon; short *o*: soccer, hollow, officer, bottom, college; short *u*: supper, summer; other: appear, pizza, occur)

78 Lesson 7 • Turn It Up!

Day 2

PRETEACH
Grammar/Writing

Run-on Sentences and Comma Splices Tell students that a run-on sentence occurs when two sentences are not joined with a conjunction. A comma splice is two sentences joined with only a comma. Write these examples on the board:

> Linda cleaned up the toys Dave and Bob took a nap.
> Cathy and Steve warmed up, Joan started jogging.

Help students understand that the first sentence is a run-on and the second is a comma splice. Lead them to correct the sentences by adding a comma and *and* to the first, and by adding *and* or *but* to the second.

GUIDED PRACTICE Have students turn to page 28 of their *Practice Books*. Tell students that in the first part of the activity, they will need to identify the subjects and predicates in order to tell whether the sentence is simple or compound. Point out that in the second activity, they will need to decide whether the sentence is a run-on or a comma splice before they add a conjunction or a comma and a conjunction.

Fluency

Fluency Practice Invite students to look at the bottom half of *Practice Book* page 27. These sentences have been broken into natural phrases. Tell students to repeat each phrase after you, mirroring your expression, phrasing, and pace. After students have repeated each sentence, invite them to practice reading the sentences to a partner.

"You Have Mail!" 79

LESSON 7

DAY AT A GLANCE — Day 3

COMPREHENSION
Preteach Prefixes, Suffixes, and Roots
Reread and Summarize "You Have Mail!"

DECODING/SPELLING
Reteach Word Parts

BUILD ROBUST VOCABULARY
Teach Words from "You Have Mail!"

GRAMMAR/WRITING
Reteach Writing Trait: Focus/Ideas

FLUENCY
Fluency Practice

Materials Needed: *Turn It Up!*

Student Edition pp. 72–78

Practice Book pp. 27, 29

Copying Master 27

30+ Minutes

PRETEACH

Comprehension

Prefixes, Suffixes, and Roots Distribute *Copying Master 27*. Have students read the information at the top of the page. Ask students to read aloud the key words in dark type with you. Ask students to read the story. Read aloud the first underlined word. Then name the part of the word that tells the basic meaning of the word. (take) Identify the prefix or suffix added to the word. (mis) Discuss the meaning of the root word (the way or idea about something) and the meaning of the prefix. (wrong) Explain that *mistake* means "the wrong way" or "wrong idea."

GUIDED PRACTICE Invite students to follow the same process as they add each underlined word to the chart. Allow time for students to share their responses.

Reread and Summarize Have students reread and summarize "You Have Mail!" in sections, as described below.

 Let's reread page 72 to recall what Grandma is going to do.
Summary: Grandma is going to write a note. Jay is impatient because he wants her to take him to the mall.

 Now let's reread pages 73–75 to recall what helpful things Jay says to Grandma and why.
Summary: Jay sees that Grandma is a bit afraid of learning to send an e-mail. Jay tells Grandma "You can do this" to encourage her.

 Last, let's reread pages 76–78 to remember what Jay thinks Grandma might buy at the mall and why she would want it.
Summary: Jay thinks Grandma should buy a laptop since she seems to like sending e-mail.

RETEACH

Decoding/Spelling

Word Parts Write the following VCCV words on the board:

| letter | slipper | bottom | classic |

Explain that when a VCCV word needs to be divided into syllables, it should be divided between the two matching consonants. When the word needs to be separated at the end of a line on a page, then a hyphen is placed after the first consonant. Ask students to rewrite each word on the board with a hyphen dividing the syllables. (let-ter, slip-per, bot-tom, clas-sic)

---

80 Lesson 7 • *Turn It Up!*

Day 3

TEACH
Build Robust Vocabulary

pp. 74–77

Words from "You Have Mail!" Have students locate the word *begged* on page 74 of "You Have Mail!" Ask a volunteer to read aloud the sentence in which this word appears. (First sentence: *"We will take it one step at a time," Jay begged.*) Explain that this means that Jay spoke in a way that showed he very much wanted Grandma to agree. Then ask students to locate and read aloud the sentence on page 76 in which *peeked* appears. (Line 3: *When she stopped, she peeked at Jay.*) Explain that this sentence means that Grandma took a quick little look at Jay. Continue by asking students to locate and read aloud the sentence on page 77 in which the word *amazed* appears. (Line 2: *You will be amazed.*) Explain that this sentence means that Gail will be so surprised at what she sees that she will hardly believe it.

Whisper one of the words to a student. Have the student act out the word. Have other students guess the word. Continue with the other words.

RETEACH
Grammar/Writing

Practice Book 29

Writing Trait: Focus/Ideas Ask students to turn to page 29 in their *Practice Book*. Explain that when writers write a story, it is important that each sentence is focused or relates to the topic of the story. The story needs to have a beginning where characters and setting are described. It needs a middle that tells events in the order that they happened. There should be an ending that wraps up the story. This order also helps to keep the ideas focused on the topic. Point out how the author of "You Have Mail!" keeps the story focused on the topic.

GUIDED PRACTICE Have a volunteer read the directions on *Practice Book* page 29. Ask students to work in pairs to complete the page.

Fluency

Practice Book 27

Fluency Practice Tell students that today they will reread the sentences on the bottom of *Practice Book* page 27. Have students locate and point to the first sentence. Tell students that everyone is going to read the sentence together. This choral reading will give students an opportunity to hear others and listen to the natural phrasing of the sentences. Choral-read each of the sentences several times.

"You Have Mail!" 81

LESSON 7

DAY AT A GLANCE — Day 4

COMPREHENSION
Reteach Prefixes, Suffixes, and Roots

DECODING/SPELLING
Reteach Words with VCCV: Same Medial Consonant

ROBUST VOCABULARY
Reteach Words from "You Have Mail!"

GRAMMAR/WRITING
Reteach Writing Form: Narrative

FLUENCY
Fluency Practice

Materials Needed: *Turn It Up!*

 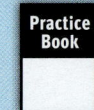

Student Edition pp. 72–78 | Practice Book p. 30 | Copying Master 28

Spelling Words: Lesson 7

1. letter	11. officer
2. ladder	12. lettuce
3. appear	13. better
4. lesson	14. slipper
5. soccer	15. bottom
6. classic	16. ribbon
7. hollow	17. summer
8. supper	18. college
9. accent	19. occur
10. pizza	20. rabbit

30+ Minutes

RETEACH

Comprehension

Prefixes, Suffixes, and Roots Remind students that a root word may have a prefix added to the beginning, or a suffix added to the end. The root is the basic part of the word. Sometimes, the root needs more word parts to be a whole word. The prefix and suffix add a new meaning to the root.

Write *misfortune* on the board. Invite students to read the word. Help students recognize the meaning by looking at each word part. (root word *fortune* means "good luck"; prefix *mis* means "wrong" or "bad"; *misfortune* means "wrong or bad luck")

GUIDED PRACTICE Write the following words on the board:

disrepair   believable   environment

Ask students to locate the prefix or suffix and root for each word. Have them use the meanings of each word part to find the meaning of the word. (*dis*—not, *repair*—to fix, *disrepair*—not fixed; *able*—can do, *believe*—to think something is true, *believable*—can think something is true; *ment*—condition of, *environ*—place or area, *environment*—condition of a place or area)

RETEACH

Decoding/Spelling

Words with VCCV: Same Medial Consonant Have students number a sheet of paper 1–19. Write the Spelling Word *ladder* on the board and point to the VCCV pattern. Tell students that each of the words you will dictate has the VCCV pattern. After students write each word, display the word so they can proofread their work.

1. letter	2. appear	3. lesson	4. soccer
5. classic	6. hollow	7. supper	8. accent
9. pizza	10. officer	11. lettuce	12. better
13. slipper	14. bottom	15. ribbon	16. summer
17. college	18. occur	19. rabbit	

Invite students to turn to page 30 in their *Practice Book*. Read the story aloud as students read along. Then have students reread one sentence at a time, circling each word that has the VCCV pattern. Then have volunteers read each numbered sentence. Tell them to choose a VCCV word they circled to complete the sentence. Instruct students to write the correct word on the line.

82 Lesson 7 • *Turn It Up!*

Day 4

RETEACH
Build Robust Vocabulary

Words from "You Have Mail!" Review the meanings of *begged*, *peeked*, and *amazed*. Then say these sentences and ask which word each sentence describes. Have students explain why.

- **Sam asked Mom if he could go to the movies in a way that showed he really, really wanted to go.** (begged)
- **The girl took a quick look out the window to see if it was raining.** (peeked)
- **Mom was so surprised at how fast I learned my spelling words that she could hardly believe it.** (amazed)

RETEACH
Grammar/Writing

Copying Master 28

Writing Form: Narrative Remind students that a narrative tells a story about events that happen to a main character. Read aloud the information about narratives at the top of *Copying Master 28*. Then read the Student Model together. Invite a volunteer to read aloud a sentence that tells something about Mary in the beginning of the story. (Possible responses: Mary was very excited; It was finally time to open her birthday presents.) Model how you can decide if this sentence focuses on the topic: **The topic of this story is that Mary is opening a birthday gift. The sentence describes Mary and tells how she is feeling on her birthday. So, I know that this sentence is focused on the story topic.**

GUIDED PRACTICE Complete the activity by having students explain their choices. Read the second activity together. Invite students to suggest ways to rewrite this sentence.

Fluency

pp. 72–78 **Fluency Practice** Have each student work with a partner to read passages from "You Have Mail!" aloud to each other. Students may select a passage that they enjoyed or choose one of the following options:

- Read page 72. (Total: 88 words)
- Read page 73. (Total: 71 words)

Encourage students to read the selected passage aloud to their partner three times. Have the student rate his or her reading on the 1–4 scale.

1	Need more practice
2	Pretty good
3	Good
4	Great!

"You Have Mail!" **83**

Preteach for LESSON 8

30+ Minutes

Day 5

VOCABULARY
Preteach slick, nimble, impressed, cease, exist, fierce

COMPREHENSION
 Preteach Author's Purpose and Perspective

DECODING/WORD ATTACK
Preteach Decode Longer Words

DECODING/SPELLING
Preteach Words with VCCV: Different Medial Consonants

GRAMMAR/WRITING
Preteach Prepositions

FLUENCY
Fluency Performance

Materials Needed: *Turn It Up!*

Student Edition pp. 72–78 | Copying Master 29

PRETEACH

Vocabulary

Copying Master 29 | **Lesson 8 Vocabulary** Explain to students that they will learn six new words that they will come across again when they read "The Pigs, the Wolf, and a Laptop." Distribute a set of Vocabulary Word Cards to each student or pair of students. Hold up the card for the first word, and ask a volunteer to read the word aloud. Have students repeat the word and hold up the matching card. Give the explanation for the word. Then ask students the first question below and discuss their responses. Continue for each Vocabulary Word.

- **What room in your school do you think is really slick?**
- **What is an activity you need nimble fingers for?**
- **Who is a person you are impressed with? What did he or she do to impress you?**
- **What activities will you cease doing when school is out?**
- **What animals exist in your community?**
- **What kinds of fierce animals have you read about?**

PRETEACH

Comprehension

pp. 72–78 **Author's Purpose and Perspective** Tell students that authors write for different reasons. An author also writes from a certain point of view, called perspective. Details and words in the selection or story are clues to this perspective. Ask students to recall what they read in "You Have Mail!" Then ask:

- **How do you think the author feels about writing letters with paper and pen?** (The author does not like letters written with paper and pen because writing them is too slow.)
- **What clues from the story make you think this is how the author feels?** (Jay says, "Your note is called 'snail mail.' It will take days.")
- **What is the author's purpose? Why?** (The author's purpose is to entertain because this is fiction. I think the author also wanted to inform readers about learning new things.)

GUIDED PRACTICE Ask students to work in pairs as they discuss a different point of view for "You Have Mail!" Tell students that the point of view has been changed. Now the author feels that e-mail is too fast and young people need to learn how to write and send letters correctly. Discuss how the story would be different. (Possible response: Grandma would not learn to send an e-mail. She would teach Jay how to write a proper letter.)

84 Preteach for Lesson 8 • *Turn It Up!*

Day 5

PRETEACH
Decoding/Word Attack

Decode Longer Words Write *comfort* on the board. Name the letters in the first syllable. Then point out the second syllable. Explain that *comfort* has the VCCV syllable pattern, but each consonant is different. The syllables are divided between these two letters.

Repeat the process with the word *father*. Point out that even though the consonants are different, they make one sound. These two consonants stay together in one syllable.

GUIDED PRACTICE Copy these words on the board: *fishing, forgiven, festival,* and *another*. Have students read each word and identify the VCCV pattern. Have them decide whether the consonants stand for one sound or two. (one sound: *sh, th;* two sounds: *rg, st*)

PRETEACH
Decoding/Spelling

Words with VCCV: Different Medial Consonants Write the following Spelling Words on the board and read them aloud. Ask students to identify the VCCV sounds.

| chapter | welcome | window | problem |
| hunger | history | mother | secret |

PRETEACH
Grammar/Writing

Prepositions Write the following sentence on the board:

> My book is under the table.

Identify the preposition. (under) Explain that a preposition shows the relationship between a noun or pronoun and another word in the sentence. Point out that the preposition shows where the book is in relation to the table.

Erase the prepositions and ask students to name different prepositions that will work in the sentence, such as *on, by,* and *beside.* Have students explain the relationship between the two nouns.

VOCABULARY
Student-Friendly Explanations

slick If something is slick, it is presented in an attractive way.

nimble If someone is nimble, he or she moves quickly, lightly, and easily.

impressed To be impressed with someone means to admire that person.

cease If you cease to do something, you stop doing it.

exist When something exists, it is a real thing that is present in the world.

fierce A fierce person or animal is angry, violent, or ready to attack.

Fluency

Fluency Performance
pp. 72–78
Invite students to read aloud the passages from "You Have Mail!" that they selected and practiced earlier. Note the number of words each student reads correctly and incorrectly. Have students rate their own oral reading on the 1–4 scale. Give students the opportunity to continue practicing and then to read the passage to you again.

"You Have Mail!" 85

LESSON 8

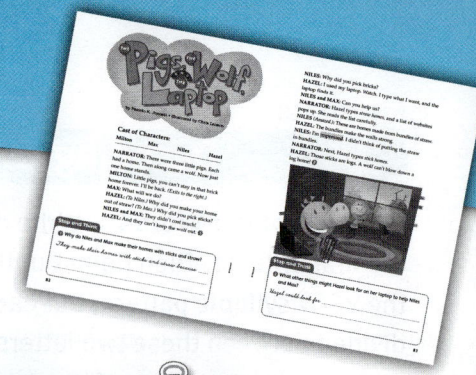

DAY AT A GLANCE — Day 1

VOCABULARY
Reteach slick, nimble, impressed, cease, exist, fierce

COMPREHENSION
Reteach Author's Purpose and Perspective

DECODING/SPELLING
Reteach Words with VCCV: Different Medial Consonants

GRAMMAR/WRITING
Preteach Prepositional Phrases

FLUENCY
Fluency Practice

Materials Needed: *Turn It Up!*

Student Edition pp. 80–81 | Practice Book p. 31 | Skill Card 8 | Copying Master 30

RETEACH — Vocabulary

pp. 80–81

Lesson 8 Vocabulary Read aloud the Vocabulary Words. Review the Student-Friendly Explanations. Have students read the news articles on pages 80 and 81. Guide students to choose the correct word to complete each sentence. If students have difficulty choosing, refer to the Student-Friendly Explanations. Ask volunteers to reread each sentence with the missing word. Then have students read aloud the completed story. (Answers for pages 80–81: 2. *exist*, 3. *cease*, 4. *fierce*, 5. *nimble*, 6. *impressed*)

RETEACH — Comprehension

Skill Card 8

Author's Purpose and Perspective Have students look at side A of *Skill Card 8: Author's Purpose and Perspective*. Read aloud the definitions of purpose and perspective. Then have a volunteer read aloud the paragraph while students follow along. Point to the chart. Ask:

- What genre is this paragraph?
- What is the author's purpose for writing this story?
- What is the author's perspective for this story?
- What are some clues that tell you the author's perspective?

Remind students that the perspective of the author affects what happens in the story. Discuss how the story could be different if the author thought that it was not a good idea to try new things because they are too hard.

GUIDED PRACTICE Now have students look at side B of *Skill Card 8: Author's Purpose and Perspective*. Review the Skill Reminder, and have a student read aloud the passage. Direct students to copy the chart on paper and complete it using details from the passage. (Title: "No New Foods"; Genre: fiction; Author's Name: Mary Roth; Author's Purpose or Purposes: to entertain; to teach a lesson about trying new things; Clues to the Author's Perspective: tried new dish once and didn't like it, tried tiny piece, emptied plate, likes new food, wants more) Then ask students how the story might change if the author thought that trying new things were not a good thing. Ask students to describe how this new perspective would affect the story.

86 Lesson 8 • Turn It Up!

Day 1

RETEACH

Decoding/Spelling

Words with VCCV: Different Medial Consonants Distribute *Copying Master 30*. Model reading each Spelling Word, and ask students to repeat them. Review the details for breaking VCCV words into syllables. Have pairs of students write the Spelling Words on index cards. Have one student draw a card and read its word aloud, and have the other student write the word; then have partners switch roles. When a student spells a word correctly, he or she initials the card and returns it to the pile. Students should work through the pile twice or until each student has had the opportunity to spell each of the words. Have students write down each word they do not spell correctly to study later.

PRETEACH

Grammar/Writing

Prepositional Phrases Explain to students that a preposition, an object of the preposition, and the words in between make a prepositional phrase. The object of a preposition is the noun that follows the preposition. Write the following sentence on the board:

> I like blankets on my bed.

Read the sentence aloud. Underline the prepositional phrase *on my bed*. Then ask a student to name the preposition. (on) Point out the object of the preposition. (bed) Write the following sentence on the board:

> I will walk you across the busy street.

Have a student read the sentence aloud. Guide students to underline the prepositional phrase (across the busy street) and circle the object of the preposition. (street)

GUIDED PRACTICE Write the following sentences on the board:

> The girls play tennis at the park.
> Bobby walked through the door.

Ask students to underline each prepositional phrase and circle the object of the preposition. (at the park, park; through the door, door)

VOCABULARY

Student-Friendly Explanations

slick If something is slick, it is presented in an attractive way.

nimble If someone is nimble, he or she moves quickly, lightly, and easily.

impressed To be impressed with someone means to admire that person.

cease If you cease to do something, you stop doing it.

exist When something exists, it is a real thing that is present in the world.

fierce A fierce person or animal is angry, violent, or ready to attack.

Fluency

Fluency Practice Have students turn to *Practice Book* page 31. Read the words in the first column aloud. Invite students to track each word and repeat the words after you. Then have students work in pairs to read the words in the first column aloud to each other. Follow the same procedure with each of the remaining columns. After partners have practiced reading aloud the words in each of the columns, have them practice reading all of the words.

"The Pigs, the Wolf, and a Laptop" 87

LESSON 8

Day 2

VOCABULARY
Reteach slick, nimble, impressed, cease, exist, fierce

COMPREHENSION
"The Pigs, the Wolf, and a Laptop"
Build Background
Monitor Comprehension
Answers to *Think Critically* Questions

DECODING/SPELLING
Reteach Words with VCCV: Different Medial Consonants

GRAMMAR/WRITING
Preteach Longer Prepositional Phrases

FLUENCY
Fluency Practice

Materials Needed: *Turn It Up!*

Student Edition
pp. 82–89

Practice Book
pp. 31, 32

Copying Masters
29, 30

RETEACH

Vocabulary

Lesson 8 Vocabulary Have pairs of students stand next to each other, each holding a set of Vocabulary Word Cards. Read aloud the definition of one of the words. Have the two students work together to identify the word being defined and hold up that Vocabulary Word Card. Have students separate their Word Cards into those they identify correctly and those they need to study more.

Comprehension

Build Background: "The Pigs, the Wolf, and a Laptop"
Ask students to talk about times when they have searched the Internet for some helpful information. Have them describe what problem or question they had, and how they made their search.

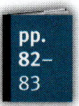
Monitor Comprehension: "The Pigs, the Wolf, and a Laptop"
Read the title of the story aloud. Then have students read pages 82–83 to find out what Hazel built her house with, and why.

After reading the pages, ask: **What did Hazel use to build her house? Why did she choose that?** (Hazel used bricks. She picked bricks because she used her laptop to learn that bricks were a strong building material.) Guide students in writing the answer to this question. **DRAW CONCLUSIONS**

Discuss the Stop and Think question on page 82: **Why did Niles and Max make their homes with sticks and straw?** (They made their homes with sticks and straw because sticks and straw didn't cost much.) Guide students in writing the answer to this question. **NOTE DETAILS**

Discuss the Stop and Think question on page 83: **What other things might Hazel look for on her laptop to help Niles and Max?** (Possible responses: Hazel could look for other ways to build homes, how to get rid of a wolf, or alarm systems.) Guide students in writing the answer to this question. **DRAW CONCLUSIONS**

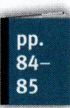
Ask: **What do you know about Alaska?** (Possible response: I know that Alaska is one of the fifty states in the United States; the weather in Alaska is cold and snowy.) **USE PRIOR KNOWLEDGE**

Discuss the Stop and Think question on page 84: **What do you think will happen next?** (Possible response: I think that the pigs will trick Milton and send him to Alaska.) Guide students in writing the answer to this question. **MAKE PREDICTIONS**

88 Lesson 8 • *Turn It Up!*

Discuss the Stop and Think question on page 85: **How do the pigs find out how to build better homes?** (Possible response: The pigs find out how to build better homes by researching on the laptop new ways to build homes.) Guide students in writing the answer to this question. **SUMMARIZE**

Ask: **What worries Milton when he is not able to blow down the houses?** (Milton is worried that no one will think he is fierce.) **NOTE DETAILS**

Discuss the Stop and Think question on page 86: **What happens after Milton finds he cannot blow the houses down?** (After Milton finds he cannot blow the houses down, he is upset, and the pigs don't know what to do.) Guide students in writing the answer to this question. **SEQUENCE**

Ask: **How do you think Milton will feel about living where there are many like him?** (Possible responses: I think he will feel more comfortable living with other wolves instead of pigs. I think he will be happy and not want to blow down houses anymore.) **CHARACTER'S EMOTIONS**

Discuss the Stop and Think question on page 87: **Do you think Milton will leave the pigs alone? Explain.** (Possible responses: I think that Milton will leave the pigs alone. He can't blow down their homes; he will move to Alaska.) Guide students in writing the answer to this question. **EXPRESS PERSONAL OPINIONS**

Discuss the Stop and Think question on page 88: **Did the author write this play to entertain you or to teach you something? Explain your answer.** (Possible response: I think the author wrote this play to entertain me. The story has funny parts, and it's a play that I could act out with friends.) Guide students in writing the answer to this question. **AUTHOR'S PURPOSE AND PERSPECTIVE**

After students finish reading the story, model the strategy of summarizing for them.

THINK ALOUD If I wanted to summarize this story, I would think about the most important parts. The pigs find a better way to build houses. That's important. The pigs discover Milton would be better off in Alaska, where there are other wolves. In the end, everyone is happy because they now have what they need. **SUMMARIZE**

VOCABULARY
Student-Friendly Explanations

slick If something is slick, it is presented in an attractive way.

nimble If someone is nimble, he or she moves quickly, lightly, and easily.

impressed To be impressed with someone means to admire that person.

cease If you cease to do something, you stop doing it.

exist When something exists, it is a real thing that is present in the world.

fierce A fierce person or animal is angry, violent, or ready to attack.

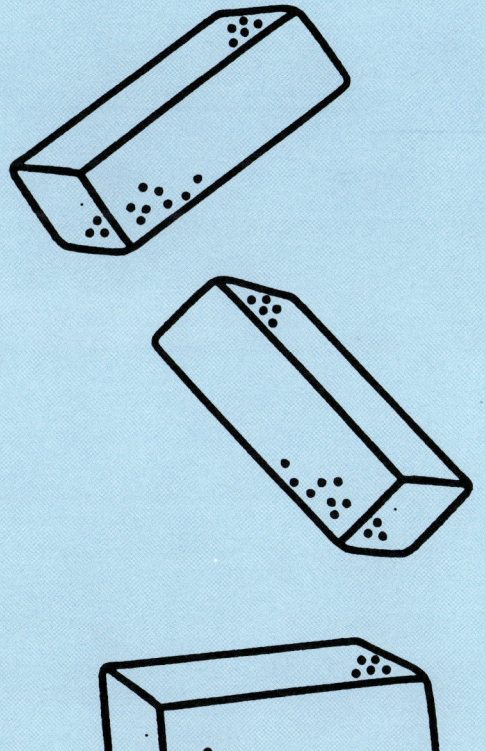

"The Pigs, the Wolf, and a Laptop" 89

Day 2

Spelling Words: Lesson 8

1. history	11. thunder
2. number	12. furnish
3. hunger	13. jersey
4. company	14. mother
5. window	15. secret
6. welcome	16. harvest
7. blanket	17. winter
8. perhaps	18. problem
9. service	19. chapter
10. subject	20. nurses

Answers to *Think Critically* Questions (page 89) Help students read and answer the *Think Critically* questions on page 89. Have students copy the graphic organizer in question 1 onto a separate sheet of paper. Then guide students in writing the answer to each question. Possible responses are provided.

1. [First] Two brother pigs seek shelter in their sister's brick home after a wolf blows down their straw and stick homes. [Next] Hazel uses her laptop to learn better ways to build homes. [Then] The pigs show Milton homes for wolves on the laptop. [Finally] Milton moves to Alaska, and the pigs live happily ever after. **PLOT**

2. This is how it is different: He used bundles of straw to make it stronger. This is how it is the same: It is still made of straw. **COMPARE AND CONTRAST**

3. The pigs want to help Milton because they feel sorry for him. They think he would be happier in a place with other wolves. **CHARACTERS' MOTIVATIONS**

RETEACH
Decoding/Spelling

Words with VCCV: Different Medial Consonants Distribute *Copying Master 30*. Have teams of students play a matching game. Have students write each two-syllable Spelling Word on a slip of paper and cut the word apart in between the syllables. Then have students spread out the word parts face-up and take turns matching word parts to make a word.

PRETEACH

Grammar/Writing

Practice Book 32 **Longer Prepositional Phrases** Briefly review prepositional phrases with students. Then write these sentences on the board:

> I read a book after I finished my chores.
>
> After I finished my chores, I read a book.

Guide students to identify how these sentences are different. (One sentence has the prepositional phrase at the beginning.) Help students understand that a comma is needed when a prepositional phrase more than a few words long is at the beginning of the sentence.

GUIDED PRACTICE Direct students to *Practice Book* page 32. Help them approach each sentence step-by-step as they circle, underline, and draw a triangle around the words as needed. Help students to recognize the appropriate use of commas.

Fluency

Practice Book 31 **Fluency Practice** Invite students to look at the bottom half of *Practice Book* page 31. These sentences have been broken into natural phrases. Tell students to repeat each phrase after you, imitating your expression, phrasing, and pace. After students have repeated each sentence, invite them to practice reading the sentences to partners.

"The Pigs, the Wolf, and a Laptop" **91**

LESSON 8

DAY AT A GLANCE — Day 3

COMPREHENSION
Preteach Locate Information
Reread and Summarize: "The Pigs, the Wolf, and a Laptop"

DECODING/SPELLING
Reteach Hear Consonant Sounds

BUILD ROBUST VOCABULARY
Teach Words from "The Pigs, the Wolf, and a Laptop"

GRAMMAR/WRITING
Reteach Writing Trait: Organization

FLUENCY
Fluency Practice

Materials Needed: *Turn It Up!*

Student Edition pp. 82–88 | Practice Book pp. 31, 33 | Copying Master 31

30+ Minutes

PRETEACH

Comprehension

Locate Information Invite students to read along as you read aloud the information at the top of *Copying Master 30*. Review the use of a library database.

GUIDED PRACTICE Ask students to look at the illustration that shows the ways to locate and research information. Have pairs of students work together to complete the chart. Review students' responses as a group.

Reread and Summarize Have students reread and summarize "The Pigs, the Wolf, and a Laptop" in sections, as described below.

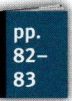
pp. 82–83
Let's reread pages 82–83 to recall how Hazel helps Niles and Max.
Summary: Hazel helps Niles and Max by using her laptop to find websites. These websites explain how to make better straw and stick homes. Hazel shares this with Niles and Max.

pp. 84–85
Now let's reread pages 84–85 to recall what the pigs find out about wolves.
Summary: The pigs find better ways to build new homes. They also discover that wolves exist in Alaska. They wonder if Milton should be living in Alaska.

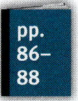
pp. 86–88
Last, let's reread pages 86–88 to remember what Milton promises.
Summary: Milton promises to leave the pigs alone. In return, the pigs tell him about Alaska. Milton moves to Alaska, where he is happy with other wolves. The pigs live safely in their new homes.

RETEACH

Decoding/Spelling

Hear Consonant Sounds Tell students that they can say a word softly and listen carefully for the consonant sounds to help them spell words correctly. Model by saying *number* aloud and then identifying the /n/, /m/, /b/, and /r/ sounds. Have students repeat the process with these words:

window	blanket	welcome
(/w/, /n/, /d/)	(/b/, /l/, /n/, /k/, /t/)	(/w/, /l/, /k/, /m/)
secret	**mother**	**problem**
(/s/, /k/, /r/, /t/)	(/m/, /th/, /r/)	(/p/, /r/, /b/, /l/, /m/)

Remind students that they can use this strategy to proofread what they write.

92 Lesson 8 • Turn It Up!

Day 3

TEACH
Build Robust Vocabulary

Words from "The Pigs, the Wolf, and a Laptop" (pp. 83–88) Have students locate the word *bundles* on page 83 of "The Pigs, the Wolf, and a Laptop." Ask a volunteer to read aloud the sentence in which this word appears. (Line 7: *These are homes made from bundles of straw.*) Explain that this means that the straw is tied or wrapped together in little bunches or groups. Continue by asking students to locate and read aloud the sentence on page 87 that includes the word *appears*. (Line 5: *The wolf website appears.*) Explain that this means that the website showed up on the screen so the pigs could see it. Then ask students to locate and read aloud the sentence on page 88 in which *splendid* appears. (First line: *What a splendid plan.*) Explain that this sentence means that the plan is wonderful.

Give each student a card with one of the words on it. Say the meaning for one of the words. Ask a student if the meaning matches his or her card. If not, the student may trade with someone who has the correct word. Continue the game until all students have had a turn.

RETEACH
Grammar/Writing

Writing Trait: Organization (Practice Book 33) Have students turn to *Practice Book* page 33. Explain that when you write an e-mail, you need to show organization by arranging ideas into a beginning, a middle, and an end. Ask a volunteer to read aloud the information at the top of the page. Point out that the author of "The Pigs, the Wolf, and a Laptop" organizes this play into a beginning, middle, and end.

GUIDED PRACTICE Complete page 33 together. Help students recognize the organizational pattern in each passage.

Fluency

Fluency Practice (Practice Book 31) Tell students that today they will reread the sentences on the bottom of *Practice Book* page 31. Have students locate and point to the first sentence. Tell students that everyone is going to read the sentence together. This choral reading will give students an opportunity to hear others and listen to the natural phrasing of the sentences. Choral-read each of the sentences several times.

"The Pigs, the Wolf, and a Laptop" 93

LESSON 8

DAY AT A GLANCE — Day 4

COMPREHENSION
Reteach Locate Information

DECODING/SPELLING
Reteach Words with VCCV: Different Medial Consonants

BUILD ROBUST VOCABULARY
Reteach Words from "The Pigs, the Wolf, and a Laptop"

GRAMMAR/WRITING
Reteach Writing Form: E-Mail

FLUENCY
Fluency Practice

Materials Needed: *Turn It Up!*

 Student Edition pp. 82–88

 Practice Book p. 34

 Copying Master 32

Spelling Words: Lesson 8

1. history	11. thunder
2. number	12. furnish
3. hunger	13. jersey
4. company	14. mother
5. window	15. secret
6. welcome	16. harvest
7. blanket	17. winter
8. perhaps	18. problem
9. service	19. chapter
10. subject	20. nurses

30+ Minutes

RETEACH
Comprehension

Locate Information   Share the following information about locating information with students:

- A **library database** can be accessed from a computer in the library or a personal computer that connects to the Internet.
- A library database lets a writer research library items by **author's name, book title, call number,** or **keyword**.
- A writer can also search for information in a **CD-ROM encyclopedia** by topic or by alphabet.
- Writers also find information in **online magazine and newspaper** articles.

Write on the board the following sentences related to the play:

> 1. "The Pigs, the Wolf, and a Laptop" is a play about three pigs. Are there other stories about three pigs?
> 2. What are bricks made of and where are they made?

Invite students to read aloud each sentence and explain what resource they might use to locate information about the topic. (Possible responses: 1. Use library database; search by keyword "three pigs." 2. Use CD-ROM encyclopedia; search "bricks" or "How are bricks made?")

RETEACH
Decoding/Spelling

 Words with VCCV: Different Medial Consonants   Ask students to number their paper 1–19. Write the Spelling Word *chapter* on the board. Point to the VCCV pattern. Explain to students that the nineteen words you will dictate all include the VCCV pattern. After students write each word, display it so they can proofread their work.

1. history	2. number	3. hunger	4. company
5. window	6. welcome	7. blanket	8. perhaps
9. service	10. subject	11. thunder	12. furnish
13. jersey	14. mother	15. secret	16. harvest
17. winter	18. problem	19. nurses	

Ask students to turn to *Practice Book* page 34. Point to the first picture and ask students to describe the picture. Read aloud the first set of sentences as students read along. Have a volunteer read aloud the sentence that best describes the picture. Repeat with each picture and set of sentences.

94 Lesson 8 • Turn It Up!

Day 4

RETEACH
Build Robust Vocabulary

Words from "The Pigs, the Wolf, and a Laptop" Review the meanings of *bundles, appear,* and *splendid.* Then say these sentences and ask which word each sentence describes. Have students explain why.

- **The class tied the newspapers into little bunches to recycle.** (bundles)
- **The bus will show up every morning at 7:30.** (appear)
- **I think the idea of going to the beach is wonderful.** (splendid)

RETEACH
Grammar/Writing

Copying Master 32

Writing Form: E-Mail Ask a volunteer to read the description of e-mail at the top of *Copying Master 32*. Read aloud the Student Model with students. Point out how each part of the e-mail fits into the boxes labeled *Beginning, Middle,* and *End.* Read aloud the following passage from the e-mail and guide students to rewrite the sentence so it is a more polite ending.

> **Send the information very quickly.**
> (Possible response: Please send the information about the dollhouse as soon as possible.)

Discuss why this revised sentence is preferable and where it should be placed in the e-mail.

GUIDED PRACTICE Guide students as they complete the questions at the bottom of the page.

Fluency

pp. 82–88 **Fluency Practice** Have each student work with a partner to read passages from "The Pigs, the Wolf, and a Laptop" aloud to each other. Students may select a passage that they enjoyed or choose one of the following options:

- Read page 82. (Total: 82 words)
- Read page 83. (Total: 94 words)

Encourage students to read the selected passage aloud to their partner three times. Have the student rate his or her reading on the 1–4 scale.

1	Need more practice
2	Pretty good
3	Good
4	Great!

"The Pigs, the Wolf, and a Laptop" 95

Preteach for **LESSON 9**

VOCABULARY
Preteach unique, infest, intervals, delicate, flexible, bond, inspires, preserve

COMPREHENSION
 Preteach Author's Purpose and Perspective

DECODING/WORD ATTACK
Preteach Decode Longer Words

DECODING/SPELLING
Preteach Words with VCCCV

GRAMMAR/WRITING
Preteach Phrases and Independent Clauses

FLUENCY
Fluency Performance

Materials Needed: *Turn It Up!*

Student Edition pp. 82–88

Copying Master 33

PRETEACH

Vocabulary

Copying Master 33

Lesson 9 Vocabulary Distribute a set of Vocabulary Word Cards to each student. Hold up the card for the first Vocabulary Word, and ask a volunteer to read the word aloud. Have students repeat the word and hold up the matching card. Give the explanation for the word. Then ask students the first question below and discuss their responses. Continue for each Vocabulary Word.

- **What is something unique about your home?**
- **What kinds of bugs might infest a building?**
- **What things are set up at regular intervals in our classroom?**
- **What are some delicate things you see at the grocery store?**
- **Do you have any toys or games that are flexible? How do they work?**
- **What bond do you share with other members of your family?**
- **What kind of music inspires you to dance or move around?**
- **How does your family preserve special pictures or papers?**

PRETEACH

Comprehension

pp. 82–88

Author's Purpose and Perspective Tell students that authors have different purposes for writing. The author's perspective can be found in his or her choice of words. Ask students to think about "The Pigs, the Wolf, and a Laptop." Ask:

- **How do you think the author feels about finding information from websites? What clues show her perspective?** (Possible response: The author feels that it is very helpful to look at websites. Hazel says "Websites can be very helpful." At the end of the story, it says "Now when they have a problem, they check what to do on the laptop.")

- **What do you think this author's perspective is about friendship? What clues help you to know?** (Possible response: The author thinks that friends need to help each other and take care of each other. Hazel helps her friends find out how to build their homes better. The pigs help the wolf find a better place to live.)

Explain that the author has a purpose for writing a story. Usually, the purpose of fiction is to entertain.

96 Preteach for Lesson 9 • *Turn It Up!*

Day 5

PRETEACH

Decoding/Word Attack

Decode Longer Words   Write *encloses* and *merchandise* on the board. Read each word aloud and then have students repeat each word after you. Point out that these words have the VCCCV pattern. Draw a line under the VCCCV letters in each word. (<u>encl</u>oses; m<u>erch</u>andise) Tell students that *encloses* is divided into syllables between *n* and the blend *cl*, and *merchandise* is divided into syllables between *r* and the blend *ch*. The two consonants that stand for the one sound are not divided. Explain that knowing this rule will make it easier for them to decode longer words.

PRETEACH

Decoding/Spelling

Words with VCCCV   Tell students that it will be easier to spell VCCCV words if they recognize how to divide the words into syllables. Write the following Spelling Words on the board and read them aloud. Ask students to identify the VCCCV pattern in each word.

monster	hundred	conflict	ostrich
kitchen	pumpkin	punctual	Thursday

PRETEACH

Grammar/Writing

Phrases and Independent Clauses   Write the following words on the board and read them aloud:

> Plays the piano.

Tell students that this group of words is a phrase because it is missing a subject. Guide a student to add a subject to make a complete sentence. Write the following sentence on the board and read it aloud:

> The girl played her drums.

Explain that this is an independent clause because it has a subject and verb. It is a complete sentence. Point out the subject and the verb.
(subject: *girl*; verb: *played*)

VOCABULARY

Student-Friendly Explanations

unique   Something is unique if it is the only one of its kind.

infest   If insects or animals infest a place, they are there in large numbers and usually cause damage.

intervals   Something that happens at regular intervals is repeated over and over with a certain amount of time in between.

delicate   If something is done in a delicate way, it is done with great care so that nothing is broken or hurt.

flexible   Something is flexible if it can bend or be bent easily.

bond   A bond is a feeling or interest that unites two or more people or groups.

inspires   If something inspires you, it makes you excited about doing something good.

preserve   To preserve something is to keep it from being harmed or changed.

Fluency

Fluency Performance
pp. 82–88   Invite students to read aloud the passages from "The Pigs, the Wolf, and a Laptop" that they selected and practiced earlier. Note the number of words each student reads correctly and incorrectly. Have students rate their own oral reading on the 1–4 scale. Give students the opportunity to continue practicing and then to read the passage to you again.

"The Pigs, the Wolf, and a Laptop"   97

DAY AT A GLANCE

Day 1

LESSON 9

30+ Minutes

VOCABULARY
Reteach *unique, infest, intervals, delicate, flexible, bond, inspires, preserve*

COMPREHENSION
 Reteach Author's Purpose and Perspective

DECODING/SPELLING
Reteach Words with VCCCV

GRAMMAR/WRITING
Preteach Dependent and Independent Clauses

FLUENCY
Fluency Practice

Materials Needed: *Turn It Up!*

Student Edition pp. 90–91 | Practice Book p. 35 | Skill Card 9 | Copying Master 34

RETEACH

Vocabulary

pp. 90–91 **Lesson 9 Vocabulary** Read aloud the Vocabulary Words. Review the Student-Friendly Explanations. Help students read the letter on page 90. Then ask students to reread the letter, choosing the correct words to complete the sentences. If students have difficulty choosing, refer to the Student-Friendly Explanations. Ask volunteers to reread each completed sentence. Repeat with the two letters on page 91. (Answers for pp. 90–91: 2. *preserve*, 3. *unique*, 4. *flexible*, 5. *delicate*, 6. *intervals*, 7. *bond*, 8. *inspires*)

RETEACH

Comprehension

  **Author's Purpose and Perspective** Have students look at side A of *Skill Card 9: Author's Purpose and Perspective*. Have volunteers read aloud the definition of author's purpose and perspective and the paragraph. Point to the chart. Ask:

- **Is this paragraph fiction or nonfiction? How do you know?** (nonfiction; gives factual information about an old barn)
- **What is the author's perspective?**
- **What are some details that show this perspective?**

Remind students that, although the usual purpose of nonfiction is to inform, an author may also have other purposes. Discuss how the writing would be different if the author only wanted to inform the reader about an old barn. (Possible response: It would not include so many details about what happened long ago. It would not ask for a donation of money.)

GUIDED PRACTICE Now have students look at side B of *Skill Card 9: Author's Purpose and Perspective*. Read aloud the Skill Reminder. Then read aloud the paragraph. Ask students to copy the chart onto their paper. Guide students to complete the chart using details from the paragraph. (Possible responses: [Author's Purpose] to persuade; [Author's Perspective] It is important to save the Little Red Schoolhouse and preserve history.; [Details] special building, very old, people work hard to care for it, children learn about history from this school, you will feel proud if you help)

98 Lesson 9 • *Turn It Up!*

Day 1

RETEACH

Decoding/Spelling

Words with VCCCV Distribute *Copying Master 34*. Have students echo-read each word and identify the VCCCV pattern. Then have students work in pairs. Each student writes a sentence for each Spelling Word but leaves a blank for the actual word. The partners then switch papers and fill in the blanks in each other's sentences. Students should give themselves one point for each correctly spelled word.

PRETEACH

Grammar/Writing

Dependent and Independent Clauses Explain that a dependent clause includes a subject and a predicate but is not a sentence because it does not include a complete thought. Write the following on the board:

> Because the store was closed.

Ask a student to read the group of words aloud. Point out that it is a dependent clause. Explain that *because* is a connecting word. Then write this:

> Mom drove down the street.

Ask a volunteer to read aloud this group of words. Explain that this is a complete thought. It is an independent clause. Demonstrate how to connect these two clauses.

> Mom drove down the street because the store was closed.

Point out how *because* connects the clauses and creates a complete sentence.

GUIDED PRACTICE Write the following sentences on the board:

> The baby started to cry when the phone rang.
> After school is over, my brother plays ball.

Help students identify the dependent and independent clause in each one. (dependent clauses: when the phone rang, After school is over; independent clauses: The baby started to cry, my brother plays ball)

VOCABULARY

Student-Friendly Explanations

unique Something is unique if it is the only one of its kind.

infest If insects or animals infest a place, they are there in large numbers and usually cause damage.

intervals Something that happens at regular intervals is repeated over and over with a certain amount of time in between.

delicate If something is done in a delicate way, it is done with great care so that nothing is broken or hurt.

flexible Something is flexible if it can bend or be bent easily.

bond A bond is a feeling or interest that unites two or more people or groups.

inspires If something inspires you, it makes you excited about doing something good.

preserve To preserve something is to keep it from being harmed or changed.

Fluency

Fluency Practice Have students turn to *Practice Book* page 35. Read the words in the first column aloud. Invite students to track each word and repeat the words after you. Then have students work in pairs to read the words in the first column aloud to each other. Follow the same procedure with each of the remaining columns. After partners have practiced reading aloud the words in each of the columns, have them practice reading all of the words.

"Raising a Barn" 99

LESSON 9

DAY AT A GLANCE
Day 2

VOCABULARY
Reteach unique, infest, intervals, delicate, flexible, bond, inspires, preserve

COMPREHENSION
"Raising a Barn"
Build Background
Monitor Comprehension
Answers to *Think Critically* **Questions**

DECODING/SPELLING
Reteach Words with VCCCV

GRAMMAR/WRITING
Preteach Complex Sentences

FLUENCY
Fluency Practice

Materials Needed: *Turn It Up!*

Student Edition pp. 92–99

Practice Book pp. 35, 36

Copying Masters 33, 34

RETEACH

Vocabulary

Copying Master 33 **Lesson 9 Vocabulary** Have students place their Vocabulary Word Cards face-up so all words are visible. Read a definition and ask students to hold up the Vocabulary Word Card that matches. Check students' responses. Invite students to place the correctly matched words in one pile and the rest in a different pile. Play the game several times.

Comprehension

Build Background: "Raising a Barn"
Invite students to talk about their experiences with rebuilding or remodeling a building. Has their family put in a new kitchen or repainted a bedroom or added a room? Ask students to describe any ways they were able to help with the project.

pp. 92–93

Monitor Comprehension: "Raising a Barn"
Read the title of the story aloud. Then have students read pages 92–93 to find out what is the first step in raising a barn.

After reading the pages, ask: **What is the first step in raising a barn?** (The first step is to take away the old planks.) **NOTE DETAILS**

Discuss the Stop and Think question on page 92: **Why might a barn need to be replaced?** (Possible responses: A barn might need to be replaced when it sags or when bugs infest it.) Guide students in writing the answer to this question. **MAIN IDEA AND DETAILS**

Ask: **What does the author mean when she writes that barns are raised "by hand"?** (Possible response: Doing something "by hand" means that the work is done with simple tools and not big machines or electricity.) **FIGURATIVE LANGUAGE**

Discuss the Stop and Think question on page 93: **Why does the farmer trade to get supplies?** (Possible response: The farmer trades for supplies because he or she can save money by trading.) Guide students in writing the answer to this question. **MAKE INFERENCES**

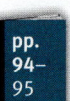
pp. 94–95

Discuss the Stop and Think question on page 94: **Small children cannot help raise the barn. Why do their parents bring them to the barn raising?** (Possible responses: Parents bring their children to the barn raising because they can watch and learn how to raise a barn.) Guide students in writing the answer to this question. **DRAW CONCLUSIONS**

100 Lesson 9 • Turn It Up!

Ask: **Would you like to be a volunteer who helps raise the barn or one who makes all of the lunches? Explain.** (Possible response: I would like to help make the lunches because I like to cook and help my mom in the kitchen.) **EXPRESS PERSONAL OPINIONS**

Discuss the Stop and Think question on page 95: **Why do they call this "raising" a barn?** (Possible responses: They call this "raising" a barn because they raise up each frame and put it in place.) Guide students in writing the answer to this question. **DRAW CONCLUSIONS**

 pp. 96–97

Discuss the Stop and Think question on page 96: **Why is moving the planks to the top a delicate job?** (Possible response: Moving the planks to the top is a delicate job because they are flexible and can crack.) Guide students in writing the answer to this question. **VOCABULARY**

Discuss the Stop and Think question on page 97: **What would happen if the intervals on the frame were not marked?** (Possible response: If the intervals were not marked, the planks might be nailed too close together or too far apart.) Guide students in writing the answer to this question. **MAKE PREDICTIONS**

Tell students: **Look back over pages 96 and 97 and briefly describe the different jobs that the teams do to help complete the barn raising.** (Possible response: The jobs include making the frames, raising the frames, building the top of the barn with planks, and finishing the top. Then the planks are nailed to the walls.) **SUMMARIZE**

 page 98

Discuss the Stop and Think question on page 98: **How does the author show you that barn raising is hard work?** (The author shows me that barn raising is hard work when she tells me the frames and planks are heavy, or that planks must be lifted in place carefully. It is hard work because people rest at noon and work until dark, or because workers are tired by the end.) Guide students in writing the answer to this question. 🎯 **AUTHOR'S PURPOSE**

Read aloud the last paragraph on page 98. Model the strategy of understanding the author's perspective by examining the author's word choice.

(THINK ALOUD) **When I read this paragraph, I wonder if the author thinks that people enjoy raising barns. Then I see that the author says the people are tired, but they are smiling. The author shows that the people are happy. So, now I know that the author does think that people enjoy the barn raising.** 🎯 **AUTHOR'S PERSPECTIVE**

VOCABULARY

Student-Friendly Explanations

unique Something is unique if it is the only one of its kind.

infest If insects or animals infest a place, they are there in large numbers and usually cause damage.

intervals Something that happens at regular intervals is repeated over and over with a certain amount of time in between.

delicate If something is done in a delicate way, it is done with great care so that nothing is broken or hurt.

flexible Something is flexible if it can bend or be bent easily.

bond A bond is a feeling or interest that unites two or more people or groups.

inspires If something inspires you, it makes you excited about doing something good.

preserve To preserve something is to keep it from being harmed or changed.

"Raising a Barn" 101

Day 2

Spelling Words: Lesson 9

1. monster	11. purchase
2. complete	12. merchant
3. hundred	13. pumpkin
4. exchange	14. angry
5. sandwich	15. Thursday
6. surprise	16. ostrich
7. applause	17. punctual
8. although	18. address
9. conflict	19. chestnut
10. mattress	20. luncheon

page 99 **Answers to *Think Critically* Questions** Help students read and answer the *Think Critically* questions on page 99. Have students copy the graphic organizer in question 1 onto a separate sheet of paper. Then guide students in writing the answer to each question. Possible responses are provided.

1. [Evidence] People are smiling. They have a bond. They are working for free. Many have helped to raise other barns. **AUTHOR'S PURPOSE**

2. Most people learn how to raise a barn when they watch others do it and help out. **DRAW CONCLUSIONS**

3. People still raise barns by hand because they like working together, they want to keep doing an old tradition, or they think the best barns are raised by hand. **MAKE INFERENCES**

RETEACH
Decoding/Spelling

Copying Master 34 **Words with VCCCV** Direct students to work in small groups to create a funny song title. Ask them to choose at least two Spelling Words. Then have them write several sentences that will be song lyrics. Provide the following example for students:

Thursday Luncheon with My Ostrich

Thursday is my luncheon day. I have lunch with Ostrich Jay.

Ostrich Jay knows my address. We meet in my kitchen, no less.

I have a chicken sandwich on rye. Ostrich Jay has pumpkin pie.

We love our Thursday Luncheon Day!

Tell students that their lyric sentences should be complete but can have silly ideas. Encourage students to use as many Spelling Words as possible. When the lyrics are completed, invite group members to read their songs aloud together.

102 Lesson 9 • Turn It Up!

Day 2

PRETEACH

Grammar/Writing

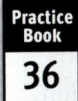 **Complex Sentences** Tell students that a complex sentence has an independent clause and at least one dependent clause. Write these complex sentences on the board:

> Tara was glad for a break after washing the windows.
> After washing the windows, Tara was glad for a break.

Have a student read each sentence aloud. Then have volunteers underline the independent clauses and circle the dependent clauses. (Tara was glad for a break (after washing the windows.) (After washing the windows,) Tara was glad for a break.) Point out that when the dependent clause comes at the beginning of the sentence, a comma separates it from the independent clause.

GUIDED PRACTICE Direct students to *Practice Book* page 36. Ask students to read aloud the first word group. Direct them to determine whether a clause needs to be underlined, whether a comma needs to be added, and whether it is a complex sentence or a phrase. Repeat this process with each group of words.

Fluency

Fluency Practice Invite students to look at the bottom half of *Practice Book* page 35. These sentences have been broken into natural phrases. Tell students to repeat each phrase after you, mirroring your expression, phrasing, and pace. After students have repeated each sentence, invite them to practice reading the sentences to a partner.

"Raising a Barn" 103

LESSON 9

DAY AT A GLANCE — Day 3

COMPREHENSION
Preteach Locate Information
Reread and Summarize "Raising a Barn"

DECODING/SPELLING
Reteach Words with VCCCV

BUILD ROBUST VOCABULARY
Teach Words from "Raising a Barn"

GRAMMAR/WRITING
Reteach Writing Trait: Organization

FLUENCY
Fluency Practice

Materials Needed: *Turn It Up!*

Student Edition pp. 92–98 | Practice Book pp. 35, 37 | Copying Master 35

30+ Minutes

PRETEACH
Comprehension

Copying Master 35

Locate Information Direct students to read aloud the top of *Copying Master 35* and the passage. Explain that these questions can be answered by searching the appropriate source for information.

GUIDED PRACTICE Guide students to read each question in the passage and complete the chart.

Reread and Summarize Have students reread and summarize "Raising a Barn" in sections, as described below.

pp. 92–93

Let's reread pages 92–93 to recall the first things a farmer will do to prepare to raise a barn.
Summary: As the farmer prepares to raise a new barn, the old planks are taken away, trees may be cut down for planks, and crops or animals might be traded for the materials that will be needed.

pp. 94–95

Next, let's reread pages 94–95 to remember how people "raise" a barn.
Summary: The people "raise" the barn by putting together the frames and lifting up the frames with their arms as far as they can. Other people push the frame with long poles until they are in place.

pp. 96–98

Finally, let's reread pages 96–98 to recall what the people do when they take a break and to find out when the barn is complete.
Summary: The people take a break to rest and eat lunch. Then they finish putting the sides and roof on the barn. By the end of the day, another barn has been raised.

RETEACH
Decoding/Spelling

Words with VCCCV Write the following spellings on the board:

complete	kumpleet	adres	address
Thursday	Thrusday	angery	angry
perches	purchase	allthoh	although

Have students work in pairs to identify the correct spellings and the misspellings.

104 Lesson 9 • Turn It Up!

Day 3

TEACH

Build Robust Vocabulary

Words from "Raising a Barn" Have students locate the words *planks* and *carted* on page 93 of "Raising a Barn." Ask a volunteer to read aloud the sentence in which these two words appear. (Line 4: *To start, the old planks are carted away.*) Explain that this sentence means that the first step in taking down a barn is to carry away the boards that were used to build the barn. *Cart* means to take things away in a small vehicle similar to a wagon. *Planks* are long, flat, heavy pieces of wood. Continue by asking students to locate and read aloud the sentence on page 96 in which *shift* appears. (Last sentence: *When they fit well, the planks cannot shift.*) Explain that this sentence means that the boards cannot move from one position or place to another.

Write the words on separate slips of paper and fold them. Make enough slips for each child to have one. Have each student select a slip, read the word, and use it in a sentence.

RETEACH

Grammar/Writing

Writing Trait: Organization Ask students to open their *Practice Book* to page 37. Explain that time order is a logical way to organize ideas for writing. Time-order words make it easier for the reader to understand. Have a volunteer read aloud the information at the top of the page. Suggest that the author of "Raising a Barn" uses time-order words so readers can easily understand the process of building a new barn.

GUIDED PRACTICE Complete the activities on the page together. Help students to recognize the usefulness of time-order words and time-order organization.

Fluency

Fluency Practice Tell students that today they will reread the sentences on the bottom of *Practice Book* page 35. Have students locate and point to the first sentence. Tell students that everyone is going to read the sentence together. This choral reading will give students an opportunity to hear others and listen to the natural phrasing of the sentences. Choral-read each of the sentences several times.

"Raising a Barn" 105

LESSON 9

DAY AT A GLANCE
Day 4

COMPREHENSION
Reteach Locate Information

DECODING/SPELLING
Reteach Words with VCCCV

BUILD ROBUST VOCABULARY
Reteach Words from "Raising a Barn"

GRAMMAR/WRITING
Reteach Writing Form: Explanatory Paragraph

FLUENCY
Fluency Practice

Materials Needed: *Turn It Up!*

Student Edition pp. 92–98 | Practice Book p. 38 | Copying Master 36

Spelling Words: Lesson 9

1. monster	11. purchase
2. complete	12. merchant
3. hundred	13. pumpkin
4. exchange	14. angry
5. sandwich	15. Thursday
6. surprise	16. ostrich
7. applause	17. punctual
8. although	18. address
9. conflict	19. chestnut
10. mattress	20. luncheon

30+ Minutes

RETEACH
Comprehension

Locate Information Remind students about the following electronic sources for information:

- Users can find information they need in a library database.
- A library database is searched by author's name, by book title, by call number, or by a link.
- Users can also find information in a CD-ROM encyclopedia.
- The CD-ROM encyclopedia is searched by subject or by alphabet letter.

GUIDED PRACTICE Write on the board the following questions about "Raising a Barn":

> What do a poplar tree and its leaves look like?
> What types of roofs do barns have?

Ask students to read each question. Have them decide what source they would use, and then explain how they would search that source. (CD-ROM encyclopedia by subject "poplar"; library database by keyword "barn roof")

RETEACH
Decoding/Spelling

Practice Book 38 **Words with VCCCV** Ask students to number a sheet of paper 1–17. Write *conflict* on the board and point to the VCCCV pattern. Tell students that the first thirteen words you will dictate have a cluster or digraph in the second syllable. Then write *pumpkin* and again point out the VCCCV pattern. Explain that the next four words will have a cluster or digraph in the first syllable. Write *exchange* and explain that this word also has the VCCCV pattern, but the three consonants make one sound together. After students write each word, write the word on the board so they can proofread their work.

1. monster	2. complete	3. hundred	4. surprise
5. applause	6. although	7. mattress	8. purchase
9. merchant	10. angry	11. ostrich	12. address
13. luncheon	14. sandwich	15. Thursday	16. punctual
17. chestnut			

Have students look at the picture at the top of *Practice Book* page 38. Ask a student to read the first sentence and follow the directions given. Have students work together to complete the page.

106 Lesson 9 • Turn It Up!

Day 4

RETEACH

Build Robust Vocabulary

Words from "Raising a Barn" Review the meanings of *planks*, *carted*, and *shift*. Then say these sentences and ask which word each sentence describes. Have students explain why.

- The house was made of long, heavy pieces of wood. (planks)
- The children cleaned up the park and took the trash away in small wagons. (carted)
- Please move the position of those books from the right side of the shelf to the left side. (shift)

RETEACH

Grammar/Writing

Copying Master 36

Writing Form: Explanatory Paragraph Tell students that an explanatory paragraph is written to explain an event or a process. The ideas can be organized in sequence or time order. Point out that time-order words should be used. Provide *Copying Master 36* for students. Ask a student to read the description at the top of the page. Read through the Student Model together. Write the following sentence on the board:

> The builders need to gather wooden logs and find pieces in many sizes.

Model for students how this sentence can be improved by including time-order words.

> First, the builders need to gather wooden logs. Next, they should find pieces in many sizes.

GUIDED PRACTICE Complete the activity by asking students to circle time-order words and add a time-order word to a sentence.

Fluency

Fluency Practice (pp. 92–98) Have each student work with a partner to read passages from "Raising a Barn" aloud to each other. Students may select a passage that they enjoyed or choose one of the following options:

- Read page 92. (Total: 76 words)
- Read page 96. (Total: 94 words)

Encourage students to read the selected passage aloud to their partner three times. Have the student rate his or her reading on the 1–4 scale.

1	Need more practice
2	Pretty good
3	Good
4	Great!

"Raising a Barn" 107

Preteach for LESSON 10

DAY AT A GLANCE
Day 5

VOCABULARY
Preteach comprehend, pliable, solitary, scan, vulnerable, exuberant, mature, lumbers, encircle, nurture

COMPREHENSION
 **Reteach** Plot: Conflict and Resolution

DECODING/WORD ATTACK
Reteach Decode Syllable Pattern Consonant -*le*

DECODING/SPELLING
Reteach Words with Consonant -*le*

GRAMMAR/WRITING
Reteach Compound Subjects and Predicates, Compound Sentences

FLUENCY
Fluency Performance

Materials Needed: *Turn It Up!*

Student Edition pp. 92–98 | Skill Card 10 | Copying Masters 37, 38

30+ Minutes

PRETEACH
Vocabulary

Copying Master 37

Lesson 10 Vocabulary Distribute a set of Vocabulary Word Cards to each student. Hold up the card for the first word, and ask a student to read it aloud. Have students repeat the word and hold up the matching card. Then ask students the first question below and discuss their responses. Continue for each Vocabulary Word.

- What can you do when you don't **comprehend** a story?
- If an object is **pliable**, what can you do with it?
- What is a **solitary** activity or game you enjoy?
- Why would a student **scan** the playground?
- When have you felt **vulnerable**?
- What kinds of events make you **exuberant**?
- When will you be **mature**? How will you know?
- What **lumbers** around after dark?
- What game calls for you to **encircle** a person in the middle?
- What kind of animal would you like to **nurture** back to health?

RETEACH
Comprehension

Skill Card 10

Plot: Conflict and Resolution Review with students that plot is made up of story elements. Remind them that story elements move the story from the conflict to the resolution. Have students look at side A of *Skill Card 10: Review: Plot: Conflict and Resolution.* Ask volunteers to read the information and the story aloud. Discuss the story events. Guide students to identify the conflict and its resolution.

GUIDED PRACTICE Guide students in copying the chart onto a separate sheet of paper. Have them use information from the story to fill in the chart. (Conflict: Dennis was not doing well in school. Story Elements: Dennis is playing a lot of sports after school. His grades are not very good. Resolution: Dennis and his parents decide it is best that he drop football.)

108 Preteach for Lesson 10 • *Turn It Up!*

Day 5

RETEACH

Decoding/Word Attack

Decode Syllable Pattern Consonant -le Write *purple* on the board and read it aloud. Have students repeat it and ask them which syllable is stressed. (the first, *pur*) Remind students that the vowel sound in the second syllable is called a schwa, and the sound it makes is neither long nor short. Explain that they divide a word into syllables before the consonant plus *-le*. Help students blend the word parts to say *purple*. Repeat the activity with *mishandle* and *untangle*.

RETEACH

Decoding/Spelling

Words with Consonant -le Distribute *Copying Master 38*. Write *castle* on the board. Divide it into syllables, and ask students to identify the schwa sound they hear in the second syllable. Continue with the other consonant *-le* words in this lesson: *handle, ruffle, icicle, fable*.

[Copying Master 38]

RETEACH

Grammar/Writing

Compound Subjects and Predicates, Compound Sentences Review with students that a compound subject is two or more subjects joined by *and* or *or*. A compound predicate has two or more predicates joined with *and* or *or*. When a compound subject or predicate has three or more subjects, use commas to separate them. Then review that a compound sentence is two or more complete thoughts joined by a comma and a conjunction. Remind students that when two sentences run together without any punctuation, it is called a run-on sentence. When two sentences are joined together with a comma and no conjunction, it is called a comma splice. Then write these sentences on the board:

> Michael hikes, bikes, or swims after school.
> Steve and Sarah sometimes join him.
> Steve likes swimming, but Sarah prefers hiking.

Have a student read each sentence aloud. Guide them as they determine the compound part in each sentence. (compound predicate, compound subject, compound sentence)

VOCABULARY

Student-Friendly Explanations

comprehend If you comprehend something, you understand it.

pliable Something that is pliable is easy to move or bend without breaking.

solitary To live in a solitary way is to be alone most of the time.

scan To scan a place is to look carefully over the entire area for something specific.

vulnerable A person or animal that is vulnerable is weak and unprotected and at risk of being harmed.

exuberant If someone is exuberant, he or she is full of excitement, energy, and happiness.

mature A mature person or animal is fully grown and behaves like an adult.

lumbers When a person or animal lumbers, it moves in a slow or clumsy way.

encircle To encircle a place or thing means to surround it.

nurture If you nurture a living thing, you care for it while it is growing and developing.

Fluency

Fluency Performance [pp. 92–98] Invite students each to read aloud from "Raising a Barn" a passage that they selected and practiced earlier. Note the number of words each student reads correctly and incorrectly. Have students rate their own oral reading on the 1–4 scale. Allow each student to read the passage to you again.

"Raising a Barn" 109

LESSON 10

Day 1

30+ Minutes

VOCABULARY
Reteach comprehend, pliable, solitary, scan, vulnerable, exuberant, mature, lumbers, encircle, nurture

COMPREHENSION
 Reteach Author's Purpose and Perspective

DECODING/WORD ATTACK
Reteach Decode Longer Words

DECODING/SPELLING
Reteach Words with VCCV

GRAMMAR/WRITING
Reteach Compound Subjects and Predicates, Compound Sentences

FLUENCY
Fluency Practice

Materials Needed: *Turn It Up!*

Student Edition pp. 100–101 | Practice Book pp. 39, 40 | Skill Card 10 | Copying Master 38

RETEACH
Vocabulary

pp. 100–101

Lesson 10 Vocabulary Read aloud the Vocabulary Words and the Student-Friendly Explanations. Then have students turn to pages 100–101 in their books and read the directions aloud. Remind students that they should read each sentence to themselves with the word they chose to be sure it makes sense. If students have difficulty choosing the correct word, refer to the Student-Friendly Explanations. After students have completed the pages, have volunteers take turns reading aloud each sentence. (Answers for pages 100–101: 2. *scan*, 3, *pliable*, 4. *vulnerable*, 5. *nurture*, 6. *encircle*, 7. *solitary*, 8. *lumbers*, 9. *mature*, 10. *comprehend*, 11. Possible response: When I am exuberant I am full of excitement, energy, and happiness. 12. Possible response: If something is pliable, it is easy to move or bend without breaking.)

RETEACH
Comprehension

  **Author's Purpose and Perspective** Have students look at side B of *Skill Card 10: Review: Author's Purpose and Perspective*. Have a student read the information at the top. Remind them that using clues and details from the text can help determine the author's purpose and perspective.

GUIDED PRACTICE Guide students as they copy the survey onto a separate sheet of paper. Have them complete the survey with details from the story. (Title: The Trouble with TV, Genre: Narrative, Author's Purpose: to get television to stop airing junk food commercials. Clues to the author's perspective: The author says she doesn't like television commercials, especially those with junk food. She feels that these commercials are misleading because they show thin, beautiful people eating junk food. She feels that kids would be healthier, and her programs would be more fun to watch, if junk food commercials weren't allowed.)

110 Lesson 10 • Turn It Up!

Day 1

RETEACH
Decoding/Word Attack

Decode Longer Words Write *happy* on the board and read it aloud. Have students repeat it. Underline the double consonants in the middle of the word. Tell students that when a word has the VCCV pattern, the double consonants stand for one sound. The word is divided between the two consonants. (hap/py) Repeat with *attendant* and *juggling*. (at/ten/dant, jug/gling)

RETEACH
Decoding/Spelling

Copying Master 38 — **Words with VCCV** Have students review *Copying Master 38* and identify the VCCV words with like consonants. Remind students that when a word has the VCCV syllable pattern, the first syllable usually has a short vowel sound. Write *soccer* on the board. Have a student read the word and divide it into syllables. (soc/cer) Continue with the rest of the VCCV words from this lesson: *appear, hollow, issue, college,* and *accent*. Remind students that dividing words into syllables will help them spell the words.

RETEACH
Grammar/Writing

Practice Book 40 — **Compound Subjects and Predicates, Compound Sentences** Review *compound subjects, compound predicates,* and *compound sentences*. Discuss with students how they can identify simple subjects and predicates to determine if a sentence has compound parts.

GUIDED PRACTICE Have students turn to *Practice Book* page 40. Ask a student to read the activity directions aloud. Have pairs of students work together to complete the page. Allow time for students to share their responses.

VOCABULARY
Student-Friendly Explanations

comprehend If you comprehend something, you understand it.

pliable Something that is pliable is easy to move or bend without breaking.

solitary To live in a solitary way is to be alone most of the time.

scan To scan a place is to look carefully over the entire area for something specific.

vulnerable A person or animal that is vulnerable is weak and unprotected and at risk of being harmed.

exuberant If someone is exuberant, he or she is full of excitement, energy, and happiness.

mature A mature person or animal is fully grown and behaves like an adult.

lumbers When a person or animal lumbers, it moves in a slow or clumsy way.

encircle To encircle a place or thing means to surround it.

nurture If you nurture a living thing, you care for it while it is growing and developing.

Fluency

Practice Book 39 — **Fluency Practice** Have students turn to *Practice Book* page 39. Read the words in the first column aloud. Invite students to track each word and repeat the words after you. Then have students work in pairs to read the words in the first column aloud to each other. Follow the same procedure with each of the remaining columns.

"Joan's Eagle" 111

LESSON 10

DAY AT A GLANCE
Day 2

30+ Minutes

VOCABULARY
Reteach *comprehend, pliable, solitary, scan, vulnerable, exuberant, mature, lumbers, encircle, nurture*

COMPREHENSION
"Joan's Eagle"
Build Background
Monitor Comprehension
Answers to *Think Critically* Questions

DECODING/WORD ATTACK
Reteach Decode Longer Words

DECODING/SPELLING
Reteach Words with VCCV

GRAMMAR/WRITING
Reteach Phrases, Clauses, and Complex Sentences

FLUENCY
Fluency Practice

Materials Needed: *Turn It Up!*

Student Edition pp. 102–109 | Practice Book p. 39 | Copying Masters 37, 38

RETEACH

Vocabulary

Copying Master 37 — **Lesson 10 Vocabulary** Distribute a set of Vocabulary Word Cards to each student. Read aloud a Student-Friendly Explanation, saying "blank" in place of the Vocabulary Word. Have students hold up and read the matching card. Repeat for each of the words.

Comprehension

Build Background: "Joan's Eagle"
Ask students to share about an experience they have had on hikes or nature walks. What kinds of things did they see? Did they come across any animals? What did they learn? What should they do if they come across an abandoned or injured animal?

pp. 102–103 **Monitor Comprehension: "Joan's Eagle"**
Read aloud the title of the story. Then have students read pages 102–103 to find out why Joan is exuberant.

After reading the pages, ask: **Why is Joan exuberant?** (Possible response: Justin has asked her to go hiking with him. She likes hiking.) DRAW CONCLUSIONS

Discuss the Stop and Think question on page 102: **Why do you think Justin expects Joan to moan and groan?** (I think Justin expects Joan to moan and groan because he knows that she often gets tired and complains.) Guide students in writing the answer to this question. MAKE INFERENCES

Ask: **Is Justin older than Joan?** (Yes) **How do you know?** (He invited her to go hiking, and he knows more about where they are going, so I think he has probably been there before.) DRAW CONCLUSIONS

Discuss the Stop and Think question on page 103: **Why does Justin think Joan might be upset?** (Justin thinks Joan might be upset because she may not see any eagles.) Guide students in writing the answer to this question. PLOT: CONFLICT AND RESOLUTION

pp. 104–105 Discuss the Stop and Think question on page 104: **Why might Joan mistake a crow for an eagle?** (Joan might mistake a crow for an eagle because they are both big dark-colored birds.) Guide students in writing the answer to this question. MAKE COMPARISONS

Ask: **What could be making the peeping sound?** (A baby bird could be making the sound.) USE PRIOR KNOWLEDGE

112 Lesson 10 • *Turn It Up!*

Read the first three lines on page 105 to show how your voice inflection changes for each punctuation mark.

THINK ALOUD When I read the first three lines, I notice there are three different punctuation marks at the end of the sentences: an exclamation mark, a question mark, and a period. I need to make sure my voice reflects each mark so I understand the emotion each character is having. READING WITH EXPRESSION

Discuss the Stop and Think question on page 105: **What do you think will happen to the baby eagle?** (I think the baby eagle will be saved by the Snows.) Guide students in writing the answer to this question. MAKE PREDICTIONS

pp. 106–107

Ask: **Why can't the adult eagles get the chick into the nest?** (Possible responses: The adults need their wings to fly, so they wouldn't be able to carry the chick. They can't pick it up with their beaks.) MAKE INFERENCES

Discuss the Stop and Think question on page 106: **What would you do if you found a baby animal alone and in danger? Why?** (Possible responses: I would call an adult who knows about animals. I would not touch it because the parents might reject it.) Guide students in writing the answer to this question. USE PRIOR KNOWLEDGE

Ask: **Why is Joan afraid of a big animal lumbering by?** (She is afraid it will harm the eagle chick.) CHARACTER'S MOTIVATIONS

Discuss the Stop and Think question on page 107: **Does Joan have a good solution to the chick's problem? How can you tell?** (Possible response: Joan does not have a good solution because she doesn't know anything about caring for baby eagles. I can tell because the Snows object to her taking the bird.) Guide students in writing the answer to this question. PLOT: CONFLICT AND RESOLUTION

page 108

Discuss the Stop and Think question on page 108: **Do you think Justin is sorry he took Joan on the hike with him? Explain your answer.** (Possible response: I think Justin is not sorry. Joan got to see an eagle, and they both learned a lot about eagles.) Guide students in writing the answer to this question. MAKE JUDGMENTS

Ask: **Why does Joan feel good about herself?** (She helped save a chick, and Mom and Dad will be proud.) SUMMARIZE

VOCABULARY

Student-Friendly Explanations

comprehend If you comprehend something, you understand it.

pliable Something that is pliable is easy to move or bend without breaking.

solitary To live in a solitary way is to be alone most of the time.

scan To scan a place is to look carefully over the entire area for something specific.

vulnerable A person or animal that is vulnerable is weak and unprotected and at risk of being harmed.

exuberant If someone is exuberant, he or she is full of excitement, energy, and happiness.

mature A mature person or animal is fully grown and behaves like an adult.

lumbers When a person or animal lumbers, it moves in a slow or clumsy way.

encircle To encircle a place or thing means to surround it.

nurture If you nurture a living thing, you care for it while it is growing and developing.

"Joan's Eagle" 113

Day 2

Spelling Words: Lesson 10

1. castle	11. accent
2. handle	12. service
3. ruffle	13. jersey
4. icicle	14. mother
5. fable	15. problem
6. soccer	16. subject
7. appear	17. complete
8. hollow	18. mattress
9. classic	19. purchase
10. college	20. luncheon

 page 109 **Answers to *Think Critically* Questions** Help students read and answer the *Think Critically* questions on page 109. Then guide students in writing the answer to each question. Possible responses are provided.

1. I think the author feels that most people don't know how to take care of eagles and should get help instead.  **Author's Purpose and Perspective**

2. Joan's problem is solved when she gets to see the eagle chick. **Plot: Conflict and Resolution**

3. The author tells me that the nests are high in trees, that they are big dark birds, and that if I come across a baby eagle I should get help instead of picking it up. **Make Inferences**

RETEACH
Decoding/Word Attack

Decode Longer Words Write *window* and *brother* on the board. Have students read the words aloud. Explain that both words follow the VCCV syllable pattern, but the words are divided differently. In *window*, each consonant in the middle stands for its own sound. The syllables are divided between the two consonants. (win/dow) In *brother*, the two consonants make one sound, /th/. The consonants *th* stay in the same syllable when *brother* is divided. (bro/ther)

RETEACH
Decoding/Spelling

 Copying Master 38 **Words with VCCV** Have students identify the VCCV words with different medial consonants. Write *service* on the board. Have a student divide the word into syllables. (ser/vice) Repeat with *mother, problem, jersey,* and *subject*. (mo/ther, prob/lem, jer/sey, sub/ject) Have volunteers explain the rules for dividing each word.

114 Lesson 10 • Turn It Up!

Day 2

RETEACH
Grammar/Writing

Phrases, Clauses, and Complex Sentences Remind students that a prepositional phrase is made up of a preposition, the object of the preposition, and any other words in between. Then review dependent clauses and independent clauses. Remind students that a complex sentence is made up of an independent clause and one or more dependent clauses. Write these sentences on the board:

> We went hiking in the woods.
> As we were hiking, we saw some deer.

Guide students to identify the prepositional phrase (in the woods), the dependent clause (As we were hiking), and the independent clause (we saw some deer). Then ask them to name the complex sentence (the second sentence).

Fluency

Fluency Practice Invite students to look at the bottom half of *Practice Book* page 39. These sentences have been broken into natural phrases. Tell students to repeat each phrase after you, mirroring your expression, phrasing, and pace. After students have repeated each sentence, invite them to practice reading the sentences to a partner.

"Joan's Eagle" **115**

LESSON 10

DAY AT A GLANCE
Day 3

COMPREHENSION
Reteach Prefixes, Suffixes, and Roots
Reread and Summarize "Joan's Eagle"

DECODING/WORD ATTACK
Reteach Decode Longer Words

DECODING/SPELLING
Reteach Words with VCCCV

BUILD ROBUST VOCABULARY
Teach Words from "Joan's Eagle"

GRAMMAR/WRITING
Reteach Phrases, Clauses, and Complex Sentences

FLUENCY
Fluency Practice

Materials Needed: *Turn It Up!*

Student Edition pp. 102–108   Practice Book pp. 39, 41   Copying Masters 38, 39

30+ Minutes

RETEACH
Comprehension

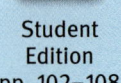 Copying Master 39

Prefixes, Suffixes, Roots Distribute *Copying Master 39*. Remind students that looking for prefixes, suffixes, and roots can help them figure out the meaning of unfamiliar words. Read the definitions at the top of the page.

GUIDED PRACTICE Have a volunteer read the passage aloud as the group listens and looks for words with prefixes and suffixes. Then have students complete the activity. Allow time for students to share their answers.

Reread and Summarize Have students reread and summarize "Joan's Eagle" in sections, as described below.

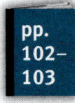
pp. 102–103

Let's read pages 102–103 to recall who Joan is.
Summary: Joan is going on a hike with Justin. She is excited and boasts that she will see an eagle. Justin hopes she won't be disappointed if they don't see anything but trees.

pp. 104–105

Let's read pages 104–105 to find out if Joan finds any eagles.
Summary: Joan thought a crow was an eagle, but then she spotted a nest in the tree. They realize a baby eagle has fallen out of its nest. They meet the Snows, who watch eagles all the time.

pp. 106–108

Let's read pages 106–108 to find out what's going to happen to the baby eagle.
Summary: Joan wants to nurse it back to health at home. The Snows, who know more about eagles, suggest that they take it to a man at the animal park. Joan is happy that she got to see a baby eagle.

RETEACH
Decoding/Word Attack

Decode Longer Words Write *northern* and *instinct* on the board. Have students read the words aloud and identify the CVVVC syllable pattern in each. Remind them that when they have a word with the CVVVC pattern, letters that stand for one sound stay together. Guide students in dividing the words into syllables, pointing out the *th* digraph and the *st* blend. (nor/thern, in/stinct) Repeat with *mattress* and *exchange*.

---

116 Lesson 10 • Turn It Up!

Day 3

RETEACH

Decoding/Spelling

 **Words with VCCCV** Have students review *Copying Master 38* and name the words with the VCCCV pattern. (complete, mattress, purchase, and luncheon) Write the words on the board. Have students identify the VCCCV in each word. Point out the blends or digraphs that should stay together when they divide the words. (pl, tr, ch, ch) Ask volunteers to divide the words into syllables. (com/plete, mat/tress, pur/chase, lun/cheon)

TEACH

Build Robust Vocabulary

 Words from "Joan's Eagle" Have students locate the words *moaning* and *groaning* on page 102 of the story. Ask a volunteer to read aloud the sentence in which this word appears. (Line 6: *We'll be on a path, so no moaning and groaning.*) Explain that *moaning* is a long, low sound that means someone feels sick or is in pain. Explain that *groaning* is a deep, long sound that means someone is in pain or sad. Point out that both words mean almost the same thing. Then ask students to locate and read aloud the sentence on page 104 in which *peeping* appears. (Line 9: *I hear peeping.*) Explain that this means that the baby eagle made a short, quiet, high sound.

Ask students the following questions: When and where might you hear moaning and groaning? (Possible responses: when someone is sick; at a doctor's office) When and where might you hear peeping? (Possible responses: when a bird is nearby; in the woods)

RETEACH

Grammar/Writing

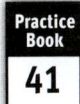 **Phrases, Clauses, and Complex Sentences** Review phrases, clauses, and complex sentences with students. Then write this clause on the board:

> Because the eagle was hurt

Ask a volunteer to read the clause aloud and to explain what type it is. (dependent) Then invite volunteers to suggest ways to make the clause a complex sentence. (Possible response: Because the eagle was hurt, it couldn't fly.)

GUIDED PRACTICE Have students turn to page 41 in their *Practice Book* and read the instructions. Ask students to work in pairs to complete the page.

Fluency

 **Fluency Practice** Tell students that today they will reread the sentences on the bottom of *Practice Book* page 39. Have students locate and point to the first sentence. Tell students that everyone is going to read the sentence together. This choral reading will give students an opportunity to hear others and listen to the natural phrasing of the sentences. Choral-read each of the sentences several times.

"Joan's Eagle" 117

LESSON 10

DAY AT A GLANCE — Day 4

COMPREHENSION
Reteach Locate Information

DECODING/SPELLING
Cumulative Review

BUILD ROBUST VOCABULARY
Reteach Words from "Joan's Eagle"

GRAMMAR/WRITING
Cumulative Review

FLUENCY
Fluency Practice

Materials Needed: *Turn It Up!*

 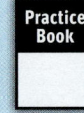 

Student Edition pp. 102–108 | Practice Book p. 42 | Copying Master 40

Spelling Words: Lesson 10

1. castle	11. accent
2. handle	12. service
3. ruffle	13. jersey
4. icicle	14. mother
5. fable	15. problem
6. soccer	16. subject
7. appear	17. complete
8. hollow	18. mattress
9. classic	19. purchase
10. college	20. luncheon

RETEACH
Comprehension

Locate Information Review types of electronic sources with students.

- To find information in a library database, users can search by author's name, book title, call number, keyword, or link.
- To find information in a CD-ROM encyclopedia, users can search by subject or by clicking on a letter of the alphabet.
- Online magazines and newspapers can be found by using a search engine. Some require you to pay a fee to view articles.

Discuss the steps they would take to find out more about their state capital.

- **What source would you use to find out about the early days of your state capital?** (CD-ROM encyclopedia or books in the library)
- **What source would you use to find out your state capital's population?** (look at an online newspaper)
- **What source would you use to find out about your state capital's mayor?** (an online newspaper or magazine)

RETEACH
Decoding/Spelling

Practice Book 42

Cumulative Review Have students number a sheet of paper 1–16. Write *castle* on the board. Tell students that the first four words you dictate will have the -əl sound. After students write each word, display it so they can proofread their work. Repeat this procedure using *soccer* for VCCV words with like consonants, *service* for VCCV words with unlike consonants, and *mattress* for VCCCV words.

1. handle	2. ruffle	3. icicle	4. fable
5. appear	6. hollow	7. hollow	8. classic
9. college	10. accent	11. jersey	12. mother
13. problem	14. subject	15. purchase	16. luncheon

Have students turn to page 42 in their *Practice Book*. Ask a volunteer to read the directions aloud. Point out that students should identify the sentence that best matches each picture. Once students have completed the page, invite them to identify the Spelling Words in the sentences.

---

118 Lesson 10 • Turn It Up!

Day 4

RETEACH

Build Robust Vocabulary

Words from "Joan's Eagle" Review the meanings of *moaning, groaning,* and *peeping*. Then say these sentences and ask which word each sentence describes. Have students explain why.

- **The baby bird made little, high sounds when it got hungry.** (peeping)
- **Dad made a low, long sound when he woke up after his operation.** (moaning)
- **Nan made a deep, low sound when she heard that her friend could not come to visit.** (groaning)

RETEACH

Grammar/Writing

Copying Master 40

Cumulative Review Have students recall the grammar skills they learned in this lesson. Discuss examples for each skill.

- compound subjects and predicates
- simple and compound sentences
- phrases and prepositional phrases
- dependent and independent clauses
- complex sentences

GUIDED PRACTICE Distribute *Copying Master 40* to each student. Invite a volunteer to read the directions. Then have students proofread each sentence, underline the mistakes, and write each sentence correctly. Allow time for students to share their responses with the class.

Fluency

pp. 102–108

Fluency Practice Have each student work with a partner to read passages from "Joan's Eagle" aloud to each other. Remind students to:

- vary their intonation to keep the interest of their listeners.
- pause between groups of words that go together.

Encourage partners to read the selected passages aloud three times. Have the students rate their own reading on the 1–4 scale.

1	Need more practice
2	Pretty good
3	Good
4	Great!

"Joan's Eagle" 119

Preteach for **LESSON 11**

DAY AT A GLANCE
Day 5

VOCABULARY
Preteach predators, traits, lure, avoid, mimic, obvious, resemble, deceptive

COMPREHENSION
 Preteach Text Structure: Cause and Effect

DECODING/WORD ATTACK
Preteach Decode Words with the VCV Pattern

DECODING/SPELLING
Preteach Words with VCV

GRAMMAR/WRITING
Preteach Common Nouns

FLUENCY
Fluency Performance

Materials Needed: *Turn It Up!*

Student Edition pp. 102–108

Copying Master 41

30+ Minutes

PRETEACH
Vocabulary

Copying Master 41

Lesson 11 Vocabulary Distribute a set of Vocabulary Word Cards to each student or pair of students. Hold up the card for the first Vocabulary Word, and ask a volunteer to read the word aloud. Have students repeat the word and hold up the matching card. Give the explanation for the word. Then ask students the first question below and discuss their responses. Continue for each of the Vocabulary Words.

- What **predators** have you seen at a zoo or in a movie?
- What **traits** do you think a student should have?
- What items in a store might **lure** you inside?
- What danger do you try to **avoid**?
- What person or animal do you like to **mimic**?
- Do you make it **obvious** to others when you are sad? How?
- What famous person do you think you **resemble**? Why?
- Is it **deceptive** to wear a costume? Why or why not?

PRETEACH
Comprehension

pp. 102–108

Text Structure: Cause and Effect Explain to students that cause and effect is one way an author can choose to organize ideas. A cause is an action or event that makes something else happen. An effect is what happens as a result. Certain clue words can help you identify cause-and-effect relationships. Ask students to remember what they read in "Joan's Eagle." Then ask:

- **The effect is that Joan wants to take the eagle home. What was the cause of this?** (The eagle had fallen out of its nest. As a result, Joan wanted to take it home.)

GUIDED PRACTICE Help students reread page 104 of "Joan's Eagle" and analyze text for cause-and-effect structure. Ask: **What causes the branch to bob up and down?** (A large crow landed on the branch.)

120 Preteach for Lesson 11 • *Turn It Up!*

Day 5

PRETEACH

Decoding/Word Attack

Decode Words with the VCV Pattern Write *native* and *vanish* on the board. Explain that VCV words might divide the syllable before or after the consonant. Read aloud *native* and divide it into syllables. (na/tive) Repeat with *vanish*. (van/ish) Then explain that if the first vowel is a long vowel sound, the syllable breaks before the consonant. If the first vowel is a short vowel sound, then the break is after the consonant. Suggest that when students are not sure if it is a long or short vowel sound, they can pronounce the word both ways to decide what sounds best. Model again with *radio* and *radish*.

PRETEACH

Decoding/Spelling

Words with VCV Explain to students that when a word has a VCV syllable pattern, the first syllable may have a short or long vowel sound. Write the following words on the board:

begin	vanish	legal	suburb
paper	relish	virus	moment

Read them aloud, stressing the first vowel sound. Then assist volunteers in locating the VCV patterns. Have students state whether the first vowel sounds are long or short. (Long vowel sounds: begin, paper, legal, virus, moment; Short vowel sounds: vanish, relish, suburb)

PRETEACH

Grammar/Writing

Common Nouns Write the following sentence on the board:

> My brother lost a quarter in the sand.

Point out that a common noun is a word that names any person, place, thing, or idea. Explain that common nouns begin with a lowercase letter unless they begin a sentence. Read the sentence aloud. Invite volunteers to underline common nouns. (brother, quarter, sand)

VOCABULARY

Student-Friendly Explanations

predators Predators are animals that kill and eat other animals.

traits Traits are particular qualities or characteristics of a person or thing.

lure If something lures you, it makes you want to go to it, even though it is dangerous or could get you in trouble.

avoid If you avoid a person or thing, you keep away from them.

mimic If you mimic a person or thing, you try to act or look exactly like that person or thing.

obvious If something is obvious, it is so easily seen or understood that no one has to explain it.

resemble If you resemble someone, you look similar to him or her.

deceptive If something is deceptive, it tries to make you believe something that is not true.

Fluency

pp. 102–108 **Fluency Performance** Invite students to read aloud the passages from "Joan's Eagle" that they selected and practiced earlier. Note the number of words each student reads correctly and incorrectly. Have students rate their own oral reading on the 1–4 scale. Give students the opportunity to continue practicing and then to read the passage to you again.

"Joan's Eagle" 121

LESSON 11

DAY 1

VOCABULARY
Reteach *predators, traits, lure, avoid, mimic, obvious, resemble, deceptive*

COMPREHENSION
 Reteach Text Structure: Cause and Effect

DECODING/SPELLING
Reteach Words with VCV

GRAMMAR/WRITING
Preteach Proper Nouns

FLUENCY
Fluency Practice

Materials Needed: *Turn It Up!*

Student Edition pp. 110–111 | Practice Book p. 43 | Skill Card 11 | Copying Master 42

RETEACH
Vocabulary

Lesson 11 Vocabulary Read aloud the Vocabulary Words and the Student-Friendly Explanations. Read aloud with students the diary entry on page 110. Help students complete each sentence with the correct Vocabulary Word. Invite volunteers to read each completed sentence. If students have difficulty choosing correct words, refer to the Student-Friendly Explanations. Continue for the diary entry on page 111. **(Answers for pages 110–111: 2. *predators*, 3. *avoid*, 4. *traits*, 5. *obvious*, 6. *mimics*, 7. *lure*, 8. *deceptive*)**

RETEACH
Comprehension

Text Structure: Cause and Effect Have students look at side A of *Skill Card 11: Text Structure: Cause and Effect*. Read aloud the definition of cause and effect. Read aloud the passage with students. Point to the two cause-and-effect charts. Explain that there are two different causes shown in the charts, and an effect is listed for each. Ask:

- What is one cause shown in a chart?
- What is the effect that happened as a result of this cause?
- Explain another cause and effect that is shown in a second chart.

Explain to students that there are clue words that can help them recognize cause-and-effect relationships in writing. Point out clue words such as *then*, *because*, and *as a result*.

GUIDED PRACTICE Now have students look at side B of *Skill Card 11: Text Structure: Cause and Effect*. Have volunteers read aloud the information at the top and then read the story. Direct students to draw two charts similar to the ones on the *Skill Card*. Guide students as they complete the charts with cause-and-effect relationships from the passage. Invite volunteers to share their responses. **(Possible responses: Cause: The waves were huge. Effect: The ship's engines failed. Cause: Water flooded the *Republic*. Effect: The ship started to sink.)**

122 Lesson 11 • Turn It Up!

Day 1

RETEACH

Decoding/Spelling

Words with VCV Distribute *Copying Master 42*. Model reading the Spelling Words and have students repeat them. Review the instructions for VCV words, and then have students complete the following activity. This activity is based on the traditional Memory Game. Pairs of students make game cards using the lesson's Spelling Words with the VCV missing; a dash appears in place of each VCV. After a student matches two cards, he or she must supply the correct missing letters to keep the game cards. If the wrong letters are supplied, the opponent gets the game cards and the next turn.

PRETEACH

Grammar/Writing

Proper Nouns Explain that a proper noun names a particular person, place, thing, or idea. Proper nouns may name buildings, songs, organizations, magazines, and works of art. Write the following sentence on the board:

> The Museum of Science has a display about space.

Ask a student to read the sentence aloud. Then ask: **Which words tell the name of a particular place?** (Museum of Science) Underline *Museum of Science* and explain that this is a proper noun that names a place. Explain that the important words in a proper noun should begin with a capital letter. However, short words, such as *of*, *the*, *a*, and *it*, are not capitalized.

GUIDED PRACTICE Write the following sentence on the board:

> My friend, _____, went to _____ to buy some presents.

Invite students to complete the sentence with proper nouns. Have students write the proper nouns on the board. (Possible response: My friend, Brian, went to Hanson's Gifts to buy some presents.)

VOCABULARY

Student-Friendly Explanations

predators Predators are animals that kill and eat other animals.

traits Traits are particular qualities or characteristics of a person or thing.

lure If something lures you, it makes you want to go to it, even though it is dangerous or could get you in trouble.

avoid If you avoid a person or thing, you keep away from them.

mimic If you mimic a person or thing, you try to act or look exactly like that person or thing.

obvious If something is obvious, it is so easily seen or understood that no one has to explain it.

resemble If you resemble someone, you look similar to him or her.

deceptive If something is deceptive, it tries to make you believe something that is not true.

Fluency

Fluency Practice Have students turn to *Practice Book* page 43. Read the words in the first column aloud. Invite students to track each word and repeat the words after you. Then have students work in pairs to read the words in the first column aloud to each other. Follow the same procedure with each of the remaining columns. After partners have practiced reading aloud the words in each of the columns, have them practice reading all of the words.

"Born for Snow" 123

LESSON 11

DAY AT A GLANCE
Day 2

30+ Minutes

VOCABULARY
Reteach predators, traits, lure, avoid, mimic, obvious, resemble, deceptive

COMPREHENSION
"Born for Snow"
Build Background
Monitor Comprehension
Answers to *Think Critically* **Questions**

DECODING/SPELLING
Reteach Words with VCV

GRAMMAR/WRITING
Preteach Abbreviations

FLUENCY
Fluency Practice

Materials Needed: *Turn It Up!*

Student Edition pp. 112–119 | Practice Book pp. 43, 44 | Copying Masters 41, 42

RETEACH

Vocabulary

Lesson 11 Vocabulary Have students work together in pairs with a set of Vocabulary Word Cards. Ask students to place the cards in a bag. One student will draw a word and give the other student a clue. The "guesser" determines the word based on the clue. Model if necessary. Ask students to play the game several times.

Copying Master 41

Comprehension

Build Background: "Born for Snow"
Ask students to share their experiences with cold weather and snow. Have they lived in an area that has snow in the winter? Have they seen movies or television shows that take place in cold or snowy areas? Invite students to describe games they have played in snow or winter sports they have tried.

Monitor Comprehension: "Born for Snow"
 pp. 112–113

Read the title of the story aloud. Then have students read pages 112–113 to find out where the Arctic is located.

After reading the pages, ask: **Where is the Arctic located?** (The Arctic is located near the North Pole.) **NOTE DETAILS**

Discuss the Stop and Think question on page 112: **What do you think you will learn about the animals that live in the Arctic?** (Possible response: I think I will learn how these animals stay warm; how these animals find food in winter.) Guide students in writing the answer to this question. **MAKE PREDICTIONS**

Discuss the Stop and Think question on page 113: **Why do some Arctic animals sleep through the coldest months?** (Possible response: Some Arctic animals sleep through the coldest months because then they do not need to find food; they can stay warm in their nests or dens.) Guide students in writing the answer to this question. **MAKE INFERENCES**

Ask: **How does spring in your area compare to spring in the Arctic?** (Possible response: In my area, we have rain in the spring and no snow. It is not very cold so I don't have to wear my heavy coat. Spring lasts several months. Spring in the Arctic is a very short season. The air is a bit warmer, but I don't think a person could wear a light jacket there.) **USE PRIOR KNOWLEDGE**

124 Lesson 11 • *Turn It Up!*

Day 2

Discuss the Stop and Think question on page 114: **What does the lemming do to stay warm in the Arctic? How does the walrus stay warm?** (The lemming digs tunnels in the snow and the walrus has thick blubber.) Guide students in writing the answer to this question. **MAKE COMPARISONS**

Discuss the Stop and Think question on page 115: **How can blending in help a hunting animal like the Arctic fox?** (Possible response: Blending in helps a hunting animal by making it hard for the animals it hunts to see it; the fox can sneak up easily if it can't be seen.) Guide students in writing the answer to this question. **DRAW CONCLUSIONS**

Read aloud the paragraph under "Fox in Summer." Model the strategy of using context to make inferences about the changes in the color of the fox.

THINK ALOUD **When I read this paragraph, I was not sure why the gray color of the fox would mimic melting snow. I think snow is very white and clean. Then I think about how snow looks when it starts to melt. There might be dirt from the ground showing in spots where the snow is gone. This dirt can make the snow look gray. Finally, I can see in my mind how melting snow can look gray like the fox.** **MAKE INFERENCES**

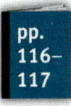

Discuss the Stop and Think question on page 116: **Why can't Arctic animals hide behind a tree?** (Possible response: Arctic animals can't hide behind a tree because the land there is quite flat.) Guide students in writing the answer to this question. **CAUSE AND EFFECT**

Ask: **What does the author mean by the word *deceptive*?** (Possible response: The author means that when you look at the white snow, you might believe that it is just snow. There could be white animals in the snow that your eyes don't see.) **VOCABULARY**

Discuss the Stop and Think question on page 117: **What two traits help the musk ox live in the Arctic?** (Possible response: Two traits that help the musk ox live in the Arctic are sharp horns to fight with and two coats to keep it warm.) Guide students in writing the answer to this question. **NOTE DETAILS**

Discuss the Stop and Think question on page 118: **What are other animals that use color or patterns to survive?** (Possible response: Other animals that use color or patterns to survive are butterflies, baby deer, zebras, leopards, and tigers.) Guide students in writing the answer to this question. **MAKE CONNECTIONS**

VOCABULARY
Student-Friendly Explanations

predators Predators are animals that kill and eat other animals.

traits Traits are particular qualities or characteristics of a person or thing.

lure If something lures you, it makes you want to go to it, even though it is dangerous or could get you in trouble.

avoid If you avoid a person or thing, you keep away from them.

mimic If you mimic a person or thing, you try to act or look exactly like that person or thing.

obvious If something is obvious, it is so easily seen or understood that no one has to explain it.

resemble If you resemble someone, you look similar to him or her.

deceptive If something is deceptive, it tries to make you believe something that is not true.

"Born for Snow" 125

Day 2

Spelling Words: Lesson 11

1.	begin	11.	paper
2.	vanish	12.	pilot
3.	bonus	13.	raven
4.	legal	14.	rival
5.	event	15.	relish
6.	moment	16.	silent
7.	motive	17.	solar
8.	native	18.	spider
9.	suburb	19.	super
10.	mimic	20.	virus

page 119 **Answers to *Think Critically* Questions** Help students read and answer the *Think Critically* questions on page 119. Have students copy the graphic organizer in question 1 onto a separate sheet of paper. Then guide students in writing the answer to each question. Possible responses are provided.

1. [Effect] Animals need special ways to stay warm. There is little food for animals to eat. **CAUSE AND EFFECT**

2. These are some supporting details: Some animals sleep all winter. Some animals have traits that help them catch food. **MAIN IDEA AND DETAILS**

3. The author described many kinds of Arctic animals because she wanted to show the different ways animals survive in the Arctic. **AUTHOR'S PURPOSE**

RETEACH

Decoding/Spelling

Copying Master 42 **Words with VCV** Ask students to think about the VCV patterns in the Spelling Words. Encourage students to look at *Copying Master* 42 for review. Then play the Draw the Raven game. The object of this game is to be the first team to draw all of the parts of a raven: head, beak, eye, two wings, two feet. Divide the group into teams. Alternate dictating Spelling Words to each team. If the player spells a word correctly, he or she draws one of the body parts of a raven on the board. Continue playing until one team completes the drawing.

> Day 2

PRETEACH

Grammar/Writing

Abbreviations Explain that an abbreviation is a short way to write a word. Almost all abbreviations have a period at the end. The first letter is capitalized if the abbreviation also stands for a title or part of a proper noun.

GUIDED PRACTICE Direct students to *Practice Book* page 44. Read aloud the first sentence. Invite a student to rewrite the sentence, with corrected punctuation and capitalization, on the board. Have students rewrite the sentence in their own books. Continue guiding students to complete the rest of the sentences in the same manner.

Fluency

Fluency Practice Invite students to look at the bottom half of *Practice Book* page 43. These sentences have been broken into natural phrases. Tell students to repeat each phrase after you, mirroring your expression, phrasing, and pace. After students have repeated each sentence, invite them to practice reading the sentences to partners.

"Born for Snow" 127

LESSON 11

DAY AT A GLANCE
Day 3

COMPREHENSION
Preteach Reference Sources

Reread and Summarize "Born for Snow"

DECODING/SPELLING
Reteach Checking Twice

BUILD ROBUST VOCABULARY
Teach Words from "Born for Snow"

GRAMMAR/WRITING
Reteach Writing Trait: Conventions

FLUENCY
Fluency Practice

Materials Needed: *Turn It Up!*

Student Edition pp. 112–118

Practice Book pp. 43, 45

Copying Master 43

30+ Minutes

PRETEACH
Comprehension

Reference Sources Distribute *Copying Master* 43 to students. Have a volunteer read aloud the information at the top of the page. Explain that these are sources that authors use to research information for their writing. Certain kinds of information can be found in each source.

GUIDED PRACTICE Read aloud the passage as students read along with you. Invite students to reread sentences with underlined words. Guide students to complete the chart. Encourage students to share their responses.

Reread and Summarize Have students reread and summarize "Born for Snow" in sections, as described below.

pp. 112–113

First, let's reread pages 112–113 to recall what the seasons are like for the animals in the Arctic.
Summary: The seasons in the Arctic are always cold. In winter, days are short. In the spring, it is not quite as cold and some snow melts. In the fall, the weather begins to get cold again.

pp. 114–116

Next, let's reread pages 114–116 to remember how some animals survive in the Arctic.
Summary: Some animals turn white in winter to blend in. Some blend in to keep from being caught by other animals. Others blend in to hunt. Some animals, like the walrus, have blubber to keep warm.

pp. 117–118

Last, let's reread pages 117–118 to recall how other animals survive the Arctic cold.
Summary: Musk ox have large horns for protection. Some birds fly away for winter. Birds have a layer of down to keep them warm. If we were to visit this place, we would have to wear warm clothing.

RETEACH
Decoding/Spelling

Checking Twice Write the following sentences on the board:

> My dad makes a coin vannish.
>
> There is a bonnus prize in my cereal box.

Have students proofread each sentence twice to locate misspelled Spelling Words. (vanish, bonus)

---

128 Lesson 11 • Turn It Up!

Day 3

TEACH
Build Robust Vocabulary

pp. 115–117 **Words from "Born for Snow"** Have students locate the word *spotting* on page 115 of "Born for Snow." Ask a volunteer to read aloud the sentence in which this word appears. (First sentence: *Foxes have a hard time spotting white rabbits and white lemmings.*) Explain that this sentence means that foxes have a hard time seeing the animals in the snow. Continue by asking students to locate and read aloud the sentence on page 115 in which the word *vanish* appears. (Line 7: *A white fox seems to vanish in the snow.*) Explain that this sentence means that white foxes seem to disappear suddenly. When something vanishes, you can no longer see it. Then refer students to page 117 to locate and read aloud the sentence in which *sheds* appears. (Line 8: *When the snow melts, the musk ox sheds the inside coat.*) Explain that this sentence means that the musk ox loses the hair that makes up its inside coat.

Write each word on a card. Write *see, disappear,* and *lose* on three other cards. Have students match the synonyms and tell why they made each pair.

RETEACH
Grammar/Writing

 **Writing Trait: Conventions** Read aloud the instruction at the top of *Practice Book* page 45 with students. Invite students to look at the graphic organizer that helps to explain the concept. Explain that conventions are the correct ways to punctuate and capitalize words.

GUIDED PRACTICE Complete the activities on this page with students. Help them to recognize that cause-and-effect sentences are often complex and need proper conventions to make them easier to understand.

Fluency

Fluency Practice Tell students that today they will reread the sentences on the bottom of *Practice Book* page 43. Have students locate and point to the first sentence. Tell students that everyone is going to read the sentence together. This choral reading will give students an opportunity to hear others and listen to the natural phrasing of the sentences. Choral-read each of the sentences several times.

LESSON 11

DAY AT A GLANCE — Day 4

COMPREHENSION
Reteach Reference Sources

DECODING/SPELLING
Reteach Words with VCV

BUILD ROBUST VOCABULARY
Reteach Words from "Born for Snow"

GRAMMAR/WRITING
Reteach Writing Form: Cause-and-Effect Compositions

FLUENCY
Fluency Practice

Materials Needed: *Turn It Up!*

Student Edition pp. 112–118 | Practice Book p. 46 | Copying Master 44

Spelling Words: Lesson 11

1. begin	11. paper
2. vanish	12. pilot
3. bonus	13. raven
4. legal	14. rival
5. event	15. relish
6. moment	16. silent
7. motive	17. solar
8. native	18. spider
9. suburb	19. super
10. mimic	20. virus

30+ Minutes

RETEACH
Comprehension

Reference Sources Remind students that authors go to a variety of reference sources to collect information for their writing. List these reference sources on the board: *almanac, atlas, dictionary, encyclopedia, nonfiction book, magazine, Internet, thesaurus*. Read aloud the following research tasks. Invite volunteers to choose the correct reference source for each task.

- locate a place (atlas)
- research a specific topic (encyclopedia, Internet, nonfiction book, or magazine)
- locate specific facts or check current facts (almanac)
- find synonyms and antonyms (thesaurus)
- locate meanings and spellings of words (dictionary)

GUIDED PRACTICE Guide students to identify a good reference source to use in answering each question below. Use the list above. Encourage students to explain their choices.

- Where is the Arctic located? (atlas, encyclopedia)
- What is another word for *cold*? (thesaurus, dictionary)
- What other kinds of foxes live in cold areas? (encyclopedia, nonfiction book or magazine, Internet)
- What does the word *resemble* mean? (dictionary)
- What is the population of the Arctic? (almanac)

RETEACH
Decoding/Spelling

Words with VCV Ask students to number a sheet of paper 1–18. Write the Spelling Word *begin* on the board and point out the VCV pattern. Explain that the first fifteen words you will dictate include a VCV syllable pattern with a long vowel sound in the first syllable. After students write each word, display the correct word so students can proofread their work. Write the word *vanish* on the board. Explain that the next three words you dictate will have the VCV syllable pattern with a short vowel sound in the first syllable.

1. bonus	2. legal	3. event	4. moment
5. motive	6. native	7. paper	8. pilot
9. raven	10. rival	11. silent	12. solar
13. spider	14. super	15. virus	16. suburb
17. mimic	18. relish		

130 Lesson 11 • Turn It Up!

Have students turn to page 46 in their *Practice Book*. Read the story together. Then guide students as they read aloud each sentence and choose the word that best completes it. Remind students that understanding the VCV patterns will help them correctly spell each word.

RETEACH
Build Robust Vocabulary

Words from "Born for Snow" Review the meanings of *spotting*, *vanish*, and *sheds*. Then say these sentences and ask which word each sentence describes. Have students explain why.

- **My dad is good at seeing unusual birds in our yard.** (spotting)
- **"I bet these cookies will disappear fast," Mom told her three children.** (vanish)
- **Snakes lose their skin as they grow.** (shed)

RETEACH
Grammar/Writing

Copying Master 44

Writing Form: Cause-and-Effect Compositions Distribute *Copying Master 44* to students. Invite a volunteer to read the description at the top. Then read the Student Model aloud with the students. Write the following sentences on the board:

> The predator usually gives up and runs away. He does not want to get hurt.

Model for students how these sentences can be improved as a cause-and-effect sentence.

> The predator usually gives up and runs away because he does not want to get hurt.

GUIDED PRACTICE Help students complete the activities at the bottom of the page. Allow time for students to share their responses with other students.

Fluency

pp. 112–118

Fluency Practice Have each student work with a partner to read passages from "Born for Snow" aloud to each other. Students may select passages that they enjoyed or choose one of the following options:

- Read page 116. (Total: 96 words)
- Read page 117. (Total: 93 words)

Encourage students to read the selected passages aloud to their partners three times. Have each student rate his or her reading on the 1–4 scale.

1	Need more practice
2	Pretty good
3	Good
4	Great!

"Born for Snow" 131

Preteach for LESSON 12

Day 5

VOCABULARY
Preteach constant, gradually, depths, immediate, contract, revealed, eruption

COMPREHENSION
 Preteach Text Structure: Cause and Effect

DECODING/WORD ATTACK
Preteach Decode Longer Words

DECODING/SPELLING
Preteach Words with Prefixes *re-*, *un-*, *non-*

GRAMMAR/WRITING
Preteach Singular and Plural Nouns

FLUENCY
Fluency Performance

Materials Needed: *Turn It Up!*

Student Edition pp. 112–118

Copying Master 45

PRETEACH
Vocabulary

Lesson 12 Vocabulary Distribute a set of Vocabulary Word Cards to each student. Hold up the card for the first Vocabulary Word, and ask a volunteer to read the word aloud. Have students repeat the word and hold up the matching card. Give the explanation for the word. Then ask students the first question below and discuss their responses. Continue for each Vocabulary Word.

- What might happen if you were a **constant** TV watcher?
- What food do you like to eat **gradually**?
- What is in the **depths** of your backpack?
- When you study, would you like **immediate** results? Why?
- What might make a balloon **contract**?
- Has a magician **revealed** a secret to you?
- Is it funny if a full trash bag has an **eruption**? Why?

PRETEACH
Comprehension

pp. 112–118

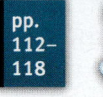 **Text Structure: Cause and Effect** Explain that authors write their ideas in a way that shows causes and effects. An effect happens as a result of a cause. Clue words help make writing clear by signaling a cause-and-effect relationship. Invite students to recall "Born for Snow." Then ask:

- What Arctic animals did you read about? (lemming, walrus, fox, polar bear, musk ox, and snow geese)
- What cause-and-effect clue words do you recall from the story? (if, when, then)

Point out that one cause might have more than one effect. Invite students to look at page 113. Then ask:

- The coming of spring is a cause. What effects happen as a result of this cause? (The effects are that it is not as cold, the snow melts a little, the grass and plants grow, and animals find more to eat.)

GUIDED PRACTICE Ask students to reread the section below and guide them to respond to the question.

- Pages 115–116: What cause-and-effect relationship is described in the sections titled "Fox in Winter" and "Polar Bear"? (Because the animals have white coats, they can hide from animals that might attack them, and they cannot be seen by the animals they want to attack.)

132 Preteach for Lesson 12 • *Turn It Up!*

Day 5

PRETEACH
Decoding/Word Attack

Decode Longer Words   Explain that the prefixes *re-*, *un-*, and *non-* begin many words. Write the word *relaunch* on the board. Ask a volunteer to read the word aloud and name the prefix. (*re-*) Then ask a student to read the root word. (*launch*) Write *unimportant* and *nonstop* on the board. Repeat the procedure for each word.

GUIDED PRACTICE   Write *unfamiliar*, *recapture*, and *nonviolent* on the board. Guide students to decode the syllables in each word and then blend them to read the word. (*un/fa/mil/iar, re/cap/ture, non/vi/o/lent*)

PRETEACH
Decoding/Spelling

Words with Prefixes *re-*, *un-*, *non-*   Explain to students that *re-*, *un-*, and *non-* are prefixes that are added to a root word. Write each word below on the board. Read them aloud with students. Invite volunteers to name each prefix and root word.

retell	unchain	nonmetal
replace	unpleasant	nontoxic

PRETEACH
Grammar/Writing

Singular and Plural Nouns   Write the following sentence on the board:

> There is a tree in my yard.

Read the sentence aloud. Explain that *tree* is a singular noun. Invite a student to underline *tree*. Then write the following sentence on the board:

> There are two trees in my yard.

Ask: **What is the plural noun in this sentence?** (*trees*) **How do you know?** (*The letter s was added.*) Invite volunteers to suggest different singular and plural nouns to replace *tree*. (Possible responses: *bush, bushes; bike, bikes; flower, flowers*)

VOCABULARY
Student-Friendly Explanations

constant   If something is constant, it happens regularly without stopping.

gradually   Something that happens gradually happens very slowly over time.

depths   The depths of something are its deepest parts.

immediate   An immediate event is one that happens right away.

contract   To *contract* means "to get smaller by shrinking."

revealed   When something is revealed, it was hidden but can now be seen.

eruption   An eruption happens when something bursts through a surface.

Fluency

pp. 112–119   Fluency Performance   Invite students each to read aloud from "Born for Snow" a passage that they selected and practiced earlier. Note the number of words each student reads correctly and incorrectly. Have students rate their own oral reading on the 1–4 scale. Give each student the opportunity to continue practicing and then to read the passage to you again.

"Born for Snow"   133

LESSON 12

Day 1

VOCABULARY
Reteach constant, gradually, depths, immediate, contract, revealed, eruption

COMPREHENSION
 Reteach Text Structure: Cause and Effect

DECODING/SPELLING
Reteach Words with Prefixes re-, un-, non-

GRAMMAR/WRITING
Preteach Plural Nouns: Change -y to -ies

FLUENCY
Fluency Practice

Materials Needed: *Turn It Up!*

Student Edition pp. 120–121 | Practice Book p. 47 | Skill Card 12 | Copying Master 46

RETEACH
Vocabulary

pp. 120–121 **Lesson 12 Vocabulary** Read aloud the Vocabulary Words and the Student-Friendly Explanations. Have students read the selection on page 120 of the *Student Edition*. Invite students to look at the diagram. Guide students to complete the sentences on page 121 by selecting the correct word in dark type. Have volunteers read each completed sentence aloud. (Answers for page 121: 2. *contract*, 3. *gradually*, 4. *revealed*, 5. *eruption*, 6. *immediate*, 7. *constant*)

RETEACH
Comprehension

  **Text Structure: Cause and Effect** Have students look at side A of *Skill Card 12: Text Structure: Cause and Effect*. Read the definitions of text structure, causes, and effects. Have a volunteer read aloud the passage. Direct students to look at the charts. Ask:

- **What is a cause in this story?**
- **What are the two effects that happened as a result of this cause?**

Ask students to identify another cause and the two effects that resulted from the cause in the story. Point out to students that there may be more than one effect that results from one cause.

GUIDED PRACTICE Now have students look at side B of *Skill Card 12: Text Structure: Cause and Effect*. Have a volunteer read aloud the information at the top of the page. Then read the passage aloud with students. Guide students in copying the two charts and completing them with the causes and effects from the passage. Invite volunteers to share their responses. (Cause: It was raining. Effects: Phil couldn't play outside; he was bored. Cause: It stopped raining. Effects: Phil ran outside to play with his friends; he wasn't bored anymore.)

134 Lesson 12 • *Turn It Up!*

Day 1

RETEACH

Decoding/Spelling

Words with Prefixes *re-*, *un-*, *non-* Distribute *Copying Master 46*. Model reading the Spelling Words and have students repeat them. Review the instruction for adding prefixes to words, and then have students complete the following activity. Have students work in pairs. Each student writes a sentence for each Spelling Word but leaves a blank for the actual word. The partners then switch papers and fill in the blanks in each other's sentences. Students should give themselves one point for each correctly spelled word.

Copying Master 46

PRETEACH

Grammar/Writing

Plural Nouns: Change *-y* to *-ies* Explain that when a singular noun ends with a consonant and *y*, the *y* will be changed to *ies* to form the plural. Write the following sentence on the board:

> Aaron saw one bunny hopping by.

Ask a volunteer to read the sentence aloud. Have a student identify the singular noun that ends in a consonant and *y*. (bunny) Write the following sentence on the board:

> Aaron saw three bunnies hopping by.

Ask a student to read the sentence aloud. Ask a volunteer to identify the plural noun that ends in *ies*. (bunnies) Invite a student to underline the consonant and *y* and the *ies* in each word. Explain that when there is a consonant before the *y*, the plural is made by changing the *y* to *ies*.

GUIDED PRACTICE Write the following sentences on the board:

> When Carolyn came home, she found one kitty on the sofa and two _____ on the chair.
>
> Dave saw one fly on the window and three _____ on the door.

Invite students to complete each sentence with the plural form of the underlined singular noun. (kitties, flies)

VOCABULARY

Student-Friendly Explanations

constant If something is constant, it happens regularly without stopping.

gradually Something that happens gradually happens very slowly over time.

depths The depths of something are its deepest parts.

immediate An immediate event is one that happens right away.

contract To *contract* means "to get smaller by shrinking."

revealed When something is revealed, it was hidden but can now be seen.

eruption An eruption happens when something bursts through a surface.

Fluency

Fluency Practice Have students turn to *Practice Book* page 47. Read the words in the first column aloud. Invite students to track each word and repeat the words after you. Then have students work in pairs to read the words in the first column aloud to each other. Follow the same procedure with each of the remaining columns. After partners have practiced reading aloud the words in each of the columns, have them practice reading all of the words.

Practice Book 47

"When the Earth Moves" 135

LESSON 12

VOCABULARY
Reteach constant, gradually, depths, immediate, contract, revealed, eruption

COMPREHENSION
"When the Earth Moves"
Build Background
Monitor Comprehension
Answers to *Think Critically* **Questions**

DECODING/SPELLING
Reteach Prefix and Root Word Puzzles

GRAMMAR/WRITING
Preteach Irregular Plural Nouns

FLUENCY
Fluency Practice

Materials Needed: *Turn It Up!*

Student Edition pp. 122–129 | Practice Book pp. 47, 48 | Copying Masters 45, 46

RETEACH

Vocabulary

Lesson 12 Vocabulary Provide Vocabulary Word Cards for each student. Have partners each secretly choose a word from their cards. Have one student use the word in a question, such as **Why do some people seem to like having constant noise in the room?** Have the partner answer the question, identifying the word that was chosen and using the word in the answer. Then have partners switch roles and repeat the activity several times.

Comprehension

Build Background: "When the Earth Moves"
Invite students to share any experiences they may have had with volcanoes or earthquakes. If they have not personally experienced these events, ask them to share information they already know about them. Have they read any interesting books or magazine articles?

Monitor Comprehension: "When the Earth Moves"
Read the title of the story aloud. Then have students read pages 122–123 to find out how thick Earth's crust is.

After reading the pages, ask: **How thick is Earth's crust?** (Earth's crust is 50 miles thick in some places, but it is thinner in other places.) **NOTE DETAILS**

Discuss the Stop and Think question on page 122: **What is Earth's crust made of?** (Earth's crust is made of layers of rock and dirt.) Guide students in writing the answer to this question. **NOTE DETAILS**

Ask: **How many plates is Earth's crust broken into?** (Earth's crust is broken into seven big plates and many small plates.) **NOTE DETAILS**

Discuss the Stop and Think question on page 123: **What happens that can make new mountains?** (Possible response: New mountains can be made when melted rock erupts from cracks in the crust.) Guide students in writing the answer to this question.
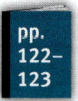 **CAUSE AND EFFECT**

 Discuss the Stop and Think question on page 124: **How are these mountains different from the ones you read about on page 123?** (Possible response: These mountains are different because they are made when blocks of rock rise up.) Guide students in writing the answer to this question. **MAKE COMPARISONS**

136 Lesson 12 • Turn It Up!

Day 2

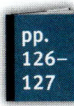
pp. 126–127

Discuss the Stop and Think question on page 125: **How does an earthquake happen?** (Possible response: An earthquake happens when the plates slip or crack all of a sudden.) Guide students in writing the answer to this question. SUMMARIZE

Ask: **Why don't we feel every earthquake that happens?** (Possible response: We don't feel every earthquake because some send out small waves and are too small to feel.) NOTE DETAILS

Ask: **Why do many earthquakes happen along the West Coast?** (Possible response: Many earthquakes happen along the West Coast because two big plates press together there.) CAUSE AND EFFECT

Read aloud the two paragraphs on page 126. Model the strategy of using cause-and-effect relationships to understand the information.

THINK ALOUD When I first read this page, I didn't understand about the "special instrument." Then I remembered reading on the previous page that earthquakes cause waves. I bet those waves cause the instrument to make those squiggly lines in the second photograph. So, the instrument records the waves. And keeping records over a period of time would reveal where earthquakes happen most often. Keeping records is the cause, and knowing where earthquakes are likely to happen is the effect. CAUSE AND EFFECT

Discuss the Stop and Think question on page 126: **How do you think people can stay safe during an earthquake?** (Possible response: I think people can stay safe during an earthquake if they go to a safe place until the earthquake stops.) Guide students in writing the answer to this question. MAKE PREDICTIONS

Discuss the Stop and Think question on page 127: **Why should you cover yourself during an earthquake?** (Possible response: I should cover myself during an earthquake because it will protect me from falling things.) Guide students in writing the answer to this question. MAKE INFERENCES

page 128

Ask: **The picture shows a can opener, a flashlight, batteries, and a radio. Why would you need these things?** (Possible response: You would need these things because you might lose your electricity and these things don't need electricity to work.) MAKE INFERENCES

Discuss the Stop and Think question on page 128: **What else do you think should be in an emergency kit?** (Possible responses: I think an emergency kit should also have pet food if you have pets; games to play; clothes; books to read.) Guide students in writing the answer to this question. PERSONAL RESPONSE

VOCABULARY
Student-Friendly Explanations

constant If something is constant, it happens regularly without stopping.

gradually Something that happens gradually happens very slowly over time.

depths The depths of something are its deepest parts.

immediate An immediate event is one that happens right away.

contract To *contract* means "to get smaller by shrinking."

revealed When something is revealed, it was hidden but can now be seen.

eruption An eruption happens when something bursts through a surface.

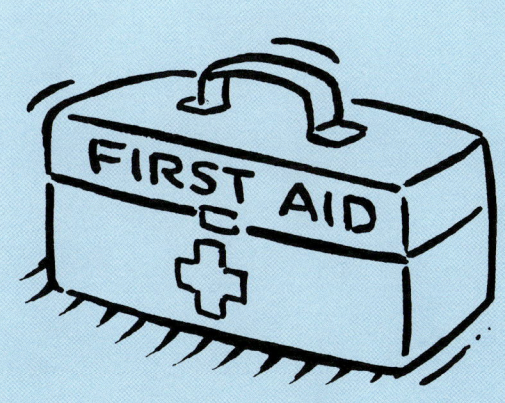

"When the Earth Moves" 137

Day 2

Spelling Words: Lesson 12

1. reuse
2. restart
3. retell
4. resend
5. replace
6. uncork
7. unstuck
8. unannounced
9. unpleasant
10. unchain
11. unfit
12. nonprofit
13. nonmetal
14. recall
15. nontoxic
16. unwelcome
17. reproduce
18. retrace
19. uninvited
20. reapply

page 129 Answers to *Think Critically* Questions

Help students read and answer the *Think Critically* questions on page 129. Have students copy the graphic organizer in question 2 on a separate sheet of paper. Then guide students in writing the answer to each question. Possible responses are provided.

1. Learning about past earthquakes can help us predict where future earthquakes might happen. **DRAW CONCLUSIONS**

2. [Effect] The waves are felt for hundreds of miles; people and animals can be harmed; trees fall; roads crack; homes are destroyed.
 **CAUSE AND EFFECT**

3. The author tells me about Earth's movements so I know what is happening and can be prepared. **AUTHOR'S PURPOSE**

RETEACH

Decoding/Spelling

Copying Master 46

Prefix and Root Word Puzzles Ask students to think about the prefix and root word parts of the Spelling Words. Have small groups of students each write four Spelling Words on individual paper strips. Direct students to cut apart each prefix and root word, using a different pattern for each cut. For example, one cut might be straight, one might be slanting to the right, one slanting to the left, one curvy, and so on. Have students take turns matching up a prefix and root word like puzzle pieces. The student reads the prefix, root word, and complete word aloud. If correct, the student keeps the pair. If incorrect, the pieces are mixed back into the pile. Students can use the top of *Copying Master 46* to check accuracy. If time allows, have small groups trade word strips and repeat the activity.

138 Lesson 12 • Turn It Up!

PRETEACH

Grammar/Writing

 Irregular Plural Nouns Explain that some nouns don't follow a pattern for forming plurals. Some of these nouns do not change at all when plural, while others have special spellings. Write these phrases on the board:

one sheep, six sheep
one child, several children
a tomato, many tomatoes
one loaf, two loaves

Have volunteers read each phrase aloud. Then guide students to discover how each noun changed, if at all, from its singular to its plural form.

GUIDED PRACTICE Ask students to look at *Practice Book* page 48 and read aloud the first pair of sentences. Guide students to determine the plural form of the noun that will complete the second sentence. Continue guiding students to determine the missing plural form in each pair of sentences.

Fluency

 Fluency Practice Invite students to look at the bottom half of *Practice Book* page 47. These sentences have been broken into natural phrases. Tell students to repeat each phrase after you, imitating your expression, phrasing, and pace. After students have repeated each sentence, invite them to practice reading the sentences to a partner.

"When the Earth Moves" 139

LESSON 12

DAY AT A GLANCE
Day 3

COMPREHENSION
Preteach Reference Sources
Reread and Summarize "When the Earth Moves"

DECODING/SPELLING
Reteach Root Words

BUILD ROBUST VOCABULARY
Teach Words from "When the Earth Moves"

GRAMMAR/WRITING
Reteach Writing Trait: Conventions

FLUENCY
Fluency Practice

Materials Needed: *Turn It Up!*

Student Edition pp. 122–128 | Practice Book pp. 47, 49 | Copying Master 47

30+ Minutes

PRETEACH
Comprehension

Reference Sources Distribute *Copying Master 47*. Have a student read the information at the top of the page. Have another student read aloud the passage. Then read the list of reference sources listed above the chart with students.

GUIDED PRACTICE Guide students to determine the reference source that would be best to use to answer each question. Assist students in completing the chart. Encourage students to share and explain their choices.

Reread and Summarize Have students reread and summarize "When the Earth Moves" in sections, as described below.

pp. 122–124

Let's reread pages 122–124 to recall what happens when Earth's plates move.
Summary: When the plates move, cracks form that let magma escape in an eruption. They also create new landforms as they twist and bend.

pp. 125–126

Now let's reread pages 125–126 to remember how earthquakes happen and why they are recorded.
Summary: Earthquakes happen when the plates slip or crack suddenly. Instruments record earthquakes so we can understand past events and know where they might happen in the future.

pp. 127–128

Last, let's reread pages 127–128 to find out how to stay safe during earthquakes.
Summary: To stay safe inside during earthquakes, you should drop, cover, and hold. Stay away from things that can fall if you are outside. It helps to prepare an emergency kit before an earthquake.

RETEACH
Decoding/Spelling

Root Words Write the root words *pleasant*, *start*, and *metal* in a column on the board. In another column, list the prefixes *re-*, *un-*, and *non-*. Invite students to read the root words and then write the correct prefix in front of each. Ask students to read aloud the new words. Explain that breaking a word into parts can help them spell the whole word correctly.

140 Lesson 12 • Turn It Up!

Day 3

TEACH

Build Robust Vocabulary

pp. 126–128

Words from "When the Earth Moves" Have students locate the word *predict* on page 126 of "When the Earth Moves." Ask a volunteer to read aloud the sentence in which this word appears. (Line 4: *We can use these records to predict where an earthquake may happen*.) Explain that this sentence means that we can use where earthquakes happened in the past to guess where they will happen in the future. Continue by asking students to locate and read aloud the sentence on page 127 in which *duck* appears. (Line 5: *Second, cover yourself with your arms or duck under strong furniture*.) Explain that in this sentence *duck* means "to bend down and get under the table quickly." Then ask students to locate and read aloud the sentence on page 128 in which *disaster* appears. (Line 5: *Be prepared for what happens after a big earthquake or any natural disaster*.) Explain that *disaster* means "an event that causes a lot of harm or damage."

Have students write each word on a card. Ask them to write the word's meaning on the back of the card. Have pairs use the cards as flash cards to quiz each other. Tell them to show words sometimes and meanings other times.

RETEACH

Grammar/Writing

Practice Book 49

Writing Trait: Conventions Direct students to read the information at the top of *Practice Book* page 49. Explain that a common noun does not begin with a capital letter, while a proper noun does begin with a capital letter.

GUIDED PRACTICE Guide students to complete the activities on this page as directed. Help students to explain why each noun is or is not capitalized.

Fluency

Practice Book 47

Fluency Practice Tell students that today they will reread the sentences on the bottom of *Practice Book* page 47. Have students locate and point to the first sentence. Tell students that everyone is going to read the sentence together. This choral reading will give students an opportunity to hear others and listen to the natural phrasing of the sentences. Choral-read each of the sentences several times.

"When the Earth Moves" 141

LESSON 12

DAY AT A GLANCE: Day 4

COMPREHENSION
Reteach Reference Sources

DECODING/SPELLING
Reteach Words with Prefixes *re-, un-, non-*

BUILD ROBUST VOCABULARY
Reteach Words from "When the Earth Moves"

GRAMMAR/WRITING
Reteach Writing Form: Informational Paragraph

FLUENCY
Fluency Practice

Materials Needed: *Turn It Up!*

Student Edition pp. 122–128 | Practice Book p. 50 | Copying Master 48

Spelling Words: Lesson 12

1. reuse	11. unfit
2. restart	12. nonprofit
3. retell	13. nonmetal
4. resend	14. recall
5. replace	15. nontoxic
6. uncork	16. unwelcome
7. unstuck	17. reproduce
8. unannounced	18. retrace
9. unpleasant	19. uninvited
10. unchain	20. reapply

30+ Minutes

RETEACH
Comprehension

Reference Sources Remind students that authors use a variety of reference sources for nonfiction writing. Point out that these reference sources help authors find information and check the information they have. List *almanac, atlas, dictionary, encyclopedia, Internet, nonfiction books, magazines*, and *thesaurus* on the board. Model how to choose a reference source to find certain information. Say: **If I want to learn more about Earth's crust, I might look in an encyclopedia or search the Internet. Both sources contain facts and information about science topics.**

Guide students to identify the best reference sources to use to find answers for the questions below. Ask students to explain their responses.

- **What are the most recent earthquakes to hit the West Coast?** (almanac, Internet, magazines)
- **What states are located along the West Coast?** (atlas)
- **What does an earthquake feel like?** (nonfiction books, magazines)
- **How does that special instrument work to measure earthquakes?** (encyclopedia, nonfiction books)
- **What does the word *landform* mean?** (dictionary)
- **Are there other interesting words I can use in place of *rocks*?** (thesaurus)

RETEACH
Decoding/Spelling

Words with Prefixes *re-, un-, non-* Have students number a sheet of paper 1–17. Write the Spelling Word *resend* on the board, and point out the prefix. Explain to students that the first eight words will include the prefix *re-*. Repeat this process with the prefixes *un-* and *non-*, using these example words: *uninvited* (seven words) and *nontoxic* (two words).

1. reuse	2. restart	3. retell	4. replace
5. recall	6. reproduce	7. retrace	8. reapply
9. uncork	10. unstuck	11. unannounced	12. unpleasant
13. unchain	14. unfit	15. unwelcome	16. nonprofit
17. nonmetal			

Ask students to turn to *Practice Book* page 50. Read the instructions at the top of the page. Read aloud the passage as students read along. Invite volunteers to reread the passage aloud. Guide students to complete the questions at the bottom of the page and share their responses.

142 Lesson 12 • *Turn It Up!*

Day 4

RETEACH
Build Robust Vocabulary

Words from "When the Earth Moves" Review the meanings of *predict, duck,* and *disaster*. Then say these sentences and ask which word each sentence describes. Have students explain why.

- **Dan is always late, so I guess that he will not show up on time for the play.** (predict)
- **When the rain started, Mom bent down and got under my umbrella.** (duck)
- **The wind storm blew down trees and caused damage to houses and stores.** (disaster)

RETEACH
Grammar/Writing

Copying Master 48

Writing Form: Informational Paragraph Explain to students that an informational paragraph gives information about a topic. The information is made up of details that support, or tell about, the topic. Authors need to use conventions such as capitalizing proper nouns to make their writing clear. Distribute *Copying Master 48*. Have a volunteer read the description of an informational paragraph. Read the Student Model together. Write the following sentence from the passage on the board:

> Eruptions might scare some people.

Explain that this sentence does not include details that support the topic. Point out that the best way to improve the passage is to delete this sentence.

GUIDED PRACTICE Complete this activity by having students underline and correct sentences according to the directions at the bottom of the page. Invite students to share their responses and explain their choices.

Fluency

pp. 122–128

Fluency Practice Have each student work with a partner to read passages from "When the Earth Moves" aloud to each other. Students may select a passage that they enjoyed or choose one of the following options:

- Read page 127. (Total: 80 words)
- Read page 128. (Total: 80 words)

Encourage students to read the selected passage aloud to their partner three times. Have the student rate his or her reading on the 1–4 scale.

1	Need more practice
2	Pretty good
3	Good
4	Great!

"When the Earth Moves" 143

Preteach for LESSON 13

Day 5

VOCABULARY
Preteach treacherous, drudgery, plunge, smoldering, altered, scoffed, skeptically, discouraged

COMPREHENSION
 Preteach Draw Conclusions

DECODING/WORD ATTACK
Preteach Decode Longer Words

DECODING/SPELLING
Preteach Words with Suffixes

GRAMMAR/WRITING
Preteach Singular Possessive Nouns

FLUENCY
Fluency Performance

Materials Needed: *Turn It Up!*

Student Edition pp. 122–128

Copying Master 49

PRETEACH

Vocabulary

Lesson 13 Vocabulary Distribute a set of Vocabulary Word Cards to each pair of students. Hold up the card for the first Vocabulary Word, and ask a volunteer to read the word aloud. Have students repeat the word and hold up the matching card. Give the explanation for the word. Then ask students the first question below and discuss their responses. Continue for each Vocabulary Word.

(Copying Master 49)

- Who is a character in a book you've read who did a **treacherous** thing?
- What is a task you do at home that you would describe as **drudgery**? Why do you feel that way?
- What is the highest **plunge** into water you've ever taken?
- Where might you see something **smoldering**?
- When was the last time you **altered** your appearance? What did you do?
- When is a time you **scoffed** at something?
- What is something you've been told that made you react **skeptically**?
- When was a time when you felt **discouraged**?

PRETEACH

Comprehension

  **Draw Conclusions** Remind students that authors do not always explain everything in what they write. Readers must figure out some things for themselves. Model for students how to draw conclusions. First, they must identify and use information in the story. Then, they must recall what they already know. Finally, they put these things together to draw conclusions about the story. Copy the following chart onto the board to demonstrate how to draw a conclusion.

(pp. 122–128)

Story Detail	What I Know	Conclusion
A police siren is sounding.	Police use sirens when responding to an emergency.	There's a police emergency nearby.

144 Preteach for Lesson 13 • *Turn It Up!*

Day 5

PRETEACH

Decoding/Word Attack

Decode Longer Words Write *excitement* on the board and read it aloud. Have students repeat the word. Remind students that many words end in suffixes, including *-able, -ible, -ment,* and *-less*. Have students identify the suffix in *excitement*. (*-ment*) Then cover up the suffix and ask them to identify the root word they see. (*excite*) Repeat the procedure for *government*.

GUIDED PRACTICE Write the following words on the board: *requirement, comfortable, hopelessness*. Guide students to break each word into syllables and read it. Have students identify the suffix in each word. (re/quire/ment, com/fort/a/ble, hope/less/ness)

PRETEACH

Decoding/Spelling

Words with Suffixes Tell students that a suffix is a word part that is added to the end of a word. Write each of the words below on the board and read them aloud:

> like (able)   response (ible)   silly (ness)   fear (less)

Then add the suffix indicated and write the new word. Have a volunteer read aloud each new word, underline the suffix, and tell whether or not the word changed when the suffix was added. (lik*able*, respons*ible*, silli*ness*, fear*less*)

PRETEACH

Grammar/Writing

Singular Possessive Nouns Write the following sentences on the board and read them aloud:

> That cat belongs to Robert. That is Robert's cat.

Explain that each sentence tells who owns, or possesses, something. Circle the apostrophe and *s* in the second sentence and note that *Robert* is a singular noun. Point out that *Robert's cat* replaces the words *cat belongs to Robert*. Now erase *Robert's*, and have volunteers suggest other singular nouns that make sense in the sentence. (Possible responses: Jack's, my uncle's, Ms. Smith's) Write each suggestion on the board, and have students help you form the possessives.

VOCABULARY

Student-Friendly Explanations

treacherous Something treacherous is dangerous and unpredictable.

drudgery Drudgery is hard and unpleasant or boring work.

plunge If you plunge into something, you rush into it suddenly.

smoldering Something smoldering is burning slowly from the inside, without flames.

altered When something has been altered, it has been changed.

scoffed If you scoffed at something, you spoke about it in a mocking or critical way.

skeptically If you speak skeptically about something, you express doubt about whether it is true.

discouraged If something discouraged you, it made you believe things weren't going to turn out as you hoped.

Fluency

pp. 122–128

Fluency Performance Invite students to read aloud the passages from "When the Earth Moves" that they selected and practiced earlier. Note the number of words each student reads correctly and incorrectly. Have students rate their own oral reading on the 1–4 scale. Give students the opportunity to continue practicing and then to read the passage to you again.

"When the Earth Moves" 145

LESSON 13

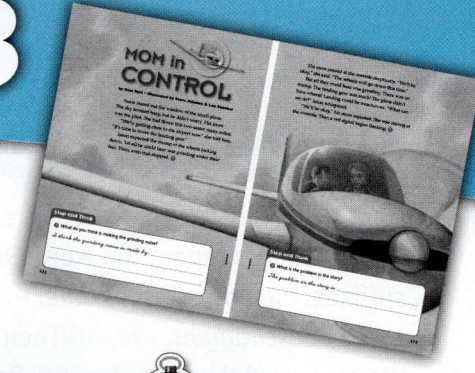

DAY AT A GLANCE — Day 1

30+ Minutes

VOCABULARY
Reteach *treacherous, drudgery, plunge, smoldering, altered, scoffed, skeptically, discouraged*

COMPREHENSION
Reteach Draw Conclusions

DECODING/SPELLING
Reteach Words with Suffixes

GRAMMAR/WRITING
Preteach Plural Possessive Nouns

FLUENCY
Fluency Practice

Materials Needed: *Turn It Up!*

Student Edition pp. 130–131 | Practice Book p. 51 | Skill Card 13 | Copying Master 50

RETEACH
Vocabulary

pp. 130–131

Lesson 13 Vocabulary Read aloud the Vocabulary Words, displaying each Word Card and the Student-Friendly Explanations. Then have students read the story and fill in the blanks on pages 130–131 of their books. Have volunteers read aloud the sentences, adding the word they inserted. Then ask them to complete the two questions at the end of the story. Ask volunteers to share their answers. If students are unable to complete the questions, refer to the Student-Friendly Explanations. (Answers for pages 130–131: 2. *treacherous*, 3. *smoldering*, 4. *scoffed*, 5. *discouraged*, 6. *plunge*, 7. *drudgery*, 8. *altered*, 9.-10. Responses will vary.)

RETEACH
Comprehension

Skill Card 13

Draw Conclusions Have students look at side A of *Skill Card 13: Draw Conclusions*. Have a volunteer read aloud the explanation and then the passage. Ask:

- **Who are the characters in the story?** (a girl named Kayla and her parents)
- **Where does the story take place?** (at a spelling bee)

Now guide students through the graphic organizer, pointing out the details the author has supplied. Have students find each listed detail in the paragraph, and ask if they agree with the statements listed in the second box. Then read the conclusion. Have a volunteer explain how the information in the first two boxes provides a basis for the conclusion drawn in the third box.

GUIDED PRACTICE Now have students look at side B of *Skill Card 13: Draw Conclusions*. Ask a volunteer to read the Skill Reminder. Then have another volunteer read the passage aloud as students follow along. Guide students as they copy the graphic organizer and complete it with details from the passage. (Story Detail: Rafael can't concentrate; head pounding; very thirsty; eyes watery; forehead both hot and cold; hand shaking. What I Know [Possible response]: When I feel like Rafael does, I'm usually getting sick. Conclusions [Possible response]: Ms. Larson thinks Rafael might be sick. She'll send him to the nurse's office.)

146 Lesson 13 • Turn It Up!

Day 1

RETEACH

Decoding/Spelling

 **Words with Suffixes** Distribute *Copying Master 50*. Focus students' attention on the *-able* and *-ible* words in this lesson's list. Model reading these Spelling Words and have students repeat them: *likable, removable, printable, adorable, comfortable, durable, usable, invisible, responsible,* and *horrible*. Then write the words on the board and have students copy them. Ask students to identify each root word and which ones changed when *-ible* or *-able* were added. (Only *comfortable* and *printable* do not change.) Have volunteers explain the change to each root. (Some dropped the final *e*, while *horrible* dropped the *-or*.) Read each word one more time and have students circle the root in each word.

Now write the words *durable* and *invisible*, explaining that sometimes words with *-ible* and *-able* have roots that are harder to recognize.

PRETEACH

Grammar/Writing

Plural Possessive Nouns Tell students that when a plural noun ends in *s,* we form the possessive by adding an apostrophe. When a plural noun does not end in *s,* we form the possessive by adding an apostrophe and an *s*. Write these examples on the board:

> six pilots' caps
> four men's coats

Have volunteers read the phrases aloud. Explain that each shows something owned by more than one person or thing. Ask: **How do these forms vary?** (Possible response: When a plural noun ends in *s,* it gets only an apostrophe. When a plural noun does not end in *s,* it gets an apostrophe and an *s*.)

GUIDED PRACTICE Write the following plurals on the board: *women, planes, runways, boys, parents*. Have students work in pairs. Have one student name something that belongs to each group of things or people. Have the other student write how to change the plurals into plural possessives. (women's, planes', runways', boys', parents')

VOCABULARY
Student-Friendly Explanations

treacherous Something treacherous is dangerous and unpredictable.

drudgery Drudgery is hard and unpleasant or boring work.

plunge If you plunge into something, you rush into it suddenly.

smoldering Something smoldering is burning slowly from the inside, without flames.

altered When something has been altered, it has been changed.

scoffed If you scoffed at something, you spoke about it in a mocking or critical way.

skeptically If you speak skeptically about something, you express doubt about whether it is true.

discouraged If something discouraged you, it made you believe things weren't going to turn out as you hoped.

Fluency

 **Fluency Practice** Have students turn to *Practice Book* page 51. Read the words in the first column aloud. Invite students to track each word and repeat the words after you. Then have students work in pairs to read the words in the first column aloud to each other. Follow the same procedure with each of the remaining columns. After partners have practiced reading aloud the words in each of the columns, have them practice reading all of the words.

"Mom in Control" 147

LESSON 13

DAY AT A GLANCE — Day 2

 30+ Minutes

VOCABULARY
Reteach treacherous, drudgery, plunged, smoldering, altered, scoffed, skeptically, discouraged

COMPREHENSION
"Mom in Control"
Build Background
Monitor Comprehension
Answers to *Think Critically* Questions

DECODING/SPELLING
Reteach Words with Suffixes

GRAMMAR/WRITING
Preteach Possessive Nouns

FLUENCY
Fluency Practice

Materials Needed: *Turn It Up!*

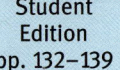

Student Edition pp. 132–139

Practice Book pp. 51, 52

Copying Masters 49, 50

RETEACH

Vocabulary

Copying Master 49

Lesson 13 Vocabulary Give each pair of students a set of Word Cards. Have pairs use the cards to practice using context to find the meaning of words. Model this procedure: Have one student take a card from the pile, read the word and then use the word in a sentence. For example, if the word were *brisk*, say: **The fall weather is so brisk that I need a coat, a hat, and gloves.** Have students take turns with the eight words. Conclude by having volunteers say a sentence for each word.

Comprehension

Build Background: "Mom in Control"
Ask students to share experiences they have had with a parent or adult relative in which the adult did something they admire. What happened? What qualities did the adult show? Do they think it's important to have adult role models? Why?

pp. 132–133

Monitor Comprehension: "Mom in Control"
Read the title of the story aloud. Then have students read pages 132–133 to find out who the main characters are and where they are.

After reading the pages, ask: **Who are the main characters? Where are they?** (The main characters are a boy named Jason and his mom, a pilot. They are in a small airplane.) **NOTE DETAILS**

Discuss the Stop and Think question on page 132: **What do you think is making the grinding noise?** (Possible response: I think the grinding noise is made by a motor trying to lower the wheels.) Guide students in writing the answer to this question.  **DRAW CONCLUSIONS**

Ask: **Why is it a problem if a plane's wheels won't go down?** (Possible response: Planes need their landing gear to land safely.) **CAUSE AND EFFECT**

Discuss the Stop and Think question on page 133: **What is the problem in the story?** (Possible response: The problem in the story is that the wheels won't come down, so the pilot will have to make a crash landing.) Guide students in writing the answer to the question. **NOTE DETAILS**

Ask: **How do you think Jason felt when he heard the grinding noise and saw the flashing red light?** (Possible response: Jason probably felt scared.) **CHARACTER'S EMOTIONS**

148 Lesson 13 • *Turn It Up!*

pp. 134–135

Discuss the Stop and Think question on page 134: **Why is Jason's mom getting discouraged?** (Possible response: Jason's mom is getting discouraged because the wheels won't go down.) Guide students in writing the answer to this question. DRAW CONCLUSIONS

Ask: **What does Jason's mom mean when she says "This is 3308"?** (3308 is the identification number of her plane.) MAKE INFERENCES

Discuss the Stop and Think question on page 135: **What does Jason's mom mean when she says "I have lost my wheels"?** (Possible response: Jason's mom means that her landing gear isn't working.) Guide students in writing the answer to this question. FIGURATIVE LANGUAGE

Read aloud the last paragraph on page 135. Model the strategy of reading ahead to understand a story.

(THINK ALOUD) **The controller in the story says that they are getting the trucks out. At first, I didn't understand this. If a plane is going to crash land, wouldn't they want to get everything out of the way? But then I turned the page and read that they are fire trucks. If there's a crash, there could be a fire, so having fire trucks nearby makes sense.** READ AHEAD

 pp. 136–137

Discuss the Stop and Think question on page 136: **Why do you think fire trucks are at the airport?** (Possible response: I think fire trucks are at the airport because there is a risk of fire.) Guide students in writing the answer to this question. MAKE INFERENCES

Discuss the Stop and Think question on page 137: **Why do you think Jason's mom is so calm?** (Possible response: I think Jason's mom is calm because she knows what to do in an emergency.) Guide students in writing the answer to this question. MAKE INFERENCES

Ask: **What might have made the wheels come down at the last minute?** (Possible responses: Something was holding them back and it might have become unstuck; trying several times might have worked them loose; something blocking them from coming down might have fallen off the plane.) USE PRIOR KNOWLEDGE

 page 138

Discuss the Stop and Think question on page 138: **What message does the author want you to understand from this story?** (Possible response: The author wants me to understand that it is important to stay calm when something bad happens.) Guide students in writing the answer to this question. THEME

Ask: **Have you ever had an experience like Jason's? Describe what happened.** (Answers will vary.) IDENTIFY WITH CHARACTERS

VOCABULARY

Student-Friendly Explanations

treacherous Something treacherous is dangerous and unpredictable.

drudgery Drudgery is hard and unpleasant or boring work.

plunge If you plunge into something, you rush into it suddenly.

smoldering Something smoldering is burning slowly from the inside, without flames.

altered When something has been altered, it has been changed.

scoffed If you scoffed at something, you spoke about it in a mocking or critical way.

skeptically If you speak skeptically about something, you express doubt about whether it is true.

discouraged If something discouraged you, it made you believe things weren't going to turn out as you hoped.

"Mom in Control" 149

Day 2

Spelling Words: Lesson 13

1.	likable	11.	tidiness
2.	removable	12.	silliness
3.	printable	13.	excitement
4.	adorable	14.	government
5.	comfortable	15.	requirement
6.	durable	16.	loneliness
7.	usable	17.	harmless
8.	invisible	18.	hopeless
9.	responsible	19.	fearless
10.	darkness	20.	horrible

Answers to *Think Critically* Questions
page 139

Help students read and answer the *Think Critically* questions on page 139. Have students copy the graphic organizer in question 2 onto a separate sheet of paper. Then guide students in writing the answer to each question. Possible responses are provided.

1. I think Jason will say that he doesn't want to go. **CHARACTER**

2. [3.] Mom tells the controller her problem, and the controller tells her to lower her speed so there is time to prepare for an emergency landing.
   [4.] The wheels go down, and the plane lands safely. **MAIN IDEA AND DETAILS**

3. I think the title for this story is a good one because Mom knew what she was doing. **MAKE JUDGMENTS**

RETEACH
Decoding/Spelling

Words with Suffixes   Distribute *Copying Master 50* to each student. Draw students' attention to the *-ness*, *-ment*, and *-less* words on this lesson's list. Model reading these Spelling Words and have students repeat them: *darkness, tidiness, silliness, loneliness, excitement, government, requirement, harmless, hopeless,* and *fearless*. Then write the words on the board and have students copy them. Ask students to identify each root word. Then point out the root words that changed when a suffix was added. (tidy, silly, and lonely) Have volunteers explain the change to each root. (The *y* changed to *i* before the suffix *-ness* was added.)

150 Lesson 13 • Turn It Up!

Day 2

PRETEACH

Grammar/Writing

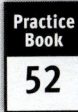 **Possessive Nouns** Remind students of these rules, and write the examples on the board:

- Form a singular possessive noun by adding *'s*. (Sam—Sam's, cat—cat's)
- Form the possessive of a plural noun that ends in *s* by adding only an apostrophe. (stores—stores'; the stores' windows)
- Form the possessive of a plural noun that does not end in *s* by adding *'s*. (geese—geese's; the geese's honking)

GUIDED PRACTICE Direct students' attention to page 52 in their *Practice Books*. Invite volunteers to select the correct word for each sentence and explain their choice. If time permits, have students work in pairs to write new sentences using the correct answer to each sentence.

Fluency

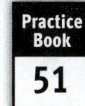 **Fluency Practice** Invite students to look at the bottom half of *Practice Book* page 51. These sentences have been broken into natural phrases. Tell students to repeat each phrase after you, mirroring your expression, phrasing, and pace. After students have repeated each sentence, invite them to practice reading the sentences to a partner.

"Mom in Control" 151

LESSON 13

DAY AT A GLANCE
Day 3

COMPREHENSION
Preteach Predict Outcomes
Reread and Summarize "Mom in Control"

DECODING/SPELLING
Reteach Words with Suffixes

BUILD ROBUST VOCABULARY
Teach Words from "Mom in Control"

GRAMMAR/WRITING
Reteach Writing Trait: Sentence Fluency

FLUENCY
Fluency Practice

Materials Needed: *Turn It Up!*

Student Edition pp. 132–138 | Practice Book pp. 51, 53 | Copying Masters 50, 51

30+ Minutes

PRETEACH
Comprehension

 Copying Master 51

Predict Outcomes Distribute *Copying Master 51*. Have students listen as a volunteer reads the information at the top of the page about predicting outcomes.

GUIDED PRACTICE Have students read the story and complete the activity. Allow time for students to explain what they have added to the chart.

Reread and Summarize Have students reread and summarize "Mom in Control" in sections, as described below.

 pp. 132–133

Let's reread pages 132–133 to recall who is in this story, where they are, and what happens to put them in danger.
Summary: Jason is flying in a small plane with his mom, who is the pilot. When she tries to lower the landing gear in preparation to land, the wheels won't go down.

 pp. 134–135

Now let's reread pages 134–135 to remember how Jason and his mom react to the danger.
Summary: Jason thinks he smells something burning, but his mom tells him not to worry. She radios the airport to tell them they are in trouble. Jason is scared but his mom is calm and knows what to do.

 pp. 136–138

Last, let's reread pages 136–138 to find out what happens.
Summary: Fire trucks gather near the runway, but Jason's mom is finally able to get the wheels to go down. They land safely, thanks to his mom's ability to keep her cool in a tough situation.

RETEACH
Decoding/Spelling

 Copying Master 50

Words with Suffixes Write on the board the words listed below:

| tidy (+ness) | like (+able) | lonely (+ness) | fear (+less) |
| print (+able) | response (+ible) | dark (+ness) | excite (+ment) |

Have students add the indicated suffix to each root. Invite volunteers to tell if the root word changed, and if so, how it changed. (tidiness, likable, loneliness, fearless, printable, responsible, darkness, excitement)

152 Lesson 13 • *Turn It Up!*

Now ask students to complete the activity at the bottom of *Copying Master 50*. Have pairs of students write the Spelling Words on index cards. Have one student draw a card and read its word aloud and the other student write the word; then have partners switch roles. When a student spells a word correctly, he or she initials the card and returns it to the pile. Students should work through the pile twice or until each student has had the opportunity to spell each of the words. Have students write down each word they do not spell correctly to study later.

TEACH

Build Robust Vocabulary

pp. 132–138 **Words from "Mom in Control"** Have students locate the word *grinding* on page 132 of "Mom in Control." Ask a volunteer to read aloud the sentence in which this word appears. (Line 7: *Yet all he could hear was grinding under their feet*.) Explain that this sentence means Jason heard something that sounded like two hard things rubbing together. Continue by asking students to locate and read aloud the sentence on page 138 in which the word *relief* appears. (Line 7: *What a relief!*) Explain that this sentence means that Jason felt good and was no longer tense and scared.

Put the words on separate slips of paper. Have students draw a slip. Ask each student to say a sentence that includes the word but to say "blank" instead of the word. Ask the group to tell which word belongs in the blank.

RETEACH

Grammar/Writing

Practice Book 53 **Writing Trait: Sentence Fluency** Have students turn to page 53 in their *Practice Book*. Explain that when they write, it is important to vary their sentences. Some should be short and others long. If a writer uses sentences that are all alike, the writing seems "clunky," or is not fluent. Ask a volunteer to read the information on the *Practice Book* page. Ask students for more examples of each kind of sentence.

GUIDED PRACTICE Complete the page together. Have volunteers share their answers to Parts A, B, and C. Discuss other possible answers to Part B, and have students suggest other ways to vary sentences in their paragraphs.

Day 3

Fluency

Practice Book 51 **Fluency Practice** Tell students that today they will reread the sentences on the bottom of *Practice Book* page 51. Have students locate and point to the first sentence. Tell students that everyone is going to read the sentence together. This choral reading will give students an opportunity to hear others and listen to the natural phrasing of the sentences. Choral-read each of the sentences several times.

"Mom in Control" 153

LESSON 13

DAY AT A GLANCE
Day 4

30+ Minutes

COMPREHENSION
Reteach Predict Outcomes

DECODING/SPELLING
Reteach Words with Suffixes

BUILD ROBUST VOCABULARY
Reteach Words from "Mom in Control"

GRAMMAR/WRITING
Reteach Writing Form: Friendly Letter

FLUENCY
Fluency Practice

Materials Needed: *Turn It Up!*

Student Edition pp. 132–138 | Practice Book p. 54 | Copying Master 52

Spelling Words: Lesson 13

1. likable	11. tidiness
2. removable	12. silliness
3. printable	13. excitement
4. adorable	14. government
5. comfortable	15. requirement
6. durable	16. loneliness
7. usable	17. harmless
8. invisible	18. hopeless
9. responsible	19. fearless
10. darkness	20. horrible

RETEACH

Comprehension

Predict Outcomes pp. 132–138 Remind students that when you predict outcomes, you figure out future events in a story. Review with students this information about predicting outcomes:

- Good readers often think about what might happen next as they read.
- Good readers look for story clues about what might happen in a story.
- Good readers think about what they already know from real life.
- Good readers use both the story clues and what they already know to make predictions about what might happen next.

Explain that they now know what happens in the story and can go back and find clues that could have helped them predict the outcome. Refer students to page 132 of their books. Ask them what the title of this story is. ("Mom in Control") Ask them how this title could have helped them predict an outcome of the story before they read it. (Possible response: I know from the title that a mom will be in control of whatever happens.)

GUIDED PRACTICE Have students reread pages 134–135. Have them identify clues that could have helped them predict the outcome of the story. (Possible responses: His mom smiled, which is a clue that things will work out; Jason complained about chores, a clue that he will get another chance to do them.)

RETEACH

Decoding/Spelling

Words with Suffixes Practice Book 54 Have students number a sheet of paper 1–15. Write the Spelling Word *likable* on the board and circle the *-able* suffix. Point out that the first six words you will say end with this suffix. Remind students that when they spell a word with a suffix, they sometimes have to change the spelling of the root word. After students write each word, display it so they can proofread their work. Repeat, using these examples: *darkness, horrible, fearless* and *requirement*.

1. removable	2. adorable	3. usable	4. printable
5. comfortable	6. durable	7. loneliness	8. silliness
9. tidiness	10. responsible	11. invisible	12. hopeless
13. harmless	14. government	15. excitement	

Have students turn to page 54 in their *Practice Books*. Have students read the story with you. Then ask them to complete the questions at the bottom of the page. Review the correct answers with the group.

154 Lesson 13 • *Turn It Up!*

Day 4

RETEACH
Build Robust Vocabulary

Words from "Mom in Control" Review the meanings of the words *grinding* and *relief*. Then say these sentences and ask which word each sentence describes. Have students explain why.

- **Dad put oil on the lawnmower parts so they would stop rubbing together and making a noise.** (grinding)
- **"I feel good now that I have finished all that homework," said Heather.** (relief)

RETEACH
Grammar/Writing

Copying Master 52

Writing Form: Friendly Letter Tell students we write letters to communicate with other people. Letters are organized in a certain way and need to include parts such as a greeting and a closing. Point out that students can make their letters more interesting by using different kinds of sentences. They can use both long and short sentences. Distribute *Copying Master 52* and have a volunteer read the information about letters. Then read the Student Model together, discussing each of the features.

Write on the board the following sentences from the letter:

> I couldn't see anything, and, boy, I was clueless, and I kept bumping into branches and rocks and trees.

Model for students how the sentence can be improved by breaking it into separate sentences.

> I couldn't see anything. Boy, I was clueless! I kept bumping into branches and rocks and trees.

GUIDED PRACTICE Complete the activity by having students answer the questions. Allow time for students to discuss their answers.

Fluency

pp. 132–138

Fluency Practice Have each student work with a partner to read passages from "Mom in Control" aloud to each other. Students may select a passage that they enjoyed or choose one of the following options:

- Read page 135. (Total: 72 words)
- Read page 137. (Total: 74 words)

Encourage students to read the selected passage aloud to their partner three times. Have the student rate his or her reading on the 1–4 scale.

1	Need more practice
2	Pretty good
3	Good
4	Great!

"Mom in Control" 155

Preteach for **LESSON 14**

DAY AT A GLANCE
Day 5

VOCABULARY
Preteach hermit, fascinated, occasionally, timid, peculiar, drab, trembling, dashed

COMPREHENSION
 **Preteach** Draw Conclusions

DECODING/WORD ATTACK
Preteach Decode Longer Words

DECODING/SPELLING
Preteach Words with Ending /ən/

GRAMMAR/WRITING
Preteach Pronouns and Antecedents

FLUENCY
Fluency Performance

Materials Needed: *Turn It Up!*

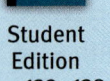 

Student Edition pp. 132–138

Copying Master 53

PRETEACH
Vocabulary

Copying Master 53 — **Lesson 14 Vocabulary** Distribute a set of Vocabulary Word Cards to each pair of students. Hold up the word card for the first Vocabulary Word, and ask a volunteer to read the word aloud. Have students repeat the word and hold up the matching card. Give the explanation for the word. Then ask students the first question below and discuss their responses. Continue for each Vocabulary Word.

- Where might a **hermit** live?
- What is something that you are **fascinated** by?
- What is a task you have to do **occasionally**?
- What animal do you consider **timid**?
- When was the last time you did or said something **peculiar**?
- What colors do you think are **drab**?
- What is one thing that might make you start **trembling**?
- If a person **dashed** from one place to another, what did he or she do?

PRETEACH
Comprehension

pp. 132–138  **Draw Conclusions** Recall with students how to draw a conclusion about something an author has not explained:

- Start with clues from the story.
- Think about what you know from your own experiences.
- Finally, put them together to draw a conclusion.

Now ask students to recall "Mom in Control." Note that on page 132 it says that Jason "expected the thump of the wheels." Ask: **What does it mean to expect something?** (It means you know about something that's going to happen, probably because you've seen it happen before.) Say: **So, if Jason expected to hear the wheels, and we know what it means to expect something, what can we conclude?** (Possible response: Jason has flown with his mom before and knows how the wheels should sound.)

156 Preteach for Lesson 14 • *Turn It Up!*

Day 5

PRETEACH
Decoding/Word Attack

Decode Longer Words Write the word *certain* on the board, and have a volunteer read it aloud. Remind students that the vowel sound in the second, unstressed, syllable is called the *schwa* sound. Ask students which letters in the word *certain* stand for the /ən/ sound. (ain) Then repeat the procedure with *chicken*. Point out that the /ən/ sound can be spelled in different ways.

GUIDED PRACTICE Write the following words on the board: *apron, swollen, fountain, orphan*. Guide students to say each word and divide it into syllables. Have students identify the syllable with the /ən/ sound and the letters that make the sound. Then have students blend the sounds to read the word. (a/pron, swol/len, foun/tain, or/phan)

PRETEACH
Decoding/Spelling

Words with Ending /ən/ Read aloud the words *button* and *even*. Ask students what sound they hear at the end of the words. (/ən/) Circle the letters that stand for this sound in each word. (on, en) Repeat with *cardigan* and *certain*. Help students understand that the /ən/ can be spelled in several different ways.

PRETEACH
Grammar/Writing

Pronouns and Antecedents Write these sentences:

> Kim saw the campfire. She walked over to it.

Read the sentences aloud. Explain that the sentences show the use of pronouns, words that take the place of one or more nouns. Draw an arrow from *Kim* to *she* and explain how the word *she* takes the place of the word *Kim*. Do the same for *campfire* and *it*. Now write this sentence on the board:

> Kim saw the campfire and walked over to it.

Draw an arrow from *campfire* to *it*. Explain that a pronoun's antecedent is the noun or nouns to which the pronoun refers. Label *it* as the pronoun and *campfire* as the noun to which it refers, or the antecedent.

VOCABULARY
Student-Friendly Explanations

hermit A hermit is a person who lives alone, often far from a community.

fascinated When you are fascinated by something, you are very interested in it and pay close attention to it.

occasionally If something happens occasionally, it happens once in a while.

timid A timid person is shy and unsure of himself or herself.

peculiar Something that is peculiar is strange and unusual, usually not in a good way.

drab Something drab looks dull and lacks color.

trembling If something is trembling, it is shaking slightly.

dashed If someone dashed away, they quickly and suddenly ran away.

Fluency

pp. 132–138 Fluency Performance Invite students to read aloud the passages from "Mom in Control" that they selected and practiced earlier. Note the number of words each student reads correctly and incorrectly. Have students rate their own oral reading on the 1–4 scale. Give students the opportunity to continue practicing and then to read the passage to you again.

"Mom in Control" 157

DAY AT A GLANCE
Day 1

VOCABULARY
Reteach *hermit, fascinated, occasionally, timid, peculiar, drab, trembling, dashed*

COMPREHENSION
 Reteach Draw Conclusions

DECODING/SPELLING
Reteach Words with Ending /ən/

GRAMMAR/WRITING
Preteach Pronouns and Antecedents

FLUENCY
Fluency Practice

Materials Needed: *Turn It Up!*

| Student Edition pp. 140–141 | Practice Book p. 55 | Skill Card 14 | Copying Master 54 |

LESSON 14

RETEACH
Vocabulary

pp. 140–141

Lesson 14 Vocabulary Read aloud the Vocabulary Words as you write each word on the board. Read aloud the Student-Friendly Explanations. Then have students read the story. Guide them to fill in the blanks on page 141 by selecting the correct word in dark type. Have volunteers read the sentences, adding the word they chose. If some students are unable to complete the sentences, refer to the Student-Friendly Explanations. (Answers for page 141: 2. *trembling*, 3. *dashed*, 4. *peculiar*, 5. *hermits*, 6. *fascinated*, 7. *drab*, 8. *timid*)

RETEACH
Comprehension

Draw Conclusions Have students look at side A of *Skill Card 14: Draw Conclusions*. Have a volunteer read the explanation of how to draw conclusions. Then read the passage aloud as students follow along. Ask:

- Who are the characters in the story? (Liz, Mark, and Anita)
- Where does the story take place? (in a church)
- What happens? (Liz and Mark see Anita walk down a church aisle.)

Now guide students through the graphic organizer, pointing out the different details the author has supplied. Then read the conclusion. Have a volunteer explain how the information in the first two boxes provides a basis for the conclusion drawn.

GUIDED PRACTICE Now have students look at side B of *Skill Card 14: Draw Conclusions*. Read the Skill Reminder. Then have a student read the passage aloud. Guide students in copying the graphic organizer and completing it with details from the story. (Top box: Mom was talking on the phone while she baked; The cookies are too salty. Middle box: People who talk on the phone sometimes don't pay attention. Sugar and salt look alike. Bottom box: Jenna's mom put salt into the cookie dough instead of sugar.) Then ask students to describe a conclusion they could draw if the cookies were dark brown and burned. (Jenna's mom had baked the cookies too long because she was talking on the phone.)

158 Lesson 14 • *Turn It Up!*

Day 1

RETEACH
Decoding/Spelling

Words with Ending /ən/ Distribute *Copying Master 54*. Model reading these Spelling Words and have students repeat them: *chicken, cardigan, even, listen, orphan, pollen, siren, swollen,* and *driven*. Then write the words on the board. Ask students to identify the sound they hear at the end of each word (/ən/) and the letter combinations that represent the sound. (*-an* and *-en*)

Now ask volunteers to take turns sorting the words into two groups, based on the letters that form the /ən/ sound. Have them write a word in one of two columns on the board. Have them also add the words to the correct column in the chart on *Copying Master 54*.

PRETEACH
Grammar/Writing

Pronouns and Antecedents Write the following sentence on the board:

> The man walked down the road and Kim waved to him.

Have a volunteer read the sentence. Identify the pronoun and its antecedent. (pronoun—him; antecedent—man) Then explain that pronouns must agree with their antecedents in two ways:

- A pronoun must agree with its antecedent in *number*. Pronouns can be *singular* or *plural*.

- A pronoun must agree with its antecedent in *gender*. Pronouns can be *masculine* or *feminine*.

Refer students to the sentence on the board. Ask them to identify the number and gender of the pronoun. (singular, male)

GUIDED PRACTICE Write the following sentences on the board:

> Kim asked the girls where they lived.
> Lynnie looked for Rick. Then Lynnie saw him by the fire.

Have volunteers identify the pronoun and antecedent, as well as the number and gender of the pronoun in each sentence. (pronoun: they; antecedent: girls; plural, feminine. pronoun: him; antecedent: Rick; singular, masculine)

VOCABULARY
Student-Friendly Explanations

hermit A hermit is a person who lives alone, often far from a community.

fascinated When you are fascinated by something, you are very interested in it and pay close attention to it.

occasionally If something happens occasionally, it happens once in a while.

timid A timid person is shy and unsure of himself or herself.

peculiar Something that is peculiar is strange and unusual, usually not in a good way.

drab Something drab looks dull and lacks color.

trembling If something is trembling, it is shaking slightly.

dashed If someone dashed away, they quickly and suddenly ran away.

Fluency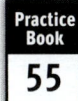

Fluency Practice Have students turn to *Practice Book* page 55. Read the words in the first column aloud. Invite students to track each word and repeat the words after you. Then have students work in pairs to read the words in the first column aloud to each other. Follow the same procedure with each of the remaining columns. After partners have practiced reading aloud the words in each of the columns, have them practice reading all of the words.

"Just Down the Road" 159

LESSON 14

DAY AT A GLANCE
Day 2

30+ Minutes

VOCABULARY
Reteach hermit, fascinated, occasionally, timid, peculiar, drab, trembling, dashed

COMPREHENSION
"Just Down the Road"
Build Background
Monitor Comprehension
Answers to *Think Critically* Questions

DECODING/SPELLING
Reteach Words with Ending /ən/

GRAMMAR/WRITING
Preteach Pronouns and Antecedents

FLUENCY
Fluency Practice

Materials Needed: *Turn It Up!*

Student Edition pp. 142–149

Practice Book pp. 55, 56

Copying Masters 53, 54

RETEACH

Vocabulary

Copying Master 53

Lesson 14 Vocabulary Ask students to answer the questions below. Record their ideas on the board, and then go back and have students use the word meanings to explain their answers. As students explain an answer, have them hold up that word's Vocabulary Word Card.

1. How might a **hermit** spend his or her day?
2. What kinds of animals are you **fascinated** by?
3. What are some TV programs you watch **occasionally**?
4. What advice would you give to someone who is **timid** about speaking in public?
5. Have you ever had a **peculiar** experience? Explain.
6. Describe some birds you think are **drab**.
7. How might you help someone who was **trembling** from the cold?
8. If a cat **dashed** from one room to another, what might be the reason?

Comprehension

Build Background: "Just Down the Road"
Ask students to describe a time when they met a fascinating person. Why was the person fascinating? Did they become friends?

pp. 142–143

Monitor Comprehension: "Just Down the Road"
Read the title of the story aloud. Then have students read pages 142–143 to find out who the main characters are, where they are, and what they are doing.

After students read the first page, ask: **What characters have we met?** (Kim, her grandfather, and a husband and wife) **What are they doing?** (Kim is talking to the husband and wife, who are watching the skaters.) SUMMARIZE

Discuss the Stop and Think question on page 142: **Where does the story happen?** (The story happens outdoors near a skating pond at night.) Guide students in writing the answer to this question. NOTE DETAILS

Ask: **How are the couple dressed?** (They are wearing hats and scarves, but no coats.) NOTE DETAILS

Discuss the Stop and Think question on page 143: **Why is it peculiar that the husband and wife are not wearing coats?** (Possible response: It's peculiar they are not wearing coats because the weather is cold and other people are wearing coats.) CAUSE AND EFFECT

160 Lesson 14 • *Turn It Up!*

Day 2

Read aloud the last paragraph on page 143. Model the strategy of analyzing the author's craft.

THINK ALOUD The author describes the wife's scarf in some detail. There must be a reason for pointing out this scarf and how it's different from Kim's. I'll keep this scarf in mind as I read. I think the author wants us to notice it because it might be important later in the story. **AUTHOR'S CRAFT**

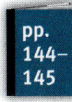
pp. 144–145

Discuss the Stop and Think question on page 144: **What has Kim learned about the husband and wife so far?** (Possible responses: Kim has learned that they are nice people, live nearby, are not cold, and do not want a snack before they leave.) Guide students in writing the answer to this question. **SUMMARIZE**

Discuss the Stop and Think question on page 145: **What do you think Kim will do the next day?** (Possible responses: I think Kim will try to find out more about the husband and wife; try to find their house.) Guide students in writing the answer to this question. **MAKE PREDICTIONS**

pp. 146–147

Ask: **What does Kim mean when she says that she likes to be alone occasionally?** (Possible response: She means she likes to be alone every now and then.) **VOCABULARY**

Discuss the Stop and Think question on page 146: **Why do you think Kim cannot find the home of the husband and wife?** (Possible response: I think Kim cannot find their home because they do not live in a home.) Guide students in writing the answer to this question.
 DRAW CONCLUSIONS

Discuss the Stop and Think question on page 147: **What does Kim spot by the side of the road?** (Kim spots the wife's bright scarf, then a flashlight.) Guide students in writing the answer to this question. **NOTE DETAILS**

Ask: **What do you think happened to the couple? Why?** (Possible response: They disappeared because they are not real people.)
 DRAW CONCLUSIONS

page 148

Discuss the Stop and Think question on page 148: **Why did the husband and wife melt?** (Possible response: The husband and wife melted because the sun came out, and it was warm enough to melt the snow.) Guide students in writing the answer to this question. **CAUSE AND EFFECT**

Ask: **Have you ever read a story like this one? How was it similar?** (Answers will vary.) **CONNECTING TEXTS**

VOCABULARY
Student-Friendly Explanations

hermit A hermit is a person who lives alone, often far from a community.

fascinated When you are fascinated by something, you are very interested in it and pay close attention to it.

occasionally If something happens occasionally, it happens once in a while.

timid A timid person is shy and unsure of himself or herself.

peculiar Something that is peculiar is strange and unusual, usually not in a good way.

drab Something drab looks dull and lacks color.

trembling If something is trembling, it is shaking slightly.

dashed If someone dashed away, they quickly and suddenly ran away.

"Just Down the Road" 161

Spelling Words: Lesson 14

1.	apron	11.	gallon
2.	button	12.	horizon
3.	canyon	13.	listen
4.	certain	14.	orphan
5.	chicken	15.	pardon
6.	cardigan	16.	pollen
7.	cotton	17.	prison
8.	dragon	18.	siren
9.	even	19.	swollen
10.	fountain	20.	driven

page 149 **Answers to *Think Critically* Questions** Help students read and answer the *Think Critically* questions on page 149. Have students copy the graphic organizer in question 2 onto a separate sheet of paper. Then guide students in writing the answer to each question. Possible responses are provided.

1. Kim is friendly, curious, caring, and polite. **CHARACTER**
2. [2.] She tries to find their home. [3.] She finds the scarf and flashlight. **PLOT**
3. These are the clues in the story: They wore only scarves; they were not cold; they stayed away from the fire and didn't want a snack; they were not clear about where they lived.  **DRAW CONCLUSIONS**

RETEACH

Decoding/Spelling

 Words with Ending /ən/ Distribute *Copying Master 54*. Model reading these Spelling Words and have students repeat them: *apron, button, canyon, certain, cotton, dragon, fountain, gallon, horizon, pardon,* and *prison*. Then write the words on the board and have students copy them into their notebooks. Ask students to identify the sound they hear at the end of each word (/ən/) and the letter combination that represents the sound. (*-ain* and *-on*)

Now ask volunteers to take turns sorting the words into two groups, based on the letters that form the /ən/ sound. Have them write a word in one of two columns on the board. Have them also add the words to the correct column in the chart on *Copying Master 54*. Conclude by reading each word one more time and having students circle in their notebooks the letters that form the /ən/ sound.

Day 2

PRETEACH

Grammar/Writing

Practice Book 56 **Pronouns and Antecedents** Remind students that the noun or pronoun to which a pronoun refers is called the pronoun's antecedent. A pronoun and its antecedent must agree in number; they must both be singular or both be plural. They must agree in gender; they must both be masculine or feminine. Use this sentence to review:

When the girls arrived, they looked worried.

Help students name the pronoun and its antecedent and identify both words as plurals. (they, girls)

GUIDED PRACTICE Direct students' attention to page 56 in their *Practice Books*. Invite volunteers to select the correct word for each sentence and explain their choice. If time permits, have students work in pairs to write new sentences using the correct answer to each sentence.

Fluency

Practice Book 55 **Fluency Practice** Invite students to look at the bottom half of *Practice Book* page 55. These sentences have been broken into natural phrases. Tell students to repeat each phrase after you, mirroring your expression, phrasing, and pace. After students have repeated each sentence, invite them to practice reading the sentences to a partner.

"Just Down the Road" 163

LESSON 14

DAY AT A GLANCE — Day 3

COMPREHENSION
Preteach Predict Outcomes
Reread and Summarize "Just Down the Road"

DECODING/SPELLING
Reteach Words with Ending /ən/

BUILD ROBUST VOCABULARY
Teach Words from "Just Down the Road"

GRAMMAR/WRITING
Reteach Writing Trait: Sentence Fluency

FLUENCY
Fluency Practice

Materials Needed: *Turn It Up!*

Student Edition pp. 142–148 | Practice Book pp. 55, 57 | Copying Masters 54, 55

30+ Minutes

PRETEACH
Comprehension

Predict Outcomes Distribute *Copying Master 55*. Have students listen as you read the information at the top of the page about predicting outcomes.

GUIDED PRACTICE Have students read the story and complete the activity. Allow time for students to share and explain what they have added to the chart.

Reread and Summarize Have students reread and summarize "Just Down the Road" in sections, as described below.

pp. 142–143 **Let's reread pages 142–143 to recall who is in this story, where they are, and who they meet.**
Summary: Kim and her grandfather are at a skating pond one chilly night, where they meet an unusual couple. The husband and wife don't seem to mind the cold.

pp. 144–145 **Now let's reread pages 144–145 to remember what happens after the couple leave.**
Summary: Kim and her grandfather talk with the couple for a while. Then the husband and wife leave for their home, "just down the road." Kim wonders where their home might be.

pp. 146–148 **Last, let's reread pages 146–148 to find out what happens when Kim and her grandfather look for the couple's home the next day.**
Summary: They can't find the home, but Kim sees the wife's scarf and a flashlight in a pile of snow. Her grandfather explains that the couple melted in the sun. Kim decides to build a new snow girl.

RETEACH
Decoding/Spelling

Words with Ending /ən/ Write on the board each of the partially spelled words below. Also write the four letter combinations that form the /ən/ sound **(-ain, -an, -en, on)**.

| apr____ | ev____ | cardig____ | cert____ |
| fount____ | chick____ | cott____ | orph____ |

Have students write the letters that correctly complete each word. **(apron, even, cardigan, certain, fountain, chicken, cotton, orphan)** Conclude by having students read each word along with you.

164 Lesson 14 • Turn It Up!

Now ask students to complete the activity at the bottom of *Copying Master 54*. This activity is based on the traditional Memory Game. Pairs of students make game cards using the lesson's Spelling Words with vowels missing; a dash appears in place of each vowel. After a student matches two cards, he or she must supply the correct missing letters to keep the game cards. If the wrong letter is supplied, the opponent gets the game cards and the next turn.

TEACH

Build Robust Vocabulary

pp. 142–147

Words from "Just Down the Road" Have students locate the word *replied* on page 142 of "Just Down the Road." Ask a volunteer to read aloud the sentence in which this word appears. (Line 5: *"Yes," replied the wife with a bright smile*.) Explain that this sentence means that the wife said something to answer what Kim had asked. Continue by asking students to locate and read aloud the sentence on page 147 in which the word *spotted* appears. (Line 5: . . .*Kim spotted something bright by the side of the road*.) Explain that this sentence means that all of a sudden Kim saw something by the side of the road.

Ask each student to write the words on cards. Give an explanation of each word and have students hold up the correct card.

RETEACH

Grammar/Writing

Practice Book 57

Writing Trait: Sentence Fluency Have students turn to page 57 in their *Practice Book*. Explain that when writers write, it is important for them to vary their sentences. Some should be short and others long. Writers should also use different kinds of sentences, including simple and compound. Ask a volunteer to read the information on the *Practice Book* page. Ask students for examples of each of the four kinds of sentences.

GUIDED PRACTICE Complete the page together. Have volunteers share their answers to Parts A, B, and C.

Fluency

Practice Book 55

Fluency Practice Tell students that today they will reread the sentences on the bottom of *Practice Book* page 55. Have students locate and point to the first sentence. Tell students that everyone is going to read the sentence together. This choral reading will give students an opportunity to hear others and listen to the natural phrasing of the sentences. Choral-read each of the sentences several times.

"Just Down the Road" 165

LESSON 14

DAY AT A GLANCE
Day 4

COMPREHENSION
Reteach Predict Outcomes

DECODING/SPELLING
Reteach Words with Ending /ən/

BUILD ROBUST VOCABULARY
Reteach Words from "Just Down the Road"

GRAMMAR/WRITING
Reteach Writing Form: Pourquoi Tale

FLUENCY
Fluency Practice

Materials Needed: *Turn It Up!*

Student Edition pp. 142–148

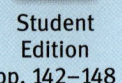
Practice Book p. 58

Copying Master 56

Spelling Words: Lesson 14

1. apron		11. gallon
2. button		12. horizon
3. canyon		13. listen
4. certain		14. orphan
5. chicken		15. pardon
6. cardigan		16. pollen
7. cotton		17. prison
8. dragon		18. siren
9. even		19. swollen
10. fountain		20. driven

30+ Minutes

RETEACH

Comprehension

Predict Outcomes Remind students that when they predict outcomes they figure out future events in a story. Review with them this information about predicting outcomes:

- Good readers often think about what might happen next as they read.
- Good readers look for story clues about what might happen next.
- Good readers think about what they already know from real life.
- Good readers use both the story clues and what they already know to make predictions about what might happen next.

Explain that they now know what happens in the story and can go back and find clues that could have helped them predict the outcome. Now refer students to page 143. Ask them to find three clues that could help them make a prediction about what will happen in the story. (The couple stayed away from the fire, wore only scarves, and said they were not cold.)

Ask how these clues could have helped them predict the outcome of the story. (Possible response: Everybody else was cold and near the fire; they were wearing fewer clothes than everyone else.)

RETEACH Have students reread pages 144–145. Have them work with a partner to identify and explain two clues on this spread that help them predict the outcome of the story. (Possible responses: The couple didn't want a snack; they were not clear about where they lived.)

RETEACH

Decoding/Spelling

Words with Ending /ən/ Have students number a sheet of paper 1–16. Write the Spelling Word *apron* on the board and circle the letters that stand for the ending /ən/ sound. Then do the same for *even, certain,* and *orphan*. Remind students that the /ən/ sound can be spelled in these four different ways in the words you will dictate.

1. prison	2. canyon	3. cardigan	4. dragon
5. listen	6. pardon	7. button	8. siren
9. cotton	10. chicken	11. swollen	12. gallon
13. driven	14. pollen	15. horizon	16. fountain

Have students turn to page 58 in their *Practice Book*. Ask them to complete the items on the page. Review the correct answers with the class. If necessary, have volunteers describe the pictures.

166 Lesson 14 • Turn It Up!

Day 4

RETEACH
Build Robust Vocabulary

Words from "Just Down the Road" Review the meanings of *replied* and *spotted*. Then say these sentences and ask which word each sentence describes. Have students explain why.

- **The students answered the teacher's question.** (replied)
- **Megan suddenly saw her friend in the crowd.** (spotted)

RETEACH
Grammar/Writing

Copying Master 56

Writing Form: Pourquoi Tale Tell students that a pourquoi tale is a story used by native people to explain why natural events, such as the changing of the seasons, occur. Have them name some examples they know. Explain that, as with other kinds of writing, these tales benefit from sentence variety and the use of new and interesting vocabulary words. Distribute *Copying Master 56* and have a volunteer read the information about pourquoi tales. Then read the student model together, discussing the text in balloons. Write on the board the following sentences from the tale:

> Then they would pull it again and again. They did it just to make the monkey mad.

Model for students how the sentences can be improved by rewriting them to make one sentence.

> Then they would pull it again and again, just to make the monkey mad.

GUIDED PRACTICE Complete the activity by having students answer the four questions. Allow time for students to discuss their answers.

Fluency

pp. 142–148

Fluency Practice Have each student work with a partner to read passages from "Just Down the Road" aloud to each other. Students may select a passage that they enjoyed or choose one of the following options:

- Read page 143. (Total: 83 words)
- Read page 147. (Total: 84 words)

Encourage students to read the selected passage aloud to their partner three times. Have the student rate his or her reading on the 1–4 scale.

1	Need more practice
2	Pretty good
3	Good
4	Great!

"Just Down the Road" 167

Preteach for LESSON 15

DAY AT A GLANCE
Day 5

VOCABULARY
Preteach *intrepid, seasoned, guidance, undoubtedly, cherish, hoist, delectable, pristine, fragile, privilege*

COMPREHENSION
Preteach Text Structure: Cause and Effect

DECODING/WORD ATTACK
Preteach Decode Longer Words

DECODING/SPELLING
Preteach Words with VCV

GRAMMAR/WRITING
Preteach Nouns

FLUENCY
Fluency Performance

Materials Needed: *Turn It Up!*

Student Edition pp. 142–148   Skill Card 15   Copying Master 57

PRETEACH
Vocabulary

Lesson 15 Vocabulary Distribute a set of Vocabulary Word Cards to each student. Hold up the card for the first word, and ask a volunteer to read it aloud. Have students repeat the word and hold up the matching card. Give the explanation for the word. Then ask students the first question below and discuss their responses. Continue for each of the Vocabulary Words.

- What is an example of something an **intrepid** person might do?
- Are you **seasoned** at any special task or activity? Which one?
- What **guidance** would you give someone who asked you to recommend a book to read?
- What is something that will **undoubtedly** happen this afternoon?
- What is a memory that you especially **cherish**?
- What is something that you would need to **hoist**?
- What is a food you consider **delectable**?
- Is your bedroom **pristine**? Why or why not?
- What would happen if you dropped something **fragile**?
- What is a **privilege** you have earned?

PRETEACH
Comprehension

Text Structure: Cause and Effect Have students look at side A of *Skill Card 15: Review–Text Structure: Cause and Effect*. Ask them to recall what they have learned about cause and effect. Read the passage aloud as students read along. Then ask:

- Who is this story about? (a girl named Lena and her family)
- What activity does the family like to do together? (take camping trips)
- What event does the author describe that happened one day? (The family's food bag is ripped open and eaten by a bear.)
- What clue words does the author use to signal a cause-and-effect relationship? (as a result)

GUIDED PRACTICE Guide students in copying the charts onto a separate sheet of paper and completing them with a cause and effect from the passage. (Possible response: Effect: Lena learned to love camping, too. Cause: Lena's family was too tired from their hike to hang up their food bag.)

168 Preteach for Lesson 15 • Turn It Up!

Day 5

PRETEACH

Decoding/Word Attack

Decode Longer Words Write *begin* and *mimic* on the board. Ask a volunteer to pronounce the words and to divide them into syllables. (be/gin, mim/ic) Guide students to discover the open syllable, with its long vowel sound, in *begin*, and the closed syllable, with its short vowel sound, in *mimic*. Continue with *legal, paper, suburb,* and *relish*. (le/gal, pa/per, sub/urb, rel/ish)

PRETEACH

Decoding/Spelling

Words with VCV Write *native* on the board. Draw a slash between the syllables (na/tive) and pronounce the word. Then do the same for *vanish*. (van/ish) Ask students which word contains the V/CV pattern. (native) Point out that the first syllable is an open syllable, with a long vowel sound. Then guide students as they pronounce these words and divide them into syllables: *event, rival, solar,* and *moment*. (e/vent, ri/val, so/lar, mo/ment)

PRETEACH

Grammar/Writing

Nouns Have students recall what they have learned about common and proper nouns. Write these nouns on the board: *cat, kittens, Felix, nation, Canada, trucks, car, Dodge,* and *countries*. Then make a three-column chart on the board labeled *singular common nouns, proper nouns*, and *plural nouns*. Invite volunteers to place each of the nouns under one of the headings. (singular common: cat, nation, car; proper: Felix, Canada, Dodge; plural: kittens, trucks, countries)

Then write the following sentences on the board.

> My friends are taking a trip to Michigan.
>
> That state is popular with campers.

For each sentence, have volunteers identify the nouns and the noun type. (friends: plural, common; trip: singular, common; Michigan: singular, proper; state: singular, common; campers: plural, common)

VOCABULARY

Student-Friendly Explanations

intrepid A person who is intrepid acts brave because he or she has no fear.

seasoned A person who is seasoned at something has a lot of experience.

guidance Someone who gives guidance provides help and advice.

undoubtedly If something will undoubtedly happen, it will definitely happen.

cherish If you cherish something, it means a lot to you and you care for it lovingly.

hoist To hoist something is to raise it, often with mechanical help.

delectable A food described as delectable tastes very good.

pristine If a place is pristine, it is clean and untouched.

fragile If a thing is fragile, it is easily broken or damaged.

privilege A privilege is a special advantage or right that only certain people can have.

Fluency

pp. 142–148 **Fluency Performance** Invite students to read aloud the passages from "Just Down the Road" that they selected. Note the number of words each student reads correctly and incorrectly. Have students rate their own oral reading on the 1–4 scale. Have students continue practicing and then read the passage to you again.

"Just Down the Road" **169**

LESSON 15

DAY AT A GLANCE — Day 1

VOCABULARY
Reteach intrepid, seasoned, guidance, undoubtedly, cherish, hoist, delectable, pristine, fragile, privilege

COMPREHENSION
 Reteach Draw Conclusions

DECODING/WORD ATTACK
Reteach Decode Longer Words

DECODING/SPELLING
Reteach Words with Prefixes re-, un-, non-

GRAMMAR/WRITING
Reteach Nouns

FLUENCY
Fluency Practice

Materials Needed: *Turn It Up!*

Student Edition pp. 150–151 | Practice Book pp. 59, 60 | Skill Card 15 | Copying Master 58

RETEACH

Vocabulary

 **Lesson 15 Vocabulary** Read aloud the Vocabulary Words and the Student-Friendly Explanations. Then have students turn to pages 150–151 in their books. Ask a volunteer to read the directions aloud. Remind students that they should read each sentence to themselves with the word they chose to be sure it makes sense. If students have difficulty choosing the correct word, refer to the Student-Friendly Explanations. After students have completed the pages, have volunteers take turns reading aloud each sentence. (Answers for pp. 150–151: 2. *cherish*, 3. *guidance*, 4. *delectable*, 5. *undoubtedly*, 6. *pristine*, 7. *fragile*, 8. *privilege*, 9. *Intrepid*, 10. *hoist*, Possible responses: 11. Someone becomes a seasoned camper after they have been camping a lot. 12. A pristine campsite is clean and untouched.)

RETEACH

Comprehension

  **Draw Conclusions** Have students look at side B of *Skill Card 15: Review: Draw Conclusions*. Ask a volunteer to read the Skill Reminder. Then read the passage aloud as students read along. Remind students that to draw a conclusion, they will need to recognize the important details in a passage and combine them with what they know from their own lives and experiences.

Discuss with students details they learn from the passage. Ask: **How are these details related?** (They show what José did to get ready for the second test and why.)

GUIDED PRACTICE Guide students in copying the chart and completing it with details from the passage. Invite students to discuss the experiences on which they based their additions to the second box. (Story Information: José wasn't happy with his last test grade, he took special care to get ready for this one; Your Own Knowledge and Experiences: not doing well one time can inspire you to do better the next time, being prepared for a test can make a big difference; Conclusions You Can Draw: José was prepared this time and got a good grade on the math test.)

170 Lesson 15 • Turn It Up!

Day 1

RETEACH

Decoding/Word Attack

Decode Longer Words Write *reuse* on the board. Ask a volunteer to underline the prefix and root, pronounce each word part, and then blend the parts to say the word. Remind students they can use their knowledge of prefixes and root words to break longer words into smaller parts. Also, remind them that a prefix forms its own syllable. Write *unwelcome, nonprofit, recall,* and *nontoxic* on the board. Ask students to copy the words, underline the prefix in each word, and rewrite the root alone. Then have volunteers blend the parts and say the words.

RETEACH

Decoding/Spelling

Copying Master 58 **Words with Prefixes re-, un-, non-** Distribute *Copying Master 58*. Have students read the Spelling Words along with you. Write *unannounced, reuse, retrace, unpleasant,* and *nonmetal* on the board. Have a volunteer draw a slash between the root word and the prefix in each. Conclude by asking students to suggest other words that use these prefixes.

RETEACH

Grammar/Writing

Practice Book 60 **Nouns** Write the following sentence on the board:

> The Empire State Building stands near many other tall buildings.

Ask a volunteer to identify the nouns and tell if they are common or proper, singular or plural. (Empire State Building: proper, singular; buildings: common, plural) Invite students to explain their answers.

GUIDED PRACTICE Have students turn to page 60 in their *Practice Books*. Ask a volunteer to read the activity directions for questions 1–5 aloud. Have students complete the first five questions and share their answers. Repeat for the last five questions.

VOCABULARY
Student-Friendly Explanations

intrepid A person who is intrepid acts brave because he or she has no fear.

seasoned A person who is seasoned at something has a lot of experience.

guidance Someone who gives guidance provides help and advice.

undoubtedly If something will undoubtedly happen, it will definitely happen.

cherish If you cherish something, it means a lot to you and you care for it lovingly.

hoist To hoist something is to raise it, often with mechanical help.

delectable A food described as delectable tastes very good.

pristine If a place is pristine, it is clean and untouched.

fragile If a thing is fragile, it is easily broken or damaged.

privilege A privilege is a special advantage or right that only certain people can have.

Fluency

Practice Book 59 **Fluency Practice** Have students turn to *Practice Book* page 59. Read the words in the first column aloud. Invite students to track each word and repeat after you. Then have pairs read aloud the words in each column. After partners have practiced reading the words in each column, have them practice reading all of the words.

"The Camping Club" 171

LESSON 15

DAY AT A GLANCE — Day 2

VOCABULARY
Reteach *intrepid, seasoned, guidance, undoubtedly, cherish, hoist, delectable, pristine, fragile, privilege*

COMPREHENSION
"The Camping Club"
Build Background
Monitor Comprehension
Answers to *Think Critically* **Questions**

DECODING/WORD ATTACK
Reteach Decode Longer Words

DECODING/SPELLING
Reteach Words with Suffixes *-able, -ible, -ness, -ment, -less*

GRAMMAR/WRITING
Reteach Possessive Nouns and Pronouns

FLUENCY
Fluency Practice

Materials Needed: *Turn It Up!*

Student Edition pp. 152–159 | Practice Book p. 59 | Copying Masters 57, 58

30+ Minutes

RETEACH

Vocabulary

Lesson 15 Vocabulary Distribute a set of Vocabulary Word Cards to each pair of students. Read aloud the Student-Friendly Explanation for one of the words, leaving out the word. Have students display and read the matching Word Card. Continue until students have matched all the words.

(Copying Master 57)

Comprehension

Build Background: "The Camping Club"
Ask students to share experiences of camping trips they have taken or read about. Who went camping? What did the campers enjoy most? What did they like the least?

Monitor Comprehension: "The Camping Club"
(pp. 152–153)
Read the title of the play aloud. Then have students read pages 152–153 to find out who this group is and what they are doing.

After reading the pages, ask: **Who are the people in the play? What are they planning?** (They are a group of friends and one child's mom; they are planning a camping trip.) **NOTE DETAILS**

Discuss the Stop and Think question on page 152: **Why might Mrs. Brown know a lot about camping?** (Possible response: Mrs. Brown might know a lot about camping because she camped when she was a girl.) Guide students in writing the answer to this question.
 **CAUSE AND EFFECT**

Ask: **Why does Kendra ask if girls can go, too?** (Possible response: She may not be sure girls can go because David shares his experiences with his father.) **CHARACTER'S MOTIVATIONS**

Discuss the Stop and Think question on page 153: **What does Mrs. Brown need the kids to do first?** (Possible response: First, Mrs. Brown needs the kids to ask their parents for permission to go.) Guide students in writing the answer to this question. **SEQUENCE**

Ask: **Jenny suggests they catch trout. Do you think it would be easy to catch and prepare a meal of fish on the camping trip? Explain your answer.** (Possible response: It would not be too easy because catching fish is not simple, and even if they caught some, they would have to clean and cook them.) **USE PRIOR KNOWLEGE**

172 Lesson 15 • Turn It Up!

Day 2

Model how to use suffixes and root words to figure out how a word is pronounced. Point out Mrs. Brown's first line on page 153.

THINK ALOUD I see the word is spelled *T-A-S-T-Y*. Usually when a vowel comes before more than one consonant, it's a short vowel. But I see that this is a special case. Why? I see that there's a suffix—*y*—at the end of a root. I also know that sometimes a final *e* drops off before you add a suffix. In this case the root is *taste*, and the final *e* did drop off. So I know the word is pronounced with a long *a* sound. PREFIXES, SUFFIXES, AND ROOT WORDS

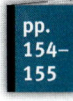 Discuss the Stop and Think question on page 154: **Why does it matter if the camping supplies are heavy?** (Possible response: It matters because the kids will have to lift them and probably carry them into camp.) Guide students in writing the answer to this question. DRAW CONCLUSIONS

Discuss the Stop and Think question on page 155: **Imagine you want to buy some camping equipment. Where could you look to learn about what to buy?** (Possible response: I would look at magazines, Scout books, or other books about camping.) Guide students in writing the answer to this question. USE REFERENCE SOURCES

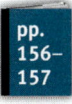 Discuss the Stop and Think question on page 156: **Why does Jenny say "Stop that"?** (Possible response: Jenny says "Stop that" because she thinks David is making strange noises.) Guide students in writing the answer to this question. DRAW CONCLUSIONS

Discuss the Stop and Think question on page 157: **Why wouldn't the kids get any sleep with the dog around?** (Possible response: The kids wouldn't get any sleep because it would want to play and run around.) Guide students in writing the answer to this question. CAUSE AND EFFECT

 Discuss the Stop and Think question on page 158: **What do the campers do to put out the fire?** (Possible response: To put out the fire, the campers put water on it, stir apart the ashes, put dirt on it, and add more water.) Guide students in writing the answer to this question. DRAW CONCLUSIONS

VOCABULARY
Student-Friendly Explanations

intrepid A person who is intrepid acts brave because he or she has no fear.

seasoned A person who is seasoned at something has a lot of experience.

guidance Someone who gives guidance provides help and advice.

undoubtedly If something will undoubtedly happen, it will definitely happen.

cherish If you cherish something, it means a lot to you and you care for it lovingly.

hoist To hoist something is to raise it, often with mechanical help.

delectable A food described as delectable tastes very good.

pristine If a place is pristine, it is clean and untouched.

fragile If a thing is fragile, it is easily broken or damaged.

privilege A privilege is a special advantage or right that only certain people can have.

"The Camping Club" 173

Day 2

Spelling Words: Lesson 15

1. event	11. comfortable
2. rival	12. horrible
3. solar	13. invisible
4. moment	14. loneliness
5. unannounced	15. requirement
6. reuse	16. fearless
7. retrace	17. cotton
8. unpleasant	18. listen
9. nonmetal	19. fountain
10. likable	20. orphan

page 159 **Answers to *Think Critically* Questions** Help students read and answer the *Think Critically* questions on page 159. Then guide students in writing the answer to each question. Possible responses are provided.

1. I think the author did not write this play to explain how to camp. I think she was writing to entertain readers. **Author's Purpose**
2. The event I think the children will remember most is the big dog running into their campsite and scaring them. **Plot**
3. I would I like to go camping because I enjoy nature. I would not like to go camping because I like the comforts of my home. **Personal Response**

RETEACH
Decoding/Word Attack

Decode Longer Words Write the word *hopeless* on the board. Underline the suffix and pronounce each word part. Have students blend the parts to say the word. Remind students that one way to decode long words is to break them into smaller parts and identify suffixes and root words. Repeat this procedure with the following words: *printable, darkness, responsible,* and *excitement*. Point out that the spelling and pronunciation of the root word may change when a suffix is added.

174 Lesson 15 • Turn It Up!

RETEACH

Decoding/Spelling

Words with Suffixes -able, -ible, -ness, -ment, -less Have students review *Copying Master 58* to identify those Spelling Words that have the suffixes *-able, -ible, -ness, -ment,* and *-less.* Write the words *likable, comfortable, horrible,* and *invisible* on the board. Have students read each word aloud as you circle the suffix in each. Point out that the pronunciation of *-able* and *-ible* are very similar. Explain that students must memorize which suffix goes with a particular root or root word.

RETEACH

Grammar/Writing

Possessive Nouns and Pronouns Have students recall that possessive nouns show ownership and are usually formed by adding apostrophe *-s* or *-s* apostrophe. Write the following phrases on the board:

> the voice of the man
> the shouts of the men
> the sound of the car
> the howling of the wolves

Review how each can be rewritten using a possessive noun. (the man's voice, the men's shouts, the car's sound, the wolves' howling)

Remind students that a pronoun takes the place of one or more nouns. Write this sentence:

> When the dog came, it scared the kids.

Guide students to identify the pronoun *it* and the word to which it refers, or its antecedent, *dog*. Follow the same procedure with these sentences:

> David heard a fly and swatted at it.
> The kids can't sleep, so they look for the dog's owner.

Fluency

Fluency Practice Invite students to look at the bottom half of *Practice Book* page 59. These sentences have been broken into natural phrases. Tell students to repeat each phrase after you, mirroring your expression, phrasing, and pace. After students have repeated each sentence, invite them to practice reading the sentences to a partner.

LESSON 15

DAY AT A GLANCE
Day 3

COMPREHENSION
Reteach Reference Sources
Reread and Summarize "The Camping Club"

DECODING/WORD ATTACK
Reteach Decode Longer Words

DECODING/SPELLING
Reteach Words with Ending /ən/

BUILD ROBUST VOCABULARY
Teach Words from "The Camping Club"

GRAMMAR/WRITING
Reteach Possessive Nouns and Pronouns

FLUENCY
Fluency Practice

Materials Needed: *Turn It Up!*

Student Edition
pp. 152–158

Practice Book
pp. 59, 61

30+ Minutes

RETEACH

Comprehension

Reference Sources Review various reference sources. Remind students that almanacs contain current facts about places, people, and events; atlases contain maps; dictionaries are used to find word meanings and spellings; encyclopedias, nonfiction books, and magazines contain information on specific topics; the Internet has both current and historical information; and a thesaurus is used to find synonyms and antonyms.

GUIDED PRACTICE Work with students to identify the best reference sources to use to answer the questions below. Have students explain their answers.

- **Where are the best places to go rock climbing?** (Internet; nonfiction books; magazine articles)
- **Where are state parks in Kentucky?** (atlas; almanac; Internet)
- **How was synthetic fleece developed?** (nonfiction books and magazines; encyclopedia; Internet)
- **What is rappelling?** (dictionary; encyclopedia; Internet)

Reread and Summarize Have students reread and summarize "The Camping Club" in sections, as described below.

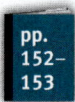
pp. 152–153
Let's reread pages 152–153 to recall who the characters are and where and when the story takes place.
Summary: It's the end of summer and Mrs. Brown suggests a camping trip. The kids are excited and start to plan the trip.

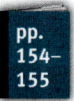
pp. 154–155
Now let's reread pages 154–155 to remember what the campers need to do first and how they begin their camping trip.
Summary: After getting permission, the camping club heads for the woods. They hike into their campsite and set up their tents.

pp. 156–158
Now let's reread pages 156–158 to find out what happens to disrupt their night in the woods and how the story ends.
Summary: The campers return a visiting dog to its owners and turn in for the night. The next day, they clean up and make sure the fire is out. They agree they would like to camp again.

176 Lesson 15 • *Turn It Up!*

Day 3

RETEACH
Decoding/Word Attack

Decode Longer Words Remind students that /ən/ can be spelled several ways: *an, ain, en, on*. Write *ripening, certainly, seasonal,* and *cardigan*. Have students underline the letters that stand for the /ən/ sound and then decode and read the words aloud.

RETEACH
Decoding/Spelling

Words with Ending /ən/ Say *rotten* and *gallon*. Have students identify the /ən/ sound at the end of the words. Write the words and have volunteers circle the letters that stand for the ending /ən/ sound. Then write the following incomplete words on the board: *driv__ drag__ orph__ mount__*. Have volunteers complete the words. (driven, dragon, orphan, mountain)

TEACH
Build Robust Vocabulary

pp. 155–157 Words from "The Camping Club" Have students locate the word *prowl* on page 155 of "The Camping Club." Ask a volunteer to read aloud the sentence in which this word appears. (Line 3: *They prowl around the forest.*) Explain that this means that they move slowly and quietly as if they don't want to be seen. Then ask students to locate and read aloud the sentence on page 157 in which *hike* appears. (Line 10: *How about a hike?*) Explain that this sentence means that Kenneth is asking if they want to take a long walk in the woods for fun.

Ask students to act out each word.

RETEACH
Grammar/Writing

Practice Book 61 Review Possessive Nouns and Pronouns Remind students that nouns that are plural, but not possessive, do not have apostrophes. Then review that a pronoun must agree with its antecedent in number and gender. Write this sentence: *Grab the plates and take it to Larry.* Have a volunteer correct the pronoun. (Grab the plates and take them to Larry.) Explain that *plates* is plural, so *them* is correct.

GUIDED PRACTICE Have students turn to page 61 in their *Practice Book*. Ask a volunteer to read aloud the directions for the first exercise. Have students complete the first exercise. Discuss their answers. Then do the same for the second exercise.

Fluency

Practice Book 59 Fluency Practice Tell students that today they will reread the sentences on the bottom of *Practice Book* page 59. Have students locate and point to the first sentence. Tell students that everyone is going to read the sentence together. This choral reading will give students an opportunity to hear others and listen to the natural phrasing of the sentences. Choral-read each of the sentences several times.

"The Camping Club" 177

LESSON 15

DAY AT A GLANCE — Day 4

COMPREHENSION
Reteach Predict Outcomes

DECODING/SPELLING
Cumulative Review

BUILD ROBUST VOCABULARY
Reteach Words from "The Camping Club"

GRAMMAR/WRITING
Cumulative Review

FLUENCY
Fluency Practice

Materials Needed: *Turn It Up!*

Student Edition
pp. 152–158

Practice Book
p. 62

Copying Masters
59, 60

Spelling Words: Lesson 15

1. event	11. comfortable
2. rival	12. horrible
3. solar	13. invisible
4. moment	14. loneliness
5. unannounced	15. requirement
6. reuse	16. fearless
7. retrace	17. cotton
8. unpleasant	18. listen
9. nonmetal	19. fountain
10. likable	20. orphan

30+ Minutes

RETEACH
Comprehension

Copying Master 59 **Predict Outcomes** Have students recall that good readers try to predict what is going to happen in a story. Distribute *Copying Master 59*, and have a volunteer read aloud the information at the top of the page.

GUIDED PRACTICE Ask students to complete the page with a partner. Invite students to share and discuss their responses with the group.

RETEACH
Decoding/Spelling

Practice Book 62 **Cumulative Review** Have students number a sheet of paper 1–16. Write the Spelling Word *event* on the board, and point to the V/CV combination. Tell students that the first three words you will dictate contain this letter pattern. After students write each word, display it so they can proofread their work. Continue to group the words by spelling rule. Use *reuse* for the prefixes *re-*, *un-*, and *non-* (4 words). Use *likable* for the suffixes *-able*, *-ible*, *-ment*, *-ness*, and *-less* (6 words). Use *cotton* for the ending /ən/ (3 words).

1. rival	2. solar	3. moment	4. unannounced
5. retrace	6. unpleasant	7. nonmetal	8. comfortable
9. horrible	10. invisible	11. loneliness	12. requirement
13. fearless	14. listen	15. fountain	16. orphan

Have students turn to page 62 in their *Practice Book*. Ask a volunteer to read the directions aloud. Once students have read the story and completed the page, invite them to identify the Spelling Words in the story.

178 Lesson 15 • Turn It Up!

Day 4

RETEACH
Build Robust Vocabulary

Words from "The Camping Club" Review the meanings of the words *prowl* and *hike*. Then say these sentences and ask which word each sentence describes. Have students explain why.

- **We saw interesting animals and plants when Dad and I took a walk in the woods for fun.** (hike)
- **The fox walked slowly and quietly into the chicken coop.** (prowled)

RETEACH
Grammar/Writing

Copying Master 60

Cumulative Review Have students recall the grammar skills they reviewed in this lesson. Discuss examples for each skill:

- common and proper nouns
- plural nouns
- possessive nouns
- pronouns and antecedents

Write these sentences on the board:

> My Family is going camping in wisconsin.
>
> Moms car is broken, so we will take my dads' van.
>
> If you see melinda, tell them we'll be back next week.

Guide students to proofread the sentences, and ask volunteers to underline the errors in each sentence. Then ask students to identify the correct word to replace each of the errors. (family, Wisconsin; Mom's, dad's; Melinda, her) Invite volunteers to rewrite each of the sentences correctly.

GUIDED PRACTICE Distribute *Copying Master 60* to each student. Have students read the directions and complete the proofreading activity. Allow time for students to share their paragraphs with the group.

Fluency

pp. 152–158

Fluency Practice Have each student work with a partner to read passages from "The Camping Club" aloud to each other. Remind students to:

- pay attention to punctuation marks to guide their pace.
- read with expression.

Encourage partners to read the selected passages aloud three times. Have the student rate his or her reading on the 1–4 scale.

1	Need more practice
2	Pretty good
3	Good
4	Great!

"The Camping Club" 179

Preteach for LESSON 16

DAY AT A GLANCE
Day 5

VOCABULARY
Preteach *tinker, hoaxer, trampled, forged, perfect, quest, barriers*

COMPREHENSION
 Preteach Fact and Opinion

DECODING/WORD ATTACK
Preteach Decode Longer Words

DECODING/SPELLING
Preteach Words Ending with /əl/

GRAMMAR/WRITING
Preteach Possessive Pronouns

FLUENCY
Fluency Performance

Materials Needed: *Turn It Up!*

Student Edition pp. 152–158

Skill Card 16

Copying Master 61

PRETEACH
Vocabulary

Lesson 16 Vocabulary Distribute a set of Vocabulary Word Cards to each student. Hold up the card for the first word, and ask a volunteer to read it aloud. Have students repeat the word and hold up the matching card. Give the explanation for the word. Then ask students the first question below and discuss their responses. Continue for each of the Vocabulary Words.

- Why do some people like to **tinker** with things?
- Would you like to be friends with a **hoaxer**? Why or why not?
- What would a flower garden look like if it were **trampled**?
- When was the last time you **forged** a friendship? What did you do?
- What is the best way to **perfect** most skills?
- What kind of **quest** do you think would be the most interesting?
- Why are **barriers** used around playgrounds?

PRETEACH
Comprehension

Fact and Opinion Tell students that writers of nonfiction sometimes include their own opinions as well as the facts. Have students look at side A of *Skill Card 16: Fact and Opinion*. Ask a volunteer to read the top of the Skill Card aloud. Then refer students to the chart, and ask:

- Is it a fact or an opinion that the New York City Marathon is the most exciting day of the year? How do you know?
- Is it a fact or an opinion that more than 35,000 runners attempt the 26.2-mile course through the five boroughs of New York City? How do you know?

Tell students that it is important to distinguish facts from opinions when they read nonfiction texts, such as magazines and biographies.

GUIDED PRACTICE Have a volunteer read aloud the passage again. Then have partners take turns making statements about the New York City Marathon, based on the passage. The listening partner should identify whether the statement is fact or opinion.

180 Preteach for Lesson 16 • Turn It Up!

Day 5

PRETEACH

Decoding/Word Attack

Decode Longer Words Write the word *cracker* on the board, and have a volunteer read it aloud. Ask which syllable receives the stress. (the first syllable, *crack-*) Remind students that the vowel sound in the second syllable is called a schwa. The schwa sound is neither long nor short, and it can be spelled with the letters *ar, er, or* or *ur*. Write *monster, inspector, polar,* and *murmur* on the board. Guide students to break each word into syllables and identify the /ər/ sound in each word. (mon/st*er*, in/spec/t*or*, so/l*ar*, mur/m*ur*)

PRETEACH

Decoding/Spelling

Words Ending with /əl/ Tell students that when words end in *-al, -el, -il,* and *-le*, they usually stand for the sound /əl/. Write *April, animal, bottle,* and *tunnel* on the board, and have students read them aloud. Ask volunteers to underline the letters that make the sound /əl/ in each word. (Apr*il*, anim*al*, bott*le*, tunn*el*) Tell students that these are some of the next lesson's Spelling Words.

PRETEACH

Grammar/Writing

Possessive Pronouns Write the following sentences on the board:

> Joe's artwork is beautiful.
> His artwork is beautiful.

Read the sentences aloud. Tell students that a possessive pronoun may replace a possessive noun or a group of nouns. In the sentence, the possessive pronoun *His* replaces the possessive noun *Joe's*. The possessive pronouns *my, your, her, his, its, our,* and *their* are used before a noun.

GUIDED PRACTICE Write these sentences on the board:

> Is this <u>the book that belongs to you</u>?
> <u>Kay's</u> books are on the table.

Guide students to substitute a possessive pronoun for the underlined possessive noun or group of words in each sentence. (Is this *your* book? *Her* books are on the table.)

VOCABULARY

Student-Friendly Explanations

tinker When you tinker with something, you try to fix or adjust it.

hoaxer Someone who tries to trick people is a hoaxer.

trampled If you trampled something, you stepped on it very hard and damaged it.

forged If you forged something together, you did it with great effort, and you hope it lasts a long time.

perfect To perfect something is to improve it so that it is the best it can be.

quest A quest is a journey with a specific purpose.

barriers Barriers are objects or people that keep you from moving ahead.

Fluency

Fluency Performance (pp. 152–158) Invite students to read aloud the passages from "The Camping Club" that they selected and practiced earlier. Have students rate their own oral reading on the 1–4 scale. Give students the opportunity to continue practicing and then to read the passage to you again.

"The Camping Club" **181**

LESSON 16

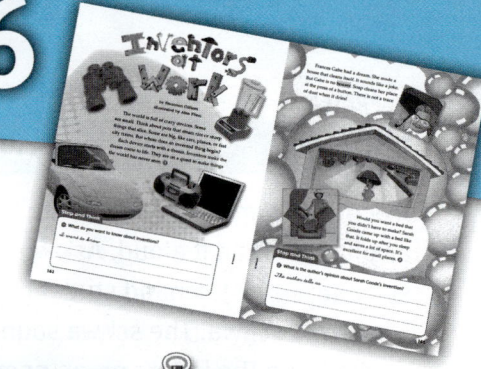

VOCABULARY
Reteach tinker, hoaxer, trampled, forged, perfect, quest, barriers

COMPREHENSION
Reteach Fact and Opinion

DECODING/SPELLING
Reteach Words Ending /əl/

GRAMMAR/WRITING
Preteach Possessive Pronouns

FLUENCY
Fluency Practice

Materials Needed: *Turn It Up!*

Student Edition pp. 160–161 | Practice Book p. 63 | Skill Card 16 | Copying Master 62

RETEACH
Vocabulary

Lesson 16 Vocabulary Read aloud the Vocabulary Words and the Student-Friendly Explanations. Read page 160 aloud with students. Ask students to complete each sentence with the correct word from the list. Have a volunteer read each completed paragraph. If students have difficulty determining correct words, refer to the Student-Friendly Explanations. Continue the same process to have students complete page 161. (Answers for pages 160–161: 2. *tinker,* 3. *forged,* 4. *trampled,* 5. *perfect,* 6. *barriers,* 7. *hoaxer*)

RETEACH
Comprehension

Fact and Opinion Have students look a side B of *Skill Card 16: Fact and Opinion*. Read the Skill Reminder. Then have a volunteer read the paragraph as students read along. Ask:

- **Ben Franklin was the best inventor. How do you know this is an opinion?** (It can't be proven; It uses the clue word *best*.)
- **Ben Franklin invented bifocals. Is this a fact or opinion? Why?** (It's a fact; I can find evidence that this really happened.)

GUIDED PRACTICE Guide students to copy and complete the chart with information from the passage. (Possible responses: Fact: Franklin invented the lightning rod; Evidence: can be proven by looking in an encyclopedia. Opinion: I believe our world today would be very different without Franklin's inventions; Evidence: a statement of belief; uses the clue words *I believe*)

182 Lesson 16 • Turn It Up!

Day 1

RETEACH

Decoding/Spelling

Copying Master 62

Words Ending with /əl/ Distribute *Copying Master 62*. Model reading the Spelling Words and have students repeat them. Then have students complete an activity based on the traditional Memory Game. Pairs of students make game cards using the lesson's Spelling Words with the last two letters missing; a dash appears in place of each *-al, -el, -il,* and *-le*. After a student matches two cards, he or she must supply the correct missing letters to keep the game cards. If the wrong letters are supplied, the opponent gets the game cards and the next turn.

PRETEACH

Grammar/Writing

Possessive Pronouns Recall with students that a possessive pronoun takes the place of a possessive noun or a group of words. Tell students that some possessive pronouns always stand alone: *mine, yours, hers, ours, theirs*. Others are used before a noun: *my, your, her, his, its, our, their*. Finally, *his* and *its* may be used alone or with a noun. Write these examples on the board:

> This is my backpack. This is mine.
>
> That gray house is Lisa's. That gray house is hers.

Help students understand that *mine* and *hers* are possessive pronouns that take the place of "my backpack" and "Lisa's."

GUIDED PRACTICE Write these sentence frames on the board:

> The Crays won the prize. The TV is ____.
>
> I wish it were ____. Do you wish it were ____?

Have volunteers complete each sentence by adding a possessive pronoun that stands alone. (theirs, mine, yours)

VOCABULARY

Student-Friendly Explanations

tinker When you tinker with something, you try to fix or adjust it.

hoaxer Someone who tries to trick people is a hoaxer.

trampled If you trampled something, you stepped on it very hard and damaged it.

forged If you forged something together, you did it with great effort, and you hope it lasts a long time.

perfect To perfect something is to improve it so that it is the best it can be.

quest A quest is a journey with a specific purpose.

barriers Barriers are objects or people that keep you from moving ahead.

Fluency

Practice Book 63

Fluency Practice Have students turn to *Practice Book* page 63. Read the words in the first column aloud. Invite students to track each word and repeat the words after you. Then have students work in pairs to read the words in the first column aloud to each other. Follow the same procedure with each of the remaining columns. After partners have practiced reading aloud the words in each of the columns, have them practice reading all of the words.

"Inventors at Work" 183

LESSON 16

DAY AT A GLANCE

Day 2

 30+ Minutes

VOCABULARY
Reteach tinker, hoaxer, trampled, forged, perfect, quest, barriers

COMPREHENSION
"Inventors at Work"
Build Background
Monitor Comprehension
Answers to *Think Critically* Questions

DECODING/SPELLING
Reteach Words Ending with /əl/

GRAMMAR/WRITING
Preteach Possessive Pronouns

FLUENCY
Fluency Practice

Materials Needed: *Turn It Up!*

Student Edition pp. 162–169 | Practice Book pp. 63, 64 | Copying Masters 61, 62

RETEACH

Vocabulary

Copying Master 61

Lesson 16 Vocabulary Distribute a set of Word Cards and a dictionary to each student. Say a word. Encourage the students to locate the word in the dictionary quickly, using the Word Card as a spelling guide. Have the student who finds the word first read the definition aloud. Continue until all the definitions have been found and read aloud.

Comprehension

Build Background: "Inventors at Work"

Ask students to think of tools and devices they use every day. How would our lives be different without these tools? What are some amazing inventions that they wish they had invented?

Monitor Comprehension: "Inventors at Work"

pp. 162–163

Read the title of the story aloud. Then have students read pages 162–163 to find out the how a new invention begins.

After reading the pages, ask: **How does a new invention begin?** (Possible response: A new invention begins with a dream, or idea.) **NOTE DETAILS**

Discuss the Stop and Think question on page 162: **What do you want to know about inventions?** (Possible responses: I want to know what some inventions are. How are inventions made? Who are some inventors?) Guide students in writing the answer to this question. **EXPRESS PERSONAL OPINIONS**

Ask: **Have you ever used any of the devices shown on page 162? For what purpose?** (Responses will vary.) **MAKE CONNECTIONS**

Ask: **What did Frances Gabe invent?** (a house that cleaned itself) **Why do you think she did this?** (Possible response: She didn't have time to clean.) **NOTE DETAILS/CHARACTER'S MOTIVATIONS**

Discuss the Stop and Think question on page 163: **What is the author's opinion about Sarah Goode's invention?** (The author tells us it is excellent for small places.) Guide students in writing the answer to this question. **FACT AND OPINION**

---

184 Lesson 16 • Turn It Up!

Day 2

Read aloud page 164. Model how you adjust your reading rate to better understand a difficult passage.

THINK ALOUD It wasn't until I read this page slowly that I was able to think about the importance of each detail. By adjusting my reading rate, I was able to picture Carver and the problems he faced. I also realized that the second paragraph follows a sequence of events. By adjusting my reading rate, I was able to understand that Carver became the "Plant Doctor" because of the effects the Civil War had on the land. ADJUST READING RATE

Discuss the Stop and Think question on page 164: **What do you think George Washington Carver will make from plants?** (Possible response: Carver will use plants to make new foods, products, or clothing.) Guide students in writing the answer to this question. MAKE PREDICTIONS

Discuss the Stop and Think question on page 165. **What did Carver do before he started inventing new things?** (Carver spent his time studying plants, thinking of new ideas, and taking notes.) Guide students in writing the answer to this question. SEQUENCE

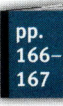

Discuss the Stop and Think question on page 166: **How do you think Jackson felt about his new flavors for ice cream?** (Possible response: I think Jackson felt proud because he had met his goal to make choice ice cream.) Guide students in writing the answer to this question. MAKE INFERENCES

Ask: **What kind of a person do you think Augustus Jackson was?** (Possible response: I think he was smart and hard-working.) CHARACTER'S TRAITS

Discuss the Stop and Think question on page 167: **Which mouse trap would you buy? Explain your answer.** (Possible response: I would buy the second one because it doesn't hurt the mice.) Guide students in writing the answer to this question. EXPRESS PERSONAL OPINIONS

Discuss the Stop and Think question on page 168: **Why does the author ask what devices the world needs next?** (Possible response: The author asks what devices the world needs next because she wants me to think of new ideas for inventions.) Guide students in writing the answer to this question. AUTHOR'S PURPOSE

VOCABULARY
Student-Friendly Explanations

tinker When you tinker with something, you try to fix or adjust it.

hoaxer Someone who tries to trick people is a hoaxer.

trampled If you trampled something, you stepped on it very hard and damaged it.

forged If you forged something together, you did it with great effort, and you hope it lasts a long time.

perfect To perfect something is to improve it so that it is the best it can be.

quest A quest is a journey with a specific purpose.

barriers Barriers are objects or people that keep you from moving ahead.

"Inventors at Work" 185

Day 2

Spelling Words: Lesson 16

1. animal	11. level
2. April	12. national
3. arrival	13. normal
4. trample	14. tremble
5. bottle	15. puddle
6. camel	16. rebel
7. capital	17. single
8. couple	18. swivel
9. festival	19. tropical
10. gentle	20. tunnel

page 169 **Answers to Think Critically Questions** Help students read and answer the *Think Critically* questions on page 169. Have students copy the graphic organizer in question 1 onto a separate sheet of paper. Then guide students in writing the answer to each question. Possible responses are provided.

1. [What I Know/What I Want to Know] Responses will vary. [What I Learned] Inventions begin with a good idea; inventors work hard to make new things; inventors try to solve problems. **MAIN IDEA AND DETAILS**
2. Kness made a new mouse trap becuase he had an idea to improve the old mouse trap. **CAUSE AND EFFECT**
3. The author wrote this article to inform readers about how inventions are made. **AUTHOR'S PURPOSE**

RETEACH

Decoding/Spelling

Copying Master 62 **Words Ending with /əl/** Remind students that the /əl/ sound comes at the end of the word. Write the following headings on the board, leaving a space beneath each one: *-al, -el, -il,* or *-le*. Have a student pick a Spelling Word from *Copying Master 62*. Have the student read it aloud and write it on the board under the correct ending. Have the student circle the /əl/ sound in the word. Continue until all of the words are placed in the columns.

186 Lesson 16 • Turn It Up!

PRETEACH

Grammar/Writing

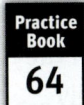 **Possessive Pronouns** Help students recall what they have learned about possessive pronouns. Use this example sentence:

<u>Sandy's</u> room is blue. <u>Her</u> room is blue.

Remind students that some possessive pronouns always stand alone: *mine, yours, hers, ours, theirs*. Others are always used before a noun: *my, your, her, his, its, our, their*. Finally, *his* and *its* may be used alone or with a noun.

Use this example sentence to review reflexive pronouns:

Taylor slipped on the ice, but caught <u>himself</u> before he fell.

Help students understand that *himself* refers to the subject, *Taylor*.

GUIDED PRACTICE Have students turn to page 64 in their *Practice Book*. Work through the first sentence together, substituting first one word and then the other into the blank to determine which is correct. Then tell students to use a similar strategy as they complete the remaining sentences.

Fluency

Fluency Practice Invite students to look at the bottom half of *Practice Book* page 63. These sentences have been broken into natural phrases. Tell students to repeat each phrase after you, mirroring your expression, phrasing, and pace. After students have repeated each sentence, invite them to practice reading the sentences to partners.

"Inventors at Work" 187

LESSON 16

DAY AT A GLANCE — Day 3

COMPREHENSION
Preteach Follow Written Directions
Reread and Summarize "Inventors at Work"

DECODING/SPELLING
Reteach Placeholder Spelling

BUILD ROBUST VOCABULARY
Teach Words from "Inventors at Work"

GRAMMAR/WRITING
Reteach Writing Trait: Voice

FLUENCY
Fluency Practice

Materials Needed: *Turn It Up!*

Student Edition pp. 162–168

Practice Book pp. 63, 65

Copying Master 63

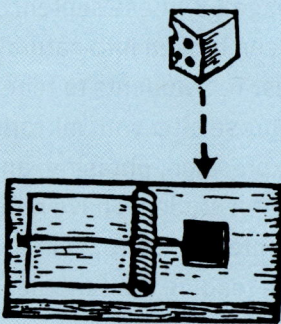

30+ Minutes

PRETEACH
Comprehension

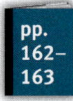 **Follow Written Directions** Distribute *Copying Master 63*. Have a student read the information in the box. Tell students that when they are following written directions, it is important that they carefully read all the steps.

GUIDED PRACTICE Have students read the directions for making chocolate ice cream. Have students work in pairs to answer the questions. Allow time for students to share their responses with the group.

Reread and Summarize Have students reread and summarize "Inventors at Work" in sections, as described below.

 Let's reread pages 162–163 to recall some examples of inventions.
pp. 162–163
Summary: Some examples of inventions are pots that steam, cars, planes, trains, and computers. Frances Gabe invented a house that cleans itself. Sarah Good invented a bed that folds up.

 Let's reread pages 164–165 to remember some facts about how George Washington Carver became an inventor.
pp. 164–165
Summary: The South was a mess after the Civil War, and Carver wanted to fix the problem. He gave advice to farmers and showed them new plants to grow. He invented things made from plants.

Let's reread pages 166–168 to recall four other inventors and their inventions.
pp. 166–168
Summary: Augustus Jackson perfected ice cream. James Atkinson made a mouse trap. Then Austin Kness made a trap that wasn't harmful to mice. Barbara Askins invented a better way to process film.

RETEACH
Decoding/Spelling

Placeholder Spelling Explain to students that if they are not sure how a word is spelled, they can leave a space for part of the word. Then they can come back to it later and check the spelling in a dictionary. Demonstrate this strategy by writing this sentence:

> My trip was to a tropi___ place.

Point out how you left a placeholder. Then model how you use a dictionary to check the spelling, and complete the word. (tropical)

188 Lesson 16 • *Turn It Up!*

Day 3

TEACH

Build Robust Vocabulary

pp. 162–168 **Words from "Inventors at Work"** Have students locate the word *devices* on page 162 of the story. Ask a volunteer to read aloud the sentence in which this word appears. (First sentence: *The world is full of crazy devices.*) Explain that this sentence means that the world is full of unusual tools and machines that were made to do certain jobs. Continue by asking students to locate and read aloud the sentence on page 165 in which *introduced* appears. (Line 4: *Over the years, he introduced many new plants for farmers to grow.*) Explain that this means that Carver told people about certain plants that they did not know about before. Then ask students to locate and read aloud the sentence on page 168 in which *process* appears. (Line 2: *She came up with an exciting process.*) Explain that this sentence means that Askins came up with a set of steps for doing something.

Play a game of Follow the Leader. Give each student a chance to select a word, say the word, and use it in a sentence. The rest of the class must repeat the word and the sentence exactly as the leader did.

RETEACH

Grammar/Writing

Practice Book 65 **Writing Trait: Voice** Have students turn to *Practice Book* page 65. Explain that when they write a story, it is important to use a personal voice to make the story more interesting. Discuss the information in the graphic organizer. Read the directions aloud. Then have a volunteer read the first sentence. Explain that voice is used to show how the character feels. The word *red-hot* appeals to the senses of sight and touch.

GUIDED PRACTICE Complete the page together. Continue to point out how the writer uses voice to show how the character felt and what she was thinking.

Fluency

Practice Book 63 **Fluency Practice** Tell students that today they will reread the sentences on the bottom of *Practice Book* page 63. Have students locate and point to the first sentence. Tell students that everyone is going to read the sentence together. This choral reading will give students an opportunity to hear others and listen to the natural phrasing of the sentences. Choral-read each of the sentences several times.

LESSON 16

DAY AT A GLANCE
Day 4

COMPREHENSION
Reteach Follow Written Directions

DECODING/SPELLING
Reteach Words Ending with /əl/

BUILD ROBUST VOCABULARY
Reteach Words from "Inventors at Work"

GRAMMAR/WRITING
Reteach Writing Form: How-To Composition

FLUENCY
Fluency Practice

Materials Needed: *Turn It Up!*

Student Edition pp. 162–168

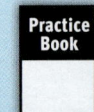
Practice Book p. 66

Copying Master 64

Spelling Words: Lesson 16

1. animal	11. level
2. April	12. national
3. arrival	13. normal
4. trample	14. tremble
5. bottle	15. puddle
6. camel	16. rebel
7. capital	17. single
8. couple	18. swivel
9. festival	19. tropical
10. gentle	20. tunnel

30+ Minutes

RETEACH
Comprehension

Follow Written Directions Have students recall what they learned about following written directions. Write on the board the materials for making a BLT sandwich:

> Materials: plate, butter knife, 2 slices of toasted bread, 2 slices of cooked bacon, lettuce, 2 slices of tomato, mayonnaise

Ask students to discuss the directions someone would need to make the sandwich. As a group, write a set of directions on the board. Discuss the order of the directions, and make corrections that would help a reader follow the directions.

RETEACH
Decoding/Spelling

Practice Book 66

Words Ending with /əl/ Have students number a sheet of paper 1–17. Write *single* on the board, and point to the /əl/ sound. Tell students that in the first six words you will dictate, the /əl/ sound is spelled like it is in *single*. After students write each word, display it so they can proofread their work. Repeat this activity for the other /əl/ sounds using these examples: *swivel* and *arrival*. Dictate *April* last, and point out it is the only Spelling Word with *-il*.

1. trample	2. gentle	3. bottle	4. couple
5. puddle	6. tremble	7. tunnel	8. rebel
9. camel	10. level	11. animal	12. festival
13. capital	14. national	15. normal	16. tropical
17. April			

Have students turn to page 66 in their *Practice Book*. Ask a volunteer to read each sentence aloud. Have students follow the sentence directions. Then have them circle all the words with the /əl/ ending sound.

190 Lesson 16 • Turn It Up!

Day 4

RETEACH
Build Robust Vocabulary

Words from "Inventors at Work" Review the meanings of *devices*, *introduced*, and *process*. Then say these sentences and ask which word each sentence describes. Have students explain why.

- Ms. Moore gave us a set of steps for making clay pots. (process)
- Carlos told us about some customs in his country that we did not know about. (introduced)
- Can you find a tool in that drawer to help me open this jar? (device)

RETEACH
Grammar/Writing

Copying Master 64

Writing Form: How-To Composition Have students turn to *Copying Master 64*. Explain to students that when authors write a how-to composition, it is important to tell the steps in order. Have a student read aloud the information about how-to compositions at the top of the page.

GUIDED PRACTICE Guide students as they complete the first question. Then have students work independently to finish the page.

Fluency

pp. 162–168

Fluency Practice Have each student work with a partner to read passages from "Inventors at Work" aloud to each other. Students may select a passage that they enjoyed or choose one of the following options:

- Read page 164. (Total: 86 words)
- Read page 167. (Total: 107 words)

Encourage students to read the selected passage aloud to their partner three times. Have the student rate his or her reading on the 1–4 scale.

1	Need more practice
2	Pretty good
3	Good
4	Great!

"Inventors at Work" 191

Preteach for **LESSON 17**

Day 5

30+ Minutes

VOCABULARY
Preteach ancestors, brilliant, exotic, graceful, mischievous, participate

COMPREHENSION
 Preteach Fact and Opinion

DECODING/WORD ATTACK
Preteach Decode Longer Words

DECODING/SPELLING
Preteach Words with Ending /ər/

GRAMMAR/WRITING
Preteach Subject Pronouns

FLUENCY
Fluency Performance

Materials Needed: *Turn It Up!*

Student Edition
pp. 162–168

Copying Master 65

PRETEACH
Vocabulary

Copying Master 65 **Lesson 17 Vocabulary**   Distribute a set of Vocabulary Word Cards to each student or pair of students. Hold up the card for the first word and have a student read it aloud. Have students find and hold up the word. Read the Student-Friendly Explanation. Then ask the first question below and discuss students' responses. Continue for each Vocabulary Word.

- What do you know about your **ancestors**?
- When are you most likely to see **brilliant** lights?
- What would be an **exotic** pet?
- Do you think dogs or cats are more **graceful**?
- How can a **mischievous** baby get into trouble?
- In what after-school activities do you **participate**?

PRETEACH
Comprehension

pp. 162–168    **Fact and Opinion**   Tell students that a **fact** is a statement that can be proved. An **opinion** tells what someone thinks or feels. An opinion cannot be proved. Clue words such as *should, must, best, worst, I think,* and *I believe* often signal opinions. Ask students to recall what they read in "Inventors at Work." Then ask:

- **What opinion does the author have about inventions?** (Possible response: People come up with some crazy devices.)
- **What is one fact about Sarah Goode's bed?** (Possible responses: It makes itself. It folds up when you are done with it.)

Explain that distinguishing fact from opinion will help students become better readers, and it will make reading more interesting.

GUIDED PRACTICE   Have students work in small groups to find facts about George Washington Carver in "Inventors at Work." (Possible responses: He was born a slave; found hundreds of uses for crops.) Have students state their opinions about Carver's life and work.

192 Preteach for Lesson 17 • *Turn It Up!*

Day 5

PRETEACH
Decoding/Word Attack

Decode Longer Words Write the word *cellar* on the board, say it, and have students repeat it. Tell students that the final syllable makes the /ər/ sound. Explain that the word endings *-ar*, *-er*, and *-or* all make the /ər/ sound. Write *corner* and *motor* as examples. Next, write *invention* and *Texan* on the board. Say them aloud and have students repeat. Underline the word endings and point out that they both make the /ən/ sound.

PRETEACH
Decoding/Spelling

Words with Ending /ər/ Tell students that the /ər/ sound at the end of some words can be spelled *ar*, *er*, or *or*. Write each of the Spelling Words below on the board and have students read each word aloud. Have volunteers underline the letters that make the /ər/ sound at the end of each word.

cellar	doctor	horror	checkers
corner	finger	master	sugar

PRETEACH
Grammar/Writing

Subject Pronouns Tell students that subject pronouns are part of the subject of a sentence. Singular subject pronouns are *I, you, he, she,* and *it*. Plural subject pronouns are *we, you,* and *they*. Write the following sentences on the board:

Patrick scored five points. He helped the team win.

Tell students that the subject pronoun *he* takes the place of the noun *Patrick*. The word *he* is a singular subject pronoun. Then write these sentences: *The fans were happy. They went wild.* Underline *They* and point out that it replaces *fans*. Explain that *they* is a plural subject pronoun.

VOCABULARY
Student-Friendly Explanations

ancestors The people who came before you in your family are your ancestors.

brilliant Things that are brilliant are very bright and often shiny.

exotic Something exotic is unusual and interesting because it came from a far-away place.

graceful If a person is graceful, he or she moves in a smooth way that is nice to look at.

mischievous Someone who is mischievous likes to play tricks on other people.

participate If you participate in a game, you are involved in it.

Fluency

pp. 162–168

Fluency Performance Invite students each to read aloud from "Inventors at Work" a passage that they selected and practiced earlier. Note the number of words each student reads correctly and incorrectly. Have students rate their own oral reading on the 1–4 scale. Give each student the opportunity to continue practicing and then to read the passage to you again.

LESSON 17

VOCABULARY
Reteach *ancestors, brilliant, exotic, graceful, mischievous, participate*

COMPREHENSION
 Reteach Fact and Opinion

DECODING/SPELLING
Reteach Words with Ending /ər/

GRAMMAR/WRITING
Preteach Object Pronouns

FLUENCY
Fluency Practice

Materials Needed: *Turn It Up!*

Student Edition pp. 170–171 | Practice Book p. 67 | Skill Card 17 | Copying Master 66

RETEACH
Vocabulary

Lesson 17 Vocabulary Read aloud the Vocabulary Words and the Student-Friendly Explanations. Then have students read the first postcard on page 170. Guide them to fill in the blanks using a word from the list. Have a student read the completed postcard aloud. Continue until all the postcards have been filled in. If students are unable to give reasonable responses, refer to the Student-Friendly Explanations. (Answers for pages 170–171: 2. *mischievous*, 3. *brillant*, 4. *participate*, 5. *exotic*, 6. *graceful*)

RETEACH
Comprehension

  **Fact and Opinion** Have students look at side A of *Skill Card 17: Fact and Opinion*. Have a volunteer read aloud the definition at the top of the card. Then have a student read the passage aloud while others follow along. Direct students to look at the chart and ask:

- What is one fact about Piedmont Park?
- What does the author think about living in Atlanta?

GUIDED PRACTICE Now have students look at side B of *Skill Card 17: Fact and Opinion*. Read the Skill Reminder aloud. Then have a volunteer read the story while the rest of the group follows along. Guide students in copying the chart and filling it in with facts, opinions, and evidence. (Possible responses: Facts: In 1912, the city of Tokyo, Japan, gave cherry trees to Washington, D.C. A Cherry Blossom Festival is held each year in early spring. Tourists come from all over the world. The celebration includes a parade, a ten-mile road race, and a street festival. Evidence: can be proven by reading a history book or encyclopedia; something that can really be seen. Opinions: The blooming trees are an amazing sight. The festival is the best time to be in Washington, D.C. Evidence: tells how the writer thinks or feels; cannot be proved; includes signal word *best*)

194 Lesson 17 • *Turn It Up!*

Day 1

RETEACH

Decoding/Spelling

Words with Ending /ər/ Distribute *Copying Master 66*. Model reading each Spelling Word and have the students repeat after you. Have a volunteer read the instruction for recognizing the /ər/ sound. Have students complete the following activity. Have pairs of students write the Spelling Words on index cards. Have one student draw a card and read its word aloud; the other student writes the word. Then have the partners switch roles. When a student spells a word correctly, he or she initials the card and returns it to the pile. Students should work through the pile twice or until each student has had the opportunity to spell each word. Have students write down each word they do not spell correctly to study later.

PRETEACH

Grammar/Writing

Object Pronouns Tell students that an object pronoun must be used after an action verb or a preposition. Singular object pronouns include *me, you, him, her,* or *it*. Plural object pronouns include *us, you,* and *them*. Write the following sentences on the board:

Heather bought Pete and Sue a gift. She gave it to them today.

Have a student read the sentences aloud. Point out the object pronouns. Explain that *it* replaces *gift* and *them* replaces *Pete* and *Sue*. Guide students to identify each pronoun as singular or plural. (it: singular; them: plural)

VOCABULARY

Student-Friendly Explanations

ancestors The people who came before you in your family are your ancestors.

brilliant Things that are brilliant are very bright and often shiny.

exotic Something exotic is unusual and interesting because it came from a faraway place.

graceful If a person is graceful, he or she moves in a smooth way that is nice to look at.

mischievous Someone who is mischievous likes to play tricks on other people.

participate If you participate in a game, you are involved in it.

Fluency

Fluency Practice Have students turn to *Practice Book* page 67. Read the words in the first column aloud. Invite students to track each word and repeat the words after you. Then have students work in pairs to read the words in the first column aloud to each other. Follow the same procedure with each of the remaining columns. After partners have practiced reading aloud the words in each column, have them practice reading all of the words.

"The Artist's Life"

LESSON 17

DAY AT A GLANCE — Day 2

VOCABULARY
Reteach ancestors, brilliant, exotic, graceful, mischievous, participate

COMPREHENSION
"The Artist's Life"
Build Background
Monitor Comprehension
Answers to *Think Critically* **Questions**

DECODING/SPELLING
Reteach Words with Ending /ər/

GRAMMAR/WRITING
Preteach Subject and Object Pronouns

FLUENCY
Fluency Practice

Materials Needed: *Turn It Up!*

Student Edition pp. 172–179   Practice Book pp. 67, 68   Copying Masters 65, 66

30+ Minutes

RETEACH
Vocabulary

Copying Master 65

Lesson 17 Vocabulary   Distribute a set of Vocabulary Word Cards to each pair of students. Have one student make up a true-or-false statement using one Vocabulary Word. For example: *The graceful dancer stumbled onto the stage.* (false) Or, *The mischievous puppy dug up the flower garden.* (true) Have the partner say whether the statement is true or false. Then have students reverse roles and continue until they have used all six words.

Comprehension

Build Background: "The Artist's Life"
Ask students to tell about a time when they were told they have a talent or a time they felt creative. What did they do about it? Did anyone help them to develop their talent or encourage them to be creative?

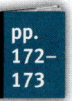
pp. 172–173

Monitor Comprehension: "The Artist's Life"
Read the title of the story aloud. Then have students read pages 172–173 to find out about Georgia O'Keeffe's life.

After reading page 173, ask: **What do you learn about Georgia O'Keeffe's life?** (Possible response: She made art well into her old age.) **NOTE DETAILS**

Discuss the Stop and Think question on page 173: **Why do you think Georgia O'Keeffe painted large works? Underline the words on the page that tell you.** (Possible response: I think Georgia O'Keeffe painted large works because they would show what she liked about the land. Students should underline the last sentence on page 172.) Guide students in writing the answer to this question. **NOTE DETAILS**

Ask: **Where is one place Georgia O'Keeffe probably lived?** (New Mexico) **How do you know?** (Possible response: It says she painted "the land around her" and then mentions New Mexico.) **DRAW CONCLUSIONS**

Ask: **How do you think the author feels about Georgia O'Keeffe?** (Possible response: I think the author admires her work because he uses the word *graceful*.) **AUTHOR'S VIEWPOINT/VOCABULARY**

196 Lesson 17 • Turn It Up!

pp. 174–175

Read aloud page 174. Model adjusting reading rate to help students understand this strategy for monitoring comprehension.

THINK ALOUD When I read this page, I realized that I was not really understanding the information. I asked myself how I could keep track of all the information. As I continued to read, I slowed down my reading rate. By adjusting my reading rate, I was able to remember and understand important information about Diego Rivera. **MONITOR COMPREHENSION/ADJUST READING RATE**

Ask: How do you think Diego Rivera felt when the man asked him to change his painting? (Possible responses: He felt angry; sad.) **MAKE CONNECTIONS**

Discuss the Stop and Think question on page 175: **In Diego Rivera's opinion, what is the best art?** (In Diego Rivera's opinion, the best art is art that challenges the way we think.) Guide students in writing the answer to this question. **RETELL**

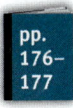
pp. 176–177

Discuss the Stop and Think question on page 176: **How did Faith Ringgold's mom help her become an artist?** (Possible response: Faith Ringgold's mom helped her become an artist when she encouraged her to make art.) Guide students in writing the answer to this question. **DRAW CONCLUSIONS**

Ask: What detail supports the third paragraph's topic statement, "Artists often show the same thing in more than one artwork"? ("Ringgold shows bridges in many quilts.") **MAIN IDEA AND DETAILS**

page 178

Ask: What is another word for *wedge* on this page? (Possible responses: *chunk, piece*) **CONTEXT CLUES**

Discuss the Stop and Think question on page 178: **How do you think the author feels about artists?** (Possible responses: I think the author respects artists; thinks artists are important.) Guide students in writing the answer to this question. **AUTHOR'S PERSPECTIVE**

VOCABULARY
Student-Friendly Explanations

ancestors The people who came before you in your family are your ancestors.

brilliant Things that are brilliant are very bright and often shiny.

exotic Something exotic is unusual and interesting because it came from a far-away place.

graceful If a person is graceful, he or she moves in a smooth way that is nice to look at.

mischievous Someone who is mischievous likes to play tricks on other people.

participate If you participate in a game, you are involved in it.

Day 2

Spelling Words: Lesson 17

1. lunar	11. honor
2. cellar	12. horror
3. collar	13. labor
4. corner	14. master
5. danger	15. motor
6. director	16. ancestors
7. doctor	17. checkers
8. dollar	18. power
9. tinker	19. regular
10. finger	20. sugar

page 179 **Answers to *Think Critically* Questions**
Help students read and answer the *Think Critically* questions on page 179. Have students copy the graphic organizer in question 2 onto a separate sheet of paper. Then guide students in writing the answer to each question. Possible responses are provided.

1. Here's how they are alike: both got an early start; both made large paintings. Here's how they are different: O'Keeffe lived in New Mexico; Rivera lived in Mexico. **COMPARE AND CONTRAST**

2. [Opinion] Ringgold's quilts show a strange and fantastic world; Ringgold uses fun shapes. [Evidence] This statement can be proven. Someone can look at the quilts and see whether they are large.  **FACT AND OPINION**

3. An artist's life affects his or her artwork because what they know and do sometimes shows up in their artwork. **MAKE INFERENCES**

RETEACH
Decoding/Spelling

Copying Master 66 **Words with Ending /ər/** Remind students that when a word ends in *-ar, -er,* or *-or,* those letters stand for the /ər/ sound. Write the following headings on the board: *-ar, -er, -or.* Have a volunteer choose a Spelling Word from *Copying Master 66*, read it aloud, and write it on the board under the correct ending. Have the student underline the letters that stand for the /ər/ sound. Continue until all of the words are placed in the appropriate columns.

198 Lesson 17 • Turn It Up!

Day 2

PRETEACH

Grammar/Writing

 **Subject and Object Pronouns** Guide students to recall the information they have learned about subject and object pronouns. Write the following sentence on the board:

Melissa and I will take the bus to school.

Tell students that *I* is a subject pronoun. *I* always comes after other nouns or pronouns in the subject of a sentence. For example, we would never say "I and Melissa...." Then write this sentence on the board:

The bus picks Melissa and me up at 8:30.

Point out that *me* is an object pronoun. *Me* always comes after other nouns and pronouns that follow an action verb or a prepositional phrase.

GUIDED PRACTICE Direct students to *Practice Book* page 68. Read the directions for each activity together. Have students work alone or in pairs to complete the page.

Fluency

Fluency Practice Invite students to look at the bottom half of *Practice Book* page 67. These sentences have been broken into natural phrases. Tell students to repeat each phrase after you, mirroring your expression, phrasing, and pace. After students have repeated each sentence, invite them to practice reading the sentences to a partner.

"The Artist's Life" 199

LESSON 17

Day 3

COMPREHENSION
Preteach Follow Written Directions
Reread and Summarize "The Artist's Life"

DECODING/SPELLING
Reteach Checking Twice

BUILD ROBUST VOCABULARY
Teach Words from "The Artist's Life"

GRAMMAR/WRITING
Reteach Writing Trait: Voice

FLUENCY
Fluency Practice

Materials Needed: *Turn It Up!*

Student Edition pp. 172–178 | Practice Book pp. 67, 69 | Copying Master 67

30+ Minutes

PRETEACH
Comprehension

Follow Written Directions Distribute *Copying Master 67*, and have a student read the information at the top of the page.

GUIDED PRACTICE Have students read the directions for making pretzels. Then have them answer the questions at the bottom of the page. Allow time for students to share their responses with others.

Reread and Summarize Have students reread and summarize "The Artist's Life" in sections, as described below.

pp. 172–173 **Let's reread pages 172–173 to remember the artistic career of Georgia O'Keeffe.**
Summary: Georgia O'Keeffe's teachers encouraged her to be an artist when she was a young girl. First, she painted. Then she worked with clay.

pp. 174–175 **Let's reread pages 173–174 to remember details about Diego Rivera.**
Summary: Diego Rivera began studying art at age ten. His father encouraged him. Someone who didn't like Rivera's artwork smashed it, but Rivera had made a copy of it.

pp. 176–178 **Let's reread pages 176–178 to find out the kind of art Faith Ringgold likes to do and also what it takes to have an artist's life.**
Summary: Faith Ringgold likes to make quilts out of fun shapes and blocks. Her quilts use brilliant colors. She includes bridges in many of her quilts. An artist's life takes work and energy, and it can begin at any age.

RETEACH
Decoding/Spelling

Checking Twice Point out to students that proofreading their writing is an important step in the writing process. Correcting misspelled words is part of proofreading. Write these sentences on the board:

> The celler door was left open. It was a dangir to go down the stairs.
>
> My dad gave me a doller to buy some sugor at the cornar store.

200 Lesson 17 • *Turn It Up!*

Have students proofread each sentence twice to find the misspelled words. Have a volunteer go to the board, put a line through one of the misspelled words, and write the word correctly above the crossed-out word. (celler/cellar; dangir/danger; doller/dollar; sugor/sugar; cornar/corner) Remind students to proofread their writing twice to check for misspelled words.

> TEACH
Build Robust Vocabulary

pp. 174–178 **Words from "The Artist's Life"** Have students locate the word *original* on page 174 of "The Artist's Life." Ask a volunteer to read aloud the sentence in which this word appears. (Line 11: *In 1933, a man asked Rivera to paint an original work of art.*) Explain that this sentence means that the man asked Rivera to paint a new picture that he did not copy from anyone. Continue by asking students to locate and read aloud the sentence in which the word *budge* appears on pages 174–175. (Last sentence on p. 174: *He told Rivera to change it, but Rivera would not budge.*) Explain that this sentence means that Rivera would not change his mind. He would not do what the man asked. Then ask students to locate and read aloud the sentence in which the word *wedge* appears on page 178. (Line 8: *You can start with some paints or a wedge of clay.*) Explain that the phrase "a wedge of clay" means a piece of clay that is thick at one end and thin at the other.

Ask yes or no questions using the words. For example, point to a duplicated handout and ask: *Is this original?* Have students explain their answers.

> RETEACH
Grammar/Writing

 Practice Book 69 **Writing Trait: Voice** Have students turn to page 69 in their *Practice Books*. Tell them that when they write an autobiography, it is important to use voice to show their characteristics and traits. Voice also can show a writer's opinions and feelings.

GUIDED PRACTICE Complete Part A and Part B of page 69 together. Allow students to complete Part C on their own, and encourage volunteers to share their responses.

Fluency

Practice Book 67 **Fluency Practice** Tell students that today they will reread the sentences on the bottom of *Practice Book* page 67. Have students locate and point to the first sentence. Tell students that everyone is going to read the sentence together. This choral reading will give students an opportunity to hear others and to listen to the natural phrasing of the sentences. Choral-read each sentence several times.

"The Artist's Life" 201

LESSON 17

DAY AT A GLANCE

COMPREHENSION
Reteach Follow Written Directions

DECODING/SPELLING
Reteach Words with Ending /ər/

BUILD ROBUST VOCABULARY
Reteach Words from "The Artist's Life"

GRAMMAR/WRITING
Reteach Writing Form: Autobiographical Composition

FLUENCY
Fluency Practice

Materials Needed: *Turn It Up!*

 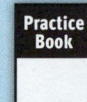 

Student Edition pp. 172–178 | Practice Book p. 70 | Copying Master 68

Spelling Words: Lesson 17

1. lunar	11. honor
2. cellar	12. horror
3. collar	13. labor
4. corner	14. master
5. danger	15. motor
6. director	16. ancestors
7. doctor	17. checkers
8. dollar	18. power
9. tinker	19. regular
10. finger	20. sugar

RETEACH
Comprehension

Follow Written Directions Review with students the following information about following written directions:

- Read the directions all the way through before you start.
- Make sure you have all the materials you need.
- Ask questions about anything that is confusing.
- Follow the steps in order.

On the board, write these directions:

> You will need: paper, pencil
>
> Directions: Draw a square in the center of the paper. Inside the square, draw a circle. Make the circle's sides touch the square's sides. Next, outside of the square, draw a triangle. Make the points of the triangle touch the edges of the paper. Finally, draw a straight line from one corner of the paper to the other.

Have all students read and follow the directions. Then ask:

- **What materials did you need?** (paper and pencil)
- **How did you know what to do first?** (Possible response: I followed the directions in order, so I drew a square in the center of the paper first.)

RETEACH
Decoding/Spelling

 **Words with Ending /ər/** Have students number a sheet of paper 1–17. Write *dollar* on the board and point to the letters that make the /ər/ sound. Tell students that in the first five words you will dictate, the /ər/ sound is spelled *-ar*. After students write each word, display it so they can proofread their work. Repeat this activity, using the examples *tinker* and *horror*.

202 Lesson 17 • *Turn It Up!*

Day 4

1. lunar	2. cellar	3. collar	4. regular
5. sugar	6. corner	7. danger	8. finger
9. master	10. checkers	11. power	12. director
13. doctor	14. honor	15. labor	16. motor
17. ancestor			

GUIDED PRACTICE Have students turn to *Practice Book* page 70 and complete the activity.

RETEACH
Build Robust Vocabulary

Words from "The Artist's Life" Review the meanings of the words *original*, *budge*, and *wedge*. Then say the following sentences, and have students tell you which word describes each sentence. Have students explain their answers.

- Ms. West asked the student to write a new story that he did not copy from a book. (original)
- Alex's sister would not change her mind about which game she wanted to play, no matter how much Alex tried to convince her. (budge)
- Dad cut a piece of cake that was thick at one end and thin at the other. (wedge)

RETEACH
Grammar/Writing

Copying Master 68

Writing Form: Autobiographical Composition Remind students that an autobiographical composition is something an author writes about him- or herself. It gives hints about the writer's attitudes and opinions. Have a student read the top of *Copying Master 68*. Ask another volunteer to read the Student Model aloud as others follow along.

GUIDED PRACTICE Have students complete the exercises at the bottom of the page. Guide them in following the directions if they need help. Have volunteers share their responses with the class.

Fluency

pp. 172–178

Fluency Practice Have each student work with a partner to read passages from "The Artist's Life" aloud to each other. Students may select a passage that they enjoyed or choose one of the following options:

- Read page 172. (Total: 93 words)
- Read page 176. (Total: 103 words)

Encourage students to read the selected passage aloud to their partner three times. Have each student rate his or her reading on the 1–4 scale.

1	Need more practice
2	Pretty good
3	Good
4	Great!

"The Artist's Life" 203

Preteach for **LESSON 18**

DAY AT A GLANCE
Day 5

VOCABULARY
Preteach bountiful, vast, stature, relentless, roused, resourceful, intentions, inadvertently

COMPREHENSION
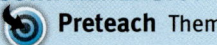 **Preteach** Theme

DECODING/WORD ATTACK
Preteach Decode Longer Words

DECODING/SPELLING
Preteach Word Parts *over-, under-, sub-*

GRAMMAR/WRITING
Preteach Adjectives

FLUENCY
Fluency Performance

Materials Needed: *Turn It Up!*

Student Edition pp. 172–178 | Skill Card 18 | Copying Master 69

PRETEACH
Vocabulary

Copying Master 69 **Lesson 18 Vocabulary** Distribute a set of Vocabulary Word Cards to each student. Hold up the card for the first word, and ask a volunteer to read it aloud. Have students repeat the word and hold up the matching card. Give the explanation for the word. Then ask students the first question below and discuss their responses. Continue for each of the Vocabulary Words.

- What would it be like to have a **bountiful** amount of money?
- What is a **vast** place you have visited?
- How much have you grown in **stature** since the first grade?
- When would it be a good time to be **relentless**?
- When was a time that you had to be **roused** from your sleep?
- What is a **resourceful** way to write if you don't have a pencil?
- What are your **intentions** for this afternoon?
- What is something that you might do **inadvertently**?

PRETEACH
Comprehension

Skill Card 18  **Theme** Have students look at side A of *Skill Card 18: Theme*. Have a volunteer read aloud the introductory paragraph. Tell students that the moral generally does not become clear until the end of the story. Then have students silently read the passage. Tell students that the setting, characters, and plot in a story work together to build the theme. Point to the chart and ask:

- **How does the setting add to the problem in this story?** (Possible response: The cottage was too small for Ocean and all his friends.)
- **How would the end of this story be different if Ocean had not invited all his friends?** (Possible response: Sun and Moon would not have moved.)
- **What did Ocean learn in this story?** (Possible response: He learned not to take advantage of his friends' kindness.)

204 Preteach for Lesson 18 • *Turn It Up!*

Day 5

PRETEACH

Decoding/Word Attack

Decode Longer Words Write *overheated* on the board. Divide the word into its word parts and ending. (over/heat/ed) Model blending these parts together to say the whole word. Tell students that the word parts *over, sub,* and *under* appear at the beginning of many longer words. Explain that recognizing word parts can help students read words that look unfamiliar at first. Write *overseeing, subscribe,* and *underhanded* on the board. Have volunteers identify the beginning word part in each word. Guide students to break the rest of each word into parts and read the whole word.

PRETEACH

Decoding/Spelling

Word Parts *over, under, sub* Write *overpass* on the board. Read the word aloud, and then draw a line between the word parts. (over/pass) Have students blend the parts to read the word. Repeat with *overreact, underwater,* and *submarine*. Help students to understand that when a word has two or more parts, knowing the separate word parts can help them know how to say or spell the word. Tell students that these are some of the next lesson's Spelling Words.

PRETEACH

Grammar/Writing

Adjectives Tell students that an adjective describes a noun or a pronoun. Adjectives tell what kind, how many, or which one. Write these sentences on the board:

> Frankie made four baskets in the game.
> Frankie is wearing red sneakers.

Guide students to identify the adjectives and identify what they tell about the nouns. (four: how many, red: what kind) Then erase the adjective in each sentence, and have students suggest different adjectives that will complete the sentence.

VOCABULARY

Student-Friendly Explanations

bountiful If you had a bountiful amount of something, you would have a lot of it.

vast A vast piece of land is very large.

stature Stature is how tall someone or something is.

relentless Something that is relentless goes on and on, and is often intense in some way.

roused To rouse people is to awaken or alert them.

resourceful A resourceful person is good at finding ways to solve problems.

intentions Things that a person plans to do are called intentions.

inadvertently If you do something inadvertently, you do it without meaning to.

Fluency

pp. 172–178 **Fluency Performance** Invite students to read aloud the passages from "The Artist's Life" that they selected and practiced earlier. Note the number of words each student reads correctly and incorrectly. Have students rate their own oral reading on the 1–4 scale. Give students the opportunity to continue practicing and then to read the passage to you again.

"The Artist's Life" 205

DAY AT A GLANCE

Day 1

VOCABULARY
Reteach *bountiful, vast, stature, relentless, roused, resourceful, intentions, inadvertently*

COMPREHENSION
Reteach Theme

DECODING/SPELLING
Reteach Word Parts *over-, under-, sub-*

GRAMMAR/WRITING
Preteach Adjectives

FLUENCY
Fluency Practice

Materials Needed: *Turn It Up!*

 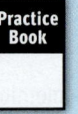  

| Student Edition pp. 180–181 | Practice Book p. 71 | Skill Card 18 | Copying Master 70 |

LESSON 18

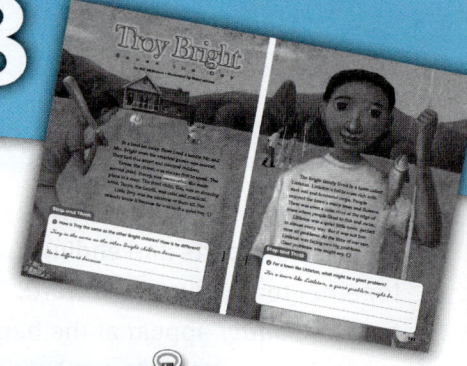

RETEACH
Vocabulary

Lesson 18 Vocabulary Read aloud the Vocabulary Words and the Student-Friendly Explanations. Then have students read the story on page 180 in their books. Guide students in completing the sentences on page 181 by selecting the correct Vocabulary Word from the list. Have a volunteer read each completed sentence aloud. If students are unable to give reasonable responses, refer to the Student-Friendly Explanations. (Answers for page 181: 2. *vast*, 3. *inadvertently*, 4. *relentless*, 5. *roused*, 6. *resourceful*, 7. *intentions*, 8. *stature*)

RETEACH
Comprehension

Theme Remind students that identifying the theme is an important skill they can apply when they read many different kinds of stories. Have students look at side B of *Skill Card 18: Theme*. Have students read the information aloud. Ask a volunteer to read the fable aloud. Remind students that the setting, characters, and plot in a story work together to build the theme. Ask:

- **What is the setting of this story?** (the woods)
- **Who are the characters in this story?** (Ant and Grasshopper)
- **What is the plot of the story?** (Ant works to gather food for the winter while Grasshopper sits in the sun. When winter comes, Ant has plenty of food, but Grasshopper is hungry.)

GUIDED PRACTICE Guide students in copying the chart and completing it. Remind students that thinking about what the characters learn can help them figure out the theme. (Possible response: Theme: Take time to prepare for the future.)

206 Lesson 18 • *Turn It Up!*

Day 1

RETEACH

Decoding/Spelling

Copying Master 70

Word Parts *over-, under-, sub-* Distribute *Copying Master 70*. Read the words aloud as students repeat them after you. Have students work in pairs. Ask each student to write a sentence for each Spelling Word but leave a blank for the actual word. The partners then switch papers and fill in the blanks in each other's sentences. Students should give themselves one point for each correctly spelled word.

PRETEACH

Grammar/Writing

Adjectives Remind students that an adjective describes a noun or pronoun. Tell them an adjective can come before the noun it describes or it can follow a verb such as *is* or *was*. Write these sentences on the board:

> The cold day made us shiver.
> The day was very cold.

Circle the adjective *cold* in both sentences. Point out that in both examples, the word describes the day. Point out how *cold* comes before the noun in the first sentence but comes after a verb in the second sentence.

GUIDED PRACTICE Write the following sentences on the board:

> The day was windy.
> Brian had on his green hat.
> Brian was happy that he had a hat.

Have students underline each adjective and circle the noun it describes. (Underline: windy, green, happy; Circle: day, hat, Brian)

VOCABULARY

Student-Friendly Explanations

bountiful If you had a bountiful amount of something, you would have a lot of it.

vast A vast piece of land is very large.

stature Stature is how tall someone or something is.

relentless Something that is relentless goes on and on, and is often intense in some way.

roused To rouse people is to awaken or alert them.

resourceful A resourceful person is good at finding ways to solve problems.

intentions Things that a person plans to do are called intentions.

inadvertently If you do something inadvertently, you do it without meaning to.

Fluency

Practice Book 71

Fluency Practice Have students turn to *Practice Book* page 71. Read the words in the first column aloud. Invite students to track each word and repeat the words after you. Then have students work in pairs to read the words in the first column aloud to each other. Follow the same procedure with each of the remaining columns. After partners have practiced reading aloud the words in each of the columns, have them practice reading all of the words.

"Troy Bright Saves the Day" 207

LESSON 18

DAY AT A GLANCE — Day 2

VOCABULARY
Reteach *bountiful, vast, stature, relentless, roused, resourceful, intentions, inadvertently*

COMPREHENSION
"Troy Bright Saves the Day"
Build Background
Monitor Comprehension
Answers to *Think Critically* Questions

DECODING/SPELLING
Reteach Word Parts *over-, under-, sub-*

GRAMMAR/WRITING
Preteach Articles

FLUENCY
Fluency Practice

Materials Needed: *Turn It Up!*

Student Edition
pp. 182–189

Practice Book
pp. 71, 72

Copying Masters
69, 70

30+ Minutes

RETEACH

Vocabulary

Lesson 18 Vocabulary   Distribute a set of Word Cards to each pair of students. Review the meaning of each word. Then have partners work together and write a sentence for each word. Challenge students to link their sentences to the preceding sentence in some way. Have students trade sentences and ask pairs to take turns reading the sentences aloud.

(Copying Master 69)

Comprehension

Build Background: "Troy Bright Saves the Day"
Ask students why it is important to get along with other people. How can people find a way to get along when they don't agree on something? How can the actions of one group affect another?

Monitor Comprehension: "Troy Bright Saves the Day"

pp. 182–183

Read the title of the story aloud. Then have students read pages 182–183 to find out who Troy Bright is and predict how he might save the day.

After reading the pages, ask: **Who is Troy Bright?** (Troy Bright is the youngest child in the Bright family. He is clever and quiet.) **How do you think he will save the day?** (Possible response: I think he will solve a problem that nobody else can solve.) **CHARACTER'S TRAITS**

Discuss the Stop and Think question on page 182: **How is Troy the same as the other Bright children? How is he different?** (Troy is the same as the other Bright children because he is also smart and talented. He is different because he is the youngest, he is the smartest, and he is quiet.) Guide students in writing the answer to this question. **COMPARE AND CONTRAST**

Discuss the Stop and Think question on page 183: **For a town like Littleton, what might be a giant problem?** (Possible response: For a town like Littleton, a giant problem might be something much bigger than they are.) Guide students in writing the answer to this question. **MAKE JUDGMENTS**

pp. 184–185

Discuss the Stop and Think question on page 184: **What does the author want you to know about the giants?** (The author wants me to know that the giants are like other people; they work hard and relax just like anyone else.) Guide students in writing the answer to this question. **AUTHOR'S PURPOSE**

208 Lesson 18 • Turn It Up!

Read aloud the last paragraph on page 184. Model the strategy of self-correcting by rereading and reading ahead.

THINK ALOUD The last part of this page says "when giants relax, it's not so relaxing for others nearby." I didn't understand the reason for this, but I guessed that finding out what the giants do for relaxation would be important to understanding the problem. The people of Littleton like to fish and swim, but the story did not tell what giants like to do when they relax. On the next page, it says that the giants sing their favorite tunes. Singing is one thing that the giants like to do. Then I read further to find out why their singing causes a problem. **SELF-CORRECT**

Discuss the Stop and Think question on page 185: **How do the giants cause problems for Littleton?** (The giants cause problems for Littleton when they sing too loudly and stir up a wind when they dance.) Guide students in writing the answer to this question. **SUMMARIZE**

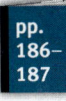
pp. 186–187

Discuss the Stop and Think question on page 186: **How would you solve Littleton's problems?** (Possible response: I would solve Littleton's problems by putting a tent around the town to keep out the wind and noise.) Guide students in writing the answer to this question. **EXPRESS PERSONAL OPINIONS**

Ask: **Why did everyone groan when even the Brights couldn't solve the problem?** (Possible response: The Brights were the smartest people around. If they couldn't solve the problem, then there was little chance anyone else could.) **MAKE INFERENCES**

Discuss the Stop and Think question on page 187: **What do you think Troy's big idea will be?** (Possible response: I think Troy's big idea will be to move the town of Littleton.) Guide students in writing the answer to this question. **MAKE PREDICTIONS**

page 188

Ask: **What do the people of Littleton learn from Troy?** (Possible responses: They learn that their neighbors are good people, and that they can work together to solve their problems; they learn that trees make a good barrier for wind and noise.) **DRAW CONCLUSIONS**

Discuss the Stop and Think question on page 188: **What message does the author want you to understand from this story?** (Possible response: The author wants me to understand that big problems need big ideas; problems with neighbors can be worked out; working together can solve many problems.) Guide students in writing the answer to this question. **THEME**

Day 2

VOCABULARY

Student-Friendly Explanations

bountiful If you had a bountiful amount of something, you would have a lot of it.

vast A vast piece of land is very large.

stature Stature is how tall someone or something is.

relentless Something that is relentless goes on and on, and is often intense in some way.

roused To rouse people is to awaken or alert them.

resourceful A resourceful person is good at finding ways to solve problems.

intentions Things that a person plans to do are called intentions.

inadvertently If you do something inadvertently, you do it without meaning to.

"Troy Bright Saves the Day" 209

Day 2

Spelling Words: Lesson 18

1. overactive
2. overbite
3. overboard
4. overdrive
5. overestimate
6. overhand
7. overheat
8. overpass
9. overreact
10. underline
11. underbrush
12. underdeveloped
13. undergo
14. underhand
15. underpass
16. underscore
17. underwater
18. submarine
19. subway
20. overact

page 189 **Answers to *Think Critically* Questions** Help students read and answer the *Think Critically* questions on page 189. Have students copy the graphic organizer in question 1 onto a separate sheet of paper. Then guide students in writing the answer to each question. Possible responses are provided.

1. [1.] Giants settle next to Littleton. [2.] The giants cause problems when they sing and dance. [3.] Troy goes to Bigville. [4.] Troy asks the giants to set up a forest to block out the noise and wind. **PLOT**

2. The giants plant a forest because it will protect Littleton from their noisy singing and windy dancing. **CAUSE AND EFFECT**

3. Troy is quiet, brave, creative, and very smart. **CHARACTER'S TRAITS**

RETEACH

Decoding/Spelling

Copying Master 70 **Word Parts *over-*, *under-*, *sub-*** Distribute *Copying Master 70* to pairs of students. For each word, have them write the prefix on one index card and the root word on another. Have them shuffle the cards and place them facedown on a table. Tell partners to take turns turning up two cards at a time. If the two cards form a Spelling Word, the student spells the word aloud, keeps the pair, and takes another turn. If the cards are not a Spelling Word, they are placed facedown again, and it is the partner's turn. The game ends when all the cards are matched.

210 Lesson 18 • Turn It Up!

Day 2

PRETEACH

Grammar/Writing

Practice Book 72

Articles Tell students that *a, an,* and *the* are special adjectives called *articles*. Explain that *a* and *an* refer to any person, place, or thing. *A* is used before a noun that begins with a consonant sound. *An* is used before a noun that begins with a vowel sound. Point out that *the* refers to a specific person, place, or thing. Write the following sentence frames on the board:

> I ate _____ orange.
> I would like _____ banana.

Guide students to choose an article to complete each sentence. (an, a) Now replace each with *the*. Point out how the sentences now refer to a specific orange or banana.

GUIDED PRACTICE Direct students attention to page 72 in their *Practice Book*. Invite volunteers to read the directions aloud. Ask students to work in pairs to complete the activities. Have pairs share their answers.

Fluency

Practice Book 71

Fluency Practice Invite students to look at the bottom half of *Practice Book* page 71. These sentences have been broken into natural phrases. Tell students to repeat each phrase after you, mirroring your expression, phrasing, and pace. After students have repeated each sentence, invite them to practice reading the sentences to partners.

"Troy Bright Saves the Day" 211

LESSON 18

DAY AT A GLANCE — Day 3

COMPREHENSION
Preteach Narrative Forms
Reread and Summarize "Troy Bright Saves the Day"

DECODING/SPELLING
Reteach Word Parts *over-*, *under-*, *sub-*

BUILD ROBUST VOCABULARY
Teach Words from "Troy Bright Saves the Day"

GRAMMAR/WRITING
Reteach Writing Trait: Ideas

FLUENCY
Fluency Practice

Materials Needed: *Turn It Up!*

Student Edition pp. 182–188 | Practice Book pp. 71, 73 | Copying Master 71

PRETEACH
Comprehension

Narrative Forms Distribute *Copying Master 71*. Have students read the information at the top of the page with you. Go over each narrative form with students. Ask students to tell about examples of each type of narrative form that they have read.

GUIDED PRACTICE Have students complete *Copying Master 71* on their own. Allow time for students to share their responses with the group.

Reread and Summarize Have students reread and summarize "Troy Bright Saves the Day" in sections, as described below.

 Let's reread pages 182–183 to recall what the characters in this story are like and where the story takes place.
Summary: The Brights are a smart family. All five of the Bright children are clever and talented. They live in a quiet little town, but they are facing a giant problem.

 Let's reread pages 184–185 to recall what the giant problem is.
Summary: New neighbors, giant neighbors, move in across the river. They make a lot of noise singing, and they stir up a great wind with their dancing. This is a problem for Littleton.

 Let's reread pages 186–188 to recall how the problem is solved.
Summary: Troy Bright saves the day by having a talk with the giants. Bigville agrees to build a forest between the towns, so the noise won't be as loud and the dancing won't cause a wind.

RETEACH
Decoding/Spelling

Word Parts *over-*, *under-*, *sub-* Write *over*, *sub*, and *under* in one column on the board. Write *water*, *act*, and *marine* in another column. Have students draw a line connecting each prefix to a root word to make a Spelling Word. (overact, submarine, underwater) Ask students to write each word on the board. Have them underline the beginning word parts and circle the root words.

212 Lesson 18 • Turn It Up!

Day 3

TEACH

Build Robust Vocabulary

pp. 182–188

Words from "Troy Bright Saves the Day" Have students locate the word *practical* on page 182 of "Troy Bright Saves the Day." Ask a volunteer to read aloud the sentence in which this word appears. (Line 7: *Tanya, the fourth, was calm and practical.*) Explain that *practical* means that Tanya had ideas that would really work. Continue by asking students to locate and read aloud the sentence on page 186 in which *suggested* appears. (Line 4: *He suggested they put cotton in their ears to block out the noise.*) Explain that this means that Trevor shared his idea. Then ask students to locate and read aloud the sentence on page 188 in which *drifts* appears. (Line 8: *Now, sometimes at night, music drifts over the trees and across the river.*) Explain that this sentence means that the music floats along slowly on the air. Things can also drift on water.

Ask each student to write the words on cards. Ask a volunteer to close his or her eyes and hold up one card without peeking. Have another student look at the word and say its meaning. Have the student holding the card tell what the word is and then open his or her eyes to check. Repeat several times.

RETEACH

Grammar/Writing

Practice Book 73

Writing Trait: Ideas Tell students that when writing to persuade, every sentence should focus on that purpose. Recall how the author of "Troy Bright Saves the Day" gives reasons why the giants should build a forest. Have students turn to page 73 in their *Practice Book*. Ask a student to read the directions aloud. Then read the paragraph together. Guide students to identify the sentence that does not focus on the main idea.

GUIDED PRACTICE Work with students to complete the rest of Part A. Have a volunteer read the Part B directions. Have students complete the section, and share their responses as a group. Then read the Part C directions and have students write sentences of their own. Invite students to share what they wrote.

Fluency

Practice Book 71

Fluency Practice Tell students that today they will reread the sentences on the bottom of *Practice Book* page 71. Have students locate and point to the first sentence. Tell students that everyone is going to read the sentence together. This choral reading will give students an opportunity to hear others and listen to the natural phrasing of the sentences. Choral-read each of the sentences several times.

"Troy Bright Saves the Day" 213

LESSON 18

DAY AT A GLANCE
Day 4

COMPREHENSION
Reteach Narrative Forms

DECODING/SPELLING
Reteach Word Parts *over, under, sub*

BUILD ROBUST VOCABULARY
Reteach Words from "Troy Bright Saves the Day"

GRAMMAR/WRITING
Reteach Writing Form: Persuasive Composition

FLUENCY
Fluency Practice

Materials Needed: *Turn It Up!*

Student Edition pp. 182–188

Practice Book p. 74

Copying Master 72

Spelling Words: Lesson 18

1. overactive	11. underbrush
2. overbite	12. underdeveloped
3. overboard	13. undergo
4. overdrive	14. underhand
5. overestimate	15. underpass
6. overhand	16. underscore
7. overheat	17. underwater
8. overpass	18. submarine
9. overreact	19. subway
10. underline	20. overact

30+ Minutes

RETEACH
Comprehension

Narrative Forms Review narrative forms and their features. Then write the following story idea on the board: *This story is about a girl who goes up into a castle to ask an ogre for a favor.* Have students identify the narrative form the author is likely to use. (fairy tale) If necessary, have students refer to Copying Master 71 to help them remember the kinds of narrative forms.

GUIDED PRACTICE Write the following story ideas on the board:

> This story tells how the moon knows what size to be in the night sky.
>
> This story is about a baby who could walk when he was just a week old.

Have students work in small groups. Ask them to read each idea and explain the kind of narrative form the writer is likely to use to tell each story. (pourquoi tale, tall tale) Encourage groups to explain their choices.

RETEACH
Decoding/Spelling

Word Parts *over, under, sub* Tell students to number a sheet of paper 1–17. Write *overboard* on the board, and point to the prefix. Tell students that the first nine words you will dictate begin with *over*. After students write each word, display it so they can proofread their work. Repeat this activity for the other words using these examples: *underpass* and *subway*.

1. overactive	2. overestimate	3. overpass
4. overact	5. overbite	6. overdrive
7. overhand	8. overheat	9. overreact
10. underscore	11. underwater	12. underhand
13. undergo	14. underdeveloped	15. underbrush
16. underline	17. submarine	

Have students turn to page 74 in their *Practice Book*. Ask a volunteer to read the passage aloud. Guide them to find and circle all the words that begin with *over, under,* and *sub*. Then have them finish the bottom of the page independently. Allow time for students to share their answers with the group.

214 Lesson 18 • Turn It Up!

Day 4

RETEACH
Build Robust Vocabulary

Words from "Troy Bright Saves the Day" Review the meanings of *practical, suggested,* and *drifted*. Then say these sentences and ask which word describes each sentence. Have students explain why.

- **I need an idea that will really work to help me keep my room neat.** (practical)
- **The little boat floated slowly down the stream.** (drifted)
- **Megan shared her idea about going on a family picnic.** (suggested)

RETEACH
Grammar/Writing

Copying Master 72

Writing Form: Persuasive Composition Tell students that one reason for writing is to convince others to do something or take action. Explain that it's important to keep their ideas focused and organized in order to persuade others. Distribute *Copying Master 72*. Have a volunteer read the description of a persuasive composition. Then read the selection and margin notes together.

GUIDED PRACTICE Invite a volunteer to find the argument in the selection. Tell students that the first sentence clearly states what the author wants the readers to do. Then work together to answer the rest of the questions.

Fluency

pp. 182–188

Fluency Practice Have each student work with a partner to read passages from "Troy Bright Saves the Day" aloud to each other. Students may select a passage that they enjoyed or choose one of the following options:

- Read page 183. (Total: 81 words)
- Read page 186. (Total: 90 words)

Encourage students to read the selected passage aloud to their partner three times. Have the student rate his or her reading on the 1–4 scale.

1	Need more practice
2	Pretty good
3	Good
4	Great!

"Troy Bright Saves the Day" **215**

Preteach for LESSON 19

Day 5

VOCABULARY
Preteach magnificent, insisted, declared, confidently, distressed, gloated, anxiously

COMPREHENSION
 Preteach Theme

DECODING/WORD ATTACK
Preteach Decode Longer Words

DECODING/SPELLING
Preteach Words with Irregular Plurals and Possessives

GRAMMAR/WRITING
Preteach Comparing with Adjectives

FLUENCY
Fluency Performance

Materials Needed: *Turn It Up!*

Student Edition pp. 182–188 | Copying Master 73

PRETEACH

Vocabulary

Lesson 19 Vocabulary Distribute a set of Vocabulary Word Cards to each student. Hold up the card for the first word, and ask a volunteer to read it. Have students repeat the word and hold up the matching card. Give the explanation for the word. Then ask students the first question below and discuss their responses. Continue for each of the Vocabulary Words.

- What part of nature do you think is **magnificent**?
- What might happen if you **insisted** on walking backward?
- What might be **declared** at a sports event?
- What topic can you speak **confidently** about?
- How might a **distressed** pet act?
- Have you ever **gloated** about winning? How did you feel afterward?
- What would you do if you were **anxiously** waiting for a letter?

PRETEACH

Comprehension

 **Theme** Explain that knowing the setting and characters' words and actions helps readers to recognize the theme. Students can understand an unstated theme by thinking about what the main character learns or how the problem gets solved. Ask students to recall "Troy Bright Saves the Day." Then ask:

- **What is the setting of the story?** (the town of Littleton, a quiet, almost perfect little town near the new town of Bigville)
- **Who are the characters in this story?** (Mr. and Mrs. Bright, Trevor, Tracey, Tim, Tanya, and Troy; the townspeople of Littleton; the giants of Bigville)
- **What is the problem in the story?** (The giants' singing voices are too loud and when they dance they create a wind, so the people of Littleton have to hide in their houses.)
- **How is the problem solved?** (Troy suggests that the giants plant more giant trees to block the wind and noise.)
- **What is the theme of this story?** (Big problems need big ideas, even if they are from little children.)

Tell students that there might be more than one theme for a story. Discuss with students other possible themes, based on what other characters in the story say and do about the problem.

216 Preteach for Lesson 19 • *Turn It Up!*

Day 5

PRETEACH

Decoding/Word Attack

Decode Longer Words Write *goldfishes* on the board. Have a volunteer read it aloud. Ask students to name letters that stand for the inflected ending. (*-es*) Then have a student name the singular form of goldfishes. (*goldfish*) Repeat the procedure with *fixtures*. Explain that words that end in inflections *-s* or *-es* are the plural forms of some words.

PRETEACH

Decoding/Spelling

Words with Irregular Plurals and Possessives Explain that an apostrophe and *s* are usually added to plural nouns to form the possessive, as in the Spelling Words *baby's, class's, mouse's,* and *woman's*. If the plural noun ends in *s*, then just add an apostrophe, such as in *babies', classes',* and *fishes'*. Help students understand that some nouns stay in the same form for singular and plural, such as *sheep* and *moose*.

PRETEACH

Grammar/Writing

Comparing with Adjectives Write the following sentences on the board:

> My dog is small, but your dog is smaller.
>
> The book is funny, but this book is funniest of all.

Read the sentences aloud with students. Tell students that the first sentence compares two things, so *-er* is added. Explain that the second sentence compares more than two things, so *-est* is added. Explain that when an adjective ends in *-y*, the *y* is changed to *i* before *-er* or *-est* is added.

VOCABULARY

Student-Friendly Explanations

magnificent Something magnificent is very beautiful and impressive.

insisted If you insisted on something, you said it very firmly and you refused to change your mind.

declared Something that has been declared has been announced in a clear way.

confidently When you do something confidently, you are sure about what you are doing.

distressed Someone who is distressed feels very sad and helpless.

gloated If someone gloated, he or she bragged about something in a mean way.

anxiously If you waited anxiously for something, you worried about how it would turn out.

Fluency

pp. 182–188 **Fluency Performance** Invite students each to read aloud from "Troy Bright Saves the Day" a passage that they selected and practiced earlier. Note the number of words each student reads correctly and incorrectly. Have students rate their own oral reading on the 1–4 scale. Give each student the opportunity to continue practicing and then to read the passage to you again.

"Troy Bright Saves the Day" 217

LESSON 19

VOCABULARY
Reteach *magnificent, insisted, declared, confidently, distressed, gloated, anxiously*

COMPREHENSION
 Reteach Theme

DECODING/SPELLING
Reteach Words with Irregular Plurals and Possessives

GRAMMAR/WRITING
Preteach Comparing with Adjectives

FLUENCY
Fluency Practice

Materials Needed: *Turn It Up!*

  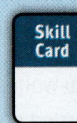 

Student Edition pp. 190–191 | Practice Book p. 75 | Skill Card 19 | Copying Master 74

RETEACH
Vocabulary

Lesson 19 Vocabulary Read aloud the Vocabulary Words and the Student-Friendly Explanations. Read the story aloud on pages 190–191. Guide students to complete the story by selecting the correct Vocabulary Word from the list. If students have difficulty choosing the correct word, refer to the Student-Friendly Explanations. Invite volunteers to reread each sentence with the correct word. Then ask students to read aloud the completed story. (Answers for pages 190–191: 2. *magnificent*, 3. *gloated*, 4. *insisted*, 5. *distressed*, 6. *anxiously*, 7. *confidently*)

RETEACH
Comprehension

  **Theme** Have students look at side A of *Skill Card 19: Theme*. Have a volunteer read aloud the definition. Then have another volunteer read the passage aloud. Point out the chart. Explain that this chart shows the characters' actions and motivations, as well as the theme or message. Ask:

- What actions do the characters perform that reveal the theme?
- What motivations do the characters have for their actions?
- Based on these actions and motivations, what is the theme?

Remind students that a story might have more than one theme.

GUIDED PRACTICE Now have students look at side B of *Skill Card 19: Theme*. Ask volunteers to read aloud the information and the story. Guide students as they copy the chart and complete it. Invite volunteers to share their responses. (Possible responses: Characters' Actions: Ted offers to help look for the car. Ted looks in many places. Ted finds the car. Characters' Motivations: Ted wants to be helpful. Theme: When we work together, we win.)

218 Lesson 19 • Turn It Up!

Day 1

RETEACH

Decoding/Spelling

Copying Master 74

Words with Irregular Plurals and Possessives Distribute *Copying Master 74*. Echo-read the Spelling Words with students. Then have students work in pairs. Each student writes a sentence for each Spelling Word but leaves a blank for the actual word. The partners then switch papers and fill in the blanks in each other's sentences. Students should give themselves one point for each correctly spelled word.

PRETEACH

Grammar/Writing

Comparing with Adjectives Explain that for longer adjectives *more* and *most* are added when making comparisons. Write the following sentence on the board:

> The dress my sister wore is <u>more</u> glamorous than mine.

Invite a volunteer to read the sentence aloud. Explain that *glamorous* is an adjective. Tell students that since it is a longer word, *more* is used with it to compare one thing with another. Then write this sentence on the board:

> That woman wore the <u>most</u> glamorous dress at the party.

Have a volunteer read aloud the sentence. Tell students that *most* is used with longer adjectives when comparing to two or more things.

GUIDED PRACTICE Write the following sentences on the board:

> Bananas are _____ popular than oranges.
> We saw the _____ amazing fireworks ever!

Invite students to add *more* or *most* to each sentence. (more, most)

VOCABULARY

Student-Friendly Explanations

magnificent Something magnificent is very beautiful and impressive.

insisted If you insisted on something, you said it very firmly and you refused to change your mind.

declared Something that has been declared has been announced in a clear way.

confidently When you do something confidently, you are sure about what you are doing.

distressed Someone who is distressed feels very sad and helpless.

gloated If someone gloated, he or she bragged about something in a mean way.

anxiously If you waited anxiously for something, you worried about how it would turn out.

Fluency

Practice Book 75

Fluency Practice Have students turn to *Practice Book* page 75. Read the words in the first column aloud. Invite students to track each word and repeat the words after you. Then have students work in pairs to read the words in the first column aloud to each other. Follow the same procedure with each of the remaining columns. After partners have practiced reading aloud the words in each of the columns, have them practice reading all of the words.

"An Awful Mess" 219

LESSON 19

30+ Minutes

DAY AT A GLANCE — Day 2

VOCABULARY
Reteach magnificent, insisted, declared, confidently, distressed, gloated, anxiously

COMPREHENSION
"An Awful Mess"
Build Background
Monitor Comprehension
Answers to *Think Critically* Questions

DECODING/SPELLING
Reteach Possessive Pictures

GRAMMAR/WRITING
Preteach Comparing with Adjectives

FLUENCY
Fluency Practice

Materials Needed: *Turn It Up!*

Student Edition
pp. 192–199

Practice Book
pp. 75, 76

Copying Masters
73, 74

RETEACH

Vocabulary

Copying Master 73

Lesson 19 Vocabulary Divide the group into teams. Provide each team with a set of Vocabulary Word Cards. Read a definition from the Student-Friendly Explanations aloud, without stating the word. Have each team decide which word fits the definition and send one team member to the board to write it. Tell students that each team member must write at least one word. Repeat definitions as necessary to provide all students with several opportunities to write a Vocabulary Word.

Comprehension

Build Background: "An Awful Mess"
Ask students to share their experiences with making a mess that needed to be cleaned up. Did they make the mess by themselves or with others? Did they clean it up alone or with help? What did they learn from the experience?

pp. 192–198

Monitor Comprehension: "An Awful Mess"
Read the title of the story aloud. Then have students read pages 192–193 to find out about the setting for the story.

After reading the pages, ask: **What is the setting for the story?** (Possible responses: It is a hot, humid day at the end of a workday; The characters are on a lawn.) **NOTE DETAILS**

Have students think about the actions of the workers. Ask: **How do the workers behave when they see the nice lawn?** (Possible responses: When the workers see the lawn, they each say they saw it first. They act selfishly.) **How do you think they should behave?** (Possible response: I think they should all be willing to share the lawn. They should say that they all found it together.) **EXPRESS PERSONAL OPINIONS**

Discuss the Stop and Think question on page 192: **How do you know the workers take a nap?** (Possible response: I know this because the last line says they fell asleep.) Guide students in writing the answer to this question. **NOTE DETAILS**

Discuss the Stop and Think question on page 193: **Why are the workers upset?** (Possible response: The workers are upset because they slept too long and their feet are tangled.) Guide students in writing the answer to this question. **CAUSE AND EFFECT**

---

220 Lesson 19 • *Turn It Up!*

Day 2

pp. 194-195

Discuss the Stop and Think question on page 194: **How do the workers act when they discover they have a problem?** (Possible response: When the workers discover they have a problem, they cry and fight about it.) Guide students in writing the answer to this question. **THEME**

Ask: **Why does Paula tease the workers?** (Possible response: Paula teases the workers because she thinks they are not serious about being stuck and might be teasing her.) **DRAW CONCLUSIONS**

Discuss the Stop and Think question on page 195: **What do you think will happen next?** (Possible response: I think Paula will help the workers.) Guide students in writing the answer to this question. **MAKE PREDICTIONS**

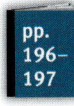
pp. 196-197

Discuss the Stop and Think question on page 196: **How do you think these workers usually act when they have a problem?** (Possible response: I think the workers usually worry too much and cry.) Guide students in writing the answer to this question. **GENERALIZE**

Discuss the Stop and Think question on page 197: **How would you describe Paula?** (Possible responses: Paula is clever, helpful, smart, and calm.) Guide students in writing the answer to this question. **CHARACTER'S TRAITS**

page 198

Discuss the Stop and Think question on page 198: **How does the author make you laugh with this story?** (Possible response: The author makes me laugh when he tells about the silly things the rabbits do.) Guide students in writing the answer to this question. **AUTHOR'S PURPOSE**

Read aloud page 198. Model the strategy of recognizing a message or moral in the story.

THINK ALOUD When I read that the workers think they have learned a lesson, I wondered what it might be. The workers say that they learned to never, ever fall asleep on the lawn. But I expected that they might have learned to stay calm to solve a problem or maybe they learned that they need to work together to solve problems. I think this is what the author wants readers to learn. **THEME**

VOCABULARY
Student-Friendly Explanations

magnificent Something magnificent is very beautiful and impressive.

insisted If you insisted on something, you said it very firmly and you refused to change your mind.

declared Something that has been declared has been announced in a clear way.

confidently When you do something confidently, you are sure about what you are doing.

distressed Someone who is distressed feels very sad and helpless.

gloated If someone gloated, he or she bragged about something in a mean way.

anxiously If you waited anxiously for something, you worried about how it would turn out.

"An Awful Mess" 221

Day 2

Spelling Words: Lesson 19

1.	babies'	11.	fishes'
2.	baby's	12.	goose's
3.	child's	13.	geese
4.	children	14.	jeans
5.	classes'	15.	mouse's
6.	class's	16.	mice
7.	sheep	17.	teeth
8.	feet	18.	women
9.	elk	19.	woman's
10.	fish	20.	moose

Answers to *Think Critically* Questions Help students read and answer the *Think Critically* questions on page 199. Have students copy the graphic organizer in question 3 onto a separate sheet of paper. Then guide students in writing the answer to each question. Possible responses are provided.

1. Paula helps the rabbits when she pokes each foot. Then the rabbits can tell which foot belongs to whom. PLOT
2. The rabbits are silly, foolish, and make a big deal out of things. CHARACTERS' TRAITS
3. [Theme] It is best to stay calm when solving a problem. THEME

RETEACH

Decoding/Spelling

Possessive Pictures Have students work in small groups. Write the following pairs of phrases on the board. Ask group members to write the phrase pairs on strips of paper. Suggest that students refer to *Copying Master 74* to check spellings.

> the jacket of the woman/the jackets of the women
>
> the wing of the goose/the wings of the geese
>
> the teacher of the class/the teachers of the classes
>
> the field of the sheep/the fields of the sheep

Invite group members to take turns writing the possessive forms of the noun phrases. (the woman's jacket/the women's jackets; the goose's wing/the geese's wings; the class's teacher/the classes' teachers; the sheep's field/the sheep's fields) Ask each student to choose one set of phrases and draw side-by-side pictures to illustrate both. Have students share their drawings.

Day 2

PRETEACH

Grammar/Writing

Practice Book 76

Comparing with Adjectives Write *better, best, worse,* and *worst* on the board. Explain that these words are the comparative forms of *good* and *bad*. Point out that these comparative adjectives are never used with *more* or *most*. Explain that *better* and *worse* compare two things while *best* and *worst* compare more than two things.

GUIDED PRACTICE Direct students to page 76 in their *Practice Books*. Invite a volunteer to read the sentence with the correct comparison word and write the word on the board. Guide students to complete the rest of the sentences by circling and writing the correct words.

Fluency

Practice Book 75

Fluency Practice Invite students to look at the bottom half of *Practice Book* page 75. These sentences have been broken into natural phrases. Tell students to repeat each phrase after you, mirroring your expression, phrasing, and pace. After students have repeated each sentence, invite them to practice reading the sentences to a partner.

"An Awful Mess" 223

LESSON 19

DAY AT A GLANCE
Day 3

COMPREHENSION
Preteach Narrative Forms
Reread and Summarize "An Awful Mess"

DECODING/SPELLING
Reteach Use a Dictionary

BUILD ROBUST VOCABULARY
Teach Words from "An Awful Mess"

GRAMMAR/WRITING
Reteach Writing Trait: Ideas

FLUENCY
Fluency Practice

Materials Needed: *Turn It Up!*

Student Edition pp. 192–198

Practice Book pp. 75, 77

Copying Master 75

30+ Minutes

PRETEACH
Comprehension

Narrative Forms Distribute *Copying Master 75*. Have students read the information at the top of the page with you. Explain that characters, settings, and events might not be realistic in these narrative forms.

GUIDED PRACTICE Invite students to read the story with you. Point out that this is a fable. Guide students to complete the chart with the details from the story. Have volunteers share their responses.

Reread and Summarize Have students reread and summarize "An Awful Mess" in sections, as described below.

pp. 192–194

First, we will reread pages 192–194 to recall the awful mess the workers get into.
Summary: The workers fall asleep on the nice lawn for a nap. They oversleep and wake up with their feet tangled. They are afraid they will be stuck on the lawn forever.

pp. 195–196

Next, let's reread pages 195–196 to remember what Paula does and how she feels about it.
Summary: The workers are upset because they can't tell their feet apart. Paula teases the workers. This makes the workers even more upset. Paula regrets teasing them.

pp. 197–198

Finally, we will reread pages 197–198 to remember how the workers' problem is solved.
Summary: Paula pokes each foot with a stick so that each worker can draw in his or her foot and untangle their legs.

RETEACH
Decoding/Spelling

Use a Dictionary Explain to students that a dictionary allows them to check for the correct spelling of words. Write *elk, mouse, baby,* and *woman* on the board. Invite students to work in pairs to write the plural, singular possessive, and plural possessive form of each noun. Have them check the spelling in a dictionary. (elk, elk's, elk's; mice, mouse's, mice's; babies, baby's, babies'; women, woman's, women's)

224 Lesson 19 • Turn It Up!

Day 3

TEACH

Build Robust Vocabulary

pp. 192–193

Words from "An Awful Mess" Have students locate the word *humid* on page 192 of "An Awful Mess." Ask a volunteer to read aloud the sentence in which this word appears. (Line 3: *"It is so awfully hot and humid," said one*.) Explain that this sentence means that it was a hot and sticky day with lots of dampness in the air. Continue by asking students to locate and read aloud the sentence in which the word *bawled* appears on page 193. (Line 6: *"Wait! We can't go anyplace," bawled one*.) Explain that this means that the worker cried out with a loud voice. Then ask students to locate and read aloud the sentence in which the word *scrawny* appears on page 193. (Line 8: *There were ten scrawny feet*.) Explain that this sentence means that the feet were skinny.

Ask students: **Which word tells how something feels?** (humid) **Which tells how something sounds?** (bawled) **Which tells how something looks?** (scrawny) Have them explain their answers.

RETEACH

Grammar/Writing

Practice Book 77

Writing Trait: Ideas Ask students to turn to *Practice Book* page 77. Explain that all ideas in a fable need to be focused. Ask a volunteer to read the information at the top of the page. Point out how the author of "An Awful Mess" has focused his ideas and events to lead to the resolution of the conflict.

GUIDED PRACTICE Complete the activities on *Practice Book* page 77 together. Encourage volunteers to share the sentences they write.

Fluency

Practice Book 75

Fluency Practice Tell students that today they will reread the sentences on the bottom of *Practice Book* page 75. Have students locate and point to the first sentence. Tell students that everyone is going to read the sentence together. This choral reading will give students an opportunity to hear others and to listen to the natural phrasing of the sentences. Choral-read each sentence several times.

"An Awful Mess" 225

LESSON 19

DAY AT A GLANCE
Day 4

COMPREHENSION
Reteach Narrative Forms

DECODING/SPELLING
Reteach Words with Irregular Plurals and Possessives

BUILD ROBUST VOCABULARY
Reteach Words from "An Awful Mess"

GRAMMAR/WRITING
Reteach Writing Form: Fable

FLUENCY
Fluency Practice

Materials Needed: Turn It Up!

Student Edition pp. 192–198 | Practice Book p. 78 | Copying Master 76

Spelling Words: Lesson 19

1. babies'	11. fishes'
2. baby's	12. goose's
3. child's	13. geese
4. children	14. jeans
5. classes'	15. mouse's
6. class's	16. mice
7. sheep	17. teeth
8. feet	18. women
9. elk	19. woman's
10. fish	20. moose

30+ Minutes

RETEACH
Comprehension

Narrative Forms Remind students that there are a variety of imaginative narrative forms that authors use in literature. These include fables, folktales, fairy tales, myths, tall tales, and pourquoi tales. These forms have settings and characters that might not seem realistic, and events that would not really happen. Have volunteers read page 192 of "An Awful Mess" and explain what seems unrealistic. (Jackrabbits do not really use saws and work at jobs; jackrabbits do not really speak.)

pp. 192–198

RETEACH
Decoding/Spelling

Words with Irregular Plurals and Possessives Have students number a sheet of paper 1–16. Write *sheep* on the board. Tell students that the first four words you will dictate are spelled the same for both the singular and plural form. After students write each word, display the word so they can proofread their spellings. Then write *children* on the board. Explain that the next five words will be words that change their spelling in the plural form. Then list *baby's* and *babies'* on the board. Tell students that the last seven words will be singular and plural possessive forms.

Practice Book 78

1. elk	2. fish	3. jeans	4. moose
5. feet	6. geese	7. mice	8. teeth
9. women	10. child's	11. classes'	12. class's
13. fishes'	14. goose's	15. mouse's	16. woman's

Ask students to turn to *Practice Book* page 78. Have students read the first set of sentences and look at the picture. Guide students to choose the sentence that best describes the picture. Have students complete the remaining sentences.

226 Lesson 19 • Turn It Up!

Day 4

RETEACH
Build Robust Vocabulary

Words from "An Awful Mess" Review the meanings of the words *humid*, *bawled*, and *scrawny*. Then say these sentences and ask which word describes each sentence. Have students explain why.

- Liz's hair gets frizzy on sticky, damp days. (humid)
- "Run!" the coach cried out loudly. (bawled)
- The stray cat looked too thin, so Pam gave him some good food. (scrawny)

RETEACH
Grammar/Writing

Copying Master 76

Writing Form: Fable Distribute *Copying Master 76* to students. Choose a volunteer to read the instruction at the top of the page. Explain that the moral is usually stated clearly in a fable. Read aloud the Student Model together with the students. Write on the board the following sentence from the passage:

> "Basketball is an exciting sport for roosters."

Explain that this sentence does not lead to the moral. Model for students how to improve this sentence:

> "Looking good for basketball is important to roosters."

GUIDED PRACTICE Guide students to complete the activities on the bottom of the page. Invite volunteers to share their responses.

Fluency

pp. 192–198

Fluency Practice Have each student work with a partner to read passages from "An Awful Mess" aloud to each other. Students may select a passage that they enjoyed or choose one of the following options:

- Read page 193. (Total: 81 words)
- Read page 197. (Total: 92 words)

Encourage students to read the selected passage aloud to their partner three times. Have the student rate his or her reading on the 1–4 scale.

1	Need more practice
2	Pretty good
3	Good
4	Great!

"An Awful Mess"

Preteach for LESSON 20

DAY AT A GLANCE
Day 5

VOCABULARY
Preteach *ominous, confound, miserable, gracious, beams, self-assurance, monitor, exposed, installed, looming*

COMPREHENSION
 Preteach Theme

DECODING/WORD ATTACK
Preteach Decode Longer Words

DECODING/SPELLING
Preteach Words with Ending /əl/

GRAMMAR/WRITING
Preteach Pronouns

FLUENCY
Fluency Performance

Materials Needed: *Turn It Up!*

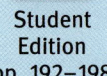
Student Edition pp. 192–198

Skill Card 20

Copying Master 77

PRETEACH

Vocabulary

Copying Master 77 — **Lesson 20 Vocabulary** Distribute a set of Vocabulary Word Cards to each student. Hold up the card for the first word, and have a student read it aloud. Have other students repeat the word and hold up the matching card. Give the explanation for the word. Then ask students the first question below and discuss their responses. Continue for each of the Vocabulary Words.

- Why is a car on the side of the road **ominous**?
- What game do you play that can **confound** you?
- How might a sprained ankle make you feel **miserable**?
- When was the last time you did something **gracious**?
- If your mom **beams** at you, what might you have just done?
- What is something you do that shows you have **self-assurance**?
- How would you **monitor** the amount of snow that falls?
- What could happen if you were **exposed** to a foreign language?
- Why might someone have **installed** a new washing machine?
- How do you feel when you see a thunderstorm **looming** in the distance?

PRETEACH

Comprehension

 **Theme** On side A of *Skill Card 20: Review—Theme,* have a student read the information at the top. Remind students that knowing what a story's theme is will help readers better understand the story. Have a volunteer read aloud the passage. Ask:

- **What does the reader learn from this fable?** (Possible response: Just because something doesn't go your way doesn't mean it isn't good.)
- **How does knowing the setting, characters, and plot help you understand the theme of this fable?** (Possible response: I understand that though the fox couldn't reach the grapes, that doesn't mean they are sour.)

GUIDED PRACTICE Guide students in copying the chart onto a separate sheet of paper. Have them fill in the chart. (Setting: orchard; Character: fox; Plot: The fox tries hard but can't reach grapes.; Theme: Don't be a sore loser.) Ask students if they ever wanted something, but when they didn't get it, they said they didn't want it anymore.

228 Preteach for Lesson 20 • *Turn It Up!*

Day 5

PRETEACH
Decoding/Word Attack

Decode Longer Words Write *singer* on the board and read it aloud. Have students repeat it and tell how many syllables they hear. (2) Review which letters stand for the /ər/ ending. (er) Have students tell you what the root word is. (sing) Remind students they can use their knowledge of inflected endings to decode a word. Repeat the activity with these words: *monitor, polar, dipper*.

PRETEACH
Decoding/Spelling

Words with Ending /əl/ Write the words *arrival, gentle, national, single,* and *level* on the board. Have students read each word aloud as you circle the letters that stand for the /əl/ sound. Point out that there are several spellings for the /əl/ sound. Explain to students that they must memorize which spelling goes with each word.

PRETEACH
Grammar/Writing

Pronouns Review the types of pronouns listed below. Then guide students to give examples of each type of pronoun, and write them on the board.

Subject pronouns: *I, you, he, she, it, we, you, they*
Object pronouns: *me, us, them, you, him, her, it*
Possessive pronouns: *my, his, her, your, our, their, its*
Possessive pronouns that stand alone: *his, hers, mine, yours, ours, theirs*
Reflexive pronouns: *himself, herself, itself, myself, yourself, themselves, ourselves, yourselves*

Then write the following sentences on the board:

> Gary and I were ready to play with it.
> We asked Mark to bring a game with him.
> He wanted to play with us, too.

Have students draw a circle around each subject pronoun and a box around each object pronoun. (circle *I*, box *it*; circle *We*, box *him*; circle *He*, box *us*)

VOCABULARY
Student-Friendly Explanations

ominous Something ominous is a sign of trouble or a warning.

confound If you confound a person, you surprise or confuse him.

miserable A person who feels miserable feels uncomfortable and unhappy.

gracious Someone who is gracious is pleasant and polite.

beams Someone who beams is grinning.

self-assurance People who have self-assurance are confident and sure of themselves.

monitor When you monitor something, you regularly check its progress.

exposed A thing that has been exposed has been uncovered and lost its protection from its surroundings.

installed If you installed a piece of equipment, you put it in to make it ready for use.

looming When an event is looming, it seems likely to happen soon.

Fluency

pp. 192–198
Fluency Performance Invite students each to read aloud from "An Awful Mess" a passage that they practiced earlier. Note the number of words each student reads correctly. Have each students rate their own reading on the 1–4 scale. Have each student continue practicing and then read the passage to you again.

"An Awful Mess" 229

LESSON 20

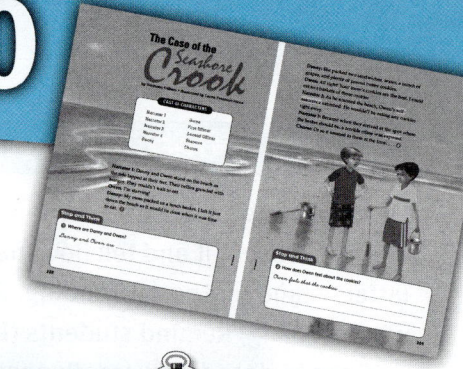

DAY AT A GLANCE — Day 1

VOCABULARY
Reteach ominous, confound, miserable, gracious, beams, self-assurance, monitor, exposed, installed, looming

COMPREHENSION
 Preteach Fact and Opinion

DECODING/WORD ATTACK
Reteach Decode Longer Words

DECODING/SPELLING
Preteach Words with Ending /ər/

GRAMMAR/WRITING
Reteach Pronouns

FLUENCY
Fluency Practice

Materials Needed: *Turn It Up!*

Student Edition pp. 200–201 | Practice Book pp. 79, 80 | Skill Card 20 | Copying Master 78

RETEACH: Vocabulary

Lesson 20 Vocabulary (pp. 200–201) Read aloud the Vocabulary Words and the Student-Friendly Explanations. The have students turn to pages 200–201 in their books. Ask a student to read the directions aloud. Remind students that they should read each sentence to themselves with the word they chose to be sure it makes sense. If students have difficulty choosing the correct word, refer to the Student-Friendly Explanations. After students have completed the pages, have volunteers take turns reading aloud each sentence. (Answers for pages 200–201: 2. *gracious*, 3. *beams*, 4. *self-assurance*, 5. *miserable*, 6. *installed*, 7. *looming*, 8. *monitor*, 9. *confound*, 10. *ominous*, 11.–12. Responses will vary.)

PRETEACH: Comprehension

 **Fact and Opinion** On side B of *Skill Card 20: Review—Fact and Opinion*, ask a student to read the Skill Reminder. Then have a volunteer read the passage aloud as students follow along. Remind students that writers use facts and opinions while writing nonfiction to make it more interesting. Discuss with students facts and opinions from the article. Ask: **How do Red Sox fans feel about their team?** (Possible response: They think their team is the greatest.) Guide students to understand how to distinguish fact from opinion. Remind them that signal words sometimes guide readers to opinions.

GUIDED PRACTICE Guide students in copying the chart and completing it. (Possible facts: (1) In 1920 the Red Sox sold Babe Ruth to the Yankees. (2) They went 86 years without a World Series win. (3) The Red Sox fans would wait until 2004 for a World Series win. (4) The Red Sox beat the Cardinals. Evidence: History books, encyclopedias, or eyewitnesses could prove that these events happened. Possible opinions: (1) The Boston Red Sox are the greatest baseball team. (2) It is one of the best rivalries in all of sports. (3) The 86 years with no Series wins were "agonizing." Evidence: Statements reflect the beliefs or feelings of the writer; cannot be proved. The signal words *greatest* and *best* imply statement of opinion.)

230 Lesson 20 • Turn It Up!

Day 1

RETEACH
Decoding/Word Attack

Decode Longer Words Write *doctor* on the board. Ask a volunteer to read it aloud. Ask students which syllable receives the stress. (the first) Repeat with *nation*. Point out that /ər/ and /ən/ can have different spellings, but their sounds are always the same. Then write the following words on the board:

```
char-ac-ter     an-i-ma-tion
schol-ar        vis-ion
```

Have a student read the first word aloud. Ask how many syllables are in the word. Tell students that if they divide longer words into syllables, they will be able to decode them. Tell them that knowing /ər/ and /ən/ sounds will help them decode words. Continue the activity with the rest of the words.

PRETEACH
Decoding/Spelling

Copying Master 78 **Words with Ending /ər/** Distribute *Copying Master 78*. Have students echo-read the Spelling Words with you. Have students identify the words that end in /ər/. Write them on the board. Have students read each word aloud as you circle the letters that stand for the /ər/ sound. Point out that there are several spellings for the /ər/ sound.

RETEACH
Grammar/Writing

 **Pronouns** Review the types of pronouns. Write these sentences on the board:

```
Can you help Callie and I with this homework?
Mine homework is complete.
```

Have students identify the pronoun in each sentence. (I, Mine) Guide students to understand that the first sentence needs an object pronoun to be correct. (Me) The second sentence needs a possessive pronoun that does not stand alone. (My) Ask volunteers to read each corrected sentence.

GUIDED PRACTICE Have students turn to page 80 in their *Practice Book*. Have students work in pairs to proofread each sentence and make corrections. Allow time for pairs to share their responses.

VOCABULARY
Student-Friendly Explanations

ominous Something ominous is a sign of trouble or a warning.

confound If you confound a person, you surprise or confuse him.

miserable A person who feels miserable feels uncomfortable and unhappy.

gracious Someone who is gracious is pleasant and polite.

beams Someone who beams is grinning.

self-assurance People who have self-assurance are confident and sure of themselves.

monitor When you monitor something, you regularly check its progress.

exposed A thing that has been exposed has been uncovered and lost its protection from its surroundings.

installed If you installed a piece of equipment, you put it in to make it ready for use.

looming When an event is looming, it seems likely to happen soon.

Fluency

 **Fluency Practice** Have students turn to *Practice Book* page 79. Read the words in the first column aloud. Invite students to track each word and repeat it. Then have pairs read the words in the first column aloud. Follow the same procedure with each column.

"The Case of the Seashore Crook" **231**

LESSON 20

DAY AT A GLANCE
Day 2

VOCABULARY
Reteach *ominous, confound, miserable, gracious, beams, self-assurance, monitor, exposed, installed, looming*

COMPREHENSION
"The Case of the Seashore Crook"
Build Background
Monitor Comprehension
Answers to *Think Critically* Questions

DECODING/WORD ATTACK
Reteach Decode Longer Words

DECODING/SPELLING
Preteach Words Parts *over-, under-, sub-*

GRAMMAR/WRITING
Preteach Adjectives and Articles

FLUENCY
Fluency Practice

Materials Needed: *Turn It Up!*

Student Edition
pp. 202–209

Practice Book
p. 79

Copying Masters
77, 78

30+ Minutes

RETEACH

Vocabulary

Lesson 20 Vocabulary Distribute a set of Word Cards to each student or pair of students. Read aloud the Student-Friendly Explanation for one of the words, leaving out the word. Have students display and read the matching Word Card. Continue until students have matched all the words.

Copying Master 77

Comprehension

Build Background: "The Case of the Seashore Crook"
Ask students to share their experiences of mysteries they may have been involved in. How was the mystery solved? What clues did they find? Who solved the mystery?

Monitor Comprehension: "The Case of the Seashore Crook"
Read the title of the story aloud. Then have students read pages 202–203 to find out what "crime" Danny and Owen uncover.

pp. 202–203

After reading the pages, ask: **What "terrible crime" do they think has been exposed?** (Possible response: Danny and Owen can't find the picnic basket, so they probably think someone has stolen it.) **PLOT**

Discuss the Stop and Think question on page 202: **Where are Danny and Owen?** (Danny and Owen are at the beach.) Guide students in writing the answer to this question. **SETTING**

Ask: **Why does the author write *"Or so it seemed to them at the time..."*?** (Possible response: She makes it sound more like a mystery; she wants the reader to turn the page to find out.) **WRITER'S CRAFT**

Discuss the Stop and Think question on page 203: **How does Owen feel about the cookies?** (Owen feels that the cookies are the best. He says he could eat two baskets of them.) Guide students in writing the answer to this question. **FACT AND OPINION**

pp. 204–205

Discuss the Stop and Think question on page 204: **Why do Danny and Owen look up and down the beach?** (Possible response: Danny and Owen look up and down the beach because they are looking for hints. They think a crook has stolen their basket.) Guide students in writing the answer to this question. **CHARACTERS' MOTIVATIONS**

Ask: **Why are Danny and Owen lucky two police officers are nearby?** (Possible responses: If someone really did steal the basket, they can report the crime.) **DRAW CONCLUSIONS**

---

232 Lesson 20 • *Turn It Up!*

Day 2

Discuss the Stop and Think question on page 205: **What do the officers tell Danny and Owen?** (The officers tell Danny and Owen not to assume a crook took the basket.) Guide students in writing the answer to this question. **SUMMARIZE**

Ask: **What is *foul play*?** (*Foul play* means "a crime.") **CONTEXT CLUES**

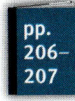
pp. 206–207

Ask: **What is one clue the police officers find while trying to solve the mystery?** (Possible responses: There were no footprints. They didn't see anyone prowling around.) **PLOT**

Ask: **Why wouldn't a crook know Danny's mom was a good cook?** (Possible response: It's unlikely a crook would know Danny's mom. A crook would probably never have tasted her cookies.) **DRAW CONCLUSIONS**

Discuss the Stop and Think question on page 206: **What do you think happened to the basket?** (Possible responses: I think the basket was stolen; misplaced; carried off by the waves.) Guide students in writing the answer to this question. **MAKE PREDICTIONS**

Discuss the Stop and Think question on page 207: **What was the ominous sound they heard?** (The ominous sound was the crash of a wave on the shore.) Guide students in writing the answer to this question. **VOCABULARY**

Model the strategy of recognizing the theme of a story.

THINK ALOUD As I think about the characters and the problem in this story, I realize that Danny and Owen right away think that someone stole their basket. But they find no evidence. Then the problem is solved when they see the basket in the water. It's a good thing they didn't accuse anyone of the crime. I think the theme might be that we shouldn't jump to conclusions. **THEME**

page 208

Ask: **What kind of person is Shannon?** (Possible response: She is helpful.) **CHARACTER'S TRAITS**

Ask: **What is Shannon doing when she holds up the cookies?** (Possible responses: She is showing that she has the basket. She is teasing the boys.) **SUMMARIZE**

Discuss the Stop and Think question on page 208: **What lesson do the boys learn?** (Possible responses: The boys learn that they shouldn't assume something is stolen just because it is missing. They need to put their basket up away from the waves.) Guide students in writing the answer to this question. **THEME**

VOCABULARY
Student-Friendly Explanations

ominous Something ominous is a sign of trouble or a warning.

confound If you confound a person, you surprise or confuse him.

miserable A person who feels miserable feels uncomfortable and unhappy.

gracious Someone who is gracious is pleasant and polite.

beams Someone who beams is grinning.

self-assurance People who have self-assurance are confident and sure of themselves.

monitor When you monitor something, you regularly check its progress.

exposed A thing that has been exposed has been uncovered and lost its protection from its surroundings.

installed If you installed a piece of equipment, you put it in to make it ready for use.

looming When an event is looming, it seems likely to happen soon.

"The Case of the Seashore Crook" 233

Day 2

Spelling Words: Lesson 20

1. arrival	11. overheat
2. gentle	12. underbrush
3. national	13. undergo
4. single	14. subway
5. level	15. sheep
6. collar	16. class's
7. doctor	17. fishes'
8. pasture	18. women
9. power	19. jeans
10. overboard	20. fish

page 209 **Answers to *Think Critically* Questions** Help students read and answer the *Think Critically* questions on page 209. Guide students in writing the answer to each question. Possible responses are provided.

1. The picnic basket ends up in the water because the high tide picked up the basket and carried it out to sea. CAUSE AND EFFECT
2. There are no footprints because there was no crook; the high tide washed all the footprints away. DRAW CONCLUSIONS
3. The mystery was that the boys' picnic basket was missing and they thought it was stolen. The mystery was solved when they found that the waves had carried the basket away. PLOT

RETEACH
Decoding/Word Attack

Decode Longer Words Write *underhand* on the board. Ask students to find the common word part *under*, and the root word *hand*. Model blending these parts. Then write the following words on the board:

over-whelm   sub-marine   under-pass

Ask students to identify the word parts in *overwhelm*. Have students blend the word parts to read the whole word. Repeat with the other words.

PRETEACH
Decoding/Spelling

Copying Master 78 **Word Parts *over-, under-, sub-*** Have students review *Copying Master 78* to identify those Spelling Words that have the word parts *over, under,* and *sub*. Review their meanings with students. Write *overboard, overheat, underbrush, undergo,* and *subway* on the board. Have students read each word aloud as you draw a slash between the word parts. Remind students that these word parts are short words that they already know how to spell.

Day 2

PRETEACH

Grammar/Writing

Adjectives and Articles Remind students that adjectives describe nouns and can be used to compare nouns. Have them recall that *a, an,* and *the* are articles that come before nouns. Remind students that when an adjective ends in *y,* they need to change the *y* to *i* before adding *-er* or *-est*. Write *pink, beautiful,* and *stormy* on the board. Guide students to write the correct form of the word used to compare two and the correct form of the word used to compare more than two. (pinker, pinkest; more beautiful, most beautiful; stormier, stormiest)

Write the following sentences on the board:

> We had a fantastic treat waiting for us at the house.
>
> Mom makes the best cookies of all.
>
> Each of the kids got three cookies and a napkin.

Guide students to identify the adjectives and articles in each sentence. (adjectives: fantastic, best, three; articles: a, the, the, the, a) Then ask students to identify the adjective that compares. (best)

Fluency

Fluency Practice Invite students to look at the bottom half of *Practice Book* page 79. These sentences have been broken into natural phrases. Tell students to repeat each phrase after you, mirroring your expression, phrasing, and pace. After students have repeated each sentence, invite them to practice reading the sentences to partners.

Practice Book **79**

"The Case of the Seashore Crook" **235**

LESSON 20

DAY AT A GLANCE — Day 3

COMPREHENSION
Preteach Follow Written Directions
Reread and Summarize "The Case of the Seashore Crook"

DECODING/WORD ATTACK
Reteach Decode Longer Words

DECODING/SPELLING
Preteach Words with Irregular Plurals and Possessives

BUILD ROBUST VOCABULARY
Teach Words from "The Case of the Seashore Crook"

GRAMMAR/WRITING
Reteach Adjectives and Articles

FLUENCY
Fluency Practice

Materials Needed: *Turn It Up!*

Student Edition pp. 202–208

Practice Book pp. 79, 81

 30+ Minutes

PRETEACH

Comprehension

Follow Written Directions Have students recall that written directions tell how to make or do something. Then discuss the steps for following directions.

- Read all the steps to make sure you understand what to do. Ask questions about anything you do not understand.
- Gather all the materials you need before you begin.
- Follow all the steps in order.

GUIDED PRACTICE Write the following recipe on the board:

> **Cinnamon and Sugar!**
>
> **Ingredients:** 1 soft taco shell, butter, cinnamon, sugar
>
> **Instructions:** Spread the butter on the taco shell. Then sprinkle cinnamon and sugar on the shell. Finally, put it in the microwave for 20 seconds. **Now enjoy!**

Have a student read aloud the recipe. Ask if there are any questions about the recipe. Talk about what could happen if they don't follow directions in order, or if they don't gather all the ingredients before they start.

Reread and Summarize Have students reread and summarize "The Case of the Seashore Crook" in sections, as described below.

 pp. 202–203 **Let's reread pages 202–203 to find out who the boys are in the story and what is going on.**
Summary: The boys are Owen and Danny. They are hungry, but their lunch basket isn't on the beach where Danny left it.

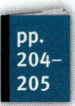 **pp. 204–205** **Let's reread pages 204–205 to find out who helps and what the boys think they could have done to prevent what they think is thievery.**
Summary: Two police officers help the boys. Danny thinks he should have kept a better lookout. Owen says they should have installed an alarm. The officers tell them not to assume someone stole the basket.

 pp. 206–208 **Let's reread pages 206–208 to find out how the mystery is solved and how the boys get their lunch back.**
Summary: One of the police officers and Danny see the basket in the water, so it must have been carried out to sea. Danny's sister is in a kayak, and she brings the basket back to shore.

236 Lesson 20 • Turn It Up!

RETEACH

Decoding/Word Attack

Decode Longer Words Write *sandwich/sandwiches* on the board, and read each aloud. Have students repeat the words and tell how many syllables they hear in each word. Ask students to tell how the singular *sandwich* was made plural. **(by adding -es)** Remind students they can use their knowledge of *-s* and *-es* endings to decode a word. Repeat the activity with *relatives, finishes,* and *circuses.*

PRETEACH

Decoding/Spelling

Words with Irregular Plurals and Possessives Remind students how to form possessive plural nouns. Review using the plural nouns *sheep* and *jeans*. **(sheep's, jeans')** Write these sentences on the board:

> The (jeans's/jeans') hems were torn out.
>
> Is the (womens's/women's) game at 7:30?
>
> Have you changed the (fishes/fishes') water lately?

Have students choose the word that correctly completes each sentence. **(jeans', women's, fishes')**

TEACH

Build Robust Vocabulary

 Words from "The Case of the Seashore Crook" Have students locate *lapped* on page 202 of "The Case of the Seashore Crook." Ask a volunteer to read aloud the sentence in which it appears. (Line 1: *Danny and Owen stood on the beach as the tide lapped at their feet.*) Explain that this sentence means that the waves gently splashed their feet. Have students turn to a partner and make up a sentence using the word *lapped*.

RETEACH

Grammar/Writing

Adjectives and Articles Review adjectives and articles with students. Remind students that the adjectives *good* and *bad* become *better* and *worse* when comparing two things. They become *best* and *worst* when comparing more than two things.

GUIDED PRACTICE Have students turn to *Practice Book* page 81. Have students work in pairs to proofread each sentence and make corrections.

Fluency

Fluency Practice Tell students that today they will reread the sentences on the bottom of *Practice Book* page 79. Have students locate and point to the first sentence. Tell students that everyone is going to read the sentence together. This choral reading will give students an opportunity to hear others and to listen to the natural phrasing of the sentences. Choral-read each of the sentences several times.

LESSON 20

DAY AT A GLANCE
Day 4

30+ Minutes

COMPREHENSION
Preteach Imaginative Literature

DECODING/SPELLING
Cumulative Review

BUILD ROBUST VOCABULARY
Reteach Words from "The Case of the Seashore Crook"

GRAMMAR/WRITING
Cumulative Review

FLUENCY
Fluency Practice

Materials Needed: *Turn It Up!*

Student Edition pp. 202–208 | Practice Book p. 82 | Copying Masters 79, 80

Spelling Words: Lesson 20

1. arrival	11. overheat
2. gentle	12. underbrush
3. national	13. undergo
4. single	14. subway
5. level	15. sheep
6. collar	16. class's
7. doctor	17. fishes'
8. pasture	18. women
9. power	19. jeans
10. overboard	20. fish

PRETEACH
Comprehension

Copying Master 79 — **Imaginative Literature** Have students recall that all imaginative literature is fiction. Distribute *Copying Master 79*, and have a volunteer read the information at the top of the page. Have students recall the characteristics of imaginative literature.

GUIDED PRACTICE Ask students to complete the page with partners. Invite students to share their answers with the class.

RETEACH
Decoding/Spelling

Practice Book 82 — **Cumulative Review** Have students number a sheet of paper 1–16. Write *arrival* on the board, and point to the /əl/ sound. Tell students that the first four words you will dictate have the /əl/ sound. After students write each word, display it so they can proofread their work. Repeat, using *collar* for /ər/ words (three words). Use *overboard* for word parts *over, under, sub* (four words). Use *sheep* for irregular plurals and possessives (five words).

1. gentle	2. national	3. single	4. level
5. doctor	6. pasture	7. power	8. overheat
9. underbrush	10. undergo	11. subway	12. class's
13. fishes'	14. women	15. jeans	16. fish

Have students turn to *Practice Book* page 82. Ask a student to read the directions aloud. Point out that the students should study each picture and identity the sentence that best matches the picture. Invite them to identify the Spelling Words in the sentences.

238 Lesson 20 • Turn It Up!

Day 4

RETEACH
Build Robust Vocabulary

Words from "The Case of the Seashore Crook" Review the meaning of *lapped*. Then say these sentences and ask which sentence reflects the meaning of the word *lapped*. Have students explain why.

- **The waves gently splashed against the side of the rowboat.** (This sentence describes *lapped*. *Lapped* means "gently splashed.")
- **The waves crashed against the shore and carried sand and pebbles back into the sea.**

RETEACH
Grammar/Writing

Copying Master 80

Cumulative Review Have students recall the grammar skills they learned in this lesson. Discuss examples for each skill:

- subject, object, possessive, and reflexive pronouns
- adjectives that tell how many, which one, or what kind
- comparative adjectives
- articles

GUIDED PRACTICE Distribute *Copying Master 80* to each student. Invite a student to read the directions. Then have students proofread each sentence. Ask them to underline the mistakes, write an adjective if there is a line for it, and rewrite the sentences correctly. Allow time for students to share their work.

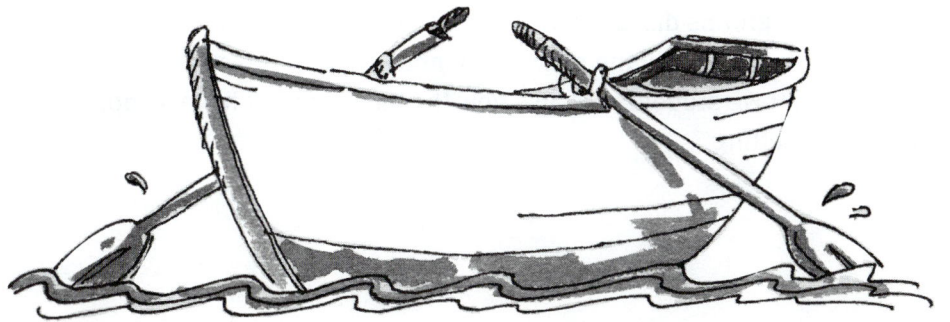

Fluency

pp. 202–208

Fluency Practice Have each student work with a partner to read passages from "The Case of the Seashore Crook" aloud to each other. Remind students to:

- vary their pace to fit the action of the story.
- read aloud with appropriate phrasing by pausing between groups of words that go together.

Encourage students to read the selected passage aloud to their partner three times. Have the student rate his or her reading on the 1–4 scale.

1	Need more practice
2	Pretty good
3	Good
4	Great!

"The Case of the Seashore Crook" 239

Preteach for LESSON 21

DAY AT A GLANCE
Day 5

VOCABULARY
Preteach consisted, prideful, intends, snatched, recalls, select

COMPREHENSION
Preteach Character, Setting, and Plot

DECODING/WORD ATTACK
Preteach Decode Longer Words

DECODING/SPELLING
Preteach Words with Suffixes *-ant, -ent, -eer, -ist, -ian*

GRAMMAR/WRITING
Preteach Verbs

FLUENCY
Fluency Performance

Materials Needed: *Turn It Up!*

Student Edition pp. 202–208

Copying Master 81

30+ Minutes

PRETEACH
Vocabulary

Copying Master 81

Lesson 21 Vocabulary Distribute a set of Vocabulary Word Cards to each student or pair of students. Hold up the card for the first Vocabulary Word, and ask a volunteer to read the word aloud. Have students repeat the word and hold up the matching card. Give the explanation for the word. Then ask students the first question below and discuss their responses. Continue for each Vocabulary Word.

- If your salad **consisted** of greens, what was in it?
- What makes your parents **prideful**?
- If someone **intends** to take a nap, how does that person look?
- Have you ever **snatched** the last cookie? Explain how you did it.
- Who clearly **recalls** what we did yesterday?
- What **select** group of books is your favorite?

PRETEACH
Comprehension

pp. 202–208

Character, Setting, and Plot Tell students that knowing who the characters in a story are and where the story takes place will help them better understand what happens. Ask students to recall what they read in "The Case of the Seashore Crook." Then ask:

- Who are the characters in the story? (Danny and Owen)
- What is the setting? (a beach near the ocean)

Then explain that the plot is the series of events in a story. Tell students that the characters and the setting affect the plot. Then ask:

- **What is the plot of the story?** (Danny set the picnic basket on the beach. Later, they can't find their basket. They think someone stole it. They look for clues. They finally find it floating in the ocean.)
- **Would the boys have lost their basket if they hadn't been on the beach? Explain.** (Possible response: No. The ocean waves were the reason that the boys lost their picnic basket.)

GUIDED PRACTICE Now tell students that the setting has been changed to a park. Have groups discuss how the plot would be different. (There are no big waves to carry away the basket. Shannon couldn't rescue the basket in her kayak.) Have students discuss how the basket might have disappeared in the new setting.

240 Preteach for Lesson 21 • *Turn It Up!*

Day 5

PRETEACH
Decoding/Word Attack

Decode Longer Words Write the word *different* on the board. Have students repeat the word after you. Draw a line between each syllable. (dif/fer/ent) Explain that a suffix always stays together as a syllable, and it's always the last syllable in a word. Point out the suffix in the word *different*. (-ent) Then ask students to identify the root word. (differ) Repeat the procedure with *confident*. (con/fid/ent) Note that sometimes the suffix *-ian* is pronounced as two syllables.

PRETEACH
Decoding/Spelling

Words with Suffixes -ant, -ent, -eer, -ist, -ian Tell students that a suffix is a word part added to the end of a word. Write the following words on the board and read them aloud:

cool (coolant)	confide (confident)	engine (engineer)
cycle (cyclist)	piano (pianist)	music (musician)

Point out that when you add suffixes, you sometimes have to make a spelling change to the root word, such as dropping a final vowel.

PRETEACH
Grammar/Writing

Verbs Write the following sentence on the board:

> Jan ran to the library.

Read the sentence aloud. Tell students that the verb *ran* tells what the subject, Jan, did. Underline *ran*. Then write this sentence on the board:

> Jan opened the door.

Ask: What is the verb in this sentence? (opened) How do you know? (It tells what Jan did.) Have a volunteer underline *opened*. Now erase the verb in each sentence. Ask students to suggest different verbs that fit in each sentence. (Possible responses: walked, skipped, drove; closed, slammed, pushed) Record the sentences on the board.

VOCABULARY
Student-Friendly Explanations

consisted If something consisted of a few things, it was made up of those things.

prideful If you are prideful, you feel great because of something you did.

intends If a person intends to do something, he or she plans to do it.

snatched If you snatched something from a person, you grabbed it quickly and suddenly.

recalls When a person recalls something, he or she remembers it.

select A select group is one that is very special and one of the best.

Fluency

Fluency Performance (pp. 202–208) Invite students each to read aloud from "The Case of the Seashore Crook" a passage that they selected and practiced earlier. Note the number of words each student reads correctly and incorrectly. Have students rate their own oral reading on the 1–4 scale. Give each student the opportunity to continue practicing and then to read the passage to you again.

"The Case of the Seashore Crook" 241

DAY AT A GLANCE

Day 1

 30+ Minutes

LESSON 21

VOCABULARY
Reteach consisted, prideful, intends, snatched, recalls, select

COMPREHENSION
Reteach Character, Setting, and Plot

DECODING/SPELLING
Reteach Words with Suffixes -ant, -ent, -eer, -ist, -ian

GRAMMAR/WRITING
Preteach Verb Phrases and Main Verbs

FLUENCY
Fluency Practice

Materials Needed: *Turn It Up!*

Student Edition pp. 210–211 | Practice Book p. 83 | Skill Card 21 | Copying Master 82

RETEACH
Vocabulary

pp. 210–211 **Lesson 21 Vocabulary**   Read aloud the Vocabulary Words and the Student-Friendly Explanations. Then have students turn to the story on page 210 of their books. Read the story aloud as students follow along. Guide them in completing the sentences on page 211 by selecting the correct word in dark type. Have a volunteer read each completed sentence aloud. If students are unable to give reasonable responses, refer to the Student-Friendly Explanations. (Answers for page 211: 2. *consisted*, 3. *intends*, 4. *select*, 5. *snatched*, 6. *prideful*, 7. *recalls*)

RETEACH
Comprehension

Character, Setting, and Plot   Have students look at side A of *Skill Card 21: Character, Setting, and Plot*. Read the definitions of character, setting, and plot. Then have a volunteer read the passage aloud as students read along. Point to the chart. Ask:

- Who are the characters in this story?
- What is the setting?
- What is the plot of the story?

Remind students that the setting of a story can affect what happens in the plot. Discuss how the plot would be different if the story took place in a park on the weekend instead of at school on a weekday.

GUIDED PRACTICE   Now have students look at side B of *Skill Card 21: Character, Setting, and Plot*. Have volunteers read aloud the Skill Reminder, then the story. Guide students in copying the chart and completing it with the narrative elements of the story. (Characters: Jake, Luke, Paul; Setting: the park; Plot: The boys each walk their dog every day. They all feel this takes too much time. They decide to take turns walking all three dogs.)

Then ask students how the story might be different if the setting were a city sidewalk instead of a park. Invite them to explain how this new setting would affect the plot events. (Possible responses: The boys may not be able to take turns because there isn't as much space. It may not take as much time to walk the dogs.)

242 Lesson 21 • *Turn It Up!*

Day 1

RETEACH

Decoding/Spelling

Suffixes -ant, -ent, -eer, -ist, -ian Distribute *Copying Master 82*. Model reading the Spelling Words and have students repeat them. Review the instructions for adding suffixes to words and then have students complete the following activity. Have students work in pairs to write the Spelling Words on index cards. Ask one student to draw a card and read its word aloud. The other student writes the word. When a student spells the word correctly, he or she initials the card and returns it to the pile. Then have students trade roles. Students should work through the pile until each has had an opportunity to spell each of the words. Remind students to write down the words they misspell to study later.

PRETEACH

Grammar/Writing

Verb Phrases and Main Verbs Remind students that a verb shows action and tells what the subject of a sentence does. Write the following sentence on the board:

> Ben sang.

Ask a volunteer to read the sentence aloud. Then ask: **Which word tells what Ben did?** (sang) Underline the word *sang*. Then write this sentence on the board:

> Ben is singing.

Ask a volunteer to read the sentence aloud. Then underline *is singing*. Tell students that a verb can be made up of two or more words. This is called a *verb phrase*. Explain that *singing* is the main verb in the phrase.

GUIDED PRACTICE Write the following sentences on the board and ask students to identify the verb phrase and the main verb. (am listening, listening; were talking, talking; was playing, playing; has been looking, looking)

> I am listening.
> We were talking.
> Our team was playing.
> Shawna has been looking for you.

VOCABULARY

Student-Friendly Explanations

consisted If something consisted of a few things, it was made up of those things.

prideful If you are prideful, you feel great because of something you did.

intends If a person intends to do something, he or she plans to do it.

snatched If you snatched something from a person, you grabbed it quickly and suddenly.

recalls When a person recalls something, he or she remembers it.

select A select group is one that is very special and one of the best.

Fluency

Fluency Practice Have students turn to *Practice Book* page 83. Read the words in the first column aloud. Invite students to track each word and repeat the words after you. Then have students work in pairs to read the words in the first column aloud to each other. Follow the same procedure with each of the remaining columns. After partners have practiced reading aloud the words in each of the columns, have them practice reading all of the words.

"My New Dog" 243

LESSON 21

DAY AT A GLANCE — Day 2

VOCABULARY
Reteach consisted, prideful, intends, snatched, recalls, select

COMPREHENSION
"My New Dog"
Build Background
Monitor Comprehension
Answers to *Think Critically* Questions

DECODING/SPELLING
Reteach Words with Suffixes -ant, -ent, -eer, -ist, -ian

GRAMMAR/WRITING
Preteach Helping Verbs

FLUENCY
Fluency Practice

Materials Needed: *Turn It Up!*

Student Edition pp. 212–219   Practice Book pp. 83, 84   Copying Masters 81, 82

30+ Minutes

RETEACH

Vocabulary

Copying Master 81

Lesson 21 Vocabulary Distribute a set of Vocabulary Word Cards to each student or pair of students. Read aloud the meaning of one of the Vocabulary Words and have students display and read the matching card. Continue until students have matched all the words.

Comprehension

Build Background: "My New Dog"
Ask students to share experiences they may have had with a new dog or puppy. Did they have to convince a family member that having a pet would be a good idea? If so, what reasons did they use to support this idea?

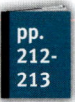

pp. 212-213

Monitor Comprehension: "My New Dog"
Read the title of the story aloud. Then have students read pages 212–213 to find out who the characters in the story are and what the life of the main character has been like up to now.

After reading the pages, ask: **Who is telling the story and what has her life been like up to now?** (Sue is telling the story. She and her dad move around a lot.) Guide students in writing the answer to the question. POINT OF VIEW/SUMMARIZE

Discuss the Stop and Think question on page 212: **How does Sue feel about moving so much?** (Possible response: Sue feels that moving a lot is not much fun and it's sometimes lonely.) Guide students in writing the answer to this question. CHARACTER'S EMOTIONS

Ask: **How do you think Sue feels about starting school?** (Possible response: I think Sue is probably nervous about being the new girl.) CHARACTER'S EMOTIONS

Ask: **Who does Sue write about in her journal?** (Sue writes about a girl she made up named Lucinda.) **Why do you think she does this?** (Possible response: She does this because she is lonely.) NOTE DETAILS/CHARACTER'S MOTIVATIONS

Discuss the Stop and Think question on page 213: **What do you think it means when Dad says "Don't stay cooped up in here"?** (Possible response: I think Dad means that she shouldn't stay inside; she needs to go outside.) Guide students in writing the answer to this question. FIGURATIVE LANGUAGE

244 Lesson 21 • Turn It Up!

Day 2

 pp. 214–215

Ask students to describe the setting in the illustration. Then discuss the Stop and Think question on page 214: **Why is the dog limping?** (Possible response: The dog is limping because he has a thorn in his paw.) Guide students in writing the answer to this question. NOTE DETAILS

Read aloud the first two paragraphs on page 214. Model the strategy of using context to confirm the meaning of the word *peered*.

THINK ALOUD When I read the page, I was not sure what *peered* meant. Sue peered down her grimy road. Then she saw something. I think *peered* must have the same meaning as *looked*. The illustration and the sentences confirm my prediction that *peered* means *looked*. USE CONTEXT TO CONFIRM MEANING

Discuss the Stop and Think question on page 215: **Why does Sue name the dog Teddy?** (Possible response: Sue names the dog Teddy because he has fur like an old teddy bear.) Guide students in writing the answer to this question. CAUSE AND EFFECT

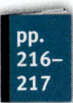 pp. 216–217

Ask: **What does Teddy do every day?** (Possible response: He visits Sue and then leaves.) GENERALIZE

Discuss the Stop and Think question on page 216: **Where does the story take place? What has happened in the story so far?** (The story takes place at Sue's new home. So far, Sue moves to a new town, and she meets Teddy.) Guide students in writing the answer to this question. NARRATIVE ANALYSIS: CHARACTER, SETTING, PLOT

Discuss the Stop and Think question on page 217: **Do you think Dad will let Teddy stay? Explain your answer.** (Possible response: I think Dad will not let Teddy stay because they move too much.) Guide students in writing the answer to this question. MAKE PREDICTIONS

 page 218

Discuss the Stop and Think question on page 218: **Why do you think Sue asks Dad if he likes dogs?** (Possible response: I think Sue asks Dad if he likes dogs because if he does, he may let her keep Teddy. If he doesn't, he won't want a dog around the house.) Guide students in writing the answer to this question. CHARACTER'S MOTIVATIONS

Ask: **What does Teddy help Sue understand about her life?** (Possible response: Teddy helps Sue realize that she wants to have a place to call home for a long period of time so she can keep Teddy.) CAUSE AND EFFECT

Ask: **How does Teddy cause Dad to change?** (Possible response: Teddy causes Dad to change by making him see that this place would be a good place to call home.) CAUSE AND EFFECT

VOCABULARY
Student-Friendly Explanations

consisted If something consisted of a few things, it was made up of those things.

prideful If you are prideful, you feel great because of something you did.

intends If a person intends to do something, he or she plans to do it.

snatched If you snatched something from a person, you grabbed it quickly and suddenly.

recalls When a person recalls something, he or she remembers it.

select A select group is one that is very special and one of the best.

"My New Dog" 245

Day 2

Spelling Words: Lesson 21

1. assistant
2. consultant
3. coolant
4. defendant
5. radiant
6. disinfectant
7. ignorant
8. absorbent
9. confident
10. different
11. engineer
12. activist
13. cyclist
14. motorist
15. pianist
16. typist
17. comedian
18. electrician
19. librarian
20. musician

page 219 **Answers to *Think Critically* Questions** Help students read and answer the *Think Critically* questions on page 219. Have students copy the graphic organizer in question 1 onto a separate sheet of paper. Then guide students in writing the answer to each question. Possible responses are provided.

1. [3] Teddy is adopted by Sue and her dad. CHARACTER, SETTING, PLOT
2. I think the author feels that moving a lot is not fun, and it's better to have a home in one place. I think the author feels this way because of the things Sue says and does. AUTHOR'S PURPOSE
3. When Dad lets Teddy in, it means that Teddy can be a part of their home and their family. CHARACTER'S MOTIVATIONS

RETEACH

Decoding/Spelling

Copying Master 82 **Words with Suffixes *-ant, -ent, -eer, -ist, -ian*** Tell students that when you add the suffix *-ant, -ent, eer, -ist,* or *-ian,* you sometimes have to make a spelling change to the root word, such as dropping a final vowel. Write the following on the board:

```
assist + ant = assistant
cycle + ist = cyclist
```

Help students see that no spelling change was necessary to add the suffix *-ant* to *assistant*. Ask: **What spelling change was necessary to add the suffix *-ist* to *cyclist*?** (Drop the final *e* from *cycle*.)

Have students take turns choosing a Spelling Word from *Copying Master 82* and writing it on the board. Then have the student write the root word and tell whether the spelling of the root word was changed.

246 Lesson 21 • Turn It Up!

Day 2

PRETEACH
Grammar/Writing

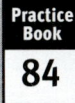 **Helping Verbs** Explain to students that a helping verb always comes before the main verb in a verb phrase. Note that there may be a word or even two between the helping verb and the main verb. Write these examples:

> The turtle will crawl out of the sand.
>
> The turtle will soon crawl out of the sand.
>
> The turtle will almost always crawl out of the sand.

Help students identify the helping verb and the main verb in each sentence.

GUIDED PRACTICE Direct students' attention to page 84 in their *Practice Book*. Read the directions for the activity together. Remind students that some sentences will have only a main verb and others will have a verb phrase. Have students work in pairs to identify the verb or verb phrase and then the helping verbs in the remaining sentences.

Fluency

Fluency Practice Invite students to look at the bottom half of *Practice Book* page 83. These sentences have been broken into natural phrases. Tell students to repeat each phrase after you, imitating your expression, phrasing, and pace. After students have repeated each sentence, invite them to practice reading the sentences to partners.

"My New Dog" 247

LESSON 21

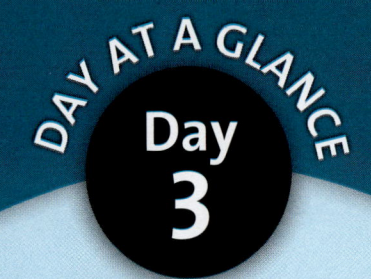

DAY AT A GLANCE

Day 3

COMPREHENSION
Preteach Make Inferences
Reread and Summarize "My New Dog"

DECODING/SPELLING
Reteach Words with Suffixes -ant, -ent, -eer, -ist, -ian

BUILD ROBUST VOCABULARY
Teach Words from "My New Dog"

GRAMMAR/WRITING
Reteach Writing Trait: Word Choice

FLUENCY
Fluency Practice

Materials Needed: *Turn It Up!*

Student Edition pp. 212–218

Practice Book pp. 83, 85

Copying Master 83

30+ Minutes

PRETEACH
Comprehension

Make Inferences Distribute *Copying Master 83* and have students read the information at the top of the page. Have a volunteer read the passage aloud as students read along. Then discuss the first inference.

GUIDED PRACTICE Ask students to read each remaining inference and support the inference with clues from the story or from what they know.

Reread and Summarize Have students reread and summarize "My New Dog" in sections, as described below.

 **pp. 212–213**
Let's reread pages 212–213 to recall what Sue's life was like.
Summary: Sue and her dad move around a lot because of his job. Sue doesn't really like it because she is always the new girl. She knows that Dad wants her to be happy.

 pp. 214–216
Now let's reread pages 214–216 to remember what happens when Sue first meets Teddy.
Summary: Teddy is limping, so Sue pulls a thorn out of Teddy's paw. They become friends immediately. Sue names the dog and gives him food. Teddy starts to visit Sue every day.

 pp. 217–218
Last, let's reread pages 217–218 to find out what happens when Sue talks to Dad about keeping Teddy.
Summary: Dad admits that he likes Teddy and welcomes the dog into the house. Dad and Sue decide to stay in this town for a while.

RETEACH
Decoding/Spelling

Word with Suffixes -ant, -ent, -eer, -ist, -ian Write the following on the board:

| type (ist) | confide (ent) | library (ian) |
| engine (eer) | piano (ist) | ignore (ant) |

Then write these words on the board:

| ignorant | engineer | typist |
| librarian | pianist | confident |

248 Lesson 21 • *Turn It Up!*

Ask students to match up each new word with its root word and suffix. Have students identify how the spelling of the root word changed when the suffix was added.

TEACH

Build Robust Vocabulary

Words from "My New Dog" (pp. 214–215) Have students locate the words *peered* and *grimy* on page 214 of "My New Dog." Ask a volunteer to read aloud the sentence in which these two words appear. (Line 3: *She peered down the grimy avenue.*) Explain that this sentence means that the girl looked down the dirty street. *Peered* means "looked hard or carefully," and *grimy* means "very dirty." Continue by asking students to locate and read aloud the sentence on page 215 in which *plopped* appears. (Last sentence: *Teddy plopped down next to the stoop.*) Explain that this sentence means that Teddy sat down quickly and heavily next to the stoop.

Ask each student to write the words on cards. Give an explanation of each word and have students hold up the correct card.

RETEACH

Grammar/Writing

Writing Trait: Word Choice (Practice Book 85) Have students turn to page 85 in their *Practice Books*. Explain that when you write a story, it is important to use specific and interesting words so readers can picture in their minds what you are saying. Discuss the information in the graphic organizer. Recall how the author of "My New Dog" uses vivid words to describe the characters' actions. Read the directions aloud. Then have a volunteer read the first sentence from the story. Point out the vivid verb *spied*. Explain that the author could have used the word *saw*, but choosing the word *spied* makes a more vivid picture in the reader's mind.

GUIDED PRACTICE Work with students to complete the rest of this section. Then have a student read the second passage aloud. Help students identify the vivid and colorful words. Have them describe what picture the words create in their mind. Then invite students to extend the story with sentences of their own.

Fluency

Fluency Practice (Practice Book 83) Tell students that today they will reread the sentences on the bottom of *Practice Book* page 83. Have students locate and point to the first sentence. Tell students that everyone is going to read the sentence together. This choral reading will give students an opportunity to hear others and listen to the natural phrasing of the sentences. Choral-read each of the sentences several times.

"My New Dog" 249

LESSON 21

DAY AT A GLANCE
Day 4

COMPREHENSION
Reteach Make Inferences

DECODING/SPELLING
Reteach Words with Suffixes -ant, -ent, -eer, -ist, -ian

BUILD ROBUST VOCABULARY
Reteach Words from "My New Dog"

GRAMMAR/WRITING
Reteach Writing Form: Narrative Paragraph

FLUENCY
Fluency Practice

Materials Needed: *Turn It Up!*

 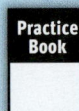 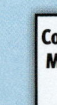

Student Edition pp. 212–218 | Practice Book p. 86 | Copying Master 84

Spelling Words: Lesson 21

1.	assistant	11.	engineer
2.	consultant	12.	activist
3.	coolant	13.	cyclist
4.	defendant	14.	motorist
5.	radiant	15.	pianist
6.	disinfectant	16.	typist
7.	ignorant	17.	comedian
8.	absorbent	18.	electrician
9.	confident	19.	librarian
10.	different	20.	musician

30+ Minutes

RETEACH
Comprehension

Make Inferences Give students the following information about making inferences:

- A writer may not explain everything that is happening in a story.
- Readers need to make inferences, or figure out things that the writer hasn't said.
- To make inferences, readers have to use clues from the story along with what they already know.

Write on the board the following sentences from "My New Dog":

> At first I didn't see the dog limping up the road.
> He could use some grooming to get his fur smooth again.
> Snatching it up, he didn't even chew it.

Have volunteers read each sentence aloud and explain what they know about the dog based on the words that are used. (Possible inferences: The dog was hurt. The dog was dirty or smelly. The dog was hungry.)

GUIDED PRACTICE Write these other sentences from "My New Dog" on the board. Invite volunteers to read the sentences aloud. Then discuss what inferences students can make about one of the characters, the setting, or what is happening in the story.

> I wish I could unpack my suitcase for good.
> I peered down my own grimy road.
> My time with Teddy made me want to have a home.

RETEACH
Decoding/Spelling

Words with Suffixes -ant, -ent, -eer, -ist, -ian Have students number a sheet of paper 1–16. Write the Spelling Word *assistant* on the board and point to the suffix. Tell students that the first six words you will dictate have the suffix *-ant*. After students write each word, display it so they can proofread their work. Repeat this activity for the other suffixes using these examples: *absorbent, puppeteer, activist,* and *comedian.*

250 Lesson 21 • Turn It Up!

1. consultant	2. coolant	3. defendant	4. radiant
5. disinfectant	6. ignorant	7. confident	8. different
9. engineer	10. cyclist	11. motorist	12. pianist
13. typist	14. electrician	15. librarian	16. musician

Have students turn to page 86 in their *Practice Books*. Read the passage together. Then read the first sentence. Invite the group to choose the word that correctly completes the sentence. If students have difficulty, encourage them to revisit the passage for the answer. Have students complete the remaining sentences in the same manner.

REVIEW

Build Robust Vocabulary

Words from "My New Dog" Review the meanings of the words *peered*, *grimy*, and *plopped*. Then say these sentences and ask which word each sentence describes. Have students explain why.

- **Jack looked carefully at the apples to decide which one he wanted.** (peered)
- **Maria's pants were very dirty after the softball game.** (grimy)
- **The dog laid down quickly and heavily on the rug to take a nap.** (plopped)

RETEACH

Grammar/Writing

Writing Form: Narrative Paragraph Explain that a narrative paragraph tells a story about something that happens to a character. When writers write a story, it is important to use specific and interesting words so readers can picture what they are saying in their minds. Distribute *Copying Master 84*. Have a volunteer read the description of a narrative paragraph. Then read the passage and the notes in the margin together.

GUIDED PRACTICE Invite a volunteer to read the first sentence aloud. Tell students that the words *shredded homework* give the reader a picture of what is being described. Have students give other examples of colorful, vivid language from the sentence. Then work through the rest of the questions in the section.

Fluency

Fluency Practice Have each student work with a partner to read passages from "My New Dog" aloud to each other. Students may select a passage that they enjoyed or choose one of the following options:

- Read page 213. (Total: 97 words)
- Read page 217. (Total: 102 words)

Encourage students to read the selected passage aloud to their partner three times. Have the student rate his or her reading on the 1–4 scale.

1	Need more practice
2	Pretty good
3	Good
4	Great!

"My New Dog" 251

Preteach for **LESSON 22**

Day 5

VOCABULARY
Preteach burst, opportunities, huddled, comforted, recognized, journey

COMPREHENSION
 Preteach Character, Setting, and Plot

DECODING/WORD ATTACK
Preteach Decode Longer Words

DECODING/SPELLING
Preteach Word Parts *in, out, down, up*

GRAMMAR/WRITING
Preteach Action Verbs

FLUENCY
Fluency Performance

Materials Needed: *Turn It Up!*

Student Edition pp. 212–218

Copying Master 85

PRETEACH
Vocabulary

Copying Master 85 | **Lesson 22 Vocabulary** Distribute a set of Vocabulary Word Cards to each student or pair of students. Hold up the card for the first Vocabulary Word, and ask a volunteer to read the word aloud. Have students repeat the word and hold up the matching card. Give the explanation for the word. The ask students the first question below and discuss their responses. Continue for each Vocabulary Word.

- When have you felt as if you were going to **burst** with excitement?
- What kinds of **opportunities** do you hope to have at school?
- When have you **huddled** with other people? Why?
- How do you feel after you have been **comforted** by someone?
- How can you tell whether someone has **recognized** you?
- Have you ever gone on a long **journey**? Where did you go?

PRETEACH
Comprehension

pp. 212–218  **Character, Setting, and Plot** Explain to students that events in a plot can affect the events that follow. Knowing this will help readers better understand and enjoy a story. Ask students to recall the story "My New Dog."

- Who are the characters in "My New Dog"? (Sue, Dad, Teddy)
- What is the setting for the story? (the country)
- What events make up the plot? (Sue is lonely because she and Dad move so often. Sue meets a stray dog. Dad agrees with Sue that they should stay in one place and raise Teddy.)
- How would the story have been different if the dog hadn't had a thorn in its paw? Explain. (Possible response: Sue would not have helped it. If the dog hadn't been limping, maybe she wouldn't have noticed it.)

GUIDED PRACTICE Have students work in pairs to reread a page of "My New Dog" and name other important plot events. (Possible responses: Sue teaches Teddy to play broom ball. Dad has work to do in the town.) Ask pairs to discuss how the story would have been different if an event had not happened or if it had happened in another way.

252 Preteach for Lesson 22 • *Turn It Up!*

Day 5

PRETEACH
Decoding/Word Attack

Decode Longer Words Write the word *incorrect* on the board, and read it aloud. Have students repeat the word after you, and ask how many syllables they hear in the word. (3) Draw lines to show where the word should be divided. (in/cor/rect) Ask students to name the beginning word part. (in) Then ask them to identify the root. (correct) Repeat the procedure with *downstairs*. Point out that the word part *down-* is the first syllable. Tell students that the word parts *in, out, up,* and *down* are often the first syllable in a word.

GUIDED PRACTICE Write the following words on the board:

> independent   outstanding   downright   uplifted

Guide students as they break each word into syllables and read the words. Ask students to identify the first word part in each word. (in/de/pen/dent, out/stand/ing, down/right, up/lift/ed)

PRETEACH
Decoding/Spelling

Word Parts *in, out, down, up* List these word parts on the board: *in, out, down, up*. Write *indirect, outbid, downstairs,* and *upwind*. Ask: **What smaller word part do you see at the beginning of *indirect*?** (in) Have students read both word parts and then blend them. Follow the same procedure for *outbid, downfall,* and *update*. Point out that the spelling of the root does not change when *in, out, down,* or *up* is added.

PRETEACH
Grammar/Writing

Action Verbs Write the following sentences on the board:

> Kate read all afternoon.
> Kate ran to the market.

Tell students that an action verb tells what the subject of a sentence does. Explain that an action verb may tell about something you can see happening. Read the first sentence together. Ask: **What word tells what Kate did?** (read) Read the second sentence together. Have students identify the action verb in this sentence. (ran) Erase the verbs in each sentence and have students suggest other action verbs that make sense.

VOCABULARY
Student-Friendly Explanations

burst When a person feels ready to burst, it means that the person is very excited and cannot wait to say something.

opportunities Opportunities are chances to do something you want to do.

huddled If people huddled together, they got close to each other in a group.

comforted If a person comforted a friend, he or she helped that friend feel better about something.

recognized If you recognized someone, you saw him or her and knew who it was.

journey A journey is a trip from one place to another that usually takes a long time.

Fluency

Fluency Performance
pp. 212–218
Invite students each to read aloud from "My New Dog" a passage that they selected and practiced earlier. Note the number of words each student reads correctly and incorrectly. Have students rate their own oral reading on the 1–4 scale. Give each student the opportunity to continue practicing and then to read the passage to you again.

"My New Dog" 253

DAY AT A GLANCE

Day 1

VOCABULARY
Reteach burst, opportunities, huddled, comforted, recognized, journey

COMPREHENSION
 Reteach Character, Setting, and Plot

DECODING/SPELLING
Reteach Word Parts: in-, out-, down-, up-

GRAMMAR/WRITING
Preteach Linking Verbs

FLUENCY
Fluency Practice

Materials Needed: *Turn It Up!*

Student Edition pp. 220–221 | Practice Book p. 87 | Skill Card 22 | Copying Master 86

LESSON 22

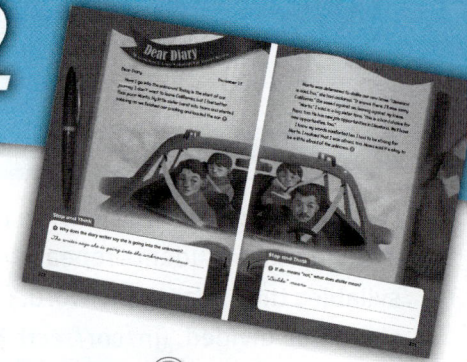

30+ Minutes

RETEACH
Vocabulary

 pp. 220–221

Lesson 22 Vocabulary Read aloud the Vocabulary Words and the Student-Friendly Explanations. Then have students read the letters on pages 220–221 of their books. Guide students in completing the sentences by selecting the correct word from the word list. Have a volunteer read each completed sentence aloud. Then have students read the completed letters along with you. If students are unable to give reasonable responses, refer to the Student-Friendly Explanations. (Answers for pages 210 and 211: 2. *burst*, 3. *opportunities*, 4. *comforted*, 5. *huddled*, 6. *recognized*)

RETEACH
Comprehension

  **Character, Setting, and Plot** Have students look at side A of *Skill Card 22: Character, Setting, and Plot*. Have a volunteer read the definitions of character, setting, and plot. Then ask a student to read the passage aloud. Point to the chart. Ask:

- **Who are the characters in this story?**
- **What is the setting?**
- **What is the problem in the story and how is it resolved?**

Remind students that the story events affect the plot. Discuss with students how the story would change if Marina had not known how to play soccer. Invite volunteers to tell how the problem might have been resolved differently. (Possible response: Naomi might have walked away. She might have asked Marina to do something else with her.)

GUIDED PRACTICE Now have students look at side B of *Skill Card 22: Character, Setting, and Plot*. Read the Skill Reminder aloud. Then have a volunteer read the story aloud while students follow along. Guide students as they copy the chart and complete it with details from the story. Ask students to discuss how the story might have been different if Carlos had fallen down. (Characters: Carlos, ski instructor, the group; Setting: ski class on a snowy hill; Plot Events: 1. Carlos watches his ski instructor. 2. He begins to ski down the hill. 3. Carlos gives a happy yell as he skis down the hill.)

254 Lesson 22 • Turn It Up!

Day 1

RETEACH

Decoding/Spelling

Word Parts: in-, out-, down-, up- Distribute *Copying Master 86*. Model reading the Spelling Words and have students repeat them. Review the instruction for adding prefixes to words, and then have students complete the following activity based on the traditional Memory Game. Pairs of students make game cards using the lesson's Spelling Words with prefixes missing; a dash appears in place of each prefix. After a student matches two cards, he or she must supply the correct missing prefix to keep the game cards. If the wrong prefix is supplied, the opponent gets the game cards and the next turn.

PRETEACH

Grammar/Writing

Linking Verbs Write the following sentences on the board:

> Jake is ten years old today.
> Jake was the line leader.

Point out that these sentences do not contain action verbs. Explain that some verbs connect the subject with words in the predicate that rename or describe the subject. These verbs are called linking verbs. Explain that *is* links *Jake* with the describing words *ten years old*. Help students understand that in the second sentence, the words *line leader* rename Jake.

GUIDED PRACTICE Write the following sentences on the board:

> Spencer was bored.
> Spencer is a big cat.
> Dave and Spencer are pals.
> I am excited about the game.
> We were late for dinner.

Ask students to identify the linking verb and tell whether the predicate renames or describes the subject. (was—describes, is—renames, are—renames, am—describes, were—describes)

VOCABULARY

Student-Friendly Explanations

burst When a person feels ready to burst, it means that the person is very excited and cannot wait to say something.

opportunities Opportunities are chances to do something you want to do.

huddled If people huddled together, they got close to each other in a group.

comforted If a person comforted a friend, he or she helped that friend feel better about something.

recognized If you recognized someone, you saw him or her and knew who it was.

journey A journey is a trip from one place to another that usually takes a long time.

Fluency

Fluency Practice Have students turn to *Practice Book* page 87. Read the words in the first column aloud. Invite students to track each word and repeat the words after you. Then have students work in pairs to read the words in the first column aloud to each other. Follow the same procedure with each of the remaining columns. After partners have practiced reading aloud the words in each of the columns, have them practice reading all of the words.

"Dear Diary" 255

LESSON 22

Day 2

VOCABULARY
Reteach burst, opportunities, huddled, comforted, recognized, journey

COMPREHENSION
"Dear Diary"
Build Background
Monitor Comprehension
Answers to *Think Critically* Questions

DECODING/SPELLING
Reteach Word Chains

GRAMMAR/WRITING
Preteach Helping Verbs

FLUENCY
Fluency Practice

Materials Needed: *Turn It Up!*

Student Edition pp. 222–229 | Practice Book pp. 87, 88 | Copying Masters 85, 86

30+ Minutes

RETEACH

Vocabulary

Lesson 22 Vocabulary Distribute a set of Word Cards for each student or pair of students. Read aloud the meaning of one of the Vocabulary Words, and have students point to and read the matching card. Continue until students have matched all the words.

Comprehension

Build Background: "Dear Diary"
Ask students to share experiences they may have had with moving. Did they move or did a friend move? Did they think the move was a good idea? Did they have special concerns or expectations about what things would be like after the move?

Monitor Comprehension: "Dear Diary"
Read the title of the story aloud. Then have students read pages 222–223 to find out where the characters are going and why.

After reading the pages, ask: **Where are the characters going? Why are they going there?** (Possible response: They are driving to Cleveland so that Eva's father will have new job opportunities.) **NOTE DETAILS**

Discuss the Stop and Think question on page 222: **Why does the diary writer say she is going into the unknown?** (Possible response: The writer says she is going into the unknown because she does not know what life in a new place will be like.) Guide students in writing the answer to this question. **MAKE INFERENCES**

Ask: **How does Eva seem to want to feel at the beginning of the story?** (Possible response: She wants to feel brave.) **CHARACTER'S EMOTIONS**

Discuss the Stop and Think question on page 223: **If *dis-* means "not," what does *dislike* mean?** (*Dislike* means "not to like.") Guide students in writing the answer to this question. **PREFIXES, SUFFIXES, AND ROOT WORDS**

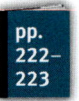

Ask students to describe the setting in the illustration. Discuss the Stop and Think question on page 224: **Why does the snow surprise Marta?** (Possible response: The snow surprises Marta because she thinks it's always sunny in California; she thinks it snows only in Cleveland.) Guide students in writing the answer to this question. **MAKE INFERENCES**

256 Lesson 22 • Turn It Up!

Day 2

Read aloud the first and second paragraphs on page 224. Model how readers create mental images about what they read.

THINK ALOUD I read that snow was drifting and swirling all around. A sign flashed a warning that chains were required. When I read this, I picture a scene in my head of white snow as far as I can see—flakes swirling around, moved by gusting winds, and a road so covered in snow that it has become too slippery for regular car tires. **CREATE MENTAL IMAGES**

Discuss the Stop and Think question on page 225: **Why does Papa put chains on the tires?** (Possible response: Papa puts chains on the tires so that the tires would not slip on the snowy highway.) Guide students in writing the answer to this question. **CAUSE AND EFFECT**

pp. 226–227

Discuss the Stop and Think question on page 226: **Why do children feel differently about snow than grown-ups do?** (Possible response: Children feel differently about snow because they can play in it; grown-ups must shovel the snow, must clean it off their cars, and have trouble getting to work.) Guide students in writing the answer to this question. **MAKE COMPARISONS**

Ask: **How does the setting change from page 226 to page 227?** (Possible response: On page 226, the setting is still the snowy highway. On page 227, they have driven farther and the land is flat, with few hills and not much to look at.) **SETTING**

Discuss the Stop and Think question on page 227: **Where does the story take place? How does this affect the plot?** (Possible response: The story takes place in a car driving across the country. Many plot events are affected by the fact that the family is driving in a car. For example, they see snow along the way. They also spend three days together, which seems to help the children feel better about moving to a new place.) Guide students in writing the answer to this question.) **CHARACTER, SETTING, PLOT**

page 228

Discuss the Stop and Think question on page 228: **Eva and Marta did not want to move to Cleveland. How do you think they feel now? Why?** (Possible response: Now Eva and Marta feel happy. They will like Cleveland after all, with help from Uncle Tony and Isabel.) Guide students in writing the answer to this question. **CONFLICT/RESOLUTION**

Ask: **How does the setting of the story change at the end?** (The story moves from inside a moving car to inside a warm and friendly home.) **How does the change in setting make you feel about Marta's and Eva's future?** (Possible response: The change in setting makes you feel that Marta and Eva will have a happy future in their new home.)
 CHARACTER, SETTING, PLOT

VOCABULARY
Student-Friendly Explanations

burst When a person feels ready to burst, it means that the person is very excited and cannot wait to say something.

opportunities Opportunities are chances to do something you want to do.

huddled If people huddled together, they got close to each other in a group.

comforted If a person comforted a friend, he or she helped that friend feel better about something.

recognized If you recognized someone, you saw him or her and knew who it was.

journey A journey is a trip from one place to another that usually takes a long time.

"Dear Diary" 257

Day 2

Spelling Words: Lesson 22

1. incomplete	11. outdated
2. indirect	12. outdoor
3. indent	13. downfall
4. instead	14. downhill
5. include	15. downpour
6. inexact	16. downstairs
7. infamous	17. update
8. outbid	18. upfront
9. outbreak	19. uphill
10. outcast	20. upwind

page 229 **Answers to *Think Critically* Questions**
Help students read and answer the *Think Critically* questions on page 229. Have students copy the graphic organizer in question 1 onto a separate sheet of paper. Then guide students in writing the answer to each question. Possible responses are provided.

1. [4.] They play games and make bracelets. [5.] They meet Isabel and Uncle Tony in Cleveland.  **CHARACTER, SETTING, PLOT**
2. Isabel makes Marta laugh when she just walks up and starts talking. **CHARACTER'S EMOTIONS**
3. In the end, Marta feels happy. She is laughing. **MAKE COMPARISONS**

RETEACH

Decoding/Spelling

Copying Master 86 **Word Chains** Have pairs of students make word chains with the Spelling Words on *Copying Master 86*. Invite students to begin by writing one word. Then, have the partner use a letter in that word to write another, and so on.

i	n	c	o	m	p	l	e	t	e
n									
d	o	w	n	p	o	u	r		
e									
n									
t									

258 Lesson 22 • Turn It Up!

Day 2

PRETEACH
Grammar/Writing

 Linking and Helping Verbs Explain that forms of the verb *be* can act as linking verbs or as helping verbs. Write these sentences:

> We are healthy.
> We were rushing to lunch.

Have a volunteer read aloud the sentences. Help students understand that in the first sentence, *are* links *We* to a describing word, *healthy*. In the second sentence, the helping verb *were* is part of the verb phrase *were rushing*.

GUIDED PRACTICE Direct students to page 88 in their *Practice Book*. Read the activity directions together. Then ask students to complete the page. Allow time for students to share their responses.

Fluency

Fluency Practice Invite students to look at the bottom half of *Practice Book* page 87. These sentences have been broken into natural phrases. Tell students to repeat each phrase after you, mirroring your expression, phrasing, and pace. After students have repeated each sentence, invite them to practice reading the sentences to partners.

"Dear Diary" 259

LESSON 22

DAY AT A GLANCE — Day 3

COMPREHENSION
Preteach Make Inferences
Reread and Summarize "Dear Diary"

DECODING/SPELLING
Reteach Word Parts

BUILD ROBUST VOCABULARY
Teach Words from "Dear Diary"

GRAMMAR/WRITING
Reteach Writing Trait: Word Choice

FLUENCY
Fluency Practice

Materials Needed: *Turn It Up!*

Student Edition pp. 222–228   Practice Book pp. 87, 89   Copying Master 87

 30+ Minutes

PRETEACH

Comprehension

 Copying Master 87

Make Inferences Distribute *Copying Master 87*, and have a volunteer read the information at the top of the page.

GUIDED PRACTICE Ask students to read the passage and make inferences. Ask: **What do you know about the characters, setting, and plot that is not explicitly stated in the passage?** Have students record their inferences in the third column, then go back and support each inference. Allow time for students to share their responses with others.

Reread and Summarize Have students reread and summarize "Dear Diary" in sections, as described below.

 pp. 222–223

Let's read pages 222–223 to recall how Eva and Marta felt about the move at the beginning of the story.
Summary: Eva and Marta are not happy about leaving California. It is especially hard for the younger Marta.

 pp. 224–226

Now let's reread pages 224–226 to remember how the girls reacted at their first sight of snow.
Summary: Their mother has to tell the girls what the snow is. Eva and Marta both got out of the car. They were cold, but excited.

pp. 227–228

Finally, let's reread pages 227–228 to find out what happens when Eva and Marta arrive at their destination.
Summary: The family is warmly welcomed by other family members in Cleveland. Marta immediately makes a new friend. Eva is reassured by her younger sister's happiness.

RETEACH

Decoding/Spelling

Word Parts Write these Spelling Words on the board:

indent	inexact	infamous	outbid
outbreak	downfall	downhill	update

Have students read each word aloud. Ask them to picture the word. Erase the word part *in*, *out*, *down*, or *up*. Call on volunteers to write each missing word part and read the word aloud again. Discuss with students how breaking a word into smaller parts helps with spelling the word.

260 Lesson 22 • *Turn It Up!*

Day 3

TEACH

Build Robust Vocabulary

page 223–224 **Words from "Dear Diary"** Have students locate the word *determined* on page 223 of "Dear Diary." Ask a volunteer to read aloud the sentence in which this word appears. (Line 1: *Marta was determined to dislike our new home.*) Explain that this sentence means that Marta showed that she was very sure she would not like the new home, and she would not change her mind. Continue by asking students to locate and read aloud the sentence on page 224 in which the words *alerted* and *required* appear. (Line 4: *A flashing sign alerted us that chains were required, so Papa pulled over.*) Explain that *alert* means to let someone know that there could be trouble or danger. Then tell students that *required* means drivers had to use chains. They had no choice about it.

Ask students to work in small groups. Have each student in the group think of a sentence for one of the words and act out its meaning. Give each group a chance to perform its sentences for the others.

RETEACH

Grammar/Writing

Practice Book 89 **Writing Trait: Word Choice** Have students turn to page 89 in their *Practice Book*. Explain that when writers write a story, it is important to use vivid, descriptive words so readers can picture exactly what is happening and how the characters felt about what happened. Ask a volunteer to read the information at the top of the page. Point out how the author of "Dear Diary" uses vivid words to describe the scenery and the characters' actions.

GUIDED PRACTICE Complete the page together. Guide students to find the vivid, descriptive words in Parts A and B. Then invite pairs to work together to complete Part C. Suggest that students look in a thesaurus for new words if they can't think of any on their own.

Fluency

Practice Book 87 **Fluency Practice** Tell students that today they will reread the sentences on the bottom of *Practice Book* page 87. Have students locate and point to the first sentence. Tell students that everyone is going to read the sentence together. This choral reading will give students an opportunity to hear others and listen to the natural phrasing of the sentences. Choral-read each of the sentences several times.

"Dear Diary" 261

LESSON 22

DAY AT A GLANCE — Day 4

COMPREHENSION
Reteach Make Inferences

DECODING/SPELLING
Reteach Word Parts: *in, out, down, up*

BUILD ROBUST VOCABULARY
Reteach Words from "Dear Diary"

GRAMMAR/WRITING
Reteach Writing Form: Diary

FLUENCY
Fluency Practice

Materials Needed: *Turn It Up!*

Student Edition pp. 222–228 | Practice Book p. 90 | Copying Master 88

Spelling Words: Lesson 22

1. incomplete	11. outdated
2. indirect	12. outdoor
3. indent	13. downfall
4. instead	14. downhill
5. include	15. downpour
6. inexact	16. downstairs
7. infamous	17. update
8. outbid	18. upfront
9. outbreak	19. uphill
10. outcast	20. upwind

30+ Minutes

RETEACH

Comprehension

 p. 227

Make Inferences Remind students about these key ideas:

- Authors do not always explain everything that is happening in a story.
- Use information from the story and what you already know to make inferences.

Read aloud the second paragraph on page 227. Model making inferences. If available, refer to a wall map of the United States.

THINK ALOUD Eva writes that as far as she could see, everything was flat. I know that Eva's family left California and that they are going to Cleveland—which is in Ohio. I can also tell from the date that the family has been traveling for two days. If I look at a map, I can infer that they are driving through the Great Plains region of the United States. I know it is flat and has few trees. MAKE INFERENCES

GUIDED PRACTICE Write the following sentences from "Dear Diary" on the board. Have volunteers read each sentence aloud and tell what they infer about the character based on the words that are used.

> My little sister burst into tears and started sobbing as we finished our packing and loaded the car.
>
> "What did you do with so much snow?" I asked her. "It's fun to play in," smiled Mama.

RETEACH

Decoding/Spelling

 Practice Book 90

Word Parts: *in, out, down, up* Have students number a sheet of paper 1–16. Write *incomplete* on the board and point to the prefix. Tell students that the first six words you will dictate have this prefix. After students write each word, display it so they can proofread their work. Repeat using these examples: *outbid, downfall, update*.

1. indirect	2. indent	3. instead	4. include
5. inexact	6. infamous	7. outbreak	8. outcast
9. outdated	10. outdoor	11. downhill	12. downpour
13. downstairs	14. upfront	15. uphill	16. upwind

Have students turn to *Practice Book* page 90. Do the first item together; then have students complete the page.

262 Lesson 22 • Turn It Up!

Day 4

RETEACH

Build Robust Vocabulary

Words from "Dear Diary" Review the meanings of *determined*, *alerted*, and *required*. Then say these sentences and ask which word each sentence describes. Have students explain why.

- Sam was very sure he would get his mom the necklace she wanted. (determined)
- The beeping smoke detector let us know that the fried chicken was burning. (alerted)
- Students must sit down when they ride the school bus. (required)

RETEACH

Grammar/Writing

Copying Master 88

Writing Form: Diary Tell students that a diary entry tells about something personal that happened to the writer. The writer uses precise words that tell exactly what happened and how he or she felt about what happened. One way writers do this is by using vivid, descriptive words. Distribute *Copying Master 88*. Have a volunteer read the description of a diary entry. Then read the Student Model together. Write on the board the following sentence from the passage:

> As we got close to our new house, I looked at our neighborhood.

Model for students how the sentence can be improved.

> As we approached our new house, I carefully examined the houses and yards of our new neighbors.

GUIDED PRACTICE Complete the activity by having students revise another sentence from the Student Model. Allow time for students to share their revised sentences with the group.

Fluency

pp. 222–228

Fluency Practice 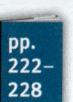 Have each student work with a partner to read passages from "Dear Diary" aloud to each other. Students may select a passage that they enjoyed or choose one of the following options:

- Read page 223. (Total: 89 words)
- Read page 227. (Total: 106 words)

Encourage students to read the selected passage aloud to their partner three times. Have the student rate his or her reading on the 1–4 scale.

1	Need more practice
2	Pretty good
3	Good
4	Great!

"Dear Diary" 263

Preteach for LESSON 23

DAY AT A GLANCE — Day 5

VOCABULARY
Preteach *forlornly, fidget, pathetic, resolved, scrounging, noble, stingy, suspicion*

COMPREHENSION
 **Preteach** Sequence: Story Events

DECODING/WORD ATTACK
Preteach Decode Longer Words

DECODING/SPELLING
Preteach Suffixes *-ation, -ition, -al, -ial*

GRAMMAR/WRITING
Preteach Present-Tense Verbs; Subject-Verb Agreement

FLUENCY
Fluency Performance

Materials Needed: *Turn It Up!*

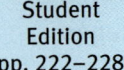

Student Edition pp. 222–228

Copying Master 89

30+ Minutes

PRETEACH — Vocabulary

Lesson 23 Vocabulary Distribute a set of Vocabulary Word Cards to each student or pair of students. Hold up the card for the first word, and ask a volunteer to read it aloud. Have students repeat the word and hold up the matching card. Give the explanation for the word. Then ask students the first question below and discuss their responses. Continue for each of the Vocabulary Words.

- When might you look **forlornly** at something?
- Who **fidgets** more, a child or an adult? Why?
- People don't like to be seen as **pathetic**. Why do you think that is?
- Have you ever **resolved** to change in some way at the start of a new year? What happened?
- When might animals be **scrounging** for food? Why?
- Why might we want **noble** character traits in our community leaders?
- Is it **stingy** or wise to have money in a savings account? Why?
- Have you ever felt **suspicious** of a friend? How did it feel?

PRETEACH — Comprehension

  **Sequence: Story Events** Remind students that events in a story occur in a certain order. Explain that the order in which story events happen is the sequence. Point out that signal words such as *first, next, then,* and *finally* can help the reader keep track of the sequence. Time words such as *this morning, noon,* or *later tonight* also help the reader keep track of the order of events.

GUIDED PRACTICE Have students think about "Dear Diary" and discuss the answers to these questions:

- **How does the story begin?** (Possible response: Eva is writing in her diary in the car.)
- **How long have Eva and her family been driving at this point?** (Possible response: Not long; it is still the first day of travel.)
- **In what special way does the author let the reader know how many days have passed since Eva's last entry?** (Possible response: Each entry begins with a date.)
- **How does the story end?** (Possible response: Eva's family arrives at her uncle's house. They are welcomed warmly. Marta makes friends with Isabel.)

264 Preteach for Lesson 23 • *Turn It Up!*

Day 5

PRETEACH

Decoding/Word Attack

Decode Longer Words Tell students that a suffix is a word part added to the end of a root word. The suffixes *-ation, -ition, -al,* and *-ial* are one syllable long. Write *reservation* on the board and guide students to determine the number of syllables and how the word should be divided. **(4; res/er/va/tion)** When readers encounter a longer word, they can try breaking it into smaller parts, such as suffixes and root words. Repeat the exercise with the words *conclusion, natural,* and *commercial.*

PRETEACH

Decoding/Spelling

Suffixes *-ation, -ition, -al, -ial* Write *admiration* on the board, and underline the suffix. **(-ation)** Circle the root *admir* and tell students that the root word is *admire.* Point out that the *e* at the end of *admire* was dropped when the suffix *-ation* was added. Explain that when *-ation, -ition, -al,* or *-ial* is added to a word, a spelling change sometimes occurs, such as dropping a final *e* or *y* before adding the suffix.

PRETEACH

Grammar/Writing

Present-Tense Verbs; Subject-Verb Agreement Write the following sentences on the board:

> Joe hears a dog bark.
> Joe hears very well.

Read the sentences aloud. Explain that a verb in the present tense tells about an action that happens now or happens over and over. Explain that in the first sentence, Joe is hearing the bark right now. *Hears* is the present tense verb. Explain that in the second sentence, *hears* is also in the present-tense, but it has the second meaning. Joe can hear very well—over and over.

VOCABULARY
Student-Friendly Explanations

forlornly If you do something forlornly, you do it in a way that shows you feel sad and lonely.

fidget People might fidget, or move around restlessly, when they are bored or nervous.

pathetic A person or thing that is pathetic is sad or helpless. You usually feel sorry for pathetic people or things.

resolved When you have resolved to do something, you have made up your mind to do it.

scrounging If an animal is scrounging, it is looking around trying to find food.

noble If you describe someone as noble, you think that person is honest and unselfish.

stingy Someone who is stingy doesn't like to spend money or share what he or she has.

suspicion If you think someone is guilty of doing something wrong, you have a suspicion about him or her.

Fluency

pp. 222–228 **Fluency Performance** Invite students each to read aloud from "Dear Diary" a passage that they selected and practiced earlier. Note the number of words each student reads correctly and incorrectly. Have students rate their own oral reading on the 1–4 scale. Give each student the opportunity to continue practicing and then to read the passage to you again.

"Dear Diary" **265**

LESSON 23

30+ Minutes

Day 1 — DAY AT A GLANCE

VOCABULARY
Reteach *forlornly, fidget, pathetic, resolved, scrounging, noble, stingy, suspicion*

COMPREHENSION
 Reteach Sequence: Story Events

DECODING/SPELLING
Reteach Suffixes *-ation, -ition, -al, -ial*

GRAMMAR/WRITING
Preteach Present-Tense Verbs; Subject-Verb Agreement

FLUENCY
Fluency Practice

Materials Needed: *Turn It Up!*

  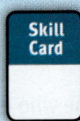 

Student Edition pp. 230–231 | Practice Book p. 91 | Skill Card 23 | Copying Master 90

RETEACH
Vocabulary

pp. 230–231

Lesson 23 Vocabulary Read aloud the Vocabulary Words and the Student-Friendly Explanations. Then have students read the story on page 230 of their books. Guide students as they complete the sentences on page 231 by selecting the correct word in dark type. Have a volunteer read each completed sentence aloud. If students get stuck, encourage them to guess the most likely word and try reading the sentence aloud with the word in place to see if it makes sense. If students are unable to give reasonable responses, refer to the Student-Friendly Explanations. (Answers for page 231: 2. *suspicion*, 3. *scrounging*, 4. *fidget*, 5. *noble*, 6. *stingy*, 7. *forlornly*, 8. *resolved*)

RETEACH
Comprehension

Sequence: Story Events Have students look at side A of *Skill Card 23: Sequence: Story Events*. Ask a volunteer to read the instruction aloud. Then read the passage aloud as students read along.

Point out that the author used the word *first* to tell the reader that the first important thing was about to happen. You may also wish to point out that the chart doesn't have room for everything that happens in the story, so the reader just writes the most important events. Review the information included on the chart.

GUIDED PRACTICE Now have students look at side B of *Skill Card 23: Sequence*. Review the Skill Reminder. Guide students in copying the chart and completing it with the key plot events of the story. Help students distinguish between key events and details by having them summarize the story as they go. (Possible responses: Event 1: Daisy gets locked outside. Event 2: Daisy learns how to use the doorbell from watching a young man. Event 3: Tom rings the bell and the door is opened.)

266 Lesson 23 • Turn It Up!

Day 1

RETEACH

Decoding/Spelling

Suffixes -ation, -ition, -al, -ial Distribute *Copying Master 90*. Model reading the Spelling Words as students repeat them. Review the instruction for adding suffixes to words, and then have students complete the following activity. Have pairs of students write the Spelling Words on index cards. Have one student draw a card and read its word aloud. Have the other student write the word; then have partners switch roles. When a student spells a word correctly, he or she initials the card and returns it to the pile. Students should work through the pile twice or until each student has had the opportunity to spell each of the words. Have students write down each word they do not spell correctly to study later.

PRETEACH

Grammar/Writing

Present-Tense Verbs; Subject-Verb Agreement Remind students that a verb in the present tense tells about an action that happens now or happens over and over. Write the following sentences on the board:

> Ben sings a song.
> Josh and Jacob sing a song.

Ask a volunteer to read the sentences aloud. Explain that in the first sentence, the subject is singular—there is only one person singing—so the verb, *sings*, ends in *s*. In the second sentence, the subject is plural—there is more than one person singing—so the verb, *sing*, has no ending.

GUIDED PRACTICE Write each of the following sentences on the board:

> The horses _____ over the fence.
> She _____ a book every night.
> Raul _____ very well.
> The boys _____ apples on the field trip.

Ask students to identify each subject and tell whether the subject is singular or plural. (horses—plural, She—singular, Raul—singular, boys—plural) Then, have volunteers suggest a verb to complete each sentence above. Have the class check to be sure that the verb agrees with the subject. (Possible responses: jump, reads, writes, collect)

VOCABULARY

Student-Friendly Explanations

forlornly If you do something forlornly, you do it in a way that shows you feel sad and lonely.

fidget People might fidget, or move around restlessly, when they are bored or nervous.

pathetic A person or thing that is pathetic is sad or helpless. You usually feel sorry for pathetic people or things.

resolved When you have resolved to do something, you have made up your mind to do it.

scrounging If an animal is scrounging, it is looking around trying to find food.

noble If you describe someone as noble, you think that person is honest and unselfish.

stingy Someone who is stingy doesn't like to spend money or share what he or she has.

suspicion If you think someone is guilty of doing something wrong, you have a suspicion about him or her.

Fluency

Fluency Practice Have students turn to *Practice Book* page 91. Read the words in the first column aloud. Invite students to track each word and repeat the words after you. Then have students work in pairs to read the words in the first column aloud to each other. Follow the same procedure with each of the remaining columns. After partners have practiced reading aloud the words in each of the columns, have them practice reading all of the words.

"Phil in the City" **267**

LESSON 23

DAY AT A GLANCE
Day 2

VOCABULARY
Reteach *forlornly, fidget, pathetic, resolved, scrounging, noble, stingy, suspicion*

COMPREHENSION
"Phil in the City"
Build Background
Monitor Comprehension
Answers to *Think Critically* Questions

DECODING/SPELLING
Reteach Suffixes *-ation, -ition, -al, -ial*

GRAMMAR/WRITING
Preteach Present-Tense Verbs; Subject-Verb Agreement

FLUENCY
Fluency Practice

Materials Needed: *Turn It Up!*

Student Edition pp. 232–239 | Practice Book pp. 91, 92 | Copying Master 89

RETEACH

Vocabulary

Copying Master 89

Lesson 23 Vocabulary Distribute a set of Words Cards to each pair of students. Have the pair lay the cards face-up between them. Have the first partner choose one of the words and use it in a sentence. Have the second partner point to the card that has the word on it. Then have students trade roles and repeat the activity until all the words have been used in a sentence and identified.

Comprehension

Build Background: "Phil in the City"
Ask students to share what they know about crickets, such as their approximate size, what they look like, and the kinds of noises they make. Then ask students to tell about any experiences they may have had with going to a strange city for the first time. What did it feel like? How did they find their way around the new city?

pp. 232–233

Monitor Comprehension: "Phil in the City"
Read the title of the story aloud. Then have students read pages 232–233 to find out what happens first in the story "Phil in the City."

After reading the pages, ask: **What was the first event in the story?** (Phil got off the bus and looked around.)  **SEQUENCE**

Ask: **What important, or key, event happened next?** (Possible response: A big cat appeared.) **SEQUENCE**

Ask: **Who are the main characters so far?** (Phil Cricket, Ralph the cat) **Where does the story take place?** (on a city sidewalk) **STORY ELEMENTS**

Discuss the Stop and Think question on page 232: **Do you think the cat will eat Phil?** (Possible response: I think the cat will not eat Phil.) Guide students in writing the answer to this question. **MAKE PREDICTIONS**

Discuss the Stop and Think question on page 233: **Think about the sentence "This cat seemed rather sophisticated." Is it a fact or an opinion? Explain your answer.** (Possible response: This sentence is an opinion. It tells what Phil thinks of Ralph the cat.) Guide students in writing the answer to this question. **FACT AND OPINION**

268 Lesson 23 • *Turn It Up!*

Day 2

Discuss the Stop and Think question on page 234: **Why does Ralph say he knows what Phil is thinking?** (Possible response: Ralph says he knows what Phil is thinking because he can tell from Phil's face that Phil doesn't trust Ralph.) Guide students in writing the answer to this question. **DRAW CONCLUSIONS**

Read aloud the first two paragraphs on page 234. Model the strategy of asking questions to improve comprehension of the story.

THINK ALOUD When I read this section, I can't help but think about what I know about cats and crickets. While I do know a few cats that are too fond of napping to bother a cricket, most of the cats I know would gobble up any cricket they met. I ask myself, "What will happen to Phil? Will he barely escape being eaten by Ralph?" Asking questions like this also help me comprehend what I read. **ASK QUESTIONS**

Discuss the Stop and Think question on page 235: **How does Ralph get to his home?** (He squeezes through a small space between the phone booth and a fence. Then he and Phil go through a small door that leads to a basement.) Guide students in writing the answer to this question. **NOTE DETAILS**

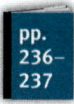

Discuss the Stop and Think question on page 236: **What happens after Phil discovers he is in a paper warehouse?** (Possible response: After Phil discovers he is in a paper warehouse, Ralph scurries behind a mound of paper.) Guide students in writing the answer to this question. **SEQUENCE**

Discuss the Stop and Think question on page 237: **Do you think Phil will find his nephew? Explain your answer.** (Possible response: I think Phil will find his nephew because Ralph will help him.) Guide students in writing the answer to this question. **MAKE PREDICTIONS**

Discuss the Stop and Think question on page 238: **In the beginning, Phil felt one way about cats. How does he feel now?** (Possible response: Now Phil feels that cats are noble and kind.) Guide students in writing the answer to this question. **CHARACTER'S EMOTIONS**

Ask: **How might the story have been different if Phil had never met Ralph?** (Possible responses: Phil would have been hungrier. It might have taken Phil a lot longer to get around. It might have taken Phil a lot longer to find the elephant in Phelps Park.) **PLOT/MAKE INFERENCES**

VOCABULARY
Student-Friendly Explanations

forlornly If you do something forlornly, you do it in a way that shows you feel sad and lonely.

fidget People might fidget, or move around restlessly, when they are bored or nervous.

pathetic A person or thing that is pathetic is sad or helpless. You usually feel sorry for pathetic people or things.

resolved When you have resolved to do something, you have made up your mind to do it.

scrounging If an animal is scrounging, it is looking around trying to find food.

noble If you describe someone as noble, you think that person is honest and unselfish.

stingy Someone who is stingy doesn't like to spend money or share what he or she has.

suspicion If you think someone is guilty of doing something wrong, you have a suspicion about him or her.

"Phil in the City" 269

Day 2

Spelling Words: Lesson 23

1. decoration	11. abdominal
2. abbreviation	12. proposal
3. admiration	13. rendition
4. association	14. disposal
5. aviation	15. emotional
6. civilization	16. environmental
7. declaration	17. denial
8. addition	18. facial
9. composition	19. judicial
10. preposition	20. testimonial

page 239 **Answers to *Think Critically* Questions** Help students read and answer the *Think Critically* questions on page 239. Have students copy the graphic organizer in question 1 onto a separate sheet of paper. Then guide students in writing the answer to each question. Possible responses are provided.

1. [Then] Ralph takes Phil to his home. [Finally] Phil finds his nephew. **SEQUENCE**
2. I know the author wrote this story to entertain me because the story has talking animals that do funny things. **AUTHOR'S PURPOSE**
3. Phil will say that he got off the bus. Then he saw a cat. He found out that the cat was nice. The cat was also generous and could sing. The cat helped him find his nephew. **PLOT**

RETEACH

Decoding/Spelling

Suffixes -ation, -ition, -al, -ial Write the following on the board:

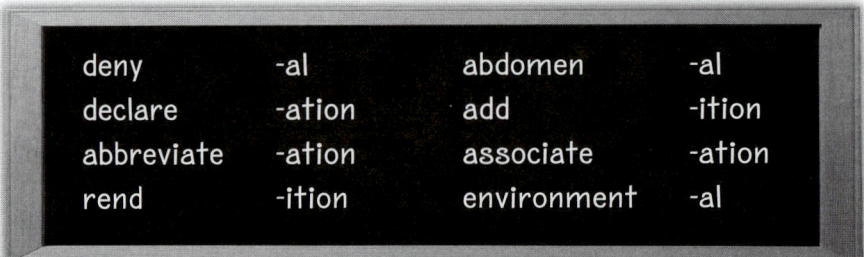

Explain that each root word is followed by a suffix. Ask students to add each suffix to the root word to form a new word. Then ask students to explain what, if any, spelling change they made to the root word.

270 Lesson 23 • Turn It Up!

Day 2

PRETEACH
Grammar/Writing

Practice Book 92

Present-Tense Verbs; Subject-Verb Agreement Explain to students that different forms of the verb *be* are used with different subjects. Write *am, is,* and *are* on the board. Point out that *am* is only used with the pronoun *I*. Note that *is* is used with singular subjects and *are* is used with plural subjects. Write these sentences on the board:

> The cat _____ by the fence.
> The cat and the cricket _____ friends.
> I _____ happy to see this.

Invite volunteers to name the form of *be* that correctly completes each sentence. (is, are, am)

GUIDED PRACTICE Have students turn to page 92 in their *Practice Book*. Read the activity directions together. Then ask students to complete the page. Allow time for students to share their answers. Reteach as necessary.

Fluency

Practice Book 91

Fluency Practice Invite students to look at the bottom half of *Practice Book* page 91. These sentences have been broken into natural phrases. Tell students to repeat each phrase after you, mirroring your expression, phrasing, and pace. After students have repeated each sentence, invite them to practice reading the sentences to partners.

"Phil in the City" 271

LESSON 23

30+ Minutes

COMPREHENSION
Preteach Use Context Clues
Reread and Summarize "Phil in the City"

DECODING/SPELLING
Reteach Suffixes *-ation, -ition, -al, -ial*

BUILD ROBUST VOCABULARY
Teach Words from "Phil in the City"

GRAMMAR/WRITING
Reteach Writing Trait: Conventions

FLUENCY
Fluency Practice

Materials Needed: *Turn It Up!*

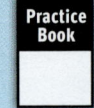

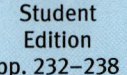

Student Edition pp. 232–238

Practice Book pp. 91, 93

Copying Master 91

PRETEACH

Comprehension

 Copying Master 91

Use Context Clues Distribute *Copying Master 91*, and have students listen as you read the information at the top of the page.

GUIDED PRACTICE Ask students to look through the passage to find the indicated words and then look for context clues that help reveal each word's meaning. Have them record their responses on the page. Invite students to check their definitions with a dictionary. Allow time for students to share their responses with others.

Reread and Summarize: "Phil in the City" Have students reread and summarize "Phil in the City" in sections, as described below.

 pp. 232–234

Let's reread pages 232–234 to recall what happens to Phil at the beginning of the story.
Summary: Phil arrives in the city and immediately meets Ralph, the cat. He is suspicious of Ralph initially, but does accept Ralph's offer of help.

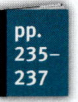 pp. 235–237

Now let's reread pages 235–237 to find out what happens when Ralph takes Phil back to his home.
Summary: Ralph leads Phil to his home in a paper warehouse. Ralph gives Phil a cracker and tells him he can help Phil find his nephew.

 page 238

Now let's reread page 238 to find out what happens when Ralph and Phil go looking for Phil's nephew.
Summary: Phil is further charmed by Ralph's talents and generosity. Ralph leads him directly to his nephew, who is glad to see Phil.

RETEACH

Decoding/Spelling

Suffixes *-ation, -ition, -al, -ial* Divide the group into two teams. Have the first player of one team spell a Spelling Word. If the player spells it correctly, he or she draws one part of a mouse's body on the board. If the word is misspelled, another team member can give the correct spelling but does not draw a part of the mouse. Alternate between the two teams until one team has completed its mouse.

272 Lesson 23 • Turn It Up!

Day 3

TEACH

Build Robust Vocabulary

Words from "Phil in the City" Have students locate the word *sophisticated* on page 233 of "Phil in the City." Ask a volunteer to read aloud the sentence in which this word appears. (Line 5: *This cat seemed rather sophisticated.*) Explain that this sentence means that the cat seemed sure of himself. He looked like he knew a lot about the world. Then ask students to locate and read aloud the sentence in which the word *triumphant* appears on page 237. (Line 5: *Ralph flashed Phil a triumphant smile.*) Explain that this sentence means that Ralph's smile showed he was proud that he had done something good.

pp. 233–237

Write *sophisticated* and *triumphant* on the board. Guide students in brainstorming situations in which a person might be described by one of these two words.

RETEACH

Grammar/Writing

Practice Book 93

Writing Trait: Conventions Have students turn to page 93 in their *Practice Book*. Explain that when writers write a story, it is important to use the correct conventions of writing. Using correct grammar, spelling, punctuation, and capitalization helps the reader better understand your writing. Ask volunteers to read the information in the boxes. Point out how the author of "Phil in the City" uses correct conventions to help the reader make sense of the story.

GUIDED PRACTICE Work with students to complete Part A and Part B. Finally, have students work in pairs to complete Part C. Allow time for volunteers to share their corrected writing.

Fluency

Practice Book 91

Fluency Practice Tell students that today they will reread the sentences on the bottom of *Practice Book* page 91. Have students locate and point to the first sentence. Tell students that everyone is going to read the sentence together. This choral reading will give students an opportunity to hear others and listen to the natural phrasing of the sentences. Choral-read each of the sentences several times.

"Phil in the City" 273

LESSON 23

DAY AT A GLANCE
Day 4

COMPREHENSION
Reteach Use Context Clues

DECODING/SPELLING
Reteach Suffixes -ation, -ition, -al, -ial

BUILD ROBUST VOCABULARY
Reteach Words from "Phil in the City"

GRAMMAR/WRITING
Reteach Writing Form: Adventure Scene

FLUENCY
Fluency Practice

Materials Needed: *Turn It Up!*

Student Edition pp. 232–238

Practice Book p. 94

Copying Master 92

Spelling Words: Lesson 23

1. decoration	11. abdominal
2. abbreviation	12. proposal
3. admiration	13. rendition
4. association	14. disposal
5. aviation	15. emotional
6. civilization	16. environmental
7. declaration	17. denial
8. addition	18. facial
9. composition	19. judicial
10. preposition	20. testimonial

30+ Minutes

RETEACH

Comprehension

Use Context Clues   Remind students that when they come to an unfamiliar word in the reading, they can use **context clues** to figure out its meaning. Review these key points:

- Context clues are words or phrases around a new word that give hints about the word's meaning.
- Some familiar words have more than one meaning. You can use context clues to figure out which meaning is intended.
- Some context clues tell what the word means; others provide hints.
- If there aren't enough hints to figure out the meaning from context, you can still use a dictionary to look up a word's meaning.

Write the following sentences on the board. Have volunteers read each sentence aloud and explain what they know about the underlined word based on the surrounding context.

- "Perhaps I can be of some help. Let me <u>introduce</u> myself. I am Ralph." (Possible response: The text doesn't say exactly what *introduce* means, but in the next line, Ralph tells Phil his name. We can infer that *introduce* has to do with telling someone who you are.)
- "That's not odd at all!" <u>exclaimed</u> Ralph. (Possible response: I know an exclamation point is used to show great emotion, so maybe *exclaimed* means to say something with great emotion.)

RETEACH

Decoding/Spelling

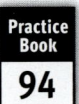

Practice Book 94

Suffixes -ation, -ition, -al, -ial   Have students number a sheet of paper 1–16. Write *decoration* on the board, and point to the suffix. Tell students that in the first six words have the suffix *-ation* at the end of the word. After students write each word, display it so they can proofread their work. Repeat this activity using these examples: *addition, abdominal, denial*.

1. abbreviation	2. admiration	3. association	4. aviation
5. civilization	6. declaration	7. composition	8. preposition
9. rendition	10. proposal	11. disposal	12. emotional
13. environmental	14. facial	15. judicial	16. testimonial

Have students turn to page 94 in their *Practice Book*. Look at the illustration together; then have a volunteer read the first sentence. Have students follow the directions. Have them complete the remaining directions in the same manner.

274 Lesson 23 • Turn It Up!

Day 4

RETEACH
Build Robust Vocabulary

Words from "Phil in the City" Review the meanings of the words *sophisticated* and *triumphant*. Then say these sentences and ask which word describes each sentence. Have students explain why.

- **The guest speaker knew a lot about the world and was very sure of herself.** (sophisticated)
- **When the girl won the race, she put her hands high in the air as a sign that she was proud of winning.** (triumphant)

RETEACH
Grammar/Writing

Copying Master 92

Writing Form: Adventure Scene Explain that an adventure scene tells a story about the adventures of a main character. The scene should begin with a sentence that gets the reader's attention, and should include time-order words and details that help the reader picture the scene. Explain that it is important to use correct conventions of writing to help the reader understand the story.

GUIDED PRACTICE Distribute *Copying Master 92*. Have a volunteer read the description of an adventure scene. Then read the notes in the margin together. Point out that the word *morning* is a time-order word that helps set the time of day for the story. Have students look for other examples of time-order words in the story. (by the time, as soon as I got there, then) Then work through the rest of the directions in the section.

Fluency

pp. 232–238

Fluency Practice Have each student work with a partner to read passages from "Phil in the City" aloud to each other. Students may select a passage that they enjoyed or choose one of the following options:

- Read page 235. (Total: 83 words)
- Read page 238. (Total: 86 words)

Encourage students to read the selected passage aloud to their partner three times. Have the student rate his or her reading on the 1–4 scale.

1	Need more practice
2	Pretty good
3	Good
4	Great!

"Phil in the City" 275

Preteach for LESSON 24

DAY AT A GLANCE — Day 5

VOCABULARY
Preteach *remarkable, suitable, advantage, extracts, withstand, stealthy*

COMPREHENSION
Preteach Text Structure: Sequence

DECODING/WORD ATTACK
Preteach Decode Longer Words

DECODING/SPELLING
Preteach Words with Suffixes in Combination

GRAMMAR/WRITING
Preteach Past-Tense Verbs

FLUENCY
Fluency Performance

Materials Needed: *Turn It Up!*

 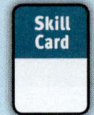 

Student Edition pp. 232–238 | Skill Card 24 | Copying Master 93

PRETEACH
Vocabulary

Lesson 24 Vocabulary Distribute a set of Vocabulary Word Cards to each student. Hold up the word card for the first Vocabulary Word, and ask a volunteer to read the word aloud. Have students repeat the word and hold up the matching card. Give the explanation for the word. Then ask students the first question below and discuss their responses. Continue for each of the Vocabulary Words.

- What would be **remarkable** about a car that ran on air?
- Would heavy hiking boots be **suitable** for P.E.? Why or why not?
- How do some humans take **advantage** of the strength of horses?
- If someone **extracts** something from your pocket, is that a good thing?
- What do you need to **withstand** very bad weather?
- Which is a better example of a **stealthy** animal: a cat or a cow? Why?

PRETEACH
Comprehension

Text Structure: Sequence Have students look at side A of *Skill Card 24: Text Structure: Sequence*. Read the information about sequence. Ask a volunteer to read the passage aloud while students follow along. Point to the chart. Discuss with students why these events were chosen for the chart and how they know the events are in the correct order. Ask students to tell other events that could be included in the sequence chart.

276 Preteach for Lesson 24 • *Turn It Up!*

> **Day 5**

> **PRETEACH**
> ### Decoding/Word Attack

Decode Longer Words Write *thankfulness, endlessly, amazingly,* and *admittedly* on the board. Divide *thankfulness* into syllables. Point out that the last two syllables are suffixes. Tell students that when they come to a longer word, they can divide the word into syllables to look for suffixes. Tell students:

- Sometimes root words or roots have two or more suffixes added.
- The inflected endings *-ed* and *-ing* can be combined with suffixes.

Have volunteers identify any suffixes in the remaining words.

> **PRETEACH**
> ### Decoding/Spelling

Words with Suffixes in Combination Write *beautifully, educationally, guiltlessly,* and *childishness* on the board, and read them aloud. Underline the suffixes in each word. Identify the root words. (beauty, educate, guilt, child) Remind students that suffixes are added, a spelling change is sometimes made to the root word, such as changing *y* to *i* or dropping a final vowel.

> **PRETEACH**
> ### Grammar/Writing

Past-Tense Verbs Write the following sentences on the board:

> Jamal played the piano yesterday.
> Natalie tried to fix the table.

Read the sentences aloud. Tell students that a verb in the past tense tells about an action that happened in the past. Explain that in this sentence, *played* is in the past tense. Explain that we add *-ed* to the end of regular verbs to form the past tense. Have students identify the past-tense verb in the second sentence. (tried) Point out that the verb's root is *try*. To change the word to the past tense, the *y* is changed to *i* before *-ed* is added.

VOCABULARY
Student-Friendly Explanations

remarkable A remarkable thing is something very special.

suitable Something is suitable if it is right for a certain use.

advantage When you take advantage, you use something available to you.

extracts Someone who extracts something carefully pulls it out.

withstand If you withstand a difficult time, you are able to get through it.

stealthy A stealthy animal is quiet and hidden as it moves about.

Fluency

pp. 232–238 **Fluency Performance** Invite students each to read aloud from "Phil in the City" a passage that they selected and practiced earlier. Note the number of words each student reads correctly and incorrectly. Have students rate their own oral reading on the 1–4 scale. Give each student the opportunity to continue practicing and then to read the passage to you again.

"Phil in the City"

LESSON 24

DAY AT A GLANCE — Day 1

VOCABULARY
Reteach *remarkable, suitable, advantage, extracts, withstand, stealthy*

COMPREHENSION
 Reteach Text Structure: Sequence

DECODING/SPELLING
Reteach Words with Suffixes in Combination

GRAMMAR/WRITING
Preteach Future-Tense Verbs

FLUENCY
Fluency Practice

Materials Needed: *Turn It Up!*

| Student Edition pp. 240–241 | Practice Book p. 95 | Skill Card 24 | Copying Master 94 |

RETEACH

Vocabulary

Lesson 24 Vocabulary Read aloud the Vocabulary Words and the Student-Friendly Explanations. Then have students read the articles and fill in the blanks on pages 240 and 241 of their books. Have a volunteer read each paragraph, adding the word they inserted. If students are unable to give reasonable responses, refer to the Student-Friendly Explanations. (Answers for pages 240–241: 2. *withstand*, 3. *advantage*, 4. *extracts*, 5. *suitable*, 6. *stealthy*)

RETEACH

Comprehension

  **Text Structure: Sequence** Have students look at side B of *Skill Card 24: Text Structure: Sequence*. Have a volunteer read the information in the box aloud. Then have a volunteer read the passage aloud while students follow along.

GUIDED PRACTICE Guide students in copying the chart and completing it with the key events from the passage. (Event 1: A cornfield ant begins life as an egg. Event 2: It then turns into a larva. Event 3: Next, the larva turns into a pupa. Event 4: Finally, the pupa becomes an adult ant.)

278 Lesson 24 • *Turn It Up!*

Day 1

RETEACH

Decoding/Spelling

Words with Suffixes in Combination Distribute *Copying Master 94*. Model reading the Spelling Words and have students repeat them. Review the instruction for adding suffixes to words, and then have students complete the following activity, which is based on the traditional Memory Game. Pairs of students make game cards using the lesson's Spelling Words with suffixes missing; a dash appears in place of each suffix. After a student matches two cards, he or she must supply the correct missing suffixes to keep the game cards. If the wrong suffixes are supplied, the opponent gets the game cards and takes the next turn.

PRETEACH

Grammar/Writing

Future-Tense Verbs Write the following sentence on the board:

> Jamal will play the piano tomorrow.

Read the sentence aloud. Remind students that a verb's tense refers to time. A verb in the future tense tells about an action that will happen in the future. Point to the sentence and ask: **What is the verb phrase in this sentence?** (will play) Explain that in this sentence, Jamal will play the piano at some point in the future. He is not playing the piano now. In the verb phrase *will play*, *will* is a helping verb that tells the reader that the playing will happen in the future.

GUIDED PRACTICE Write the following sentence frames on the board, and have students copy them:

> Hank _____ in the band.
> She _____ horses this summer.

Have students work in pairs to identify a future-tense verb phrase that can complete each sentence and write it in the blank. Invite students to take turns sharing their responses. (Possible responses: will play, will ride)

VOCABULARY

Student-Friendly Explanations

remarkable A remarkable thing is something very special.

suitable Something is suitable if it is right for a certain use.

advantage When you take advantage, you use something available to you.

extracts Someone who extracts something carefully pulls it out.

withstand If you withstand a difficult time, you are able to get through it.

stealthy A stealthy animal is quiet and hidden as it moves about.

Fluency

Fluency Practice Have students turn to *Practice Book* page 95. Read the words in the first column aloud. Invite students to track each word and repeat the words after you. Then have students work in pairs to read the words in the first column aloud to each other. Follow the same procedure with each of the remaining columns. After partners have practiced reading aloud the words in each of the columns, have them practice reading all of the words.

"Where Land and Sea Meet" 279

LESSON 24

DAY AT A GLANCE — Day 2

30+ Minutes

VOCABULARY
Reteach remarkable, suitable, advantage, extracts, withstand, stealthy

COMPREHENSION
"Where Land and Sea Meet"
Build Background
Monitor Comprehension
Answers to *Think Critically* Questions

DECODING/SPELLING
Reteach Combine Word Parts

GRAMMAR/WRITING
Preteach Conjugating Verbs

FLUENCY
Fluency Practice

Materials Needed: *Turn It Up!*

Student Edition pp. 242–249 | Practice Book pp. 95, 96 | Copying Master 93

RETEACH

Vocabulary

Lesson 24 Vocabulary Distribute a set of Word Cards to each student or pair of students. Read aloud the meaning of one of the Vocabulary Words, and have students display and read the matching Word Card. Continue until students have matched all the words.

Comprehension

Build Background: "Where Land and Sea Meet"

Ask students to share experiences they may have had with growing plants or trees. What did the plants or trees look like? Where did they grow best? Did they need a lot of light, or could they grow in shade? What new things did you learn about this plant or tree?

Monitor Comprehension: "Where Land and Sea Meet"

pp. 242–243

Read the title of the story aloud. Then have students read pages 242–243 to learn what happens where land and sea meet.

After reading the pages, ask: **What happens where land and sea meet?** (Mangrove trees grow in the water.) **MAIN IDEA AND DETAILS**

Ask: **How are mangroves like other kinds of trees? How are they different?** (All trees have roots, but mangrove roots don't grow under the ground. Instead, they grow in salt water.) **COMPARE AND CONTRAST**

Discuss the Stop and Think question on page 242: **What would you like to learn about mangrove trees?** (Possible responses: I would like to learn other reasons why mangrove trees are unusual; what kinds of animals live in a mangrove.) Guide students in writing the answer to this question. **PERSONAL RESPONSE**

Discuss the Stop and Think question on page 243: **How do mangroves make new trees?** (To make new trees, first mangroves make a lot of seeds. Each seed gets food from the mother tree. It grows into a tiny tree. When it is ready, it falls into the water. Finally it will reach new soil and grow.) Guide students in writing the answer to this question.  **TEXT STRUCTURE: SEQUENCE**

---

280 Lesson 24 • *Turn It Up!*

Day 2

 pp. 244–245

Discuss the Stop and Think question on page 244: **What are some animals that live in a mangrove forest?** (Some animals that live in a mangrove forest are crabs, fish, insects, snakes, and birds.) Guide students in writing the answer to this question. **NOTE DETAILS**

Read aloud page 244. Model the strategy of asking questions as you read.

THINK ALOUD After I read the sentence "It is the beginning of a food chain for other living things," I find myself thinking, "That's interesting. I wonder what other animals are in the food chain? What kind of animal life does the mangrove forest support?" As I continue to read, I find the answer to my question. Asking questions as I read helps me notice and remember the important details in the selection. **ASK QUESTIONS**

Discuss the Stop and Think question on page 245: **How do you think the rat snake got its name?** (Possible response: I think the rat snake got its name because it eats rats.) Guide students in writing the answer to this question. **DRAW CONCLUSIONS**

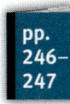 pp. 246–247

Discuss the Stop and Think question on page 246: **How do mangroves help the land?** (Mangroves help the land by preventing the land from being slowly washed into the sea, by blocking strong winds, and by protecting against tidal waves.) Guide students in writing the answer to this question. **SUMMARIZE**

Ask: **How does protecting the land also help protect the people who live nearby?** (Possible response: Protecting the land from being washed away prevents ocean-side homes from being washed away. Protecting the land from heavy winds and tidal waves also keeps the people who live there safe.) **MAKE INFERENCES**

Discuss the Stop and Think question on page 247: **What will happen if mangrove forests disappear?** (If mangrove forests disappear, the animals that live there will also disappear.) Guide students in writing the answer to this question. **CAUSE AND EFFECT**

 page 248

Discuss the Stop and Think question on page 248: **Is it better to protect the mangroves, or is it better to use the land for homes? Why?** (Possible response: I think it is better to protect the mangroves because they provide food and keep land from washing away.) Guide students in writing the answer to this question. **MAKE JUDGMENTS**

VOCABULARY

Student-Friendly Explanations

remarkable A remarkable thing is something very special.

suitable Something is suitable if it is right for a certain use.

advantage When you take advantage, you use something available to you.

extracts Someone who extracts something carefully pulls it out.

withstand If you withstand a difficult time, you are able to get through it.

stealthy A stealthy animal is quiet and hidden as it moves about.

"Where Land and Sea Meet" 281

Day 2

Spelling Words: Lesson 24

1. additional	11. guiltlessly
2. beautifully	12. joyfully
3. blissfully	13. meaningfully
4. boastfully	14. playfully
5. carefully	15. restfully
6. cheerfully	16. respectfully
7. colorfully	17. childishness
8. educational	18. truthfully
9. effortlessly	19. usefully
10. endlessly	20. powerfully

 Answers to *Think Critically* Questions Help students read and answer the *Think Critically* questions on page 249. Have students copy the graphic organizer in question 1 onto a separate sheet of paper. Then guide students in writing the answer to each question. Possible responses are provided.

1. [What I Learned] Mangroves' roots grow in water; the seeds grow into little trees on the mother tree; mangroves protect homes. **MAIN IDEA AND DETAILS**

2. I think the most interesting fact about mangroves is the way its roots grow in water; the way it makes more trees; the animals that live there. **EXPRESS PERSONAL OPINIONS**

3. I think the author wanted me to learn that mangroves are unusual trees or that it is important to protect the mangroves. **AUTHOR'S PURPOSE**

RETEACH

Decoding/Spelling

Combine Word Parts Write these word parts on the board:

bliss -ful -ly	effort -less -ly
boast -ful -ly	add -ition -al
beauty -ful -ly	educate -ion -al

Explain that the first word part in each set is the root word, and the next two word parts are suffixes. Show students how to add each combination of suffixes to the root word to form a new word. Ask a volunteer to tell which two root words will need a spelling change before the suffixes are added. (beauty, educate) Then have students work in pairs to combine the word parts to make Spelling Words.

282 Lesson 24 • Turn It Up!

Day 2

PRETEACH

Grammar/Writing

Practice Book 96 **Conjugating Verbs** Tell students that to conjugate a verb, they need to check that the form of the verb is correct, based on the tense. They also need to be sure the verb agrees with its subject. Write these sentences on the board:

> Kira clean her room now.
> I will cleaned my room later today.

Underline the verb or verb phrase in each sentence. (clean, will cleaned) Point out that in the first sentence, the verb does not agree with its subject. Cross out *clean* and write *cleans*. Then explain that in the second sentence, the verb does not agree with the tense. Cross out *cleaned* and write *clean*. Ask volunteers to name the tense of each corrected verb. (present, future)

GUIDED PRACTICE Direct students' attention to page 96 in their *Practice Book*. Have students work individually or in pairs to complete the activity. Ask volunteers to share their answers with the group.

Fluency

Practice Book 95 **Fluency Practice** Invite students to look at the bottom half of *Practice Book* page 95. These sentences have been broken into natural phrases. Tell students to repeat each phrase after you, mirroring your expression, phrasing, and pace. After students have repeated each sentence, invite them to practice reading the sentences to partners.

"Where Land and Sea Meet" 283

LESSON 24

DAY AT A GLANCE
Day 3

COMPREHENSION
Preteach Use Context Clues
Reread and Summarize "Where Land and Sea Meet"

DECODING/SPELLING
Reteach Words with Suffixes in Combination

BUILD ROBUST VOCABULARY
Teach Words from "Where Land and Sea Meet"

GRAMMAR/WRITING
Reteach Writing Trait: Conventions

FLUENCY
Fluency Practice

Materials Needed: *Turn It Up!*

Student Edition pp. 242–248

Practice Book pp. 95, 97

Copying Master 95

30+ Minutes

PRETEACH
Comprehension

Use Context Clues Distribute *Copying Master 95*, and have a student read the information at the top of the page. Ask a volunteer to read the passage aloud as students read along. Then discuss the first word and its related context clues.

GUIDED PRACTICE Ask students to use the context clues to complete the activity. Allow time for students to share their responses.

Reread and Summarize Have students reread and summarize "Where Land and Sea Meet" in sections, as described below.

pp. 242–243

Let's reread pages 242–243 to recall where mangrove tress grow and how they produce new trees.
Summary: Mangrove trees grow in coastal areas that are flooded with salt water. New seedlings form while still attached to the tree. When they are ready to take root on their own, they drop off the tree and into the water.

pp. 244–246

Let's reread pages 244–246 to remember how mangrove trees help animals and people.
Summary: The mangrove trees are the beginning of a food chain for many animals. Mangrove trees also help hold the soil in place and protect the land from strong winds and destructive waves.

pp. 247–248

Let's reread pages 247–248 to recall the problems that mangrove trees face and the solution some people have devised.
Summary: Mangrove trees are often cut down to make room for new houses and roads. Some people want to protect the mangroves, so they plant new trees and protect existing ones.

RETEACH
Decoding/Spelling

Words with Suffixes in Combination Write *add* and *additionally* on the board. Have students clap and say the number of syllables in each word. (1, 5) Tell students that it will help them to spell words with more than one suffix if they know how many syllables there are in the original root word and how many suffixes are added. Write *blissfully, effortlessly, childishness,* and *respectfully* on the board. Have students copy the words and count the number of syllables and suffixes in each word.

284 Lesson 24 • Turn It Up!

Day 3

TEACH

Build Robust Vocabulary

pp. 244–247

Words from "Where Land and Sea Meet" Have students locate the word *wildlife* on page 244 of "Where Land and Sea Meet." Ask a volunteer to read aloud the sentence in which this word appears. (Line 1: *A mangrove forest is home to many kinds of wildlife.*) Explain that this sentence means that many kinds of wild animals live in a mangrove forest. Continue by asking students to locate and read aloud the sentence in which the word *protect* appears on page 246. (Line 5: *The roots and tree trunks also protect homes during storms.*) Explain that this sentence means that the roots and trunks keep homes safe from danger during storms. Then ask students to locate and read aloud the sentence in which the word *threats* appears on page 247. (Line 3: *Two of the greatest threats to mangroves are new homes and roads.*) Explain that a "threat" is something that is likely to harm something or someone else.

Give each student a card with the letters of one of the words scrambled on it. Have students unscramble their words, read them for the group, and tell what they mean.

RETEACH

Grammar/Writing

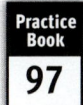
Practice Book 97

Writing Trait: Conventions Have students turn to page 97 in their *Practice Book*. Ask a volunteer to read the information at the top of the page. Point out how the author of "Where Land and Sea Meet" uses correct conventions to help the reader make sense of the story. For example, the subject-verb agreement in the sentence "They are some of the world's most unusual trees," helps readers better understand what they are reading.

GUIDED PRACTICE Work with students to complete Part A. Then read the directions for Part B, and remind students how to use proofreading marks. Have students read the passage and make corrections. Read the Part C directions, and have students write sentences of their own.

Fluency

Practice Book 95

Fluency Practice Tell students that today they will reread the sentences on the bottom of *Practice Book* page 95. Have students locate and point to the first sentence. Tell students that everyone is going to read the sentence together. This choral reading will give students an opportunity to hear others and listen to the natural phrasing of the sentences. Choral-read each of the sentences several times.

"Where Land and Sea Meet" 285

LESSON 24

DAY AT A GLANCE
Day 4

COMPREHENSION
Reteach Use Context Clues

DECODING/SPELLING
Reteach Words with Suffixes in Combination

BUILD ROBUST VOCABULARY
Reteach Words from "Where Land and Sea Meet"

GRAMMAR/WRITING
Reteach Writing Form: Descriptive Paragraph

FLUENCY
Fluency Performance

Materials Needed: *Turn It Up!*

Student Edition pp. 242–248

Practice Book page 98

Copying Master 96

Spelling Words: Lesson 24

1. additional	11. guiltlessly
2. beautifully	12. joyfully
3. blissfully	13. meaningfully
4. boastfully	14. playfully
5. carefully	15. restfully
6. cheerfully	16. respectfully
7. colorfully	17. childishness
8. educational	18. truthfully
9. effortlessly	19. usefully
10. endlessly	20. powerfully

30+ Minutes

RETEACH
Comprehension

Use Context Clues Tell students that when they come to an unfamiliar word, they can use context clues to figure out its meaning. Write on the board the following sentences from "Where Land and Sea Meet":

> They block some of the <u>force</u> of the heavy winds. The winds are less strong by the time they reach the homes nearby.

Ask: If you don't know the meaning of *force*, what are some clues that can help you figure out its meaning? (Possible response: The second sentence says that the winds are less strong by the time they reach homes nearby, so the word *force* in the first sentence probably means "strength.") Have a volunteer look up the word's meaning in a dictionary.

GUIDED PRACTICE Write on the board these sentences from "Where Land and Sea Meet":

> They are some of the word's most <u>unusual</u> trees. They have strong roots like other trees. But their roots don't spread underground. Instead, they grow in salt water.

Discuss what context clues could be useful for finding the meaning of the underlined word. (Possible response: The sentences that follow both tell how the tree is different form other trees. *Unusual* probably means "different.") Finally, have students look up the word in a dictionary and compare the dictionary definition to the one they inferred from context.

RETEACH
Decoding/Spelling

Words with Suffixes in Combination Have students number a sheet of paper 1–17. Write *beautifully* on the board, and point to the suffixes. Tell students that the first thirteen words you will say end in -*ful* and -*ly*. After students write each word, display it so they can proofread their work. Repeat for the other suffix combinations using these examples: *additional* and *effortlessly*. Finally, dictate *childishness*.

286 Lesson 24 • Turn It Up!

1. blissfully	2. boastfully	3. carefully	4. cheerfully
5. colorfully	6. joyfully	7. meaningfully	8. playfully
9. powerfully	10. restfully	11. respectfully	12. truthfully
13. usefully	14. educational	15. endlessly	16. guiltlessly
17. childishness			

Have students turn to page 98 in their *Practice Book*. Read the passage aloud as students read along with you. Then ask students to read each sentence and write the correct word to complete each sentence.

RETEACH
Build Robust Vocabulary

Words from "Where Land Meets Sea" Review the meanings of the words *wildlife, protect,* and *threats*. Then say these sentences and ask which word describes each sentence. Have students explain why.

- **Some people like to go into the woods and take photos of wild animals.** (wildlife)
- **Seatbelts keep people in cars safe from danger.** (protect)
- **A cat is likely to be a danger to a pet bird out of its cage.** (threat)

RETEACH
Grammar/Writing

Copying Master 96

Writing Form: Descriptive Paragraph Tell students that a descriptive paragraph tells about a person, place, or thing. When they write a story, it is important to use specific and interesting words, so readers can picture in their minds what is being described. Distribute *Copying Master 96*. Have a volunteer read about descriptive paragraphs. Then read the Student Model together.

GUIDED PRACTICE Have students complete the questions at the bottom of the page. Allow time for students to share their revised sentences with the group.

Fluency

pp. 242–248 Have each student work with a partner to read passages from "Where Land and Sea Meet" aloud to each other. Students may select a passage that they enjoyed or choose one of the following options:

- Read page 243. (Total: 96 words)
- Read page 246. (Total: 94 words)

Encourage students to read the selected passage aloud to their partner three times. Have the student rate his or her reading on the 1–4 scale.

1	Need more practice
2	Pretty good
3	Good
4	Great!

"Where Land and Sea Meet" 287

Preteach for LESSON 25

VOCABULARY
Preteach destinations, aspects, vigorously, reconstruct, gorgeous, festive, ornate, symbolize, expectantly, misfortune

COMPREHENSION
 Preteach Character, Setting, and Plot

DECODING/WORD ATTACK
Preteach Decode Longer Words

DECODING/SPELLING
Preteach Words with Suffixes -ant, -ent, -eer, -ist, -ian

GRAMMAR/WRITING
Preteach Main, Helping, Action, and Linking Verbs

FLUENCY
Fluency Performance

Materials Needed: *Turn It Up!*

 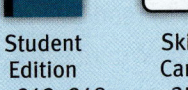 

Student Edition pp. 242–248 | Skill Card 25 | Copying Master 97

PRETEACH

Vocabulary

Lesson 25 Vocabulary Distribute a set of Vocabulary Word Cards to each student. Hold up the card for the first word, and ask a volunteer to read it aloud. Have students repeat the word and hold up the matching card. Give the explanation for the word. Then ask students the first question below and discuss their responses. Continue for each Vocabulary Word.

- What are your favorite **destinations**?
- What **aspects** of sports do you like best?
- What is an activity that you do **vigorously**?
- Why do you think some people like to **reconstruct** historic events?
- Do you think mountains are **gorgeous**? Why or why not?
- What events or times of the year seem **festive**?
- Do you prefer **ornate** or simple decorations? Why?
- What does the color red **symbolize** to you?
- What day of the year do you wait for **expectantly**? Why?
- What kind of **misfortune** could keep you out of school?

PRETEACH

Comprehension

  **Character, Setting, and Plot** Have students look at side A of *Skill Card 25: Review: Character, Setting, and Plot*. Have a volunteer read the information aloud. Have another volunteer read the passage aloud as students follow along. Point out that some plot details must be inferred. The author never says that Kiana is sick or in what way she is sick, but we can guess from Jasmine's card that Kiana is ill.

GUIDED PRACTICE Guide students in copying the story map onto a separate sheet of paper. Have students complete the story map with information from the passage. (*Characters: Jasmine, her mother, Kiana; Setting: Jasmine's home; Story Events: 1. Jasmine's mother brings Jasmine watercolor paints to comfort her. Jasmine is feeling sad because her best friend is ill. 2. Jasmine uses the paints to make Kiana a card.*)

288 Preteach for Lesson 25 • *Turn It Up!*

Day 5

PRETEACH

Decoding/Word Attack

Decode Longer Words Remind students to look for suffixes and familiar word parts when they come to a longer word. Write *pianist* on the board. Guide students to break the word into syllables (pi/a/nist), and identify the root word (piano) and the suffix (-ist). Point out that the spelling of some roots words can change when a suffix is added. Repeat this activity with *electrician, defendant,* and *different*.

PRETEACH

Decoding/Spelling

Words with Suffixes *-ant, -ent, -eer, -ist, -ian* Write the word *confident* on the board. Circle the root word *confide* and have students tell whether or not a spelling change was made when a suffix was added. (Yes, the *e* in *confide* was dropped.) Repeat the activity with *engineer, electrician,* and *radiant*.

PRETEACH

Grammar/Writing

Main, Helping, Action, and Linking Verbs Have students review main and helping verbs by examining these sentences:

> My team should win this game.

Point to the sentence. Ask: **What is the main verb?** (win) **What is the helping verb?** (should) Remind students that words such as *should, could, may, must, are,* and *have* are helping verbs. Then have students review action and linking verbs by examining these sentences:

> We played the game well.
> My team is the best.

Remind students that words such as *feel, seem, smell, sound, taste, am,* and *was* are linking verbs. Have students tell if each underlined verb is an action verb or a linking verb. (*played;* action verb: *is;* linking verb)

VOCABULARY

Student-Friendly Explanations

destinations Destinations are the places people are going to.

aspects The features and elements that make up a place are its aspects.

vigorously If you do something vigorously, you do it with enthusiasm.

reconstruct To reconstruct something that has been damaged or destroyed means to rebuild it.

gorgeous Something that is gorgeous is dazzlingly beautiful.

festive A place that looks festive looks colorful, fun, and exciting.

ornate Something that is ornate has a lot of decoration on it.

symbolize Objects or animals that symbolize something represent it. For example, doves symbolize peace.

expectantly When you wait expectantly for something, you eagerly look forward to it.

misfortune Misfortune is bad luck.

Fluency

pp. 242–248

Fluency Performance Invite students each to read aloud from "Where Land and Sea Meet" a passage that they selected and practiced earlier. Note the number of words each student reads correctly and incorrectly. Have students rate their own oral reading on the 1–4 scale. Allow students to read the passage to you again.

"Where Land and Sea Meet" 289

LESSON 25

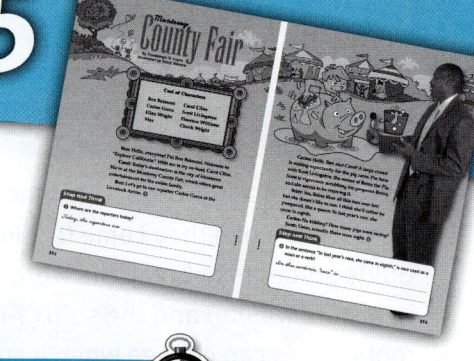

Day 1

VOCABULARY
Reteach destinations, aspects, vigorously, reconstruct, gorgeous, festive, ornate, symbolize, expectantly, misfortune

COMPREHENSION
Preteach Text Structure: Sequence

DECODING/WORD ATTACK
Preteach Decode Longer Words

DECODING/SPELLING
Preteach Word Parts: *in, out, down, up*

GRAMMAR/WRITING
Reteach Main, Helping, Action, and Linking Verbs

FLUENCY
Fluency Practice

Materials Needed: *Turn It Up!*

Student Edition pp. 250–251 | Practice Book pp. 99, 100 | Skill Card 25 | Copying Master 98

RETEACH
Vocabulary

Lesson 25 Vocabulary Read aloud the Vocabulary Words and the Student-Friendly Explanations. Then have students turn to pages 250–251 in their books. Ask a volunteer to read the directions aloud. Remind students that they should read each sentence to themselves with the word they chose to be sure it makes sense. If students have difficulty choosing the correct word, refer to the Student-Friendly Explanations. After students have completed the pages, have volunteers take turns reading aloud each sentence. (Answers for pages 250–251: 2. *expectantly*, 3. *gorgeous*, 4. *vigorously*, 5. *ornate*, 6. *symbolizes*, 7. *reconstruct*, 8. *aspect*, 9. *festive*, 10. *misfortune*, 11. It means that you are looking forward to something. 12. Responses will vary.)

PRETEACH
Comprehension

Text Structure: Sequence Have students look at side B of *Skill Card 25: Review—Text Structure: Sequence*. Ask a volunteer to read the Skill Reminder. Have another volunteer read the passage aloud.

GUIDED PRACTICE Guide students in copying the chart and completing it with the main events of the passage in the order in which they occurred. (Possible responses: Event 1: Maria is born into a large family and is well-educated; Event 2: Maria takes over running the household and the education of her brothers and sisters; Event 3: Maria writes an exceptional mathematics book that is published in 1748.)

290 Lesson 25 • Turn It Up!

Day 1

PRETEACH
Decoding/Word Attack

Decode Longer Words Write *indoor, outcome, downtime,* and *uproot* on the board. Point to each word and ask students what smaller word part they see at the beginning of it. (in, out, down, up) Remind students they can use familiar words parts such as *in, out, down,* and *up* to help them figure out longer words. Read the first and second parts of each word separately, and then blend them together to read the whole word. Write *outline, upright, inhabit,* and *downturn* on the board. Have students copy the words, then circle the word parts *in, out, down,* and *up* in each word. Have volunteers blend word parts to read each whole word.

PRETEACH
Decoding/Spelling

Copying Master 98

Word Parts *in, out, down, up* Distribute *Copying Master 98*. Have students read the Spelling Words aloud. Then ask students to identify the words that have the word parts *in, out, down,* and *up*. (inexact, outdated, downfall, upfront, upwind) Remind students that the spelling of the root word does not change when these word parts are added to a root word.

RETEACH
Grammar/Writing

Practice Book 100

Main, Helping, Action, and Linking Verbs Write the following sentence on the board:

> We was walking quickly.

Identify the verb phrase *was walking* and ask: **Is this the correct helping verb to use here?** (no) Erase *was* and invite students to name the correct verb. (were) Then write this sentence on the board:

> She play the tuba.

Identify the verb *play* and ask: **Is the action verb correct here?** (no) Have a volunteer add an *s* to the end of *play*. (plays)

GUIDED PRACTICE Have students turn to page 100 in their *Practice Book*. Ask a volunteer to read the activity directions aloud. Have students work in pairs to proofread each sentence and make corrections. Allow time for pairs to share their responses.

VOCABULARY
Student-Friendly Explanations

destinations Destinations are the places people are going to.

aspects The features and elements that make up a place are its aspects.

vigorously If you do something vigorously, you do it with enthusiasm.

reconstruct To reconstruct something that has been damaged or destroyed means to rebuild it.

gorgeous Something that is gorgeous is dazzlingly beautiful.

festive A place that looks festive looks colorful, fun, and exciting.

ornate Something that is ornate has a lot of decoration on it.

symbolize Objects or animals that symbolize something represent it. For example, doves symbolize peace.

expectantly When you wait expectantly for something, you eagerly look forward to it.

misfortune Misfortune is bad luck.

Fluency

Practice Book 99

Fluency Practice Have students turn to *Practice Book* page 99. Read the words in the first column aloud. Invite students to track each word and repeat the words after you. Then have students work in pairs to read the words in the first column aloud to each other. Follow the same procedure with each of the remaining columns. Then have them practice reading all of the words.

"Monterey County Fair" **291**

LESSON 25

Day 2

VOCABULARY
Reteach destinations, aspects, vigorously, reconstruct, gorgeous, festive, ornate, symbolize, expectantly, misfortune

COMPREHENSION
"Monterey County Fair"
Build Background
Monitor Comprehension
Answers to *Think Critically* **Questions**

DECODING/WORD ATTACK
Preteach Decode Longer Words

DECODING/SPELLING
Preteach Words with Suffixes *-ation*, *-ition*, *-al*, *-ial*

GRAMMAR/WRITING
Preteach Past-, Present-, and Future-Tense Verbs

FLUENCY
Fluency Practice

Materials Needed: *Turn It Up!*

Student Edition pp. 252–259

Practice Book p. 99

Copying Masters 97, 98

RETEACH

Vocabulary

Lesson 25 Vocabulary Distribute a set of Vocabulary Word Cards for each student. Read aloud the Student-Friendly Explanation for one of the words, leaving out the word. Have students display and read the matching Word Card. Continue until students have matched all the words.

Copying Master 97

Comprehension

Build Background: "Monterey County Fair"
Ask students to share experiences of county fairs, agricultural fairs, or state fairs they have been to. What did they see there? What did they do? What was their favorite part of the fair? Their least favorite?

Monitor Comprehension: "Monterey County Fair"
Read the title of the story aloud. Then have students read pages 252–253 to find out what is happening at the Monterey County Fair.

pp. 252–253

After reading the pages, ask: **What is one event happening at the Monterey County Fair?** (There will be pig races at the Monterey County Fair.) NOTE DETAILS

Discuss the Stop and Think question on page 252: **Where are the reporters today?** (Today, the reporters are in the city of Monterey, at the Monterey County Fair.) Guide students in writing the answer to this question. CHARACTER, SETTING, PLOT

Ask: **Why do you think Carlos chose to interview Scott?** (Possible response: He wanted to interview one of the pig owners because a pig owner would be most familiar with the history and rules of the race, as well as the contestants.) CHARACTER'S MOTIVATION

Discuss the Stop and Think question on page 253: **In the sentence "In last year's race, she came in eighth," is *race* used as a noun or a verb?** (In this sentence, *race* is used as a noun.) Guide students in writing the answer to this question. VOCABULARY

pp. 254–255

Discuss the Stop and Think question on page 254: **After Carlos does his interview, who is next? Whom does he or she interview?** (After Carlos does his interview, Ellen is next. She interviews Florence Williams.) Guide students in writing the answer to this question. SEQUENCE

Ask: **What does the phrase "took 'Best of Show'" mean?** (Possible response: It means it was judged to be the best quilt in the show.) FIGURATIVE LANGUAGE

292 Lesson 25 • Turn It Up!

Discuss the Stop and Think question on page 255: **What is an album quilt? Underline the words that tell you.** (An album quilt is made by a group of quilters. Each block has a picture that symbolizes something for the person who made it. Students should underline "An album quilt is made by a group of quilters" and "Each block symbolizes something.") Guide students in writing the answer to this question. **NOTE DETAILS**

pp. 256–257 Ask: **How is a salad related to agriculture?** (Possible response: Agriculture is the business of farming. A salad is made with farm products like lettuce, cabbage, spinach, and a variety of other vegetables.) **MAKE CONNECTIONS**

Model using the strategy of asking questions to improve comprehension.

THINK ALOUD I read that Chuck and his neighbors were trying to break a world record, but Chuck doesn't say which world record. I knew that breaking the record involved making a salad, so I asked myself, "What is so special about the salad that they are making?" Then I read more closely; they are making a *huge* salad. After looking at the photograph on page 257, I concluded they they were trying to break the world record for the largest salad.

Discuss the Stop and Think question on page 256: **Do you think Chuck and his neighbors will break the world record? Explain your answer.** (Possible response: I think Chuck and his neighbors will break the world record because it is a huge salad.) Guide students in writing the answer to this question. **MAKE PREDICTIONS**

Ask: **How might it benefit farmers in Monterey County to break the world record? What do you think they are trying to achieve?** (Possible response: If they get on the news, more people will see the salad and be curious about it. Perhaps they are trying to get more people to eat salad.) **CHARACTERS' MOTIVATIONS**

Discuss the Stop and Think question on page 257: **Name one fact you know about the salad. Then give an opinion you have about salad.** (Possible response: One fact about the salad is that it weighs more than 29,000 pounds. In my opinion, salad tastes great.) Guide students in writing the answer to this question. **FACT AND OPINION**

 Discuss the Stop and Think question on page 258: **Find the sentence, "Bad break, Max." What does this sentence mean?** (Possible response: It means that Max does not get to do what he wants.) Guide students in writing the answer to this question. **FIGURATIVE LANGUAGE**

VOCABULARY
Student-Friendly Explanations

destinations Destinations are the places people are going to.

aspects The features and elements that make up a place are its aspects.

vigorously If you do something vigorously, you do it with enthusiasm.

reconstruct To reconstruct something that has been damaged or destroyed means to rebuild it.

gorgeous Something that is gorgeous is dazzlingly beautiful.

festive A place that looks festive looks colorful, fun, and exciting.

ornate Something that is ornate has a lot of decoration on it.

symbolize Objects or animals that symbolize something represent it. For example, doves symbolize peace.

expectantly When you wait expectantly for something, you eagerly look forward to it.

misfortune Misfortune is bad luck.

"Monterey County Fair" 293

Day 2

Spelling Words: Lesson 25

1. radiant	11. admiration
2. confident	12. addition
3. engineer	13. emotional
4. typist	14. abdominal
5. electrician	15. testimonial
6. inexact	16. decoration
7. outdated	17. effortlessly
8. downfall	18. meaningfully
9. upfront	19. truthfully
10. upwind	20. carefully

page 259 **Answers to *Think Critically* Questions** Help students read and answer the *Think Critically* questions on page 259. Then guide students in writing the answer to each question. Possible responses are provided.

1. I think the reporter tells people when the fair ends because people may want to visit. They need to know how much time they have. **MAKE INFERENCES**

2. I think the main idea of this play is that there are a lot of fun things to do at the fair. I think this because the play tells about many different things to do and see. **MAIN IDEA AND DETAILS**

3. I think the author feels that a county fair is a fun way to spend a day. **AUTHOR'S PURPOSE**

PRETEACH

Decoding/Word Attack

Decode Longer Words Remind students that they can break longer words into syllables to look for word parts, such as prefixes, suffixes, and root words. Write *attention* on the board. Guide students to break the word into syllables (at/ten/tion), and identify the root word (attend) and the suffix (-tion). Then have students read the whole word. Point out that the spelling of some roots and root words can change when a suffix is added. Repeat this activity with *conclusion*, *natural*, and *commercial*.

PRETEACH

Decoding/Spelling

Copying Master 98 **Words with Suffixes -ation, -ition, -al, -ial** Have students review *Copying Master 98* to identify those Spelling Words that have the suffixes *-ation, -ition, -al,* and *-ial*. Write the words *admiration, addition, abdominal, testimonial,* and *decoration* on the board. Have students tell what the root word for each word is. (admire, add, abdomen, testimony, decorate) Point out that the root word *add* does not change spelling when the suffix *-ition* is added, but the spelling of the other root words does change when the suffixes are added. Have students identify in what way each root word changes. (*e* drops, *e* changes to *i*, *y* changes to *i*, *e* drops) Remind students that root words can change spelling in other ways when a suffix is added. Write the following root words and suffixes.

294 Lesson 25 • Turn It Up!

Day 2

PRETEACH

Grammar/Writing

Past-, Present-, and Future-Tense Verbs Remind students that when they want to talk about what is happening now or what happens over and over, writers use the present tense. Remind students that a verb's ending must agree with the subject.

- When the subject is *I, you, we, they,* a plural noun, or a compound subject, do not add an ending to the verb.
- When the subject is *he, she, it,* or a singular noun, add *s* or *es* to the verb.
- If the verb is a form of *be*, use *am* with *I*, *is* with singular subjects, and *are* with plural subjects.

Write the following sentences on the board:

> Santiago (run, runs) with his dog in the morning.
> Alissa and Melody (play, plays) basketball together.
> Bryant and Darren (is, are) brothers.

Have students tell which verb form to use in each sentence. (runs, play, are) Then remind students that *-ed* should be added to most verbs to form the past tense. To form the future tense of a verb, use *will* with the main verb. Then write the following sentence frames on the board:

> Yesterday, I _____ the dishes.
> Tomorrow, Erin _____ the dishes.

Have students change the verb *wash* to the correct tense that completes each sentence. (washed, will wash)

Fluency

Fluency Practice Invite students to look at the bottom half of *Practice Book* page 99. These sentences have been broken into natural phrases. Tell students to repeat each phrase after you, mirroring your expression, phrasing, and pace. After students have repeated each sentence, invite them to practice reading the sentences to partners.

"Monterey County Fair"

LESSON 25

DAY AT A GLANCE
Day 3

COMPREHENSION
Preteach Make Inferences
Reread and Summarize "Monterey County Fair"

DECODING/WORD ATTACK
Preteach Decode Longer Words

DECODING/SPELLING
Preteach Suffixes in Combination

BUILD ROBUST VOCABULARY
Teach Words from "Monterey County Fair"

GRAMMAR/WRITING
Reteach Past-, Present-, and Future-Tense Verbs

FLUENCY
Fluency Practice

Materials Needed: *Turn It Up!*

Student Edition pp. 252–258 | Practice Book pp. 99, 101 | Copying Masters 98, 99

PRETEACH

Comprehension

 Make Inferences Have students recall that readers need to make inferences, or figure out things that the author has not directly stated. To make inferences, readers use clues from the story along with what they already know. Distribute *Copying Master 99,* and have a volunteer read aloud the information at the top of the page.

GUIDED PRACTICE Ask students to complete the page with a partner. Invite students to share and discuss their responses with the class.

Reread and Summarize Have students reread and summarize "Monterey County Fair" in sections, as described below.

 pp. 252–254
Let's reread pages 252–254 to recall who the characters are and what they are doing.
Summary: Ben and Carol host a show called "Explore California." Carlos, a reporter, interviews Scott, the young owner of a pig who is participating in the pig race.

 page 255
Let's reread page 255 to recall what an album quilt is and how it is made.
Summary: Florence, a quilter, tells Ellen that an album quilt is made by a group of quilters and that each block symbolizes something.

pp. 256–258
Let's reread page 256–258 to recall what Chuck Wright and his neighbors are up to.
Summary: Max interviews Chuck. Chuck and his neighbors are trying to break the world record for the largest salad. Then Ben and Carol wrap up the show.

PRETEACH

Decoding/Word Attack

Decode Longer Words Remind students that sometimes root words have two or more suffixes added, or have one of the inflections *-ed* or *-ing* combined with a suffix. Write *seemingly, helpfulness, essentially,* and *childishness* on the board. Have students identify the inflected ending and suffix in *seemingly*. *(-ing, -ly)* Have students identify the suffixes in each remaining word. Then guide students to blend each root word with its suffixes to read aloud the whole word.

296 Lesson 25 • *Turn It Up!*

Day 3

PRETEACH

Decoding/Spelling

Copying Master 98

Suffixes in Combination Write *carefully* on the board. Ask students to name the suffixes. *(-ful, -ly)* Call on a volunteer to circle the root word *(care)* and tell whether a change was made when the suffixes were added. *(no)* Remind students that when they add one or more suffixes to a root word, they will sometimes have to make a spelling change to the root word. Have students review *Copying Master 98.* Then have them do this activity based on the traditional Memory Game. Pairs of students make game cards using the lesson's Spelling Words with beginning word parts or suffixes missing; a dash appears in place of each word part or suffix. After a student matches two cards, he or she must supply the correct missing letters to keep the game cards. If the wrong letter is supplied, the opponent gets the game cards and the next turn.

TEACH

Build Robust Vocabulary

pp. 252–253

Words from "Monterey County Fair" Have students locate the word *entertainment* on page 252 of "Monterey County Fair." Ask a volunteer to read aloud the sentence in which this word appears. (Line 5: *We're at the Monterey County Fair, which offers great entertainment for the entire family.*) Explain that this sentence means that the fair offers lots of things that are fun and interesting to do.

Then ask students to locate and read aloud the sentence in which the word *pampered* appears on page 253. (Line 8: *I think she'd rather be pampered, like a queen.*) Explain that this sentence means that Reina likes to be treated with lots and lots of care and special attention.

Work with students to brainstorm a list of types of entertainment and then a list of ways to be pampered.

RETEACH

Grammar/Writing

Practice Book 101

Past-, Present-, and Future-Tense Verbs Review the key points about past-, present-, and future-tense verbs. Write the following sentence on the board and have students tell how to correct it:
I always sleeps well at night. (Change *sleeps* to *sleep.*)

GUIDED PRACTICE Have students turn to page 101 in their *Practice Book.* Ask a volunteer to read the activity directions aloud. Have students work in pairs to proofread each sentence and make corrections.

Fluency

Practice Book 99

Fluency Practice Tell students that today they will reread the sentences on the bottom of *Practice Book* page 99. Have students locate and point to the first sentence. Tell students that everyone is going to read the sentence together. This choral reading will give students an opportunity to hear others and listen to the natural phrasing of the sentences. Choral-read each of the sentences several times.

"Monterey County Fair" 297

LESSON 25

DAY AT A GLANCE - Day 4

COMPREHENSION
Preteach Use Context Clues

DECODING/SPELLING
Cumulative Review

BUILD ROBUST VOCABULARY
Reteach Words from "Monterey County Fair"

GRAMMAR/WRITING
Cumulative Review

FLUENCY
Fluency Practice

Materials Needed: *Turn It Up!*

Student Edition pp. 252–258 | Practice Book p. 102 | Copying Master 100

Spelling Words: Lesson 25

1. radiant	11. admiration
2. confident	12. addition
3. engineer	13. emotional
4. typist	14. abdominal
5. electrician	15. testimonial
6. inexact	16. decoration
7. outdated	17. effortlessly
8. downfall	18. meaningfully
9. upfront	19. truthfully
10. upwind	20. carefully

PRETEACH
Comprehension

Use Context Clues Remind students that good readers use context clues to help them figure out the meaning of an unfamiliar word or a word with more than one meaning. Context clues may be found in sentences or paragraphs before or after a word. Have students reread the dialogue on pages 256–257 of "Monterey County Fair." Ask:

- **What context clues help you figure out the meaning of *record*?** (They are making a huge salad to break a record; it weighs more than 29,000 pounds.)

- **Based on the context clues, what is a likely meaning of *record*?** (Possible response: it means "something that marks the best anyone has done.")

GUIDED PRACTICE Have students work in pairs to find context clues for the meaning of the word *reigning* on page 254. Have students write down the context clues, and the likely meaning of the word. Then have them use a dictionary to confirm the word's meaning.

RETEACH
Decoding/Spelling

Cumulative Review Have students number a sheet of paper 1–16. Write *radiant* on the board and point to the suffix. Tell students that the first four words you will dictate end with the suffix *-ant*, *-ent*, *-eer*, *-ist*, or *-ian*. After students write each word, display it so they can proofread their work. Repeat this activity using *inexact* for the word parts *in*, *out*, *down*, and *up*. Use the word *admiration* for the suffixes *-ation*, *-ition*, *-al*, and *-ial*. Use *effortlessly* for the words that end with suffixes in combination.

1. confident	2. engineer	3. typist	4. electrician
5. outdated	6. downfall	7. upfront	8. upwind
9. addition	10. emotional	11. abdominal	12. testimonial
13. decoration	14. meaningfully	15. truthfully	16. carefully

Have students turn to page 102 in their *Practice Book*. Ask a volunteer to read the directions aloud. Once students have completed the page, invite them to identify the Spelling Words in the sentences.

298 Lesson 25 • *Turn It Up!*

Day 4

RETEACH
Build Robust Vocabulary

Words from "Monterey County Fair" Review the meanings of the words *entertainment* and *pampered*. Then say these sentences and ask which word describes each sentence. Have students explain why.

- **Listening to music is my favorite way to have fun.** (entertainment)
- **On Mother's Day, we gave Mom breakfast in bed and did a lot of other things to show her we care.** (pampered)

RETEACH
Grammar/Writing

Copying Master 100

Cumulative Review Have students recall the grammar skills they learned in this lesson. Discuss examples for each skill.

- verb phrases with a main verb and a helping verb
- action verbs and linking verbs
- past-, present-, and future-tense forms of a verb

GUIDED PRACTICE Distribute *Copying Master 100* to each student. Invite a volunteer to read the directions. Then have students complete the page independently. Allow time for students to share their work as a group.

Fluency

pp. 252–258

Fluency Practice Have each student work with a partner to read passages from "Monterey County Fair" aloud to each other. Remind students to:

- read aloud with an intonation appropriate for the selection.
- read at a rate that helps listeners understand the text.

Encourage partners to read the selected passage aloud three times. Have the students rate their own reading on the 1–4 scale.

1	Need more practice
2	Pretty good
3	Good
4	Great!

"Monterey County Fair" 299

Preteach for LESSON 26

DAY AT A GLANCE
Day 5

VOCABULARY
Preteach contraption, roamed, massive, submerged, elegant, obstacles, complicated, eerie

COMPREHENSION
 Preteach Main Idea and Supporting Details

DECODING/WORD ATTACK
Preteach Review Silent Letters

DECODING/SPELLING
Preteach Words with Silent Letters

GRAMMAR/WRITING
Preteach Irregular Verbs

FLUENCY
Fluency Performance

Materials Needed: *Turn It Up!*

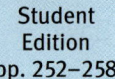

Student Edition pp. 252–258 | Skill Card 26 | Copying Master 101

30+ Minutes

PRETEACH
Vocabulary

Lesson 26 Vocabulary Distribute a set of Vocabulary Word Cards to each student or pair of students. Hold up the card for the first Vocabulary Word, and ask a volunteer to read the word aloud. Have students repeat the word and hold up the matching card. Give the explanation for the word. Then ask students the first question below and discuss their responses. Continue for each Vocabulary Word.

- What is one **contraption** that you have seen or read about?
- Which **roamed** Earth a long time ago, hills, rocks, or animals?
- If a **massive** object is in your path, should you move it or walk around it? Why?
- Where would you look to find **submerged** treasure?
- Which is more **elegant**, a rose or a garbage can? Explain your answer.
- What types of **obstacles** might you encounter on a walk in the woods?
- Which is more **complicated**, a pencil, a bowl, or a car engine?
- How would you feel if you saw something **eerie**?

PRETEACH
Comprehension

 **Main Idea and Supporting Details** Have students look at side A of *Skill Card 26: Main Idea and Supporting Details*. Read the definitions of main idea and details. Then read the passage aloud as students follow along. Ask:

- **What is the topic sentence of the selection?** (Animals that live in the Arctic rely on special features to help them survive in a cold, harsh environment.)
- **In your own words, what is the main idea of the passage?** (Possible response: Arctic animals have features that help them survive.)

Explain that identifying the main idea of the story will help students understand what the story is mostly about. Details support the main idea. Point to the diagram. Have students name the details shown on the chart and identify them in the passage.

GUIDED PRACTICE Have students work in pairs to find two other details that could be included in the diagram. Remind students to look for details that support the main idea. (The Arctic hare has grayish brown fur in the summer. The snowy owl has extra feathers and thick pads on its feet.)

300 Preteach for Lesson 26 • *Turn It Up!*

Day 5

PRETEACH

Decoding/Word Attack

Review Silent Letters Write the words *limb, honor,* and *known* on the board. Circle the letter *b* in *limb*. Say the word and ask students if they hear the letter *b* in the word. Tell students that some consonants are silent in words. Repeat the process with the silent *h* in *honor* and the silent *k* in *known*.

PRETEACH

Decoding/Spelling

Words with Silent Letters Write each of the words below on the board, and read them aloud. Ask students to tell which consonant is silent and circle the letter.

| lamb | whistle | folks | often |
| scene | knack | island | mortgage |

PRETEACH

Grammar/Writing

Irregular Verbs Write the following sentences on the board:

> Pam rang the door bell.
> Pam has rung the door bell twice.

Read the sentences aloud. Tell students that the verb *rang* is an irregular verb formed from the main verb *ring*. An irregular verb does not end with *-ed* in the past tense. Explain that some irregular verbs also use a different form when they appear with the helping verb *has, have,* or *had*. Then write these sentences on the board:

> Tess chose the red box.
> I have chosen the blue box.

Ask: What are the irregular verbs in these sentences? (chose, chosen) **How do you know?** (They do not end with *-ed*.) Have a volunteer underline the words. Ask students what main verb each was formed from. (choose) Continue by writing sentences that use the words *took* and *has taken*. Have students identify the irregular verbs and the main verb form. (take)

VOCABULARY
Student-Friendly Explanations

contraption A contraption is a strange-looking machine or device.

roamed If a creature roamed an area, it wandered around there.

massive Something massive is very large and heavy.

submerged If something is submerged, it is beneath the surface of a body of water.

elegant Something elegant is graceful and pleasing to look at.

obstacles Obstacles are things that get in your way when you are going somewhere or trying to reach a goal.

complicated Something that is complicated has many parts that are connected in ways that make it hard to understand.

eerie Something that is eerie is strange and makes people feel afraid.

Fluency

pp. 252–258 **Fluency Performance** Invite students each to read aloud from "Monterey County Fair" a passage that they selected and practiced earlier. Have students rate their own oral reading on the 1–4 scale. Give each student the opportunity to continue practicing and then to read the passage to you again.

"Monterey County Fair" **301**

DAY AT A GLANCE
Day 1

VOCABULARY
Reteach contraption, roamed, massive, submerged, elegant, obstacles, complicated, eerie

COMPREHENSION
Reteach Main Idea and Supporting Details

DECODING/SPELLING
Reteach Words with Silent Letters

GRAMMAR/WRITING
Preteach Irregular Verbs

FLUENCY
Fluency Practice

Materials Needed: *Turn It Up!*

  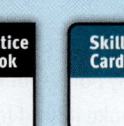 

Student Edition pp. 260–261 | Practice Book p. 103 | Skill Card 26 | Copying Master 102

LESSON 26

RETEACH
Vocabulary

Lesson 26 Vocabulary Read aloud the Vocabulary Words and the Student-Friendly Explanations. Then have students read the story and fill in the blanks on pages 260–261 of their books. Have a volunteer read each paragraph, adding the word they inserted. Then ask students to complete the word web at the end of the story. If students are unable to give reasonable responses, refer to the Student-Friendly Explanations. (Answers for pages 260–261: 2. *massive*, 3. *elegant*, 4. *obstacles*, 5. *contraptions*, 6. *complicated*, 7. *eerie*, 8. *submerged*, 9. *elegant*)

RETEACH
Comprehension

Main Idea and Supporting Details Have students look at side B of *Skill Card 26: Main Idea and Supporting Details*. Have a volunteer read the definitions of *main idea* and *supporting details*. Then have another volunteer read the passage aloud while students follow along. Ask:

- **What is the main idea of the selection?** (The first winter Olympic games were very successful.)
- **What is one supporting detail?** (Students may list any supporting detail from the passage.)

Write students' responses on the board. Tell students that they should look for main ideas and details when they read nonfiction. It will help them to understand what they read.

GUIDED PRACTICE Have students work in pairs to copy and complete the diagram on side B of *Skill Card 26: Main Idea and Supporting Details*. (Main Idea: The first winter Olympic games were very successful. Supporting Details: Almost three hundred athletes came to compete. Athletes came from sixteen different countries. There were five events at this Olympics. A decision was made to hold the Olympics every four years.)

302 Lesson 26 • Turn It Up!

Day 1

RETEACH
Decoding/Spelling

Words with Silent Letters Distribute *Copying Master 102*. Model reading the Spelling Words and have students repeat them. Review the instruction for silent letters in words and then have students complete the following activity. Have students work in pairs to write the Spelling Words on index cards. Ask one student to draw a card and read its word aloud. The other student writes the word. When a student spells the word correctly, he or she initials the card and returns it to the pile. Then have students trade roles. Students should work through the pile until each has had an opportunity to spell each of the words. Remind students to write down the words they misspell to study later.

Copying Master 102

PRETEACH
Grammar/Writing

Irregular Verbs Remind students that an irregular verb does not end in *-ed* in the past tense. Write the following sentences on the board:

> We began our chores early this morning.
> We had begun our chores by sunrise.

Ask a volunteer to read the sentence aloud. Then ask: **Which word is the irregular verb in each sentence?** (began, begun) Underline the word *had* in the second sentence. Remind students that some irregular verbs use a different form of the main verb with the helping verb *has, have,* or *had*.

Write *know, wear,* and *run* on the board. Guide students to write the past-tense form and the past-tense form with a helping verb for each verb. (know: knew, have/had known; wear: wore, have/had worn; run: ran, have/had run) Invite volunteers to use each verb or verb phrase in a sentence.

VOCABULARY
Student-Friendly Explanations

contraption A contraption is a strange-looking machine or device.

roamed If a creature roamed an area, it wandered around there.

massive Something massive is very large and heavy.

submerged If something is submerged, it is beneath the surface of a body of water.

elegant Something elegant is graceful and pleasing to look at.

obstacles Obstacles are things that get in your way when you are going somewhere or trying to reach a goal.

complicated Something that is complicated has many parts that are connected in ways that make it hard to understand.

eerie Something that is eerie is strange and makes people feel afraid.

Fluency

Fluency Practice Have students turn to *Practice Book* page 103. Read the words in the first column aloud. Invite students to track each word and repeat the words after you. Then have students work in pairs to read the words in the first column aloud to each other. Follow the same procedure with each of the remaining columns. After partners have practiced reading aloud the words in each of the columns, have them practice reading all of the words.

Practice Book 103

"Rough and Tough Enough" 303

LESSON 26

DAY AT A GLANCE
Day 2

VOCABULARY
Reteach contraption, roamed, massive, submerged, elegant, obstacles, complicated, eerie

COMPREHENSION
"Rough and Tough Enough"
Build Background
Monitor Comprehension
Answers to *Think Critically* **Questions**

DECODING/SPELLING
Reteach Words with Silent Letters

GRAMMAR/WRITING
Preteach Irregular Verbs

FLUENCY
Fluency Practice

Materials Needed: *Turn It Up!*

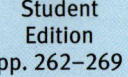

Student Edition pp. 262–269

Practice Book pp. 103, 104

Copying Masters 101, 102

30+ Minutes

RETEACH

Vocabulary

Copying Master 101

Lesson 26 Vocabulary Distribute a set of Word Cards to each student or pair of students. Read aloud the meaning of one of the Vocabulary Words. Have students display and read the matching card. Ask a volunteer to use the word in a sentence. Continue until students have matched all the words.

Comprehension

Build Background: "Rough and Tough Enough"
Ask students to share experiences they may have had going to a museum. Were they able to see bones from animals that lived long ago? Ask them to share what they know.

pp. 262–263

Monitor Comprehension: "Rough and Tough Enough"
Read the title of the story aloud. Then have students read pages 262–263 to find out what massive animal roamed Earth long ago.

After reading the pages, ask: **What massive animal roamed Earth long ago?** (Mammoths roamed Earth long ago.) **NOTE DETAILS**

Discuss the Stop and Think question on page 262: **Mammoths were large, tough animals from the past. What details support this?** (These details support the main idea: They were massive. They were able to stand the cold of the Ice Age.) Guide students in writing the answer to this question. 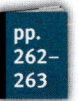 **MAIN IDEA AND DETAILS**

Ask: **What helped the mammoths stand the cold?** (They had great coats of hair. They had enough body fat to keep them warm.) **NOTE DETAILS**

Ask: **How would you describe a mammoth to someone who doesn't know what they looked like? Use the illustration on page 263 to help you.** (Possible response: A mammoth had a body like an elephant, but with shaggy hair. It also had huge curving tusks.) **GRAPHIC AIDS**

Discuss the Stop and Think question on page 263: **How did mammoths use their trunks?** (Mammoths used their trunks to eat, to smell, to knock obstacles out of the way, and to say hello.) Guide students in writing the answer to this question. **SUMMARIZE**

pp. 264–265

Read aloud the first paragraph on page 264. Model the strategy of finding the topic sentence to identify the main idea of the paragraph.

THINK ALOUD When I read the first paragraph, I looked for the topic sentence. The topic sentence can tell me the main idea. The topic sentence says that mammoths lived together in packs. Then

304 Lesson 26 • Turn It Up!

the following sentences give me more details about the packs that mammoths lived in. As I read, I find details that support the main idea. 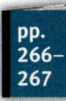 MAIN IDEA AND DETAILS

Discuss the Stop and Think question on page 264: **Why do you think mammoths roamed in packs?** (Possible responses: I think mammoths roamed in packs because it was safer for them as a group; they wanted to be with other animals.) Guide students in writing the answer to this question. MAKE INFERENCES

Discuss the Stop and Think question on page 265: **Why do you think there are no mammoths today?** (Possible responses: There are no mammoths today because they ran out of food; hunters made them extinct.) Guide students in writing the answer to this question. MAKE PREDICTIONS

pp. 266–267 Ask students to read page 266 to find out how we know about mammoths today. After reading the page, ask: **How do we know how big mammoths were?** (Possible response: We know from studying their bones.) MAKE INFERENCES

Discuss the Stop and Think question on page 266: **Why were the mammoth bones not found for thousands of years?** (Possible response: They were not found for thousands of years because they were covered by layers of water and mud.) Guide students in writing the answer to this question. DRAW CONCLUSIONS

Direct students' attention to the illustrations on page 267. Explain that these illustrations show why scientists believe that the bones were not found for thousands of years. Ask: **What events took place before we found the bones in modern times?** (Possible response: The illustrations show the mammoths at a watering hole. The hole filled with mud and the mammoths were in the mud. Their bones were left in the mud. Much later, when the mud dried, people were finally able to find them.) RETELL/GRAPHIC AIDS

page 268 Ask: **Why do you think mammoths became extinct?** (Possible response: I think hunters wiped out the animals.) EXPRESS PERSONAL OPINIONS

Discuss the Stop and Think question on page 268: **Why doesn't the author tell us why mammoths no longer walk on Earth?** (Possible responses: The author doesn't tell us why mammoths no longer walk on Earth because it is an unsolved riddle; scientists don't know the answer.) Guide students in writing the answer to this question. AUTHOR'S PURPOSE

VOCABULARY
Student-Friendly Explanations

contraption A contraption is a strange-looking machine or device.

roamed If a creature roamed an area, it wandered around there.

massive Something massive is very large and heavy.

submerged If something is submerged, it is beneath the surface of a body of water.

elegant Something elegant is graceful and pleasing to look at.

obstacles Obstacles are things that get in your way when you are going somewhere or trying to reach a goal.

complicated Something that is complicated has many parts that are connected in ways that make it hard to understand.

eerie Something that is eerie is strange and makes people feel afraid.

"Rough and Tough Enough" 305

Day 2

Spelling Words: Lesson 26

1. subtle	11. island
2. scene	12. lamb
3. climbed	13. numb
4. comb	14. often
5. exhibit	15. rustle
6. doubt	16. debt
7. folks	17. knack
8. exhaust	18. thumb
9. half	19. unknown
10. whistle	20. mortgage

page 269 **Answers to *Think Critically* Questions**
Help students read and answer the *Think Critically* questions on page 269. Have students copy the graphic organizer in question 1 onto a separate sheet of paper. Then guide students in writing the answer to each question. Possible responses are provided.

1. They roamed Earth during the Ice Age; they weighed thousands of pounds; they had powerful trunks and tusks; they died long ago.
   MAIN IDEA AND DETAILS
2. Hot Springs, South Dakota, is a good place to learn about mammoths because many mammoth bones were found there. **NOTE DETAILS**
3. I think the author wrote this article to teach readers about mammoths. **AUTHOR'S PURPOSE**

RETEACH

Decoding/Spelling

Copying Master 102 **Words with Silent Letters** Write these incomplete Spelling Words on the board:

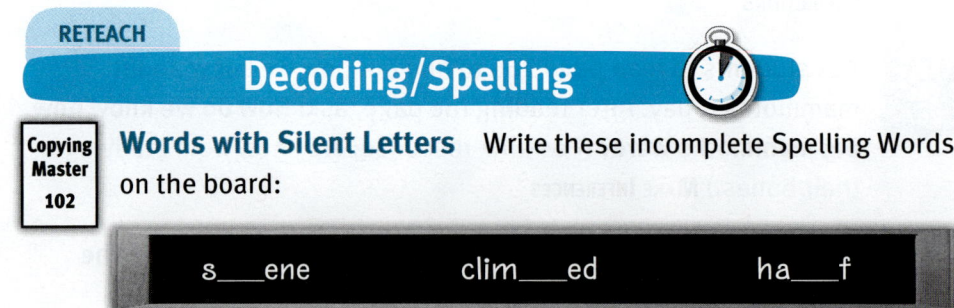

Read the words and have students read them with you. Have students complete each word by telling the missing silent letter. (scene, climbed, half)

Have pairs work together to fix the following incomplete Spelling Words. Have students complete each word by filling in the missing silent letter: *un__nown, of__en, dou__t, mor__gage, i__land,* and *ex__ibit.* (unknown, often, doubt, mortgage, island, exhibit)

306 Lesson 26 • Turn It Up!

| PRETEACH |
Grammar/Writing

Irregular Verbs Review the definition of an irregular verb. Point out that the verb *break* becomes *broke* in the past tense and *broken* when used in the past tense with the helping verb *have, has,* or *had.* Write the following sentence frames on the board:

Practice Book 104

Ask a volunteer to tell which form of the verb *break* should be used to complete each sentence. (broke, broken)

GUIDED PRACTICE Direct students' attention to page 104 in their *Practice Book*. Read the chart title and column labels to the students. Read the directions for the activity together. Have students work in pairs to complete each sentence with the correct past-tense form of the irregular verbs.

Day 2

Fluency

Fluency Practice Invite students to look at the bottom half of *Practice Book* page 103. These sentences have been broken into natural phrases. Tell students to repeat each phrase after you, mirroring your expression, phrasing, and pace. After students have repeated each sentence, invite them to practice reading the sentences to partners.

Practice Book 103

"Rough and Tough Enough" **307**

LESSON 26

DAY AT A GLANCE
Day 3

COMPREHENSION
 Preteach Paraphrase
Reread and Summarize "Rough and Tough Enough"

DECODING/SPELLING
Reteach Words with Silent Letters

BUILD ROBUST VOCABULARY
Teach Words from "Rough and Tough Enough"

GRAMMAR/WRITING
Reteach Writing Trait: Sentence Fluency

FLUENCY
Fluency Practice

Materials Needed: *Turn It Up!*

Student Edition pp. 262–268 | Practice Book pp. 103, 105 | Copying Master 103

30+ Minutes

PRETEACH
Comprehension

Paraphrase Distribute *Copying Master 103*, and have a student read the information at the top of the page. Then have a volunteer read the passage aloud as students read along. Guide students to paraphrase the first sentence by retelling it in their own words.

GUIDED PRACTICE Ask students to read the second sentence and paraphrase it. Allow students time to share their responses. Have students work in pairs to paraphrase for the remainder of the passage.

Reread and Summarize: "Rough and Tough Enough"
Have students reread and summarize "Rough and Tough Enough" in sections, as described below.

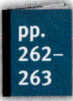
pp. 262–263
Let's reread pages 262–263 to recall why mammoths were considered rough and tough animals from the past.
Summary: Mammoths were massive animals that lived during the Ice Age. They had lots of body fat and hair to keep them warm. They also had large trunks that helped them to eat and to move large obstacles.

pp. 264–265
Now let's reread pages 264–265 to remember what life was like for mammoths.
Summary: Mammoths lived together in packs. Some would use their tusks to fight each other. Early humans hunted mammoths for their meat and bones.

pp. 266–268
Last, let's reread pages 266–268 to find out what happened to mammoths.
Summary: We know what mammoths look like because a large number of bones were found in South Dakota. Scientists are still unsure of exactly why mammoths are now extinct.

RETEACH
Decoding/Spelling

Words with Silent Letters Write the following sentences on the board:

> The foks heard a whisle.
> I dout that the exibit is open.
> Ted offen goes to the iland.

Ask volunteers to circle each misspelled word and write it correctly. (folks, whistle, doubt, exhibit, often, island)

308 Lesson 26 • Turn It Up!

Day 3

TEACH

Build Robust Vocabulary

pp. 264–266

Words from "Rough and Tough Enough" Have students locate *packs* on page 264 of "Rough and Tough Enough." Ask a volunteer to read aloud the sentence in which this word appears. (First sentence: *Mammoths lived together in packs.*) Explain that this sentence means that groups of mammoths lived and hunted for food together. Continue by asking students to locate and read aloud the sentence on page 265 in which *prized* appears. (Line 6: *Many scientists today think that the hunters prized the mammoths.*) Explain that this means that the hunters thought the mammoths were valuable and wanted them very much. Then ask students to locate and read aloud the sentence on page 266 in which *spring* appears. (Line 11: *The hole had filled with spring water and sticky clay.*) Explain that this sentence means that the hole had filled with water that flowed out of the ground.

Ask students to choose one of the words. Have individuals tell a meaning they already knew for the word and the new meaning they learned.

RETEACH

Grammar/Writing

Practice Book 105

Writing Trait: Sentence Fluency Have students turn to page 105 in their *Practice Book*. Explain that when they write a paragraph, it is important to use a variety of sentence types and lengths. This makes the writing more interesting and effective. Point out how the author of "Rough and Tough Enough" uses a variety of sentence types and lengths. Read aloud the information in the chart and the directions. Then have a volunteer read the first sentence. Point out that this sentence is short and expresses one simple idea.

GUIDED PRACTICE Work with students to complete the rest of Part A. Then read the Part B directions and sentences. Guide students to combine the two sentences to make a complex sentence. Remind students that they can use words such as *because*, *since*, *after*, *although*, and *when* to combine sentences. Read the Part C directions and have students write sentences of their own. Invite students to share what they wrote.

Fluency

Practice Book 103

Fluency Practice Tell students that today they will reread the sentences on the bottom of *Practice Book* page 103. Have students locate and point to the first sentence. Tell students that everyone is going to read the sentence together. This choral reading will give students an opportunity to hear others and listen to the natural phrasing of the sentences. Choral-read each of the sentences several times.

"Rough and Tough Enough" 309

LESSON 26

DAY AT A GLANCE
Day 4

COMPREHENSION
 Reteach Paraphrase

DECODING/SPELLING
Reteach Words with Silent Letters

BUILD ROBUST VOCABULARY
Reteach Words from "Rough and Tough Enough"

GRAMMAR/WRITING
Reteach Writing Form: Summary

FLUENCY
Fluency Practice

Materials Needed: Turn It Up!

Student Edition pp. 262–268 | Practice Book p. 106 | Copying Master 104

Spelling Words: Lesson 26

1. subtle	11. island
2. scene	12. lamb
3. climbed	13. numb
4. comb	14. often
5. exhibit	15. rustle
6. doubt	16. debt
7. folks	17. knack
8. exhaust	18. thumb
9. half	19. unknown
10. whistle	20. mortgage

30+ Minutes

RETEACH
Comprehension

Paraphrase Give students the following information about paraphrasing:
- To paraphrase, we retell a sentence or a story in our own words.
- It is important not to change the author's meaning as we paraphrase.
- Sometimes you can paraphrase by using synonyms. Other times you can paraphrase when you change the order of words and ideas.

Write the following sentences from "Rough and Tough Enough" on the board. Have volunteers read each sentence aloud. Then guide students as they paraphrase each sentence.

- **Many mammoths roamed Earth during the Ice Age.** (Possible response: Many mammoths wandered around during the Ice Age.)
- **They used their elegant trunks to reach leaves in a tree.** (Possible response: Mammoths used their great trunks to get leaves in a tree.)
- **The animal remains were submerged in water and layers of mud.** (Possible response: Mammoth bones were buried under layers of mud.)
- **We try to make sense of this complicated riddle.** (Possible response: We try to understand the answer to this puzzle.)

RETEACH
Decoding/Spelling

Words with Silent Letters Have students number a sheet of paper 1–15. Write the Spelling Word *subtle* on the board, and point to the silent letter *b*. Tell students that the first seven words you will dictate have the silent letter *b*. After students write each word, display it so they can proofread their work. Repeat this activity for the other silent letters using these examples: *exhibit, folks, whistle, knack*. Finally, dictate *scene* and *island*.

1. climbed	2. comb	3. doubt	4. lamb
5. numb	6. debt	7. thumb	8. exhaust
9. half	10. often	11. rustle	12. mortgage
13. unknown	14. scene	15. island	

Have students turn to page 106 in their *Practice Book*. Have students read the sentences. Have them do what the sentences tell them to do. Remind students to circle the words that have silent letters after they have followed the directions.

310 Lesson 26 • Turn It Up!

Day 4

RETEACH
Build Robust Vocabulary

Words from "Rough and Tough Enough" Review the meanings of *packs*, *prized*, and *spring*. Then say these sentences and ask which word each sentence describes. Have students explain why.

- The ranger warned visitors to stay away from groups of wild dogs that lived and hunted together in the forest. (packs)
- Little fish swam in the pond that formed from water that came out of the ground. (spring)
- People thought the chocolates made in the little shop were very fine and wanted very much to buy them. (prized)

RETEACH
Grammar/Writing

Writing Form: Summary Tell students that a summary retells the main idea and the most important details of a passage. When you write a summary, it is important to use a variety of sentence types and lengths. It will make the selection more interesting and effective. Distribute *Copying Master 104*. Have a volunteer read the description of a summary. Then read the Student Model together. Write on the board the following sentences from the passage:

> First, they had a great sense of smell.
> Second, their trunks were very strong.

Model for students how to combine these simple sentences into a compound sentence.

> A mammoth's trunk had a great sense of smell, and it was very strong.

GUIDED PRACTICE Complete the activity by having students revise other sentences in the summary. Allow time for students to share their revised sentences with the group.

Fluency

Fluency Practice Have each student work with a partner to read passages from "Rough and Tough Enough" aloud to each other. Students may select a passage that they enjoyed or choose one of the following options:

- Read page 266. (Total: 171 words)
- Read page 268. (Total: 99 words)

Encourage students to read the selected passage aloud to their partner three times. Have the student rate his or her reading on the 1–4 scale.

1	Need more practice
2	Pretty good
3	Good
4	Great!

"Rough and Tough Enough" 311

Preteach for LESSON 27

DAY AT A GLANCE: Day 5

VOCABULARY
Preteach ancient, distant, sentries, glistens, embedded, cascading, weary, eroding

COMPREHENSION
Preteach Main Idea and Supporting Details

DECODING/WORD ATTACK
Preteach Decode Using Structural Analysis

DECODING/SPELLING
Preteach Words with Greek and Latin Roots

GRAMMAR/WRITING
Preteach Contractions

FLUENCY
Fluency Performance

Materials Needed: *Turn It Up!*

Student Edition pp. 262–268

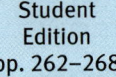
Copying Master 105

PRETEACH — Vocabulary

Lesson 27 Vocabulary Distribute a set of Vocabulary Word Cards to each student. Hold up the card for the first word, and ask a volunteer to read it aloud. Have students repeat the word and hold up the matching card. Give the explanation for the word. Then ask students the first question below and discuss their responses. Continue for each of the Vocabulary Words.

- Have you ever seen or visited something **ancient**? Describe it.
- What is a way to keep in touch with **distant** family members or friends?
- How do you think **sentries** would stand? Why do they stand that way?
- What does a lake look like when it **glistens** in the morning light?
- How do you get out a splinter **embedded** in your skin?
- Where would you go to see **cascading** water? What would it look like?
- What types of activities make you **weary**? Why?
- Have you ever seen water **eroding** a hillside? Describe what it looks like.

PRETEACH — Comprehension

Main Idea and Supporting Details Explain that identifying the main idea and the details will help students understand a selection better. Sometimes the main idea is not stated. Finding the details can help the reader determine the main idea. Ask students to reread page 265 from the selection "Rough and Tough Enough" in the *Student Edition*. Then ask:

- What are some details from this page? (Students may name any details from this page.)
- What do all these details talk about? (early humans and mammoths)
- What is one possible main idea that is not directly stated? (Possible response: Mammoths were a very important resource for early humans.)

312 Preteach for Lesson 27 • *Turn It Up!*

Day 5

PRETEACH

Decoding/Word Attack

Decode Using Structural Analysis Write *visit* and *visa* on the board. Ask students to identify the letters that are the same in both words. (*vis*) Explain that *vis* is a Latin root word. It means "to see." Tell students that they can use Latin and Greek root words to help them figure out the pronunciation and the meaning of a word. Write *revise* on the board. Point out that the prefix *re-* means "again" and the Latin root word *vis* means "to see." Show students that by knowing these parts of the word, they are able to figure out that *revise* means "to see something again."

PRETEACH

Decoding/Spelling

Words with Greek and Latin Roots Write *inspect, autograph, construct,* and *visor* on the board. Explain that these are some of the next lesson's Spelling Words. Have a volunteer read each aloud. Then tell students the meanings of these roots: *spect* means "look," *struct* means "build," *graph* means "write," and *vis* means "see." Have students match each word to its root.

PRETEACH

Grammar/Writing

Contractions Tell students that a contraction is a short way to write two words. Write *cannot* and *can't* on the board. Tell students that *can't* is a contraction. Point out how an apostrophe is used to take the place of one or more letters. Then write these word pairs on the board: *do not/don't; will not/won't;* and *could not/couldn't*. Guide students to understand how the two words change to form a contraction.

VOCABULARY

Student-Friendly Explanations

ancient Something that is ancient is very, very old.

distant Something distant is very far away.

sentries Sentries are people who stand as guards around a camp, building, or other area.

glistens Something that glistens looks wet and shiny.

embedded If an object is embedded in something, it is stuck firmly in it.

cascading Cascading water falls or rushes downward very fast.

weary If you are weary, you are very tired from working hard at something, and you want to stop.

eroding Something that is eroding is being slowly scraped away a little at a time, often by the force of moving water or strong wind.

Fluency

pp. 262–268 **Fluency Performance** Invite students each to read aloud from "Rough and Tough Enough" a passage that they selected and practiced earlier. Note the number of words each student reads correctly and incorrectly. Have students rate their own oral reading on the 1–4 scale. Give each student the opportunity to continue practicing and then to read the passage to you again.

"Rough and Tough Enough" 313

DAY AT A GLANCE
Day 1

LESSON 27

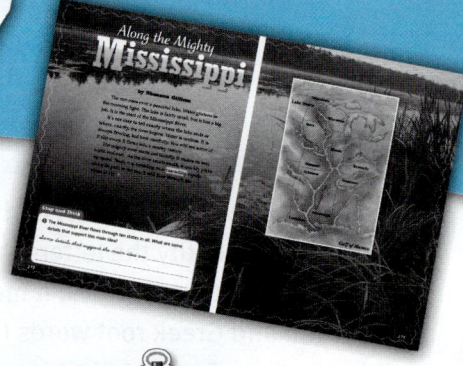

VOCABULARY
Reteach *ancient, distant, sentries, glistens, embedded, cascading, weary, eroding*

COMPREHENSION
Reteach Main Idea and Supporting Details

DECODING/SPELLING
Reteach Words with Greek and Latin Roots

GRAMMAR/WRITING
Preteach Possessive Pronouns

FLUENCY
Fluency Practice

Materials Needed: *Turn It Up!*

  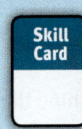 

Student Edition pp. 270–271 | Practice Book p. 107 | Skill Card 27 | Copying Master 106

RETEACH
Vocabulary

Lesson 27 Vocabulary Read aloud the Vocabulary Words and the Student-Friendly Explanations. Then have students turn to pages 270–271 of their books. Guide students as they complete the sentences on the postcards by selecting the correct Vocabulary Word and writing it in the blank. Have volunteers read each completed postcard aloud. If students are unable to give reasonable responses, refer to the Student-Friendly Explanations. (Answers for pages 270–271: 2. *cascading*, 3. *distant*, 4. *sentries*, 5. *weary*, 6. *ancient*, 7. *embedded*, 8. *eroding*)

RETEACH
Comprehension

Main Idea and Supporting Details Have students look at side A of *Skill Card 27: Main Idea and Supporting Details*. Read the definitions. Then read the paragraph aloud as students read along. Remind students that when the main idea is unstated, they need to identify the details and determine what the details mostly talk about. Suggest a possible main idea. (The Gateway Arch is a famous structure in St. Louis.)

GUIDED PRACTICE Now have students look at side B of *Skill Card 27: Main Idea and Supporting Details*. Invite volunteers to read the passage aloud. Guide students as they copy the chart and complete it with details from the paragraph. (Main idea: The alligator hole is a home for many animals; Detail: It is marked with large, broad leaves; Detail: It is clear of vegetation and muck; Detail: It is full of water during the dry season; Detail: Small animals move into the hole along with the alligator.)

314 Lesson 27 • Turn It Up!

Day 1

RETEACH

Decoding/Spelling

Words with Greek and Latin Roots Distribute *Copying Master 106*. Model reading the Spelling Words and have students repeat them. Have students look for the roots *spect, vis, struct, phon,* and *graph* in each word. Then have students complete the following activity. Have students work in pairs. Each student writes a sentence for each Spelling Word but leaves a blank for the actual word. The partners then switch papers and fill in the blanks in each other's sentences. Students should give themselves one point for each correctly spelled word.

PRETEACH

Grammar/Writing

Possessive Pronouns Tell students that possessive pronouns show ownership. Explain that some possessive pronouns are similar to contractions. Point out that one way to tell them apart is to remember that contractions have apostrophes. Write *your* and *you're* on the board. Model how *you're* is a contraction of *you are*. Explain that *your* indicates something that belongs to you. Write these sentences on the board:

> Mario put his cap on the hook.
> Shannon finished her homework.
> The snake darted into its hole.

Guide students to identify the possessive pronoun in each sentence. (his, her, its)

VOCABULARY
Student-Friendly Explanations

ancient Something that is ancient is very, very old.

distant Something distant is very far away.

sentries Sentries are people who stand as guards around a camp, building, or other area.

glistens Something that glistens looks wet and shiny.

embedded If an object is embedded in something, it is stuck firmly in it.

cascading Cascading water falls or rushes downward very fast.

weary If you are weary, you are very tired from working hard at something and you want to stop.

eroding Something that is eroding is being slowly scraped away a little at a time, often by the force of moving water or strong wind.

Fluency

Fluency Practice Have students turn to *Practice Book* page 107. Read the words in the first column aloud. Invite students to track each word and repeat the words after you. Then have students work in pairs to read the words in the first column aloud to each other. Follow the same procedure with each of the remaining columns. After partners have practiced reading aloud the words in each of the columns, have them practice reading all of the words.

"Along the Mighty Mississippi" 315

LESSON 27

30+ Minutes

DAY AT A GLANCE — Day 2

VOCABULARY
Reteach ancient, distant, sentries, glistens, embedded, cascading, weary, eroding

COMPREHENSION
"Along the Mighty Mississippi"
Build Background
Monitor Comprehension
Answers to *Think Critically* **Questions**

DECODING/SPELLING
Reteach Words with Greek and Latin Roots

GRAMMAR/WRITING
Preteach Easily Confused Words

FLUENCY
Fluency Practice

Materials Needed: *Turn It Up!*

Student Edition pp. 272–279

Practice Book pp. 107, 108

Copying Masters 105, 106

RETEACH

Vocabulary

Copying Master 105

Lesson 27 Vocabulary Divide the group into teams. Place the Vocabulary Word Cards in a bag and mix them up. Have the first team choose a card out of the bag. That player will then ask a teammate a question, such as *What word would you use to describe a person who is standing guard?* If the teammate gives the correct word the team gets a point. Have teams take turns until each word has been used by all teams.

Comprehension

Build Background: "Along the Mighty Mississippi"
Ask students to share experiences they may have had on a river or a lake. What is the river or lake like? What activities did they do there? What fish or wildlife did they see?

pp. 272–273

Monitor Comprehension: "Along the Mighty Mississippi"
Read the title of the story aloud. Then have students read page 272 to find out what this selection is mostly about.

After reading the page, ask: **What do you think this selection will be mostly about?** (Possible response: I think this selection will be about the Mississippi River.) **MAKE PREDICTIONS**

Discuss the Stop and Think question on page 272: **The Mississippi River flows through ten states in all. What are some details that support this main idea?** (Some details that support the main idea are that the mighty river makes its way north and east; the river heads south; it tumbles over rapids until it reaches the sea.) Guide students in writing the answer to this question.  **MAIN IDEA AND DETAILS**

Ask: **What information does the map give us on page 273?** (Possible response: The map gives us information about which states the Mississippi River flows through. It also shows other rivers that are connected to it.) **GRAPHIC AIDS**

Ask: **Does the water in the river stand still?** (No, it is always flowing.) **How would you know?** (You can see the water cascading along its path.) **NOTE DETAILS**

pp. 274–275

Discuss the Stop and Think question on page 274: **Why does the author share facts about the river's fish?** (The author shares facts about the river's fish because she wants to provide information about the river.) Guide students in writing the answer to this question. **AUTHOR'S PURPOSE**

316 Lesson 27 • *Turn It Up!*

Read aloud the second paragraph on page 274. Model the strategy of using context to confirm word meaning.

THINK ALOUD When I read the page, I was not sure what *sentries* meant. I remembered that it was one of our Vocabulary Words. It describes people that guard a building or camp. Then the text said the boys sit like sentries. The boys are fishing. I know that when I am fishing, I try to sit very still. I would think that *sentries* are people who are very still as they are watching something. **USE CONTEXT CLUES**

Discuss the Stop and Think question on page 275: **Why does the river get bigger and turn brown?** (Possible response: The river gets bigger and turns brown because as other rivers join it, they add more water and mud.) Guide students in writing the answer to this question. **DRAW CONCLUSIONS**

pp. 275–277

Ask: **In what ways is the river useful?** (Possible response: The river is a border, it is a "drainpipe," and it is a way to move goods.) **NOTE DETAILS**

Discuss the Stop and Think question on page 276: **Why is the river a useful way to ship goods?** (Possible response: The river is a useful way to ship goods because it is wide and deep enough for boats to pass through and it costs less than other ways of shipping.) Guide students in writing the answer to this question. **DRAW CONCLUSIONS**

Ask: **Why do you think the visitors in St. Louis stop to watch the river?** (Possible response: The visitors may like to watch the different boats on the river.) **MAKE INFERENCES**

Discuss the Stop and Think question on page 277: **Where do you think the article will take us next?** (I think the article will take us to the spot where the river flows out into the sea.) Guide students in writing the answer to this question. **MAKE PREDICTIONS**

page 278

Discuss the Stop and Think question on page 278: **How is the end of the article like the beginning?** (The end of the article is like the beginning because it uses the same words to tell how water is restless and always flowing.) Guide students in writing the answer to this question. **MAKE CONNECTIONS**

Ask: **Why do you think the author used the same text to describe the river at the end of the article?** (Possible response: The author wants to show how the water is never-ending and that it keeps moving whether it is from a small lake or into a large sea.) **AUTHOR'S PURPOSE**

Day 2

VOCABULARY
Student-Friendly Explanations

ancient Something that is ancient is very, very old.

distant Something distant is very far away.

sentries Sentries are people who stand as guards around a camp, building, or other area.

glistens Something that glistens looks wet and shiny.

embedded If an object is embedded in something, it is stuck firmly in it.

cascading Cascading water falls or rushes downward very fast.

weary If you are weary, you are very tired from working hard at something, and you want to stop.

eroding Something that is eroding is being slowly scraped away a little at a time, often by the force of moving water or strong wind.

"Along the Mighty Mississippi" 317

Day 2

Spelling Words: Lesson 27

1. respect	11. autograph
2. inspect	12. photograph
3. spectacle	13. phonics
4. spectator	14. telegraph
5. spectrum	15. paragraph
6. specific	16. visor
7. construct	17. visitor
8. destruction	18. visual
9. instruct	19. visible
10. structure	20. television

page 279 **Answers to *Think Critically* Questions** Help students read and answer the *Think Critically* questions on page 279. Have students copy the graphic organizer in question 1 onto a separate sheet of paper. Then guide students in writing the answer to each question. Possible responses are provided.

1. [Detail] The river starts out small. [Detail] As it moves along, it gets wider, deeper, and muddier. [Detail] The water splits up into channels as it approaches the sea. [Main Idea] The Mississippi River changes a lot as it moves along its path to the sea.  **MAIN IDEA AND DETAILS**

2. Once a drop of water joins the river, it takes about 90 days for it to flow with the river out to sea. **CAUSE AND EFFECT**

3. The author wrote this article to give facts about the Mississippi River, but she also uses the article to tell a kind of story about how the water in the river moves. **AUTHOR'S PURPOSE**

RETEACH
Decoding/Spelling

Copying Master 106 **Words with Greek and Latin Roots** Remind students that when they know the Greek or Latin root of a word, it is easier to determine the meaning. Write the following roots, prefixes, and suffixes on the board:

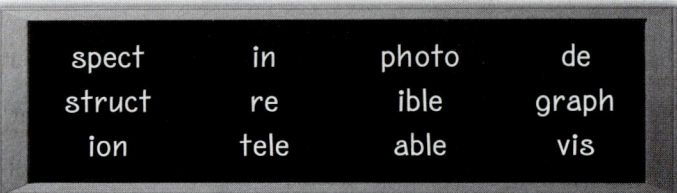

Ask students to think of some words using the prefixes, suffixes, and roots. (Possible responses: invisible, inspect, instruct, instruction, destruct, destruction, indestructible, photograph, photographable, telephoto, television) Have students take turns choosing a Spelling Word from *Copying Master 106* and writing it on the board. Then have the student underline the root word and tell what the root word means.

318 Lesson 27 • Turn It Up!

Day 2

PRETEACH

Grammar/Writing

 **Easily Confused Words** Remind students that some contractions and possessive pronouns are easily confused. Convey these reminders to students:

- *They're* is a contraction of *they are*.
  Their means "belonging to them."
  There means "that place."

- *It's* is a contraction of *it is*.
  Its means "belonging to it."

- *Who's* is a contraction of *who is*.
  Whose means "belonging to someone."

Point out that students may need to refer to these reminders as they proofread their writing.

GUIDED PRACTICE Direct students' attention to page 108 in their *Practice Book*. Invite students to read aloud each of the sentences in the activity. Ask a volunteer to choose the correct word to complete each sentence. Have students discuss how they were able to choose the correct word in each case.

Fluency

Fluency Practice Invite students to look at the bottom half of *Practice Book* page 107. These sentences have been broken into natural phrases. Tell students to repeat each phrase after you, mirroring your expression, phrasing, and pace. After students have repeated each sentence, invite them to practice reading the sentences to partners.

"Along the Mighty Mississippi" **319**

LESSON 27

DAY AT A GLANCE
Day 3

COMPREHENSION
Preteach Paraphrase, Use Graphic Aids
Reread and Summarize "Along the Mightly Mississippi"

DECODING/SPELLING
Reteach Use Word Families

BUILD ROBUST VOCABULARY
Teach Words from "Along the Mighty Mississippi"

GRAMMAR/WRITING
Reteach Writing Trait: Sentence Fluency

FLUENCY
Fluency Practice

Materials Needed: *Turn It Up!*

Student Edition pp. 272–278

Practice Book pp. 107, 109

Copying Master 107

30+ Minutes

PRETEACH
Comprehensive

Copying Master 107

Paraphrase Remind students that paraphrasing is retelling information in their own words. Tell students that they can paraphrase information by using synonyms to change the words but not change the meaning of the text.

Use Graphic Aids Distribute *Copying Master 107* and have students listen as you read the information at the top of the page. Then have a volunteer read the definition. Model how to read the graph to gather factual information.

GUIDED PRACTICE Ask students to look at the graph and answer questions about the information it presents. Allow time for students to share their responses with others.

Reread and Summarize Have students reread and summarize "Along the Mighty Mississippi" in sections, as described below.

pp. 272–273

Let's reread pages 272–273 to recall where the Mississippi River begins.
Summary: The Mississippi River begins at a lake. The waters in the river are constantly flowing. The river first goes north and east, then south. The water will flow through ten states in all.

pp. 274–275

Now let's reread pages 274–275 to recall more about the river.
Summary: The river is a map for birds heading south. The river is also a home to many kinds of fish. Farms and cities are joined by the river. The river is also a "drainpipe" for the country.

pp. 276–278

Last, let's reread pages 276–278 to recall other facts about the river.
Summary: The river is a useful way to ship goods. As the river gets close to its end, it splits into channels. The water slows down and many animals are found here. The end of the river is where the sea begins.

RETEACH
Decoding/Spelling

Use Word Families Write *telephone, telegraph,* and *television* on the board. Ask students to find the root that is common in each of the words. Tell students that a group of words sharing a root word is called a word family. Ask students what word family these words belong to. (the *tele-* word family) Tell them that *tele* means "far or distant." Ask students to write the word *telescope* on a piece of paper, looking at other words in the word family to spell the root word. Then have them use the root to figure out its possible meaning.

320 Lesson 27 • Turn It Up!

Day 3

TEACH

Build Robust Vocabulary

pp. 272–274 **Words from "Along the Mighty Mississippi"** Have students locate the word *timidly* on page 272 of "Along the Mighty Mississippi." Ask a volunteer to read aloud the sentence in which this word appears. (Line 8: *The mighty river starts out timidly.*) Explain that this sentence means that the river does not start out looking mighty. It starts out weakly as if it is scared or unsure. Continue by asking students to locate and read aloud the sentence in which the word *soar* appears on page 274. (Line 1: *High above, birds soar over the water.*) Explain that this sentence means that the birds fly very high. Then ask students to locate and read aloud the sentence in which the word *roughly* appears on page 274. (Line 7: *The river has roughly 250 kinds of fish.*) Explain that in this sentence *roughly* means "about." The river has about 250 kinds of fish.

Ask students to use the words in sentences about personal experiences. For example: *When it was icy, I walked timidly because I was afraid I would fall.*

RETEACH

Grammar/Writing

Practice Book 109 **Writing Trait: Sentence Fluency** Have students turn to page 109 in their *Practice Book*. Explain that when writers write a story, it is important to use a variety of sentence lengths and types so that the writing isn't "clunky." Ask a volunteer to read the information in the box. Point out how the author of "Along the Mighty Mississippi" used a variety of sentence lengths and types so that the sentences flow from one to the next.

GUIDED PRACTICE Complete the page together. Invite volunteers to share their sentences in Parts B and C.

Fluency

Practice Book 107 **Fluency Practice** Tell students that today they will reread the sentences on the bottom of *Practice Book* page 107. Have students locate and point to the first sentence. Tell students that everyone is going to read the sentence together. This choral reading will give students an opportunity to hear others and listen to the natural phrasing of the sentences. Choral-read each of the sentences several times.

"Along the Mighty Mississippi" **321**

LESSON 27

DAY AT A GLANCE
Day 4

COMPREHENSION
Reteach Use Graphic Aids, Paraphrase

DECODING/SPELLING
Reteach Words with Greek and Latin Roots

BUILD ROBUST VOCABULARY
Reteach Words from "Along the Mighty Mississippi"

GRAMMAR/WRITING
Reteach Writing Form: Explanatory Essay

FLUENCY
Fluency Practice

Materials Needed: Turn It Up!

 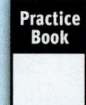 

Student Edition pp. 272–278 | Practice Book p. 110 | Copying Master 108

Spelling Words: Lesson 27

1. respect	11. autograph
2. inspect	12. photograph
3. spectacle	13. phonics
4. spectator	14. telegraph
5. spectrum	15. paragraph
6. specific	16. visor
7. construct	17. visitor
8. destruction	18. visual
9. instruct	19. visible
10. structure	20. television

30+ Minutes

RETEACH
Comprehension

page 273 **Use Graphic Aids** Remind students that graphic aids show information in pictures rather than words. Have students look at the map on page 273 of their books. Challenge students to list information they learned from the map that they did not learn from the text.

Paraphrase Remind students that when they paraphrase, they should retell information in their own words. To paraphrase,

- change the words without changing the meaning of the words.
- replace some words with synonyms or change the order of words.
- the paraphrased passage should always be about the same length as the original passage.

Write on the board these sentences from "Along the Mighty Mississippi":

> The mighty river starts out timidly.
> Visitors in St. Louis stop to watch.

Have volunteers read each sentence and paraphrase it. (Possible responses: The huge river moves slowly at first; tourists in St. Louis pause to look.)

RETEACH
Decoding/Spelling

Practice Book 110 **Words with Greek and Latin Roots** Have students number a sheet of paper 1–16. Write *respect* on the board, and point to the root word. Tell students that the first five words that you will dictate have the same root word. After students write each word, display it so they can proofread their work. Repeat this activity for the other words using these examples: *construct* (three words), *autograph* (three words), and *visor* (four words). Finally, dictate *phonics*.

1. inspect	2. spectacle	3. spectator	4. spectrum
5. specific	6. destruction	7. instruct	8. structure
9. photograph	10. telegraph	11. paragraph	12. visitor
13. visual	14. visible	15. television	16. phonics

Have students turn to page 110 in their *Practice Book*. Have students circle the letter in front of the sentence that best describes each picture.

322 Lesson 27 • Turn It Up!

Day 4

RETEACH
Build Robust Vocabulary

Words from "Along the Mighty Mississippi" Review the meanings of the words *timidly*, *soar*, and *roughly*. Then say these sentences and ask which word describes each sentence. Have students explain why.

- **The new student walked into class as if she were a little unsure of herself.** (timidly)
- **Airplanes fly high above the clouds.** (soar)
- **There are about 25 cookies in each package.** (roughly)

RETEACH
Grammar/Writing

Copying Master 108

Writing Form: Explanatory Essay Tell students that an explanatory essay gives factual information. When they write an explanatory essay it is important to make sure their sentences flow from one to the next. Distribute *Copying Master 108*. Have a volunteer read the description of the explanatory essay. Then read the Student Model together. Write on the board the following sentences from the passage:

> There are many birds along the river. There are many waterfowl along the river as well.

Model for students how these two short sentences can be combined into a longer sentence.

> There are many birds and waterfowl along the river.

GUIDED PRACTICE Complete the activity by having students answer the questions about the Student Model. Allow time for students to share their responses with the group.

Fluency

pp. 272–278

Fluency Practice Have each student work with a partner to read passages from "Along the Mighty Mississippi" aloud to each other. Students may select a passage that they enjoyed or choose one of the following options:

- Read page 272. (Total: 116 words)
- Read page 274. (Total: 89 words)

Encourage students to read the selected passage aloud to their partner three times. Have the student rate his or her reading on the 1–4 scale.

1	Need more practice
2	Pretty good
3	Good
4	Great!

"Along the Mighty Mississippi" 323

Preteach for LESSON 28

VOCABULARY
Preteach *behemoth, cordially, hearty, fanciful, scenic, colossal, illusion*

COMPREHENSION
 Preteach Figurative Language

DECODING/WORD ATTACK
Preteach Decode Longer Words

DECODING/SPELLING
Preteach Homophones

GRAMMAR/WRITING
Preteach Adverbs

FLUENCY
Fluency Performance

Materials Needed: *Turn It Up!*

Student Edition pp. 272–278

Copying Master 109

PRETEACH

Vocabulary

 Lesson 28 Vocabulary Distribute a set of Vocabulary Word Cards to each student. Hold up the card for the first word, and ask a volunteer to read it aloud. Have students repeat the word and hold up the matching card. Give the explanation for the word. Then ask students the first question below and discuss their responses. Continue for each of the Vocabulary Words.

- **What is an animal that could be called behemoth?**
- **How would you cordially invite a friend to your house?**
- **What foods might be part of a hearty meal?**
- **What fanciful characters have you read about? Describe them.**
- **What kind of place would have a scenic view?**
- **What do you think it would be like to live in a colossal house?**
- **If you saw an illusion of an ice cream cone, how would you eat it?**

PRETEACH

Comprehension

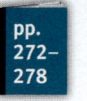  **Figurative Language** Explain that authors use figurative language to make their writing more vivid. Tell students that the author of "Along the Mighty Mississippi" used figurative language. Ask:

- **What do you think the author meant when she said "Water is restless"?** (She meant that the water is always moving.)

Tell students that this sentence is an example of personification. It is describing the water as if it were human. Identify and define other types of figurative language:

- simile: a comparison using *like* or *as*
- metaphor: a comparison that talks about one thing as if it were another
- idiom: a group of words with a special meaning
- hyperbole: a huge exaggeration

GUIDED PRACTICE Have students reread the second paragraph on page 274 of the *Student Edition*. Ask students to find a simile. (they sit like sentries) Then have students reread the first paragraph on page 275 to find another example of personification. (sleepless cities) Discuss with students how the figurative language made the writing more interesting.

324 Preteach for Lesson 28 • *Turn It Up!*

Day 1

RETEACH

Decoding/Spelling

Copying Master 110

Homophones Distribute *Copying Master 110*. Model reading the Spelling Words and have students repeat them. Review the instruction for homophones, and then have students complete the following activity. Have students work in pairs. Each student writes a sentence for each Spelling Word but leaves a blank for the actual word. The partners should then switch papers and fill in the blanks in each other's sentences. Students should give themselves one point for each correctly spelled word.

PRETEACH

Grammar/Writing

Adverbs Remind students that adverbs are words that describe verbs. Adverbs can be used to compare two or more things. Explain to students that with short adverbs, we add *-er* to compare two things or *-est* to compare more than two. Write the following sentence on the board:

> Kate finished sooner than Derek.

Ask a volunteer to read the sentence aloud. Underline *sooner*, and explain that it is an adverb that compares when two people finished.

Tell students that with longer adverbs, the word *more* is added to compare two things, and *most* is added to compare more than two. Then write the following sentence on the board:

> Of the four boys, Derek slept the most soundly.

Ask a volunteer to read the sentence aloud. Then underline the adverb. Circle the word *most* in front of the adverb. Point out that more than two things are being compared.

GUIDED PRACTICE Have students copy the following sentence frames:

> Josh woke up _____ than Billy. (earlier, earliest)
> Kira runs _____ of all. (faster, fastest)
> Michael writes _____ than Sue. (more carefully, most carefully)

Ask students to choose the correct comparing adverbs from the words in parentheses. (earlier, fastest, more carefully)

VOCABULARY

Student-Friendly Explanations

behemoth Something called behemoth is extremely large.

cordially To say something cordially is to say it in a warm, friendly way.

hearty If a meal is hearty, it is satisfying and includes plenty of good food.

fanciful Something that is fanciful is not real but comes from the imagination.

scenic A scenic place has lovely natural features, such as trees, cliffs, or bodies of water.

colossal Something that is colossal is huge.

illusion An illusion is something that is not really what it appears to be.

Fluency

Practice Book 111

Fluency Practice Have students turn to *Practice Book* page 111. Read the words in the first column aloud. Invite students to track each word and repeat the words after you. Then have students work in pairs to read the words in the first column aloud to each other. Follow the same procedure with each of the remaining columns. After partners have practiced reading aloud the words in each of the columns, have them practice reading all of the words.

"The Untold Story of Texas Kate" **327**

LESSON 28

DAY AT A GLANCE
Day 2

VOCABULARY
Reteach behemoth, cordially, hearty, fanciful, scenic, colossal, illusion

COMPREHENSION
"The Untold Story of Texas Kate"
Build Background
Monitor Comprehension
Answers to *Think Critically* Questions

DECODING/SPELLING
Reteach Homophones

GRAMMAR/WRITING
Preteach Double Negatives

FLUENCY
Fluency Practice

Materials Needed: *Turn It Up!*

Student Edition
pp. 282–289

Practice Book
pp. 111, 112

Copying Masters
109, 110

30+ Minutes

RETEACH
Vocabulary

Copying Master 109

Lesson 28 Vocabulary Distribute a set of Word Cards to each student or pair of students. Say these sentences as students hold up a Word Card that can complete the sentence.

- A stegosaurus is an animal that is _____. (behemoth)
- You are _____ invited to my party. (cordially)
- I enjoy a tasty, _____ meal. (hearty)
- A leprechaun is a _____ creature. (fanciful)
- We took several pictures of the _____ view. (scenic)
- That _____ skyscraper is 53 stories high. (colossal)
- An _____ is not really there. (illusion)

Comprehension

Build Background: "The Untold Story of Texas Kate"
Ask students to discuss what it would be like to be a giant. Note that tall tales include characters that are impossibly large, are incredibly strong, and can do things no real person could ever do.

pp. 282–283

Monitor Comprehension: "The Untold Story of Texas Kate"
Read the title of the story aloud. Then have students read pages 282–283 to find out who Texas Kate is and why her story has been untold.

Ask: Why has Kate's story been untold for so long? (Possible responses: People are scared to tell her story. People think lightning will strike if you say her name.) **MAKE INFERENCES**

Discuss the Stop and Think question on page 282: **What do we know about Kate? Underline the words on the page that tell you.** (Kate is Pecos Bill's little sister. Kate is a girl from the Old West. Students should underline the phrases "Pecos Bill," "little sister, Kate" and "story has been untold for decades.") Guide students in writing the answer to this question. **NOTE DETAILS**

Discuss the Stop and Think question on page 283: **Why does Kate head south?** (Possible response: Kate heads south because she misses her brother, Pecos Bill. She plans to join him.) Guide students in writing the answer to the question. **CAUSE AND EFFECT**

Ask: What is the first problem that Kate faces on her trip? How does she solve it? (A river is blocking her path, so she uses what she has on hand to make a boat.) **CONFLICT AND RESOLUTION**

328 Lesson 28 • *Turn It Up!*

Day 2

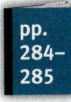
pp. 284–285

Discuss the Stop and Think question on page 284: **How does Kate feel when she sees how much she's grown?** (When she sees how much she has grown, Kate is surprised. She is not worried, but she is hungry.) Guide students in writing the answer to this question.
CHARACTER'S EMOTIONS

Read aloud the first paragraph on page 284. Model the strategy of using compare and contrast to understand how Kate changes in the story.

THINK ALOUD After I read the paragraph, I thought about how Kate changed. At the beginning of the story, it seemed that Kate was a regular-sized girl. Now after her boat ride, she has grown to over ten feet tall. That's a big change that will probably have an effect on Kate's daily life. As I read further, I'll look for details about how her life is different now. **COMPARE AND CONTRAST**

Discuss the Stop and Think question on page 285: **How does the author describe Kate's thirst? What does this mean?** (The author says Kate is as parched as a fish out of water. It means that she is really thirsty.) Guide students in writing the answer to this question.
 FIGURATIVE LANGUAGE

pp. 286–287

Discuss the Stop and Think question on page 286: **What do you think Kate will do next?** (Possible response: I think Kate will get something to eat.) Guide students in writing the answer to this question. **MAKE PREDICTIONS**

Ask: **What happened when Kate's friend gave her a sandwich? Describe what she did with it.** (She ate it very quickly.)
 FIGURATIVE LANGUAGE

Discuss the Stop and Think question on page 287: **How does Kate's friend help her?** (Kate's friend helps her when he gets the entire town to help feed her.) Guide students in writing the answer to this question. **CONFLICT AND RESOLUTION**

page 288

Discuss the Stop and Think question on page 288: **What do you find out about the narrator on this page?** (Possible responses: I found out that the narrator is Kate's friend from the story; the man Kate meets by the river.) Guide students in writing the answer to this question.
MAKE CONNECTIONS

Ask: **Why does the narrator want to tell Texas Kate's story?** (Possible responses: The narrator wants everyone to know about his friend. He wants people to know that when Texas Kate's stomach is rumbling, it sounds just like a clap of thunder.) **MAKE INFERENCES**

VOCABULARY
Student-Friendly Explanations

behemoth Something called behemoth is extremely large.

cordially To say something cordially is to say it in a warm, friendly way.

hearty If a meal is hearty, it is satisfying and includes plenty of good food.

fanciful Something that is fanciful is not real but comes from the imagination.

scenic A scenic place has lovely natural features, such as trees, cliffs, or bodies of water.

colossal Something that is colossal is huge.

illusion An illusion is something that is not really what it appears to be.

"The Untold Story of Texas Kate" 329

Day 2

Spelling Words: Lesson 28

1. there
2. they're
3. their
4. sent
5. scent
6. hour
7. our
8. seam
9. seem
10. plain
11. plane
12. piece
13. peace
14. two
15. too
16. to
17. whole
18. hole
19. pail
20. pale

Answers to *Think Critically* Questions

page 289

Help students read and answer the *Think Critically* questions on page 289. Have students copy the graphic organizer in question 1 onto a separate sheet of paper. Then guide students in writing the answer to each question. Possible responses are provided.

1. Kate is restless, she does not want to stay settled for too long, and she wants to join her brother, Bill. **CAUSE AND EFFECT**
2. Kate tells her friends that she will visit them whenever they call her name. **PLOT**
3. Kate is calm; able to do things for herself; smart; doesn't panic. **CHARACTER'S TRAITS**

RETEACH

Decoding/Spelling

Homophones Remind students that homophones are words that sound the same but have different spellings and meanings. Write the following homophones on the board:

Copying Master 110

there	their	sent	scent
hour	our	seem	seam
piece	peace	pail	pale

Organize students into pairs to play a matching game. Ask each pair of students to write the words on index cards and then place them facedown on the table. Have partners take turns picking up two cards to find a set of homophones. If homophones are found, the partner needs to use each word in a sentence. They get a point for each set of homophones they find.

330 Lesson 28 • Turn It Up!

Day 2

PRETEACH

Grammar/Writing

Practice Book 112 **Double Negatives** Tell students that words such as *never, not,* and *nowhere* are called negatives. A sentence should never have a double negative—two negative adverbs. To fix a double negative, change one of the negative words to a positive.

Shawn <u>didn't never</u> get to stay up late.
Correction: Shawn didn't <u>ever</u> get to stay up late.

GUIDED PRACTICE Direct students' attention to page 112 in their *Practice Book*. Have students work individually or in pairs to complete the activity. Ask volunteers to share their answers with the group.

Fluency

Practice Book 111 **Fluency Practice** Invite students to look at the bottom half of *Practice Book* page 111. These sentences have been broken into natural phrases. Tell students to repeat each phrase after you, mirroring your expression, phrasing, and pace. After students have repeated each sentence, invite them to practice reading the sentences to partners.

"The Untold Story of Texas Kate" **331**

LESSON 28

DAY AT A GLANCE
Day 3

COMPREHENSION
Preteach Use Graphic Aids

Reread and Summarize "The Untold Story of Texas Kate"

DECODING/SPELLING
Reteach Homophones

BUILD ROBUST VOCABULARY
Teach Words from "The Untold Story of Texas Kate"

GRAMMAR/WRITING
Reteach Writing Trait: Organization

FLUENCY
Fluency Practice

Materials Needed: *Turn It Up!*

Student Edition pp. 282–288 | Practice Book pp. 111, 113 | Copying Master 111

30+ Minutes

PRETEACH
Comprehension

Use Graphic Aids Distribute *Copying Master 111* and have a student read the information at the top of the page. Model how to read the map to gather information about a location.

GUIDED PRACTICE Ask students to look at the map and answer the questions. Allow time for students to share their responses.

Reread and Summarize: "The Untold Story of Texas Kate"
Have students reread and summarize "The Untold Story of Texas Kate" in sections, as described below.

pp. 282–283

Let's reread pages 282–283 to recall who the story is about.
Summary: This story is about Texas Kate, Pecos Bill's little sister. It happened long ago, and it is a story that has gone untold. Kate decided to go south so she could be with her brother.

pp. 284–285

Now let's reread pages 284–285 to find out what happened to Kate during her travels.
Summary: After Kate finally reached a small town, she realized that she had grown over ten feet tall. She was hungry and a villager invited her to come to his town and eat.

pp. 286–288

Last, let's reread pages 286–288 to find out if Kate was able to find something to eat.
Summary: The town fed Kate. She repaid the town by helping with odd jobs. Then, Kate decided to move on, and rode a tornado out of town.

RETEACH
Decoding/Spelling

Homophones Write the following sentences on the board:

> My family is flying on a (plain, plane) tomorrow.
> This is (there, their) house.
> Can you repair the (seam, seem) in these pants?

Ask students to compare the spellings of the homophones in the parentheses to determine which one is correct. Have volunteers circle the correct words. Then have students rewrite each sentence using the correct spelling of each homophone. (plane, their, seam)

332 Lesson 28 • *Turn It Up!*

Day 3

TEACH
Build Robust Vocabulary

pp. 282–285 **Words from "The Untold Story of Texas Kate"** Have students locate the word *murmurs* on page 282 of "The Untold Story of Texas Kate." Ask a volunteer to read aloud the sentence in which this word appears. (Line 6: *Some say lightning will strike if someone so much as murmurs her name.*) Explain that the phrase "murmurs her name" means that someone says her name very softly. If someone murmured, it would be hard to hear what he or she said. Continue by asking students to locate and read aloud the sentence on page 284 in which *fret* appears. (Line 8: *But Kate didn't want to fret about such things.*) Explain that this sentence means that Kate didn't want to worry. Then ask students to locate and read aloud the sentence on page 285 in which *parched* appears. (Line 1: *And she was as parched as a fish out of water.*) Explain that this sentence means that she felt very dry and thirsty.

Give each student a card with the letters of one of the words scrambled on it. Ask each student to unscramble his or her word and make up a sentence using it.

RETEACH
Grammar/Writing

Practice Book 113 **Writing Trait: Organization** Have students turn to page 113 in their *Practice Book*. Explain that when they write a story, it is important to organize ideas in a logical order. One way to do this is to organize ideas by cause and effect. Ask a volunteer to read the information in the box. Point out how the author of "The Untold Story of Texas Kate" organized the story in a cause-and-effect order. Read the directions aloud. Then have a volunteer read the sentences. Explain that these sentences follow a cause-and-effect order.

GUIDED PRACTICE Work with students to complete the rest of Part A by writing the number for the correct sentence order. Then read the Part B directions and sentences. Remind students to think about cause and effect. Read the Part C directions and have students write sentences of their own. Invite students to share what they wrote.

Fluency

Practice Book 111 **Fluency Practice** Tell students that today they will reread the sentences on the bottom of *Practice Book* page 111. Have students locate and point to the first sentence. Tell students that everyone is going to read the sentence together. This choral reading will give students an opportunity to hear others and listen to the natural phrasing of the sentences. Choral-read each of the sentences several times.

"The Untold Story of Texas Kate" **333**

LESSON 28

DAY AT A GLANCE
Day 4

COMPREHENSION
Reteach Use Graphic Aids

DECODING/SPELLING
Reteach Homophones

BUILD ROBUST VOCABULARY
Reteach Words from "The Untold Story of Texas Kate"

GRAMMAR/WRITING
Reteach Writing Form: Tall Tale

FLUENCY
Fluency Practice

Materials Needed: *Turn It Up!*

 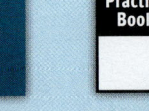 

Student Edition pp. 282–288 | Practice Book p. 114 | Copying Master 112

Spelling Words: Lesson 28

1. there	11. plane
2. they're	12. piece
3. their	13. peace
4. sent	14. two
5. scent	15. too
6. hour	16. to
7. our	17. whole
8. seam	18. hole
9. seem	19. pail
10. plain	20. pale

30+ Minutes

RETEACH
Comprehension

Use Graphic Aids Remind students that graphic aids show information in pictures rather than words. There are different kinds of graphic aids:

- A **map** shows different places.
- A **diagram** shows parts of something.
- A **graph** compares information.
- A **chart** shows different kinds of information in an easy-to-read format.

Have students discuss other graphic aids they would like to see to help them better understand "The Untold Story of Texas Kate."

Ask: **What could be shown on a diagram to help you better understand the story?** (Possible responses: how the parts were used to make Kate's clothing; a diagram showing where Kate slept and ate.)

GUIDED PRACTICE Have students recall "The Untold Story of Texas Kate." Ask volunteers to name appropriate graphic aids that would lend meaning to the story. (Possible response: A map that shows where Kate went during her travels.)

RETEACH
Decoding/Spelling

Practice Book 114

Homophones Have students number a sheet of paper 1–19. Write the Spelling Word *sent* on the board. Tell students to write the Spelling Word that is a homophone to this word. (scent) Tell students to listen carefully as you say each of the remaining words in sentences. Remind students that they have to listen to the context to determine which homophone is correct. After students write each word, display it so they can proofread their work.

1. scent	2. there	3. they're	4. their
5. hour	6. our	7. seam	8. seem
9. plain	10. plane	11. piece	12. peace
13. two	14. too	15. to	16. whole
17. hole	18. pail	19. pale	

Have students turn to page 114 in their *Practice Book*. Have volunteers take turns reading a paragraph in the story. Then have students circle the letter of the correct answer for the questions at the bottom of the page.

334 Lesson 28 • Turn It Up!

Day 4

RETEACH
Build Robust Vocabulary

Words from "The Untold Story of Texas Kate" Review the meanings of the words *murmurs, fret,* and *parched.* Then say these sentences and ask which word each sentence describes. Have students explain why.

- **When his teacher asks if he did his homework, he says, "No," very softly so she has trouble hearing him.** (murmurs)
- **Mom said, "You are a good player, so don't worry about whether you will win your game."** (fret)
- **Matt was very thirsty after running the race.** (parched)

RETEACH
Grammar/Writing

Copying Master 112

Writing Form: Tall Tale Tell students that sometimes a tall tale is used to tell how natural features, such as lakes and canyons, were created. Writers should use a cause-and-effect organization when they write a tall tale for this purpose. It makes the story more understandable and logical. Distribute *Copying Master 112*. Have a volunteer read the description of the tall tale. Then read the Student Model together. Write on the board the following sentence from the passage. Tell students this sentence is in the wrong order for cause and effect.

> Johnny's friends quickly came to his rescue.

Model how you determine the correct placement of this sentence.

(THINK ALOUD) **Johnny's friends came to his rescue before anything happened to him. This sentence should be moved to the beginning of the second paragraph. It makes more sense there.**

GUIDED PRACTICE Complete the activity by having students continue looking at the organization of the sentences in the Student Model. Allow time for students to share their responses with the group.

Fluency

pp. 282–288

Fluency Practice Have each student work with a partner to read passages from "The Untold Story of Texas Kate" aloud to each other. Students may select a passage that they enjoyed or choose one of the following options:

- Read page 283. (Total: 117 words)
- Read page 288. (Total: 119 words)

Encourage students to read the selected passage aloud to their partner three times. Have the student rate his or her reading on the 1–4 scale.

1	Need more practice
2	Pretty good
3	Good
4	Great!

"The Untold Story of Texas Kate" 335

Preteach for LESSON 29

DAY AT A GLANCE — Day 5

VOCABULARY
Preteach dedicated, determined, dainty, coddled, pitiful, endured, memorable

COMPREHENSION
Preteach Figurative Language

DECODING/WORD ATTACK
Preteach Decode Longer Words

DECODING/SPELLING
Preteach Words with Prefix + Root + Suffix

GRAMMAR/WRITING
Preteach Commas

FLUENCY
Fluency Performance

Materials Needed: *Turn It Up!*

Student Edition pp. 282–288

Copying Master 113

PRETEACH — Vocabulary

Lesson 29 Vocabulary Distribute a set of Vocabulary Word Cards to each student. Hold up the card for the first word, and ask a volunteer to read it aloud. Have students repeat the word and hold up the matching card. Give the explanation for the word. Then ask students the first question below and discuss their responses. Continue for each of the Vocabulary Words.

- What was Texas Kate **dedicated** to do?
- What is something you were **determined** to do?
- If a toddler wanted a drink, would you put it in a **dainty** cup? Explain.
- Do you think a baby or a teenager should be **coddled**? Why or why not?
- If you saw a **pitiful** puppy, what would you do?
- Talk about a famous person who has **endured** hardships to achieve goals.
- Why would a person bring a camera to a **memorable** event?

PRETEACH — Comprehension

pp. 282–288

Figurative Language Explain that writers use figurative language so they can help readers form mental images as they read. Remind students that the author of "The Untold Story of Texas Kate" used figurative language. Then ask:

- What do you think the author meant when she said that Kate "was as parched as a fish out of water"? (She meant that Kate was very thirsty.)

Remind students that this sentence is an example of a simile. It gives the readers a mental picture to show how thirsty Kate was. Guide students to identify other types of figurative language that may be found in the story.

336 Preteach for Lesson 29 • *Turn It Up!*

Day 5

PRETEACH
Decoding/Word Attack

Decode Longer Words Remind students that longer words are often made up of a root word joined with a prefix and a suffix. Write the word *unfortunately* on the board and have a volunteer read it aloud. Underline the root word *fortunate* and circle *un-* and *-ly*. Explain that by locating the root word, the prefix, and suffix, students can decode the longer word and figure out what it means.

PRETEACH
Decoding/Spelling

Words with Prefix + Root + Suffix Write *impatiently* on the board, and read it aloud. Remind students that longer words may include a root word with a prefix and a suffix. Ask a volunteer to tell you the root word of this word. (patient) Then have volunteers name the prefix and suffix. *(im-, -ly)* Remind students that when they break longer words into word parts, it will help them decode words better. Repeat with *disappearance, refreshment*, and *nonrefundable*. (dis/appear/ance, re/fresh/ment, non/re/fund/able) Explain that these are some of the next lesson's Spelling Words.

PRETEACH
Grammar/Writing

Commas Remind students that a comma is used after each item in a list of three or more things. It is also used before the conjunction in a compound sentence. A comma is also used after words such as *yes, no,* or *well* at the beginning of a sentence. Write these sentences on the board:

> Ann drove through Virginia, Maryland, and Rhode Island.
>
> She liked Maryland, but she thought Virginia was prettier.
>
> Yes, she would like to go again.

Read the sentences aloud. Guide students to identify why commas are used in each of the sentences. (commas in a list of three or more things; comma before a conjunction in a compound sentence; comma with *yes, no,* or *well*)

VOCABULARY
Student-Friendly Explanations

dedicated If you are dedicated to achieving a goal, you are devoting yourself to that purpose.

determined A determined person will do everything possible to try to accomplish a task.

dainty Something that is dainty is small and delicate.

coddled Someone who has been coddled has been treated too kindly or protected too much.

pitiful If something is pitiful, it is so sad and weak that people feel sorry for it.

endured Someone who has endured hardships has used personal strength to survive them.

memorable If something is memorable, it is worth remembering.

Fluency

Fluency Performance
pp. 282–288
Invite students each to read aloud from "The Untold Story of Texas Kate" a passage that they selected and practiced earlier. Note the number of words each student reads correctly and incorrectly. Have students rate their own oral reading on the 1–4 scale. Give each student the opportunity to continue practicing and then to read the passage to you again.

"The Untold Story of Texas Kate" 337

LESSON 29

DAY AT A GLANCE — Day 1

VOCABULARY
Reteach dedicated, determined, dainty, coddled, pitiful, endured, memorable

COMPREHENSION
 Reteach Figurative Language

DECODING/SPELLING
Reteach Words with Prefix + Root + Suffix

GRAMMAR/WRITING
Preteach Punctuating Titles

FLUENCY
Fluency Practice

Materials Needed: *Turn It Up!*

  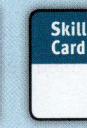 

Student Edition pp. 290–291 | Practice Book p. 115 | Skill Card 29 | Copying Master 114

RETEACH

Vocabulary

Lesson 29 Vocabulary Read aloud the Vocabulary Words and the Student-Friendly Explanations. Then have students read the diary and fill in the blanks on pages 290–291. Have volunteers read each completed diary entry aloud. If students are unable to give reasonable responses, refer to the Student-Friendly Explanations. (Answers for pages 290–291, *2. endured, 3. determined, 4. pitiful, 5. dainty, 6. dedicated, 7. memorable*)

RETEACH

Comprehension

Figurative Language  Have students look at side A of *Skill Card 29: Figurative Language*. Read the information aloud. Then have a volunteer read the passage aloud as students follow along. Point to the chart and discuss the various types of figurative language and the meaning of each one. Remind students that writers use figurative language because they want their readers to be able to picture images in their minds as they read.

GUIDED PRACTICE Now have students look at side B of *Skill Card 29: Figurative Language*. Ask volunteers to read the Skill Reminder and the story. Guide students as they copy the chart and fill it in. (Possible responses: metaphor: *buckets of rain*—it was raining hard; idiom and simile: *felt like a fish out of water*—felt uncomfortable because he was in an unfamiliar situation; personification: *bat is just aching to slap that ball*—The boy is ready to make a hit.)

338 Lesson 29 • Turn It Up!

Day 1

RETEACH
Decoding/Spelling

Copying Master 114 **Words with Prefix + Root + Suffix** Distribute *Copying Master 114*. Read the words aloud as students repeat the words after you. Then have them complete this activity based on the traditional Memory Game. Pairs of students make game cards using the lesson's Spelling Words with either a prefix or a suffix missing; a dash appears in place of each prefix or suffix. After a student matches two cards, he or she must supply the correct missing prefix to keep the game cards. If the wrong prefix or suffix is supplied, the opponent gets the game cards and the next turn.

PRETEACH
Grammar/Writing

Punctuating Titles Write these sentences on the board:

> My favorite book is Charlotte's Web.
> We sang "We Are the World."

Guide students to identify the title in each sentence. (Charlotte's Web, "We Are the World") Tell students to underline the titles of books, magazines, and movies in their writing. Explain that if they use a computer, they can put these titles in italics. Explain that quotation marks should be placed around the titles of songs, poems, stories, and articles. Capitalize the first word, last word, and all other important words in a title. Any form of the verb *to be* is considered important.

VOCABULARY
Student-Friendly Explanations

dedicated If you are dedicated to achieving a goal, you are devoting yourself to that purpose.

determined A determined person will do everything possible to try to accomplish a task.

dainty Something that is dainty is small and delicate.

coddled Someone who has been coddled has been treated too kindly or protected too much.

pitiful If something is pitiful, it is so sad and weak that people feel sorry for it.

endured Someone who has endured hardships has used personal strength to survive them.

memorable If something is memorable, it is worth remembering.

Fluency

Practice Book 115 **Fluency Practice** Have students turn to *Practice Book* page 115. Read the words in the first column aloud. Invite students to track each word and repeat the words after you. Then have students work in pairs to read the words in the first column aloud to each other. Follow the same procedure with each of the remaining columns. After partners have practiced reading aloud the words in each of the columns, have them practice reading all of the words.

"Caught in the Ice!" 339

LESSON 29

DAY AT A GLANCE
Day 2

VOCABULARY
Reteach dedicated, determined, dainty, coddled, pitiful, endured, memorable

COMPREHENSION
"Caught in the Ice!"
Build Background
Monitor Comprehension
Answers to *Think Critically* **Questions**

DECODING/SPELLING
Reteach Words with Prefix + Root + Suffix

GRAMMAR/WRITING
Preteach Punctuating Dialogue

FLUENCY
Fluency Practice

Materials Needed: *Turn It Up!*

 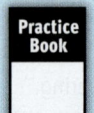 

Student Edition pp. 292–299 | Practice Book pp. 115, 116 | Copying Masters 113, 114

30+ Minutes

RETEACH
Vocabulary

Copying Master 113

Lesson 29 Vocabulary Have students play "Yes or No." Organize students in pairs. Display the Vocabulary Words. Ask students to take turns choosing a word from the list for the other to guess. The student who is guessing may ask about the part of speech, meaning of the word, the number of syllables, whether it has a certain prefix or suffix, or any other information they think may help them. However, every question can only be answered with *yes* or *no*. Encourage students to write down notes that will help them figure out the word.

Comprehension

Build Background: "Caught in the Ice!"
Ask students to discuss the weather in the winter. Have they ever been in extremely cold temperatures? When have they had experiences with snow and ice? How do the extreme conditions of winter change the way they do things?

pp. 292–293

Monitor Comprehension: "Caught in the Ice!"
Read the title of the story aloud. Then have students read pages 292–293 to find out where this story takes place.

After reading the pages, ask: **Where does this story take place?** (It takes place on board a ship heading to the South Pole.) **NOTE DETAILS**

Discuss the Stop and Think question on page 292: **Who is telling this story?** (This story is told by one of the sailors from the voyage.) Guide students in writing the answer to this question. **POINT OF VIEW**

Ask: **How do you think this sailor felt about this expedition?** (Possible response: He was a little nervous, but excited and determined, too.) **CHARACTER'S EMOTIONS**

Ask: **What happened when the ship first came in contact with the ice packs?** (The sailors had to work hard to find a path that would avoid them; the sailors became scared about problems that may occur in the future.) **CAUSE AND EFFECT**

Discuss the Stop and Think question on page 293: **Find the simile on this page. What does the author really mean?** (This is the simile on this page: Our ship was like a fly trapped in a frozen spider's web. It means the ship was stuck and could not get free.) Guide students in writing the answer to the question. **FIGURATIVE LANGUAGE**

---

340 Lesson 29 • Turn It Up!

Day 2

pp. 294–295

Discuss the Stop and Think question on page 294: **What caused the sailors to work like a team?** (The sailors worked like a team because they realized that they needed each other to stay alive.) Guide students in writing the answer to this question. **CAUSE AND EFFECT**

Read aloud the second paragraph on page 294. Model how to figure out the meaning of an idiom to understand the text better.

THINK ALOUD As I read the paragraph, I noticed the sentence *That grabbed their attention!* This is an idiom. In the story the sailor talks about how he told his fellow sailors that they could work together or perish together. If I heard that information, I would listen closely to what was being said because I would not want to die. That idiom must mean that everyone started to listen closely. **FIGURATIVE LANGUAGE**

Discuss the Stop and Think question on page 295: **What did the sailors do to keep busy?** (To keep busy, the sailors played soccer, made doghouses, held haircutting contests, and put on plays.) Guide students in writing the answer to this question. **NOTE DETAILS**

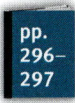
pp. 296–297

Ask: **How did you feel when you read that the sailors had lost their ship?** (Possible responses: shocked, surprised, sad) **PERSONAL RESPONSE**

Discuss the Stop and Think question on page 296: **What do you think the sailors will do without their ship?** (Possible response: I think the sailors will use the wood from the ship to make a raft.) Guide students in writing the answer to this question. **MAKE PREDICTIONS**

Discuss the Stop and Think question on page 297: **What did the sailors do after they lost their ship?** (After the sailors lost their ship, they marched over the ice, dragging their small boats with them.) Guide students in writing the answer to this question. **SEQUENCE**

page 298

Discuss the Stop and Think question on page 298: **Why do you think the author wrote about this expedition?** (Possible response: I think the author wrote about this expedition because she wanted to show how these men were able to solve the many problems they faced.) Guide students in writing the answer to this question. **AUTHOR'S PURPOSE**

Ask: **What happens at the end of the story?** (The Boss returned with help for all of the sailors that he left behind.) **TEXT STRUCTURE**

Ask: **Do you think The Boss was a good leader? Explain your judgment.** (Possible response: Yes, he was a good leader. He was dedicated to his crew and he did what he had to do to get everyone home safely.) **MAKE JUDGMENTS**

VOCABULARY
Student-Friendly Explanations

dedicated If you are dedicated to achieving a goal, you are devoting yourself to that purpose.

determined A determined person will do everything possible to try to accomplish a task.

dainty Something that is dainty is small and delicate.

coddled Someone who has been coddled has been treated too kindly or protected too much.

pitiful If something is pitiful, it is so sad and weak that people feel sorry for it.

endured Someone who has endured hardships has used personal strength to survive them.

memorable If something is memorable, it is worth remembering.

"Caught in the Ice!" **341**

Day 2

Spelling Words: Lesson 29

1. impatiently
2. disappearance
3. unhappily
4. unnaturally
5. refreshment
6. mistakenly
7. remarkable
8. nonrefundable
9. unlikely
10. unpleasantly
11. disagreement
12. inaccurately
13. incorrectly
14. irreversible
15. repayment
16. uneasily
17. unhealthy
18. unusually
19. misguidance
20. refillable

page 299 **Answers to *Think Critically* Questions** Help students read and answer the *Think Critically* questions on page 299. Have students copy the graphic organizer in question 1 onto a separate sheet of paper. Then guide students in writing the answer to each question. Possible responses are provided.

1. [Next] The Boss picks five men for a rescue mission. [Then] The rescue crew leaves the rest of the sailors behind. [Finally] The Boss returns to the island with a rescue ship. SEQUENCE

2. The men marched across the ice with the small boats because their ship was crushed by the ice; they needed to find open water. CAUSE AND EFFECT

3. The Boss is a good leader, brave, quick-thinking. CHARACTER'S TRAITS

RETEACH

Decoding/Spelling

Copying Master 114 **Words with Prefix + Root + Suffix** Remind students that a longer word can be formed from a root word joined with a prefix and a suffix. Sometimes the root word changes when a suffix is added. Write the following on the board:

```
un – happy – ly        dis – agree – ment
un – easy – ly         un – health – y
mis – guide – ance     ir – reverse – ible
```

Have students put the word parts together to write each longer Spelling Word. (unhappily, uneasily, misguidance, disagreement, unhealthy, irreversible) Ask students to describe how they had to change the root word to add the suffix, if necessary.

342 Lesson 29 • Turn It Up!

Day 2

PRETEACH
Grammar/Writing

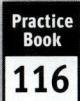 **Punctuating Dialogue** Write these sentences on the board:

> Myra asked, "Did you buy the book?"
>
> "In my opinion," said Mark, "this is a good book."

Use the sentences to explain these rules for writing dialogue:

- Use quotation marks before and after the exact words that someone says.
- Place punctuation marks at the end of the direct quotation inside the quotation marks.
- When words such as *She said* come before a quotation, put a comma between them and the first quotation mark.
- When words come after a quotation, use a comma, a question mark, or an exclamation point to separate the quotation from the rest of the sentence.

GUIDED PRACTICE Direct students' attention to page 116 in their *Practice Book*. Have students read the sentences. Ask them to rewrite the sentences using the correct punctuation.

Fluency

 Fluency Practice Invite students to look at the bottom half of *Practice Book* page 115. These sentences have been broken into natural phrases. Tell students to repeat each phrase after you, mirroring your expression, phrasing, and pace. After students have repeated each sentence, invite them to practice reading the sentences to partners.

"Caught in the Ice!" 343

LESSON 29

DAY AT A GLANCE
Day 3

COMPREHENSION
Preteach Predict Outcomes
Reread and Summarize "Caught in the Ice!"

DECODING/SPELLING
Reteach Check Sentences

BUILD ROBUST VOCABULARY
Teach Words from "Caught in the Ice!"

GRAMMAR/WRITING
Reteach Writing Trait: Organization

FLUENCY
Fluency Practice

Materials Needed: *Turn It Up!*

Student Edition pp. 292–298

Practice Book pp. 115, 117

Copying Master 115

30+ Minutes

PRETEACH
Comprehension

 **Predict Outcomes** Distribute *Copying Master 115* and have students listen as you read the information at the top of the page.

GUIDED PRACTICE Ask students to read the passage and then fill in the graphic organizer with story information, real-life knowledge, and then make a prediction. Allow time for students to share their responses with others.

Reread and Summarize Have students reread and summarize "Caught in the Ice!" in sections, as described below.

 Let's reread pages 292–293 to recall where the ship was going.
pp. 292–293
Summary: Told by one of the sailors, this selection tells of Shackleton's expedition to the South Pole. The sailors knew that the trip would not be easy. Soon, they had to deal with ice packs in the water.

 **Now let's reread pages 294–295 to find out what the sailors did while they were caught in the ice.**
pp. 294–295
Summary: At first, the sailors were miserable and unhappy, but after the narrator talked to them, they realized that they had to work together to stay alive. They also entertained themselves to keep boredom away.

 **Last, let's reread pages 296–298 to find out what happened to the sailors and their ship.**
pp. 296–298
Summary: After months in the ice, the ship split apart. The sailors took their remaining supplies and walked to open water. After reaching Elephant Island, The Boss took a team and headed out for help. He finally returned to take the sailors back home.

RETEACH
Decoding/Spelling

Check Sentences Write the following sentences on the board:

> Matthew is inusually excited today.
> Todd sat uneasyly on the airplane.

Ask students to proofread each sentence, reading each one twice. Then have a volunteer draw a line through the word that is misspelled. Ask students to spell the word correctly. (unusually, uneasily)

344 Lesson 29 • Turn It Up!

Day 3

TEACH

Build Robust Vocabulary

Words from "Caught in the Ice!" Have students locate the word *apprehension* on page 293 of "Caught in the Ice!" Ask a volunteer to read aloud the sentence in which this word appears. (Line 9: *Our earlier celebrations turned into apprehension and fear.*) Explain that *apprehension* is a feeling that something bad is about to happen. Continue by asking students to locate and read aloud the sentence in which the word *perish* appears on page 294. (Line 5: *I told my fellow sailors we could work together, or we could perish together.*) Explain that this sentence means that if the sailors didn't work together, they would die. Then ask students to locate and read aloud the sentence in which the word *dreadful* appears on page 296. (Line 4: *They sounded so dreadful that the sled dogs started howling!*) Explain that this sentence means that the music sounded very, very bad or unpleasant.

Put the words on separate cards and put the cards facedown and spread out. Ask a volunteer to pick up two cards and try use them both in one sentence. Then put the cards back, mix them up, and repeat. Do this a few times.

RETEACH

Grammar/Writing

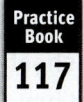 **Writing Trait: Organization** Have students turn to page 117 in their *Practice Book*. Explain that when they write a biography, it is important to organize their ideas in a sequence that makes sense. Ask a volunteer to read the information at the top of the page. Point out how the author of "Caught in the Ice!" organized the story in a sequential order.

GUIDED PRACTICE Complete the page together. Invite students to share their responses to Part C.

Fluency

Fluency Practice Tell students that today they will reread the sentences on the bottom of *Practice Book* page 115. Have students locate and point to the first sentence. Tell students that everyone is going to read the sentence together. This choral reading will give students an opportunity to hear others and listen to the natural phrasing of the sentences. Choral-read each of the sentences several times.

LESSON 29

DAY AT A GLANCE
Day 4

COMPREHENSION
Reteach Predict Outcomes

DECODING/SPELLING
Reteach Words with Prefix + Root + Suffix

BUILD ROBUST VOCABULARY
Reteach Words from "Caught in the Ice!"

GRAMMAR/WRITING
Reteach Writing Form: Biography

FLUENCY
Fluency Practice

Materials Needed: *Turn It Up!*

Student Edition pp. 292–298 | Practice Book p. 118 | Copying Master 116

Spelling Words: Lesson 29

1. impatiently	11. disagreement
2. disappearance	12. inaccurately
3. unhappily	13. incorrectly
4. unnaturally	14. irreversible
5. refreshment	15. repayment
6. mistakenly	16. uneasily
7. remarkable	17. unhealthy
8. nonrefundable	18. unusually
9. unlikely	19. misguidance
10. unpleasantly	20. refillable

30+ Minutes

RETEACH

Comprehension

 pp. 292–298

Predict Outcomes Remind students that they can predict story outcomes, or figure out what will happen next, if they think about story information and apply it to what they know from real life.

Have students predict an outcome for "Caught in the Ice!" Guide students as they make educated guesses about what they think happened to The Boss when he went looking for help. Ask: **What do we know about The Boss from the story?** (He is a good leader and is determined.) **What real-life knowledge do we know about The Boss?** (Since he was the leader of the ship he was probably very smart about how to get help.) **What do you think happened when The Boss looked for help?** (He was able to find someone to give him the ship he needed to get his men back.)

GUIDED PRACTICE Have students read aloud page 298. Ask students to predict what they think the sailors did while The Boss was gone. (Possible responses: They played games and had contests. They tried to stay positive and worked together as a team to help each other stay alive.)

RETEACH

Decoding/Spelling

 Practice Book 118

Words with Prefix + Root + Suffix Have students number a sheet of paper 1–19. Write *unhappily* on the board. Ask students to tell how the root word changed before the suffix was added. (*y* was changed to *i*) Tell students that changes were made to the root word before a suffix was added in the first three Spelling Words you will dictate. After students write each word, display it so they can proofread their work. Then dictate the remaining Spelling Words. Point out that the root words of the remaining words do not change.

1. irreversible	2. uneasily	3. misguidance
4. impatiently	5. disappearance	6. unnaturally
7. refreshment	8. mistakenly	9. nonrefundable
10. remarkable	11. unlikely	12. unpleasantly
13. disagreement	14. inaccurately	15. incorrectly
16. repayment	17. unhealthy	18. unusually
19. refillable		

Have students turn to page 118 in their *Practice Book*. Read the story. Then have students circle and write the correct word to complete each sentence at the bottom of the page.

346 Lesson 29 • *Turn It Up!*

Day 4

RETEACH

Build Robust Vocabulary

Words from "Caught in the Ice!" Review the meanings of the words *apprehension, perish,* and *dreadful.* Then say these sentences and ask which word describes each sentence. Have students explain why.

- I watched my little brother bump into the full glass of milk with a feeling that something bad was about to happen. (apprehension)
- The plant will die if no one waters it. (perish)
- Mom's new invention, spinach flavored ice cream, tasted very unpleasant. (dreadful)

RETEACH

Grammar/Writing

Copying Master 116

Writing Form: Biography Tell students that a biography is a story that tells about a person and the important events in his or her life. Explain that when they write a biography, it is important to use the correct sequence so readers will be able to follow the order in which events really happened. Distribute *Copying Master 116*. Have a volunteer read the description of the biography. Then read the Student Model together. Point out how a lack of organization in the third paragraph makes the biography difficult to understand. Guide students to realize that the second sentence is out of place.

GUIDED PRACTICE Complete the activity by having students continue looking at the sequence of the sentences in the Student Model. Have students complete the questions on their own. Allow time for students to share their responses with the group.

Fluency

pp. 292–298

Fluency Practice Have each student work with a partner to read passages from "Caught in the Ice!" aloud to each other. Students may select a passage that they enjoyed or choose one of the following options:

- Read page 292. (Total: 115 words)
- Read page 298. (Total: 113 words)

Encourage students to read the selected passage aloud to their partner three times. Have the student rate his or her reading on the 1–4 scale.

1	Need more practice
2	Pretty good
3	Good
4	Great!

"Caught in the Ice!" **347**

Preteach for LESSON 30

DAY AT A GLANCE
Day 5

VOCABULARY
Preteach *distinguished, verify, discern, dubious, descend, frantically, estimate, vicinity, abruptly, scrutinize*

COMPREHENSION
 Preteach Main Idea and Details

DECODING/WORD ATTACK
Preteach Review Silent Letters

DECODING/SPELLING
Preteach Words with Silent Letters

GRAMMAR/WRITING
Preteach Irregular Verbs, Contractions, and Possessive Pronouns

FLUENCY
Fluency Performance

Materials Needed: *Turn It Up!*

Student Edition pp. 292–298

Skill Card 30

Copying Master 117

PRETEACH
Vocabulary

Copying Master 117

Lesson 30 Vocabulary Distribute a set of Vocabulary Word Cards to each student. Hold up the card for the first word, and ask a volunteer to read it aloud. Have students repeat the word and hold up the matching card. Give the explanation for the word. Then ask students the questions below and discuss their responses. Continue for each Vocabulary Word.

- How do you think a **distinguished** person would dress for work? Why?
- How would you **verify** a person's address?
- If you are unable to **discern** something, what would you do?
- If you were **dubious** about a topic, what could you do?
- How might you **descend** to another floor in a department store?
- Talk about a time where you or a friend behaved **frantically**.
- What is an **estimate** of the number of students in the fourth grade?
- What stores are in the **vicinity** of your home?
- Why would a person **abruptly** come into the classroom?
- When might you **scrutinize** your bedroom?

PRETEACH
Comprehension

Skill Card 30

Main Idea and Details Have students look at side A of *Skill Card 30: Review: Main Idea and Details*. Have students recall what the main idea and details are in a story. Read the passage aloud as students read along. Point out that in this passage, the main idea was stated in the topic sentence. The topic sentence is usually at the beginning of the passage, and it tells the most important part of the passage.

- **What is the topic sentence in this passage?** (Queen Nefertiti reigned during the Ancient Egyptian civilization and is considered one of the most beautiful women in antiquity.)

GUIDED PRACTICE Guide students in copying the chart onto a separate sheet of paper. Have them fill in the main idea and details of the passage. (Main Idea: Queen Nefertiti was a queen during the Ancient Egyptian civilization; Detail 1: She was one of the most beautiful women in antiquity; Detail 2: She married King Akhenaton; Detail 3: She had six daughters; Detail 4: She was a very powerful queen.)

348 Preteach for Lesson 30 • Turn It Up!

Day 5

PRETEACH
Decoding/Word Attack

Review Silent Letters Write *doubt* and *knock* on the board. Circle the *b* in *doubt*. Remind students that some consonants are silent. Ask students if they hear the *b* in *debtor*. (no) Repeat the process with the initial *k* in *knock*.

PRETEACH
Decoding/Spelling

Words with Silent Letters Write *rustle* and *scene* on the board. Remind students that the *t* in *rustle* and the *c* in *scene* are silent. Point out that other letters can be silent, such as the *b* in *debt* and *numb* and the initial *k* in *knack*. Then guide students as they identify the silent letters in the following words: *debt, numb, scene, rustle,* and *knack*. Tell students that these words are part of the next lesson's Spelling Words. Have students copy the words and read each word aloud.

PRETEACH
Grammar/Writing

Irregular Verbs, Contractions, and Possessive Pronouns Have students recall that some irregular verbs show past tense by using a different form of the main verb with the helping verb *has*, *have*, or *had*. Then remind students that a contraction is a short way to write two words. An apostrophe takes the place of one or more letters. Finally, point out that possessive pronouns show ownership, and they never have apostrophes.

Then write the following sentences on the board:

> Who's/Whose coming to the game?
> Ian had torn/had teared the paper.
> That notebook on the desk is hers/her's.

Have students underline the choice to complete each sentence. (Who's, had torn, hers)

VOCABULARY
Student-Friendly Explanations

distinguished A distinguished person is very successful in a job or field.

verify If you verify something, you check it out to make sure that it's true.

discern To discern something means to see it, or to be aware that it exists.

dubious A person who is dubious is doubtful or unsure about something.

descend When you descend, you move downward.

frantically To behave frantically means to behave wildly and with great excitement.

estimate When you estimate a quantity, you make a careful guess about how many things there are.

vicinity If something is in a vicinity, it is nearby.

abruptly If you do something abruptly, you do it very suddenly.

scrutinize When you scrutinize a place, you examine it carefully, with a critical eye.

Fluency

pp. 292–298 **Fluency Performance** Invite students each to read aloud from "Caught in the Ice!" a passage that they selected and practiced earlier. Note the number of words each student reads correctly and incorrectly. Have students rate their own oral reading on the 1–4 scale. Allow each student to continue practicing and then to read the passage to you again.

"Caught in the Ice!" 349

LESSON 30

Day 1

VOCABULARY
Reteach distinguished, verify, discern, dubious, descend, frantically, estimate, vicinity, abruptly, scrutinize

COMPREHENSION
Preteach Figurative Language

DECODING/WORD ATTACK
Preteach Decode Longer Words

DECODING/SPELLING
Preteach Words with Greek and Latin Word Parts

GRAMMAR/WRITING
Reteach Irregular Verbs, Contractions, Possessive Pronouns

FLUENCY
Fluency Practice

Materials Needed: *Turn It Up!*

Student Edition pp. 300–301 | Practice Book pp. 119, 120 | Skill Card 30 | Copying Master 118

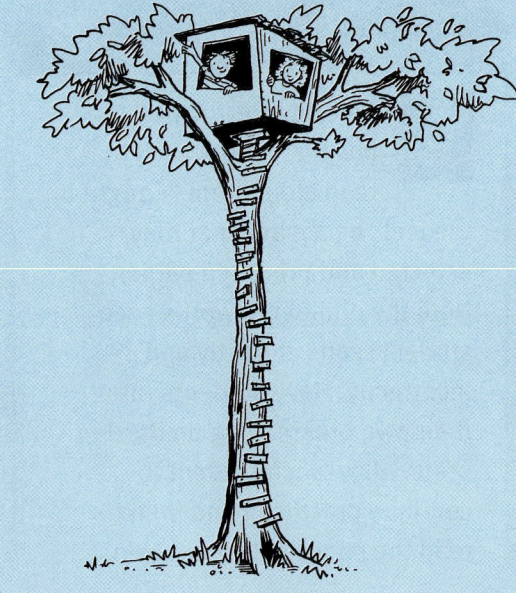

RETEACH
Vocabulary

Lesson 30 Vocabulary Read aloud the Vocabulary Words and the Student-Friendly Explanations. Then have students turn to pages 300–301 in their books. Ask a volunteer to read the directions aloud. Remind students that they should read each sentence to themselves with the word they chose to be sure it makes sense. If students have difficulty choosing the correct word, refer to the Student-Friendly definitions. After students have completed the pages, have volunteers take turns reading aloud each sentence. (Answers for pages 300–301: 2. *vicinity,* 3. *dubious,* 4. *verify,* 5. *frantically,* 6. *abruptly,* 7. *scrutinize,* 8. *descend,* 9. *discern,* 10. *estimate,* Possible responses: 11. It means that they think the mission can't be completed. 12. The person would be behaving wildly and with great excitement.)

PRETEACH
Comprehension

Figurative Language Have students look at side B of *Skill Card 30: Review: Figurative Language.* Ask a volunteer to read the Skill Reminder. Then read the passage aloud as students follow along. Remind students that writers use figurative language so their readers can picture images as they read. Review the types of figurative language.

GUIDED PRACTICE Guide students in copying the chart and completing it with details from the passage. Invite students to discuss examples of figurative language from the passage and what each means to them. (Possible responses: *the wind whistling:* personification; *that clubhouse had to be a hundred feet off the ground:* hyperbole; *I'll just take it one step at a time:* idiom)

350 Lesson 30 • Turn It Up!

Day 1

PRETEACH

Decoding/Word Attack

Decode Longer Words Remind students that many English words have Greek or Latin roots. By knowing these roots, students can use them to figure out the pronunciation and the meaning of words. Write *construction* and *destructive* on the board. Ask students to identify the letters that are the same in both. **(struct)** Remind students that *struct* is a Latin root that means "to build."

PRETEACH

Decoding/Spelling

Copying Master 118

Words with Greek and Latin Word Parts Distribute *Copying Master 118*. Read the Spelling Words aloud and have students repeat them. Then write these word parts on the board: *graph, phon, struct, spec*. Guide students to recall the meanings of the word parts. **(write, sound, build, look)** Then have students identify the words on the Spelling List that have these Greek and Latin word parts. **(paragraph, phonics, destruction, specific)**

RETEACH

Grammar/Writing

Practice Book 120

Irregular Verbs, Contractions, and Possessive Pronouns
Review irregular verbs, contractions, and possessive pronouns. Write the following sentences on the board:

> Patty bringed a yellow bag.
>
> Thomas don't know how to finish his's paragraph.

Ask volunteers to circle the errors and rewrite the sentences correctly. **(Patty brought a yellow bag. Thomas doesn't know how to finish his paragraph.)**

GUIDED PRACTICE Have students turn to page 120 in their *Practice Book*. Ask a volunteer to read the activity directions aloud. Have students work in pairs to select the correct word for each sentence. Allow time for pairs to share their responses.

VOCABULARY

Student-Friendly Explanations

distinguished A distinguished person is very successful in a job or field.

verify If you verify something, you check it out to make sure that it's true.

discern To discern something means to see it, or to be aware that it exists.

dubious A person who is dubious is doubtful or unsure about something.

descend When you descend, you move downward.

frantically To behave frantically means to behave wildly and with great excitement.

estimate When you estimate a quantity, you make a careful guess about how many things there are.

vicinity If something is in a vicinity, it is nearby.

abruptly If you do something abruptly, you do it very suddenly.

scrutinize When you scrutinize a place, you examine it carefully, with a critical eye.

Fluency

Practice Book 119

Fluency Practice Have students turn to *Practice Book* page 119. Read the words in the first column aloud. Invite students to track each word and repeat it. Then have pairs read the words in the first column aloud to each other. Follow the same procedure with each column. Then have partners practice reading all of the words.

"Beneath the Sands" 351

LESSON 30

DAY AT A GLANCE — Day 2

VOCABULARY
Reteach *distinguished, verify, discern, dubious, descend, frantically, estimate, vicinity, abruptly, scrutinize*

COMPREHENSION
"Beneath the Sands"
Build Background
Monitor Comprehension
Answers to *Think Critically* Questions

DECODING/WORD ATTACK
Preteach Use Decoding Strategies

DECODING/SPELLING
Preteach Homophones

GRAMMAR/WRITING
Preteach Adverbs and Punctuation

FLUENCY
Fluency Practice

Materials Needed: *Turn It Up!*

Student Edition pp. 302–309 | Practice Book p. 119 | Copying Master 118

30+ Minutes

RETEACH

Vocabulary

Lesson 30 Vocabulary Have a volunteer act as quizmaster and choose a Vocabulary Word for another student to define. The contestant earns 25 points for each word he or she defines correctly. If the contestant is not sure about a word, he or she can ask another student for help and still earn 25 points for a correct answer. Have students take turns acting as players and quizmasters. Continue play until each student has earned at least 100 points.

Comprehension

Build Background: "Beneath the Sands"
Discuss what students know about King Tut. Have they ever heard of King Tut? Have they ever heard about any of the treasures found in his chambers? If so, ask them to describe them.

Monitor Comprehension: "Beneath the Sands"
pp. 302–303
Read the title of the story aloud. Then have students read pages 302–303 to find out where the action takes place.

After reading the pages, ask: **Where does this story take place?** (This story takes place in Egypt. It is during the month of November in the year 1922.) **SETTING**

Discuss the Stop and Think question on page 302: **What does Carter hope to find in Egypt?** (Carter hopes to find King Tut's chambers.) Guide students in writing the answer to this question.  **MAIN IDEA AND DETAILS**

Ask: **Why does Carter believe his career will be over if he doesn't find King Tut's chambers?** (Possible response: Carter is known as a great scientist. He has to prove that he can figure out where these chambers are, unlike other scientists before him.) **MAKE INFERENCES**

Ask: **Who is Lord Carnarvon?** (Possible response: He is a wealthy man that is giving Carter money to find King Tut's chambers.) **CONTEXT CLUES/MAKE INFERENCES**

Discuss the Stop and Think question on page 303: **What does Carter mean by the phrase "throwing money"?** (Carter means that he is spending money without getting anything for it.) Guide students in writing the answer to this question. **FIGURATIVE LANGUAGE**

352 Lesson 30 • Turn It Up!

Day 2

 pp. 304–305

Discuss the Stop and Think question on page 304: **Why does the water bearer run to Carter?** (The water bearer runs to Carter because he has found something in the sand.) Guide students in writing the answer to this question. CAUSE AND EFFECT

Read aloud Narrator 3's part on page 305. Model how to figure out the character's emotions while reading the text.

THINK ALOUD After I read Narrator 3's part, I see that Carter "springs into the air and cries out." When I'm happy and excited, I jump up and down and yell out loud. The author was explaining Carter's reaction to finding the clue. I know that Carter was happy and excited. CHARACTER'S EMOTIONS

Discuss the Stop and Think question on page 305: **What do Carter and his crew do after finding the step?** (Possible response: After finding the step, Carter and his crew dig to the bottom of the steps and find a sealed door.) Guide students in writing the answer to this question. SUMMARIZE

 pp. 306–307

Ask: **Why do you think the author continues the story three weeks after the last scene?** (Possible responses: The author only wanted to write about the most important parts of the search.) AUTHOR'S PURPOSE

Discuss the Stop and Think question on page 306: **What do you think the group will find?** (Possible responses: I think the group will find King Tut's chambers; a third door; more stairs.) Guide students in writing the answer to this question. MAKE PREDICTIONS

Ask: **Why does Carter make a small hole in the door?** (Possible responses: He wanted to see what was inside; it was easier than moving the whole door.) DRAW CONCLUSIONS

Discuss the Stop and Think question on page 307: **Why is Carter awestruck?** (Possible response: Carter is awestruck because he sees amazing objects that no one has seen for thousands of years.) Guide students in writing the answer to this question. CHARACTER'S EMOTIONS

 page 308

Discuss the Stop and Think question on page 308: **How do you think the author feels about Carter's discovery?** (Possible response: I think the author feels that the discovery is interesting and important.) Guide students in writing the answer to this question. AUTHOR'S PERSPECTIVE

Ask: **Do you think Carter's discovery was important? Why or why not?** (Possible response: Yes, it was important because it helped us learn more about history.) PERSONAL RESPONSE

VOCABULARY
Student-Friendly Explanations

distinguished A distinguished person is very successful in a job or field.

verify If you verify something, you check it out to make sure that it's true.

discern To discern something means to see it, or to be aware that it exists.

dubious A person who is dubious is doubtful or unsure about something.

descend When you descend, you move downward.

frantically To behave frantically means to behave wildly and with great excitement.

estimate When you estimate a quantity, you make a careful guess about how many things there are.

vicinity If something is in a vicinity, it is nearby.

abruptly If you do something abruptly, you do it very suddenly.

scrutinize When you scrutinize a place, you examine it carefully, with a critical eye.

"Beneath the Sands" 353

Day 2

Spelling Words: Lesson 30

1. scene	11. scent
2. numb	12. pail
3. rustle	13. pale
4. debt	14. to
5. knack	15. too
6. specific	16. two
7. phonics	17. inaccurately
8. destruction	18. repayment
9. paragraph	19. misguidance
10. sent	20. unusually

page 309 **Answers to *Think Critically* Questions**   Help students read and answer the *Think Critically* questions on page 309. Then guide students in writing the answer to each question. Possible responses are provided.

1. Howard Carter is hard-working and persistent. **CHARACTER**
2. These are some details the author gives about Carter's discovery: There were four chambers filled with priceless objects; The treasures are all more than 3,000 years old.
    **MAIN IDEA AND DETAILS**
3. I think the author wants me to learn about the discovery of King Tut's tomb; what happened when the discovery was made; about some of the people who worked on this dig. **AUTHOR'S PURPOSE**

PRETEACH
Decoding/Word Attack

Use Decoding Strategies   Remind students that a compound word is made up of two words. Help students find the smaller words in *ballroom* and *stairway*. Tell students that they can use what they already know about the smaller words to figure out the meaning of each longer, compound word. Give students further practice with the compound words *bedspread*, *doorknob*, and *seacoast*. Ask volunteers to identify the two little words in each compound, and then decode, blend, and say the compound.

PRETEACH
Decoding/Spelling

Copying Master 118

Homophones   Write *sent* and *scent* on the board. Ask students what the two words have in common. Then ask how the two words are different. (The words sound the same, but are spelled differently and have different meanings.) Remind students that these kinds of words are homophones. Write the following on the board:

> Jill turned _____ when her _____ turned over.
>
> Jack wanted _____ get some water, _____, but they did not have _____ pails.

Have students identify the Spelling Words that are homophones and use them to complete these sentences. (pale, pail; to, too, two)

354 Lesson 30 • Turn It Up!

Day 2

PRETEACH

Grammar/Writing

Adverbs and Punctuation Remind students that an adverb is a word that describes a verb. It can tell how, where, or when something happened. Review the kinds of adverbs that can be used to compare two or more things. Point out that students should also avoid double negatives. Review how commas are used in a list of three or more, in a compound sentence, and after *yes* or *no* at the beginning of a sentence. Have students recall how to write titles and dialogue correctly. Then write the following sentences on the board:

> Jess dressed quick for school.
> I want to go, too, said Jimmy.

Guide students to correct the errors in each sentence. (Jess dressed quickly for school. "I want to go, too," said Jimmy.)

Fluency

Fluency Practice Invite students to look at the bottom half of *Practice Book* page 119. These sentences have been broken into natural phrases. Tell students to repeat each phrase after you, mirroring your expression, phrasing, and pace. After students have repeated each sentence, invite them to practice reading the sentences to partners.

"Beneath the Sands" 355

LESSON 30

DAY AT A GLANCE — Day 3

COMPREHENSION
Preteach Paraphrase
Reread and Summarize "Beneath the Sands"

DECODING/WORD ATTACK
Preteach Decode Root Words with Prefixes and Suffixes

DECODING/SPELLING
Preteach Words with Prefix + Root + Suffix

BUILD ROBUST VOCABULARY
Teach Words from "Beneath the Sands"

GRAMMAR/WRITING
Reteach Adverbs and Punctuation

FLUENCY
Fluency Practice

Materials Needed: *Turn It Up!*

Student Edition pp. 302–308

Practice Book pp. 119, 121

 30+ Minutes

PRETEACH

Comprehension

Paraphrase Remind students that when they paraphrase, they do not change the author's meaning. They change the order of the words and replace some of the words with synonyms. Write this sentence on the board:

> The scientists searched for days to find the cave's entrance.

Guide students to paraphrase this sentence. (Possible response: It took many days as researchers looked for the opening to the cave.)

GUIDED PRACTICE Have students reread pages 304–305 in their books. Ask them to work in pairs to paraphrase at least three lines of text. Invite pairs to share their paraphrased text with the group.

Reread and Summarize Have students reread and summarize "Beneath the Sands" in sections, as described below.

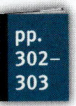 pp. 302–303
Let's reread pages 302–303 to find out what Carter is doing.
Summary: In Egypt, November 1922, Howard Carter is searching for King Tut's tomb. Many scientists doubt that he can find anything, and he wants to prove them wrong.

 pp. 304–305
Next, reread pages 304–305 to find out what happens.
Summary: The water bearer finds something in the sand and runs to Carter. Carter realizes that the water bearer has found something important. They dig and find steps that lead to a door.

 pp. 306–308
Now, reread pages 306–308 to see whether Carter was successful.
Summary: Three weeks later, Lady Herbert, Lord Carnarvon, and Carter are at a second door. Carter realizes that he has found King Tut's chambers, filled with priceless treasures.

PRETEACH

Decoding/Word Attack

Decode Root Words with Prefixes and Suffixes Remind students that some longer words are made up of a root word plus a prefix and a suffix. Have students generate a list of prefixes and suffixes that they have learned, such as *un-, dis-, re-, -able, -ly, -ful,* and *-tion*. Write *incorrectly* on the board. Underline the root word *(correct)* and circle the prefix *(in-)* and the suffix *(-ly)*.

356 Lesson 30 • Turn It Up!

Day 3

PRETEACH

Decoding/Spelling

Words with Prefix + Root + Suffix Review with students that some longer words are made up of a root with a prefix and a suffix. Remind them that when adding a suffix, sometimes there is a spelling change. Then have students work in pairs to complete the following activity. Ask students to write the Spelling Words on index cards. Have one student draw a card and read its word aloud and the other student write the word; then have partners switch roles. When a student spells a word correctly, he or she initials the card and returns it to the pile. Students should work through the pile twice. Have students write down each word they do not spell correctly to study later.

TEACH

Build Robust Vocabulary

page 302 **Words from "Beneath the Sands"** Have students locate the word *scanning* on page 302 of "Beneath the Sands." Ask a volunteer to read aloud the sentence in which this word appears. (Line 2: *He is scanning the dunes, digging, recording his finds, and digging some more.*) Explain that this means that Carter is looking over the sand dunes quickly.

Have students tell when it is necessary or appropriate to be scanning something.

RETEACH

Grammar/Writing

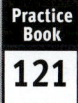 **Adverbs and Punctuation** Remind students that when they proofread, they should make sure that adverbs and punctuation are used correctly. Write these examples on the board:

> Bhavil walks more swift than Sheera.
> Bryce said, "I won't never get to go."

Guide students to proofread each sentence and correct the errors. (swiftly; won't ever *or* will never)

GUIDED PRACTICE Ask students to turn to page 121 in their *Practice Book*. Ask a volunteer to read the directions. Have students work in pairs to circle the adverbs and add the correct punctuation.

Fluency

Fluency Practice Tell students that today they will reread the sentences on the bottom of *Practice Book* page 119. Have students locate and point to the first sentence. Tell students that everyone is going to read the sentence together. This choral reading will give students an opportunity to hear others and listen to the natural phrasing of the sentences. Choral-read each of the sentences several times.

"Beneath the Sands" 357

LESSON 30

DAY AT A GLANCE
Day 4

COMPREHENSION
Preteach Use Graphic Aids

DECODING/SPELLING
Cumulative Review

BUILD ROBUST VOCABULARY
Reteach Words from "Beneath the Sands"

GRAMMAR/WRITING

FLUENCY
Fluency Practice

Materials Needed: *Turn It Up!*

 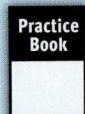 

Student Edition pp. 302–308 | Practice Book p. 122 | Copying Masters 119, 120

Spelling Words: Lesson 30

1. scene	11. scent
2. numb	12. pail
3. rustle	13. pale
4. debt	14. to
5. knack	15. too
6. specific	16. two
7. phonics	17. inaccurately
8. destruction	18. repayment
9. paragraph	19. misguidance
10. sent	20. unusually

30+ Minutes

PRETEACH
Comprehension

Use Graphic Aids Distribute *Copying Master 119* and have a volunteer read the information at the top of the page. Review the various types of graphic aids and have students explain when they would use each type.

GUIDED PRACTICE Ask students to look at the diagram and then answer the questions. Allow time for students to share their responses with others.

RETEACH
Decoding/Spelling

Cumulative Review Have students number a sheet of paper 1–16. Write *scene* on the board. Point out the silent letter *c*. Tell students that the next four words you will say have silent letters. After students write each word, display it so they can proofread their work. Continue by giving examples of other topics reviewed this week: *specific* for Greek and Latin word parts, *sent* for homophones, and *inaccurately* for prefix + root + suffix.

1. numb	2. rustle	3. debt	4. knack
5. phonics	6. destruction	7. paragraph	8. scent
9. pail	10. pale	11. to	12. too
13. two	14. repayment	15. misguidance	16. unusually

Have students turn to page 122 in their *Practice Book*. Tell students to read the sentences and then circle the letter in front of each sentence that best describes each picture. As a group, have students identify the Spelling Words that are in the sentences.

358 Lesson 30 • Turn It Up!

Day 4

RETEACH

Build Robust Vocabulary

Words from "Beneath the Sands" Review the meaning of *scanning*. Then say these sentences and ask which one accurately reflects the meaning of *scanning*. Have students explain why.

- I stared at Darby as if I had never seen her before.
- Molly quickly looked over her spelling words one more time before the test. (scanning)

RETEACH

Grammar/Writing

Copying Master 120

Cumulative Review Recall with students the grammar skills that they have reviewed this week. Discuss examples for each skill:

- irregular verbs, contractions, and possessive pronouns
- adverbs and double negatives
- punctuation in titles and dialogue.

Write these sentences on the board:

> Carter digged in the sand.
>
> The workers didnt never get a break.
>
> What do you see? they asked eager.

Guide students to proofread the sentences, and ask volunteers to underline the errors. Then ask students to correct the words and punctuation in the sentences. (Carter dug in the sand. The workers didn't ever get a break. "What do you see?" they asked eagerly.)

GUIDED PRACTICE Distribute *Copying Master 120* to each student. Invite a volunteer to read the directions. Then have students proofread each sentence, circle the mistakes, and write the sentence correctly. Allow time for students to share sentences with the group.

Fluency

pp. 302–308

Fluency Practice Have each student work with a partner to read passages from "Beneath the Sands" aloud to each other. Remind students to:

- use decoding strategies to read each word accurately when reading aloud
- read with expression that matches the content of the text

Encourage partners to read the selected passage aloud three times. Have the students rate their own reading on the 1–4 scale.

1	Need more practice
2	Pretty good
3	Good
4	Great!

"Beneath the Sands" 359

LESSON 30

DAY AT A GLANCE — Day 5

VOCABULARY
Reteach distinguished, verify, discern, dubious, descend, frantically, estimate, vicinity, abruptly, scrutinize

COMPREHENSION
 **Reteach** Main Idea and Details and Figurative Language

DECODING/SPELLING
Cumulative Review

GRAMMAR/WRITING
Cumulative Review

FLUENCY
Fluency Performance

Materials Needed: *Turn It Up!*

Student Edition pp. 302–308

Copying Master 117

30+ Minutes

RETEACH — Vocabulary

Copying Master 117

Lesson 30 Vocabulary Distribute a set of Word Cards to each student or pair of students. Read aloud or write on the board the meaning of one of the Vocabulary Words and the first letter in that word. Students match the correct word to the definition. Continue until students have matched all the words.

RETEACH — Comprehension

pp. 302–308 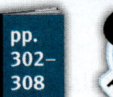 **Main Idea and Details and Figurative Language**
Remind students that the main idea is the most important idea in a passage, and details give more information about the main idea. If it is unstated, the reader needs to ask him- or herself what the details are mostly about. Then direct students' attention to page 307 and reread Carter's second line, "It's as black as night." Ask students to identify the type of figurative language. **(simile)** Have students explain what the simile means. **(Possible response: The room was so dark that it reminded Carter of the nighttime.)**

GUIDED PRACTICE Work with students to identify the main idea and details of the play. **(Main Idea: Howard Carter is a British excavator who has been searching for King Tut's chambers for many years and has finally found them.)**

360 Lesson 30 • *Turn It Up!*

RETEACH

Decoding/Spelling

Cumulative Review Remind students of the rules that apply to this lesson's Spelling Words.

GUIDED PRACTICE Say a Spelling Word and challenge a volunteer to spell the word and to state the spelling rule or skill that he or she applied to that word. For example, after spelling *scene,* the student would state that he or she had to know that it contains a silent letter, *c.* Continue for each Spelling Word.

RETEACH

Grammar/Writing

Cumulative Review Review what students have learned about irregular verbs, contractions, possessive pronouns, adverbs, and punctuating titles and dialogue.

GUIDED PRACTICE Write the following grammar words on index cards: *irregular verb, contraction, possessive pronoun, adverb, double negative, title,* and *dialogue.* Then write the following sentences on the board:

> They're going to the ball game.
>
> "I'm ready to go," said Justin.
>
> Whose car are we riding in?
>
> I want to read <u>Stuart Little</u> over summer break.
>
> She quickly wrote a note.
>
> He won't not do that again.

Read each sentence, then have a volunteer point to the card that indicates which grammar word is represented in the sentence. (contraction; contraction, dialogue; possessive pronoun; title; adverb, irregular verb; double negative)

Day 5

VOCABULARY

Student-Friendly Explanations

distinguished A distinguished person is very successful in a job or field.

verify If you verify something, you check it out to make sure that it's true.

discern To discern something means to see it, or to be aware that it exists.

dubious A person who is dubious is doubtful or unsure about something.

descend When you descend, you move downward.

frantically To behave frantically means to behave wildly and with great excitement.

estimate When you estimate a quantity, you make a careful guess about how many things there are.

vicinity If something is in a vicinity, it is nearby.

abruptly If you do something abruptly, you do it very suddenly.

scrutinize When you scrutinize a place, you examine it carefully, with a critical eye.

Fluency

pp. 302–308 **Fluency Performance** Invite students each to read aloud from "Beneath the Sands" a passage that they selected and practiced earlier. Give each partners the opportunity to continue practicing and then to read the passage to you again.

"Beneath the Sands" 361